Power

Power

Its Forms, Bases, and Uses

Dennis H. Wrong

WITH A NEW INTRODUCTION BY THE AUTHOR

TRANSACTION PUBLISHERS

New Brunswick (U.S.A.) and London (U.K.)

Fifth printing 2009

New material this edition copyright © 1995 by Transaction Publishers, New Brunswick, New Jersey. Originally published in 1979 by Harper and Row. The 1988 Preface was originally published by The University of Chicago Press.

This book is printed on acid-free paper that meets the American National Standard for Permanence of Paper for Printed Library Materials.

Library of Congress Catalog Number: 94-45957
ISBN: 978-1-56000-822-4
Printed in the United States of America

Library of Congress Cataloging-in-Publication Data

Wrong, Dennis Hume, 1923-
    Power : its forms, bases, and uses / Dennis H. Wrong ; with a new introduction by the author.
        p. cm.
    Originally published: New York : Harper and Row, 1979.
    Includes bibliographical references (p.) and index.
    ISBN 1-56000-822-9 (pbk. : acid-free paper)
        1. Power (Social sciences) I. Title.

JC33O.W76 1995
303.3'3-dc20
                                                                                            94-45957
                                                                                               CIP

Contents

Introduction to the
Transaction Edition

I originally wrote this book as a contribution to a series entitled "Key Concepts in the Social Sciences," edited by Philip Rieff and Bryan R. Wilson. Both of them were sociologists and, as I recall, they first invited me to write on "social class" or "inequality," two concepts of an essentially sociological nature. I suggested "power" as an alternative, a subject on which I had recently published an article in a sociological journal. Although it obviously has much wider connotations, at the time I thought of power primarily in sociological terms as a particular kind of relation between actors and therefore gave little attention to the wider implication of the series' focus on the social sciences in general. Some of the "key concepts" treated in other books in the series were "rationality," "social change," "individualism," "ideology," and "revolution," concepts that are by no means specifically or even distinctively sociological.

I now regret this limitation, for in the social sciences and political discourse, and even in sociology itself, it has since become if anything more common than formerly to use power as an exceedingly comprehensive term, one that virtually identifies it as the fundamental object of human striving and sees it as deeply ingrained in any and all human relations and social structures. I made an effort to take this more sweeping and inevitably ambiguous breadth of conception into account in my preface to the 1988 edition of the book, developing more fully the distinction between "power to" and "power over," which had not been entirely neglected but had been insufficiently emphasized in the first edition. The distinction remains a crucial one because conflation of the two senses of power is the source of many of the ambiguities, conceptual and rhetorical, that cling to the concept. This introduction to a new

third edition gives me an opportunity further to discuss the often pro-
miscuous recent uses of the concept.

Power has always been one of those words that everybody uses
without necessarily being able to define satisfactorily. It is treated
both as a quality or attribute possessed by individuals, groups, or
larger social structures and as an indicator of an active or interactive
process or relation between individual or collective actors. Moreover, it is also applied to physical phenomena and processes. In recent years power has tended to become an even more diffuse and
far-ranging notion in social and political theory, partly as a result of
the influence of Michel Foucault and the Nietzsche revival his writings have helped promote. It has been argued that, like "freedom" or
"justice"—those "big words which make us so unhappy," as Stephen
Dedalus called them—"power" is an "essentially contested concept,"
meaning that people with different values and beliefs are bound to
disagree over its nature and definition.[1] It is claimed therefore that
there cannot be any commonly accepted or even preferred meaning
so long as people differ on normative issues as they are likely to do
indefinitely, if not forever.

"Power," however, does not seem to me to be an inherently normative concept. Undoubtedly, conservatives, liberals, socialists, libertar-
ians, anarchists, ethnic nationalists, religious believers, and secularists
endlessly dispute over whom should have power and how much, how it
should be organized and channeled, and a host of other issues pertaining to its distribution and exercise. Accordingly, its scope and perva-
siveness, its involvement in any and all spheres of social life, give it
almost unavoidable evaluative overtones. Positive or negative, benign
or malign, auras come to envelop it, linking it still more closely to ideological controversy. Yet power as a generic attribute of social life is
surely more like the concepts of "society," "group" or "social norm"
than like such essentially and inescapably normative notions as "justice," "democracy," or "human rights." "Power" is no more or less abstract than the first set of concepts, but it bears more directly on realities that are central to the enduring moral and political differences cen-
tering on the second set. In this respect, it resembles "inequality" or
"social class," also fiercely contested concepts that are nevertheless not
by their very nature normative and value-laden.

The conflations and ambiguities to which the concept of power is
prone have their origins in three uses where the concept blends into,
merges with, or overlaps cognate terms and meanings:

1. Its most general use as a near-synonym for influence, control, rule, and domination results in its seeming to share some or all of the different shades of meaning of these terms.

2. As an attribute or quality possessed by individuals, power may be regarded as sought after, even as a fundamental object of human striving. It thus raises questions about basic human motivations involving the very nature of human nature itself.

3. Since power is unequally distributed among groups in all large-scale complex "civilized" societies, the cultures of these societies will reflect and express this inequality. The "hegemony," to use the fashionable term, of some groups over others is held to be encoded in all their modes of activity and expression, including language, the most distinctively human creation and possession of all.

I shall discuss each of these three areas in sequence in an effort to link them to prevailing arguments that cluster around the concept of power, emphasizing the more recent versions that have become common since the publication of the first edition.

The most general sense of power views it as an event or agency that produces an effect on the external world. It is therefore obviously relational, postulating something that acts on its environment and brings about some change in it. It also is of universal scope, applying to the physical world in general, including the human actors within it. Power as the capacity to produce effects may be imputed to the agency as a dispositional (in Gilbert Ryle's sense) property even when the capacity is not manifest in action. Power here resembles and includes physical force or energy, for example the explosive power seen as residing in a bomb. Power as a capacity stating a potential relation to entities in its environment is no less a relational term when it is not actually realized in overt action. I discussed this actual-potential dimension of power quite fully in the first edition.

Writers on power have often complained that the word does not exist in a verb form, at least in English. The difference between "having" and "exercising" power—a version of the actual/potential distinction—is thought to be obscured by the absence of a verb form, a problem that does not arise with "influence" or "control." Yet these terms carry slightly different shades of meaning and are therefore not really satisfactory alternatives to "power." The most famous American "how-to" book was entitled *How to Win Friends and Influence People;* one might well doubt that it would have become a best-seller if it had substituted "to control" or "to exercise power over" people for the weaker, blander "influence."

(As it was, the author, Dale Carnegie, was often accused of teaching a possibly sinister technique for manipulating innocent and trusting people.) In recent years, the noun "impact" has been converted into a verb "to impact," apparently because a word stronger than "influence" that nevertheless did not suggest conscious purpose like "control" was sought. (That "impact" as verb has become a dreadful cliché of the mass media is another matter!)

The verb "to empower" and the noun "empowerment" have also become commonplace in political debate, but they refer to the acquisition rather than to the exercise of power. What is to be acquired is "power to" rather than "power over" others; indeed, the terms are typically used with reference to groups perceived as victims or at least passive objects of the power exercised over them by others. "Empowerment" sometimes appears to refer to the mobilization of previously isolated individual actors so that they achieve collective power through solidarity and organization, a process discussed at length in Chapters 6 and 7. There may be a conflict between an individual or collective actor's "power to," here equivalent to "freedom to," and the constraints imposed by another actor's "power over." The escape from such constraints may be total, eliminating an asymmetrical power relationship altogether, or it may be partial, setting new limits to, or countering in some areas of activity, the power holder's power over the power subject. These different senses in which politics in the broadest sense involves both a struggle *for* power and *against,* or to escape *from,* power are discussed on pages 12–13.[2]

When applied to human agents, the issue of intentionality cannot be avoided. My own definition of power as a human or social phenomenon, adapted from Bertrand Russell's broader definition, was "the capacity of some persons to produce intended and foreseen effects on others." No feature of my entire discussion of power has aroused wider disagreement than my defining it as necessarily intentional.[3] The vastly consequential unintended and unanticipated effects of the decisions and actions of the powerful—statesmen, generals, bureaucrats, big capitalists, religious leaders, the media, scientific experts—immediately spring to mind and my definition is seen as ignoring all these unintended consequences. The ubiquity of unintended consequences, moreover, is widely and properly regarded as providing a major, if not *the* major, rationale for the very existence of the social sciences. Yet here I am in an excessively voluntarist fashion apparently limiting power to the shortsighted and confined effects of conscious human purposes. This can be seen as a kind of cop-out, implicitly complacent toward ignorance and resultant social evils in simply ignoring the tremendous and often malign ramifications of the unequal distribution of power in human societies. Structuralist "de-centering of the subject" provides an additional rationale for excluding the power holder's intentions from the understanding of power, but theorists who are not structuralists or poststructuralists have also challenged definitions that treat power as necessarily intentional.

My response to this argument has been to contend that for power to have important unintended consequences it must usually first be exercised in a social relation in which one actor, the power holder, produces an intended effect on another actor. I have recognized the scope and significance of "unintended influence" in the chart on page 24 that distinguishes two forms of influence, unintended and intended (equated with power), and four forms of power, namely, force, persuasion, manipulation, and authority. As one critic has observed, my concept of unintended influence is indebted to Robert Dahl and Charles Lindblom's "spontaneous field control" advanced in their compendious 1953 volume *Politics Economics and Welfare*.[4]

But to treat "power" and "influence" as synonyms is to make power, that is, the exercise of power, equivalent to the production of *any* social effect. All influences that actors have upon one another then become exercises of power. "Society" and "social interaction," the very idea of "social," become phenomena of power since they presuppose the reciprocal influence of individuals on one another. Society *is* in this view a system of power at both the macro-level of its major institutions and at the micro-level of personal relations. This corresponds more or less to the Foucauldian conception of society. If "power" is thus considered equivalent to "influence," there would seem to be no need for a specific concept of power at all. "Influence" would do all the necessary work and has the advantage of existing in both a noun and a verb form.

The widespread tendency to define power as necessarily coercive is undoubtedly inspired by a wish to avoid so broad and general an implication. I reject at some length the identification of power with coercion, with force or its threatened application, in the present book and need say no more about that here. Instead, I differentiate power from the more all-embracing concept of influence by adding the criterion of intentionality. I confess, however, to a certain sympathy with critics who react to what they see as my apparent minimization or neglect of unintended consequences, which undeniably are crucially important in as-

sessing the role of power in society. "Unintended influence" or "spontaneous field control" perhaps sound too residual, suggesting relatively
secondary effects of power. Nevertheless, the distinction between unintended and intended influence remains vital: failure to recognize it in
defining power simply collapses power into influence in all the latter's
sweeping and diffuse generality.

The concept of power continues to possess, unlike influence, overtones of coercion even among writers who do not define it as necessarily coercive. Max Weber's definition, probably the most influential one
of all, is an example: after identifying power with "the chance of a man
or a number of men to realize their own will in a social action," which
does not make power inherently coercive, he goes on to add "even against
the resistance of others who are participating in the action." Despite the
qualifying "even" in most renditions of Weber's definition, it is not
surprising that many readers have assumed that he regarded conflict
and resistance as inherent in relations of power. For writers who explicitly avoid any equation of power with coercion, the term nevertheless
manages to retain something of a malign, sinister, even demonic aura.
Indeed, it is often a rhetorical strategy to evoke just such an aura. Foucault is a case in point, which accounts for his popularity among post-
Marxists anxious not to abandon a critical, adversarial stance toward
modern society. A power relation always implies that the person subject to it does something he or she would not otherwise have done, but
it need not be something that is or is perceived as against his or her
wishes or interests.

The negative connotations of power are even more marked when it is
treated as a fundamental motive or object of human striving as in familiar allusions to "will to power," "lust for power," or "power drive." A
long tradition of political thought including Machiavelli and Hobbes
that goes back to Thrasymachus in Plato's *The Republic* has treated
these as anti-social motivations promoting hostility and conflict among
men. I have criticized the psychological assumptions on which this tradition rests at some length in the first section of chapter 9.[5] Yet many
writers in the tradition who are conventionally classified as cynics or
pessimists about human nature actually define power in a fashion that
is neutral with regard to its benign or malign uses in relation to other
human beings. Hobbes's definition of power as an individual's "present
means towards any future apparent good" is the classic example.
Nietzsche, currently fashionable because of his influence on Foucault
and other poststructuralists and so-called postmodernists, initially

equated his "will to power" with something like life force or the drive to preserve and enhance the vitality of the organism and its control over its environment. Like his contemporaries William James and Henri Bergson, he was writing at a time when the influence of Darwin on philosophy and psychology was new and at its peak. Such approaches to power begin with general statements encompassing a wide range of human motivations and then proceed fairly directly to discussion of the efforts to dominate others and the ensuing conflicts to which such efforts may sometimes give rise. What is involved is essentially a conflation or at least a slurring over of the difference between "power to," the more general category, and "power over." Only the latter, a special case of the former, suggests the potentiality of hostility, conflict, and oppression in human relations though it is only a potentiality as I have argued in contending that power is not necessarily coercive. To say that all humans seek the "power to" gratify their desires or realize their goals is to say no more than that they *have* desires and goals, that, in effect, they want to get what they want. Who could possibly dissent from such a statement? This innocuous claim nevertheless lends a specious plausibility to Nietzschean and Foucauldian assertions that humans invariably seeks to dominate and impose their will on others.

The recent tendency to see power as the most universal and pervasive feature of social life has to do with differences in collective power, or the unequal distribution of power among groups and social categories. One form this takes is to equate the unequal distribution among individuals of anything and everything that people desire and seek with inequality of power. A warrant for this may be found in Weber, who famously characterized "classes," "status groups," and "parties" as "phenomena of the distribution of power within a community." Power is clearly used here in the sense of "power to," or the capacity of individuals to satisfy their wants. To say that individuals are unequal in power is simply another way of saying that society is stratified, that some people have more income, property, status, leisure and other desiderata than other people. This is in no way objectionable unless it is assumed that more is being said: that the identification of inequalities of all kinds with inequality of power serves somehow to *explain* social inequalities and class differences rather than merely to acknowledge their existence.

Yet this assumption is often made. It conflates the aggregated unequal power of individuals encompassing inequalities of income, status, and other sought-after things with greater collective power allegedly possessed by the beneficiaries of the unequal distribution, eliding the difference between a distributive and a relational conception of power. The further assumption is made that the beneficiaries, the "haves," attain and maintain their favored position by means of the power they exercise *over* the underprivileged "have-nots." By a process of double conflation, the aggregated "power to" satisfy their wants of the most favored individuals is equated with collective power presuming a degree of solidarity and social organization exercised by them as a privileged class over a less favored subordinate class. Thus, the mere existence of inequality, of social stratification, is seen as evidence of class domination in which one class secures its superior position by some combination of ideological indoctrination, manipulation, coercion, and economic exploitation. That the lower class at least covertly resents its inferior position is recognized. This class would, it is alleged, favor a different organization of society that allocated rewards more equally if persuaded of the possibility of such an alternative. These assumptions constitute the broad core of the Marxist conception of class society; they obviously contain a large measure of truth, but they need to be argued and often qualified rather than simply assumed by being read into the very existence of social stratification as a result of equating the aggregated "power to" of individuals with the collective "power over" subordinate classes of more cohesive social classes—*Klasse für sich* in Marxist terms.

The past few decades from roughly the late 1950s to 1990 were a period in which what might be called "late Marxism" was prominent in intellectual circles, including those of academic social science. Marxists accorded greater importance to ideological indoctrination through control of culture than to political and economic coercion in accounting for the maintenance—"reproduction"—of capitalism as a social and economic order based on the rule of the bourgeoisie. Gramsci's "hegemony" was only the most favored concept of "Western Marxists" and their academic followers who paid more attention to the cultural superstructure than to the economic base. Political and economic domination of the bodies of the subordinate classes by means of physical coercion and control over the material resources required to satisfy their vital needs was less emphasized than the shaping of their consciousness by control over the agencies of cultural transmission. "Legitimation crises" or "counter-cultural revolts" rather than cumulative economic contradictions or revolutionary political mobilization were seen as the major forms of vulnerability of capitalism to fundamental change.

The collapse of communism in the early 1990s has discredited Marxism, probably for good, primarily by destroying the credibility of socialism as a more egalitarian form of society that would nevertheless secure and continue the economic progress already achieved under capitalism. Yet the general schema of some groups exercising power to their own advantage over other groups has been extended to groups other than classes, most commonly to groups distinguished by race and gender. At the same time, the view has become popular among intellectuals that knowledge, far from permitting a reflective cognitive distancing from the constraints of social reality, is itself, as Foucault in particular insisted, simply a technique or instrument by which some groups claiming superior access to it establish and secure their power over others. The "linguistic turn" in social thought has suggested a far deeper penetration of culture in the form of language into human consciousness. If the power of some groups over others is regarded as the salient feature of society, and language is the major medium both of cultural expression and transmission, then language must unavoidably reflect and reinforce social inequality. It becomes both a major medium for, and an effect of, the exercise of power. All language resembles George Orwell's "Newspeak": it cannot help but affirm the existing order and exclude the very possibility of even formulating ideas critical of that order. As a "dominant discourse" it maintains the "ideological hegemony" of the privileged by "foregrounding" them and their concerns while "marginalizing" subordinate—"subaltern"—groups. Power penetrates the very core of human consciousness. It is implicated in anything and everything that can be said, which makes everything "political" so that any lack of explicit reference to power and politics points to "silences in the text" that are held to reveal a presence confirmed by its very absence. Even Stalin, of all people, did not go so far as this when he intervened in 1950 in a controversy over linguistics in the Soviet Union to insist that language was independent of class determination grounded in the economic "base."

Whether the application of such a schema is more or less credible when extended as it is nowadays to race, gender, and other groups than in the Marxist version of the centrality of class domination need not be considered here. A prior issue is the value of this "power here, power there, power, power everywhere" perspective (apologies to Coleridge). The power reductionism that treats everything as an expression of power follows essentially from the conflation of the generic notion of "power to" with "power over," which is a social relation in which some persons possess and exercise power over others. The first is merged into the second and the concept itself acquires an oppressive, near-totalitarian ring while its diagnosticians appear to be bold rebels challenging the subtle, hidden tyranny of modern society over its subjects.

Perhaps my identity as a sociologist makes me particularly skeptical of this power reductionist or pan-power outlook, leading me to prefer a more limited conception of power.[6] A conception that sees it as one of an array or repertoire of concepts describing the diverse forms of social interaction that constitute society as a web or network constantly created and recreated in non-identical forms is doubtless more congenial to a sociologist.[7] I shall close therefore by citing several non-sociologists who have made a similar case. The late J. C. Merquior, a political philosopher, observed that "the overbroadening of the concept of power corresponds to an equal loss in depth and specificity."[8] Lawrence Stone, the historian, has written in terms entirely congruent with my own argument in the book and in this introduction to a new edition: "Since man is a social animal, and since all of social life involves some form of influence, molding, direction, or compulsion, the reduction of all social life to issues of power renders it almost impossible to make the fine intellectual, moral, and material distinctions necessary for any serious evaluation of change in history."[9] I accept the Weberian view that sociology is "Clio's handmaiden" and I cannot improve upon Stone's exemplary statement.

Dennis H. Wrong
Princeton, N.J
October 1994

Notes

1. Steven Lukes, *Power: A Radical View* (London: Macmillan, 1974), p. 9.
2. Albert O. Hirschman, *Exit, Voice and Loyalty* (Cambridge: Harvard University Press, 1970).
3. See, for example, Stewart R. Clegg, *Frameworks of Power* (London; Newbury Park, Calif.; New Delhi: Sage Publications, 1989), pp. 72–75. For a particularly lucid objection to intentionality, see John F. Gasky, "'Volume' of Power: A New Conceptualization of the Power Construct," *Sociological Spectrum* (forthcoming, 1995).
4. Gasky, "'Volume' of Power."
5. I have also discussed it at even greater length in *The Problem of Order: What Unites and Divides Society* (New York: The Free Press, 1994), chapters 4 and 5.

6. J. C. Merquior uses the term *pancratism* to refer to "a systematic reduction of all social processes to largely unspecified patterns of domination" in *Foucault* (Berkeley and Los Angeles: University of California Press, 1985), p. 115.

7. See my elaboration of this conception in chapter 3 of *The Problem of Order*.

8. Merquior, *Foucault*, p. 116.

9. Lawrence Stone, "An Exchange with Michel Foucault," *The New York Review of Books* (31 March 1983): 44.

Preface, 1988

I have come to think that I failed to give proper attention in this book to the most general uses and implications of the term "power," before passing on to its more restricted meanings in sociology and social theory. In the book's five opening paragraphs I did address myself to the equation of power with capacity or capability, mastery, and potency, all understood in the broadest possible sense. But I then went on to exclude such generalized meanings from the uses of the term in political and social theory, where power is seen as a relation between persons or groups.

I had in mind when writing these passages the story of a former colleague, a researcher and specialist in the study of community power, who became a university administrator. One of his duties was to attend dinners given by associations of the university's alumni in major American cities. On one such occasion a dignified gentleman sitting next to him asked him what his research subject was and, on learning it was "community power," launched into a long discourse on the comparative mertis of different kinds of electrical grid systems, assuming he was talking to a fellow electrical engineer. This tale sensitized me, perhaps unduly, to differentiating nature, the self, and other people as separate and distinct *objects* of power, or realms in which it might be exercised. The differences are certainly important, but they are not identical with the distinction between power as a generalized capacity to act on the world and as a specific kind of social relation. I now think that I conflated these two separate, necessary distinctions.

By the time I wrote the last chapter of the book, I had become more aware of the continuing significance to many social and political theorists of the difference between "power to" and "power over," the former equivalent to the conception of power as a capacity to act on the world or to bring about definite outcomes. I therefore introduced this distinction in my final chapter and discussed the views of power as "power to" held by several social theorists, most notably Talcott Parsons but also Anthony Giddens, C.B. Macpherson, and Robert S. Lynd.[1] However, my concentration on the debate over the nature of power between Parsons and C. Wright Mills, a debate which had initially aroused my own interest in refining the concept of power, prevented me from discussing the "power to" and "power over" distinction at its most general level. I paid particular attention to the view advanced by Parsons (but also, as I noted, implied by Marx and Engels and many later socialists) that an established organizational power structure may function as a "collective resource," making possible the attainment of goals that benefit an entire society, including the subordinate members of the power structure itself. The power to power over distinction, however, is neutral with respect to whether individuals, groups, or major institutional structures are considered the locus of power. It is also neutral on the question of who benefits, or whose interests are served, by the exercise of power. These issues have often been conflated in the contemporary discussions.

Anthony Giddens and Michel Foucault are two influential contemporary theorists who have treated power as a highly generalized capacity to produce effects or outcomes that would not otherwise have occurred. Giddens, for example, defines power as "transformative capacity" and regards an actor's achievement of outcomes by inducing the compliant actions of others as a special case exemplifying this capacity.[2] He argues that power is "logically tied to" the idea of human action or agency itself, which is presumably the basic subject matter of all the social or human sciences. Giddens insists on this fundamental connection between action and power in order to dissociate power from any inherent connection with conflict, resistance, and clashing interests, a connection which some writers have incorporated into their very definitions of power, believing mistakenly that they were following Weber's well-known definition.[3] I agree with Giddens on this score, having myself challenged in the present book the view that power is necessarily coercive, always involving the imposition of sanctions in order to overcome resistance.

However, Giddens often describes power in terms that make it virtually identical with human action or agency itself, perhaps the central concept of his social theory. His concept of agency entails freedom of choice, or the possibility that the actor might have acted differently. His notion of power, on the other hand, stresses the *effects* of action, the change it makes in an existing situation that would otherwise have remained the same. Power is action that deploys means in order to achieve outcomes. On occasion, however, Giddens defines action itself similarly.[4] The overlap between action and power seems in any case to be so great that the difference between the two concepts, making the latter a special case of the former, is obscured. This has the paradoxical effect of seeming to equate power with freedom, or the capacity to choose one's actions without external constraint. But power may be precisely such a constraint from the standpoint of persons subject to it, as the identification of power with "power over," or with an asymmetrical superior-subordinate relation, recognizes. "Power over" is unquestionably a special case of "power to," but when considered as a social relation it necessitates taking into account the standpoints of both parties to the relation. Taken into account accordingly, it *may*, not must, constrain the freedom of the subordinate party.

How do we make the transition from recognition that action virtually entails power to acknowledging the enormous inequalities of power in human society, inequalities that are intrinsic to the conception of power as an asymmetrical relation, as something possessed and exercised by some persons *over* other persons? The capacity for action, the very "power to act" as such, is a universal property of human beings (that is, of socialized human beings). An action that is literally ineffectual, that has no discernible impact whatever on the world or even on the actor's body or psyche, is nonetheless an action insofar as the actor could have acted otherwise or not at all. An attempt to exercise power, on the other hand, that is without effect is not an instance of power but of its failure or absence. The presence of effects rather than the origins of action in choice seems to be the *differentia specifica* of power as a subcategory of agency.

If power consists in the use of means or resources to achieve outcomes, then obviously there is great inequality in the distribution of these means. I agree with Giddens that power itself should not be regarded as a resource[5]: it is, rather, the mobilization by an actor, whether individual or collective, of resources such as wealth, official position, fame, skill, knowledge, etc. to produce effects. Since these resources are unequally distributed, individuals and groups are unequal in their power although equal in their ability to act in a generically human way. Inequality of power resulting from inequalities of the resources that make possible the exercise of power—including the power to augment those resources themselves—is a distributive rather than a relational phenomenon, the result of differentials in "power to" rather than "power over." Power, in short, is not a separate resource possessed by individuals or groups additional to the resources of wealth, status, skill, etc., as many sociologists have erroneously thought of it (again mistakenly believing that they were following Weber). Power is, rather, the activation of these resources in order to pursue goals or outcomes.

The unequal distribution of power is not the result of the unequal distribution of purely individual attributes and capacities, but reflects the workings of the major institutions of a society and the legitimations of these institutions. This is what makes it a proper subject for sociologists, especially students of social stratification. Power is both a generalized capacity to attain ends that is unequally distributed among the members of a society as a result of the structure of its major institutions, on the one hand, and an asymmetrical social relation among persons manifested directly in social interaction or indirectly through anticipated reactions, on the other. I think that I gave disproportionate weight to the latter relational or interactionist conception of power in Chapter One, which I only partially corrected in Chapter Nine in discussions that also dealt with other issues.

The most influential recent writer on the subject of power has undeniably been Michel Foucault. The historical perspective he brought to bear upon the asylum, the hospital, and the prison, and on the "human sciences" that have provided that rationale for these "carceral" institutions, has encouraged more systematic study of their origin and development. Foucault also advanced a general conception of power, conceiving of it as manifest not only in the "disciplinary power" rationalized by the new breed of applied social scientists, but as pervading all social relations in the form of a "micro-politics": power is "something that is exercised from innumerable points, in the interplay of nonegalitarian and mobile relations." "Power is everywhere, not because it embraces everything but because it comes from everywhere."[6]

This assertion of the ubiquity of power remains vague and allusive. Its most obvious meaning, insisted on again and again by Foucault, is that power is not concentrated or centered in the State but is diffused through many nonpolitical groups and organizations. This is a less than blinding revelation to sociologists who have typically claimed and documented the existence of power structures and power relations in the formal organizations, voluntary associations, local communities, and even small informal groups, including families, that constitute the social order as distinct from the political order. Michael Walzer has pointed out the resemblance between Foucault and the American "pluralists" of the 1950s who, though from a clearly different political standpoint, also made much of the dispersion and "de-centering" of power in society.[7]

Power is also ubiquitous, as I maintained in the very first section of the first chapter of the present book, in that it inheres in social interaction, which involves the alternation between the interactants of the exercise of power or influence over one another. But despite frequent references to "mechanisms," "tactics," and "strategies" of power at the micro level, Foucault is not an analyst of the "interaction order" in the mode of Erving Goffman,[8] whose work on total institutions has so often been compared with Foucault's. At times, however, Foucault's insistence on the omnipresence of power is reminiscent of the concept of "social control" once popular among American sociologists, connoting the self-regulated conformity to prevailing norms achieved by individuals mutually influencing one another in their everyday conduct, independent of the directives of any central authority.[9]

Foucault explicitly and repeatedly rejects a negative view of power as repression or prohibition, insisting that "what makes power hold good, and what makes it accepted, is simply the fact that it doesn't only weigh on us as a force that says no, but that it traverses and produces things, it induces pleasure, forms knowledge, produces discourse."[10] This is power as "power to," power as generalized capacity to bring about outcomes, par excellence. There is, as Giddens has noted, an affinity with Parsons's notion of power as a "collective resource."[11] If Giddens tends to blur the distinction between action and power, Foucault's conception of power is even more amorphous and implicitly all-embracing, for which Giddens himself has criticized it.[12] Occasionally, Foucault's evocative but imprecise use of the term comes close to equating it with the basic motivational energy that sets human beings in motion, that stirs them to action much as energy or force in physics is held to make work and move matter. There are echoes here of Nietzsche's "will to power" as the fundamental human motive that in Nietzsche's later work is expanded into a quasimetaphysical cosmic force throughout the universe.

Foucault's claim that there is an inherent relation between knowledge and power is his most original contribution to the study of power. Sometimes he seems to go so far as to suggest that the search for truth is dependent on a Nietzschean will to power for which knowledge is no more than a serviceable instrument. Giddens rejects this implication in charging Foucault with a "power reductionism" in which "power is seemingly prior to truth."[13] But Foucault often states no more than that "power and knowledge directly imply one another,"[14] which is surely incontestable. To strive to produce an effect on something presupposes some knowledge of the object and also generates new knowledge, whether the result is deemed a success or a failure. Foucault often writes of "power/knowledge relations" in an oblique way that results from his attempt to eliminate (in the manner of other French structuralists) the human subject as an autonomous actor standing above or outside the process of action and setting it in motion. This leads to the reification of systems of knowledge or "discourse" and power relations, considering them as if they were self-subsistent entities. Eliot Freidson is surely correct in arguing against Foucault that "knowledge cannot be treated as some fixed set of ideas or propositions organized into a discipline that is then employed mechanically by its agents. It lives only through its agents, who themselves employ ideas and techniques selectively as their tasks and perspectives dictate."[15]

Foucault's major topic, especially in his later writings, was not the power/knowledge relation as such or in general but his claim that the bodies of knowledge codified in the new human sciences have become the basis of new kinds of control and regulation of human beings by "experts"—doctors, psychiatrists, social workers, therapists of all kinds, penologists, and other professionals exercising power that is legitimated by reference to certified and credentialed formal knowledge. Foucault is hardly alone in recognizing the expansion in modern society of this new kind of authority, nor in realizing that it cannot simply be hailed as the triumphant progress of enlightenment, free of the moral ambiguities present in all power relations.

The power based on knowledge that is Foucault's subject clearly falls under the heading of what I call "competent authority" in Chapter Three. The combination of a claim both to arcane, specialized knowledge and to a primary concern for the interests of the subject endows such authority with a peculiar plausibility, particularly in an age that has condemned coercive power relations and rejected traditional legitimations of authority grounding it in divine commandment, moral absolutes, or natural law. Foucault's work strikes some readers as bold and iconoclastic for unmasking exemplars of the most characteristically modern form of authority, which operates insidiously, invoking reason, science, and self-interest—standards far removed from both coercion and moral absolutism—as grounds for legitimation.

The addition of a fuller theoretical discussion of power as a general human capacity along the lines I have just indicated is not the only revision I would make were I today to rewrite the present book. Much of Chapter Seven, notably pages 155 though 179, and all of Chapter Eight represent an effort to illustrate rather than to elaborate my conceptualizations of power with reference to the major topics of political sociology. Inevitably, political sociology has since changed: the study of voting behavior and of community power, both of which loomed large in the 1950s and 1960s and therefore also in the present book, no longer attract as much scholarly attention; nor do interpretations of social movements as products of mass society, or analyses of the fundamental nature of totalitarianism. Today I would abbreviate or eliminate altogether discussion of these topics and partly substitute for them treatment of the state as both a political actor and a unique, historically emergent kind of social structure—a prominent topic among contemporary political sociologists. I would also try to apply my conceptualizations of power to the vast subject of international relations, nuclear strategies, war and peace—"politics among the nations," as a famous textbook by Hans Morgenthau was entitled. This is hardly a new subject and my own interest in it is of long standing—if only because I am the son of a professional diplomat—but I do have the impression that there are at least faint signs that sociologists, who have, with the illustrious exception of Raymond Aron, grossly neglected world politics in the past, are at last beginning to realize that no macrosociological understanding of contemporary societies is complete without it.[17]

There are a few other changes I would make were I to rewrite *Power: Its Forms, Bases, and Uses.* No one ever writes the same book twice. But I have tried in this preface to indicate the major changes I would want to make, especially at the most general conceptual level of what is essentially a work of conceptual analysis.

Dennis H. Wrong
Princeton, N.J.
May 1988

Preface

I first became interested in the problem of how to conceptualize the elusive but indispensable notion of power in the early 1960s in connection with two debates that were going on among sociologists and political scientists at that time. At the level of empirical research, the study of the distribution of power in local communities gave rise to disagreements over whether a 'reputational' or a 'decisional' method provided the best answers to the query 'who runs this town?' More unambiguously conceptual and theoretical issues were raised by the confrontation in sociology between Talcott Parsons and C. Wright Mills and their supporters over whether power should be viewed primarily as a general social resource or as the instrument by which some groups promoted and secured their interests at the expense of other groups. This last debate was closely tied in with arguments between functionalists and conflict theorists, the former tending towards a consensual view of power as legitimate authority, the latter disposed to insist on the irreducibly coercive face of power.

These debates no longer preoccupy sociologists and political scientists in the terms in which they were first presented, although they can scarcely be said to have been resolved in the favour of either side, something that in any case rarely happens in social theory. However, they have become points of reference in contemporary discussions of structuralist as opposed to actionist theories of society, rival elucidations of the nature of group and class interests, and interpretations of the role of ideologies in shaping as well as reflecting collective world-views. I have therefore often chosen in this book to introduce topics by summarizing the debates of the 1960s while at the same time making an effort to show their relevance to and continuity with current theoretical controversies. I have also, however, in accordance with my own disposition to doubt the superiority of new to old wisdom, tried to ground my discussions in the reflections of classical political theorists, especially Aristotle, Machiavelli and Hobbes, as well as those of Dostoevsky, Freud and George Orwell. Power is too important a subject to be left to contemporary social theorists.

I have much appreciated the careful and prompt editorial attention given the manuscript by Bryan Wilson, the editor of the series of which it is part. Edward W. Lehman and Steven Lukes read nearly complete drafts and I am grateful to both of them for their trouble and for the many helpful suggestions they made; also to Eliot Freidson for his similar service with respect to part of Chapter 3. I received useful criticisms and suggestions from colleagues and students at various universities in Britain, Canada and the United States where I presented parts of the manuscript in seminars or lectures. My wife, Jacqueline, graciously allowed me to use her as a sounding-board for several ideas as well as for some of the prose included in the book.

I should like to thank the Warden and Fellows of Nuffield College, Oxford University for their hospitality in providing me as a Visiting Fellow with such comfortable and intellectually stimulating surroundings in which to complete the book in the spring and early summer of 1978. I am also indebted to the members of the Department of Sociology of the University of Manchester for their courtesies to me during a stay there in March 1978 as a Simon Visiting Professor. Last but not least, I am grateful to New York University for its generous sabbatical leave policy.

I should like to thank Columbia University Press for permission to reprint in Chapters 1–3 and 5 material that previously appeared in *Skeptical Sociology*, 1976

Dennis H. Wrong
Princeton, N.J.

CHAPTER ONE

Problems in Defining Power

The most general use of the word 'power' in English is as a synonym for capacity, skill, or talent. This use encompasses the capacity to engage in certain kinds of performance, or 'skill' in the strict sense, the capacity to produce an effect of some sort on the external world, and the physical or psychological energies underlying any and all human performances – the 'power to act' itself, as it were. Sometimes the word is used in the plural to denote the total capacities and energies – or 'faculties' – of a human being, as in reference to the increasing or failing 'powers' of a person. When power refers to the energies released by human actions, it merges into the physical concept of energy as the capacity to do work or to move matter, as in steam or electrical power. Applied in this sense to human energies, power is equated with *potency*, or an actor's general ability to produce successful performances.

The notion of controlling or acting on resistant materials is implicit in the idea of power as skill or capacity. Some writers have equated power in this general sense with *mastery*, or with the ability 'to produce observed modifications in the external world'.[1] In the case of complex physical or mental skills, the recalcitrant materials to be mastered are the actor's own body and mind rather than objects in the external environment. The actor exercises a power over himself that we usually call 'self-discipline' or 'self-control'. Freudian writers, beginning with Freud himself, habitually employ political metaphors to describe intrapsychic processes: the 'tyrannical' superego, the 'imperious' id, the 'bargaining' or 'compromising' ego.

Power as potency and, though less unambiguously, as mastery is unmistakably a 'dispositional' term in Gilbert Ryle's sense, referring not to an actual performance but to the capacity, latent in the actor even when not being exercised, to produce a particular kind of performance.[2] When we are concerned with power as a social relation between actors, it is important, as I shall argue in more detail below, to retain the dispositional sense of the term, although the sociological concept of power must not imply that it is an attribute of an actor rather than a relation between actors, whether individuals or groups.

Two famous British philosophers, separated by nearly three centuries, defined power similarly. Thomas Hobbes defined it as 'man's present means to any future apparent good',[3] while to Bertrand Russell, power was 'the production of intended effects'.[4] Hobbes's definition is clearly a dispositional one, for a man may obviously possess the means to attain a future good even when he is not engaged in employing them to that end. Russell's definition, however, lends itself to being understood as 'episodic'[5] rather than dispositional unless one adds the phrase 'the capacity for' in front of 'the production of intended effects'.

But both definitions identify power with potency or mastery and are therefore too general if one's interest is in power as a social relationship, for both cover power over the self and over nature as well as the power of men over other men. Self-mastery is, of course, a major subject for psychology, especially for psychoanalysis, but it is distinguishable from social and political power relations among individuals and groups. The relation between power over nature and power over men is also a highly important subject on which Russell made a number of acute observations over forty years ago, before the advent of computers and nuclear weapons.[6] Nowadays it is a fashionable topic among left-wing intellectuals alarmed by the possibility that the new technical and scientific intelligentsia constitutes a technocratic elite menacing human freedom.[7]. However, political and social theory requires a more restricted definition to differentiate power over nature from power over men.

Although there are hundreds, perhaps thousands, of more recent definitions of social power, or of the power of men over other men, in the literature of social science, I see no reason why we should not make do with older, simpler definitions so long as they are intellectually adequate. I shall therefore adopt a modified version of Russell's definition: *Power is the capacity of some persons to produce intended and foreseen effects on others*.[8] The terms in this definition require detailed analysis to show how they cope with major problems and confusions in the conceptual analysis of power. There are five such problems. First, there is the issue of the *intentionality* of power, and secondly, of its *effectiveness*. The *latency* of power, its dispositional nature to which I have already alluded, is a third problem. The unilateral or asymmetrical nature of power relations implied by the claim that some persons have an effect on others without a parallel claim that the reverse may also be the case is a fourth issue, to be discussed below as the problem of *asymmetry and balance* in power relations. A final question is that of *the nature of the effects produced* by power: must they be overt and behavioural, or do purely subjective, internal effects count also?

The Intentionality of Power

People exercise mutual influence and control over one another's conduct in all social interaction – in fact, that is what we mean by social interaction. It is essential, therefore, to distinguish between the exercise of power and social control in general – otherwise there would be no point in employing power as a separate concept or in identifying power relations as a distinct kind of social relation. That social control is inherent in all social interaction – at least, in all recurrent or 'patterned' social interaction – has been clearly recognized by contemporary sociologists, though some of them have minimized the degree to which resistance to the demands and expectations of others also pervades human social life. Moreover, actors nearly always belong to a larger group or community the norms and values of which they share. Even if it is often overemphasized, the influence of group norms in shaping individual conduct is a basic assumption of modern social science. If norms are the prevailing rules of conduct in a group, and are enforced by positive or negative sanctions, then does not all normatively regulated social behaviour involve power exercised by the group over the individual? Individuals, to be sure, undergo a process of socialization in the course of which they internalize many group norms. When social controls have been internalized, the concept of power as a social relation is clearly inapplicable, but to assume that most conformity to norms is the result of internalization is to adopt what I have called an 'over-socialized conception of man'.[9] Moreover, the power of the parent over the child precedes the child's internalization of parental rules; the child's superego is formed by his identification with the parents, whose commands the child eventually issues to himself without reference to their original external source. Submission to power is thus the earliest and most formative experience in human life. As R. G. Collingwood (no Freudian, to the best of my knowledge) put it:

A man is born a red and wrinkled lump of flesh having no will of its own at all, absolutely at the mercy of the parents by whose conspiracy he has

been brought into existence. That is what no science of human
community . . . must ever forget.[10]

But if to collapse the concept of power into that of social control is to
vitiate all need for a separate concept of power, it then becomes
necessary to distinguish the diffuse controls exercised by the group over
socialized individuals from direct, intentional efforts by a specific
person or group to affect another's conduct. Power is identical with
intended and effective influence. It is one of two subcategories of
influence, the other empirically larger subcategory consisting of acts
of *unintended* influence. In contrast to several recent writers, I do not
see how we can avoid restricting the term power to intentional and
effective acts of influence by some persons on the other persons. It may
be readily acknowledged that intentional efforts to influence others
often produce unintended as well as intended effects on their behaviour – a dominating and overprotective mother does not intend to
femininize the character of her son. But all social interaction produces
such unintended effects – a boss does not mean to plunge an employee
into despair by greeting him somewhat distractedly in the morning,
nor does a woman mean to arouse a man's sexual interest by paying
polite attention to his conversation at a cocktail party. The effects
others have on us, unintended by and even unknown to them, may
influence us more profoundly and permanently than direct efforts to
control our sentiments and behaviour. Dahl and Lindblom call such
unintended influence 'spontaneous field control' and sharply distinguish it from forms of deliberate control.[11]

The distinction between intentional and unintentional effects on
others may seem to be hairsplitting. Does not the elephant who dances
with the chickens exercise a power of life and death over them even
though he has no wish to trample them underfoot? Do not the acts of
governments today shape and destroy the lives of millions even though
these outcomes in no way were intended or even foreseen by
shortsighted statesmen? Yet rather than equate power with all forms of
influence, unintended as well as intended, it seems preferable to stress
the fact that the intentional control of others is likely to create a
relationship in which the power holder exercises unintended influence
over the power subject that goes far beyond what he may have wished
or envisaged at the outset.

To revert to a previous example: it is only because a mother exercises
socially approved power over her children that she may unintentionally

shape their personalities along lines that are repugnant to her and defeat her most cherished hopes. So to confine the term 'power' to the exercise of intentional control is not to make power less important or less pervasive in history and society. The study of the unintended consequences of social action may well be one of the major tasks of the social sciences,[12] but this does not preclude the necessity of carefully distinguishing between outcomes that are intended and those that are not.

Intentionality is often understood to include all outcomes that are anticipated or foreseen by the actor. But there is a difference between acting in order to achieve a certain outcome and recognizing that other effects will unavoidably result from the action which are incidental to the outcome sought by the actor.[13] These anticipated but unintended byproducts of the action may from the actor's standpoint be regarded as inconsequential, as undesirable in themselves but a price worth paying to attain the end for which the action was undertaken, or as secondary gains insufficiently attractive to justify undertaking the action. However, so long as the effects were foreseen by the actor even if not aimed at as such, they constitute an exercise of power in contrast to unanticipated (and by definition unintended) effects. There are, of course, borderline cases where the degree to which the actor may have foreseen certain consequences of his action is in doubt. Such cases often turn up in the courts where the legal assessment of responsibility is at issue. They tend to be decided according to a standard of what the actor might 'reasonably' have expected to have a given probability of happening as a result of his action; for example, the occurrence of a train accident during a brief interval when the railway signalman left his post. The difficulty of deciding in some cases just what probability an actor must have, or should have, ascribed to an unintended outcome for it to count as an expected or foreseen effect must be acknowledged. But an adequate definition of power cannot ignore the difference between intended and unintended but foreseen effects. Intention itself is, after all, sometimes legally problematical.

The Effectiveness of Power

When attempts to exercise power over others are unsuccessful, when the intended effects of the aspiring power-wielder are not in fact produced, we are confronted with an absence or a failure of power. We do not ascribe power over heavenly bodies to Chanticleer the cock, who believed that his crowing caused the sun to rise; this was merely a delusion of power on his part. When in *Henry IV, Part I* Owen Glendower boasts 'I can call spirits from the vasty deep' and Hotspur replies sceptically 'Why, so can I, or so can any man; But will they come when you do call for them?' Hotspur is questioning the reality of Glendower's power over the spirits, or perhaps the very existence of a spirit world. When an attempted exercise of power fails, although similar attempts may have been successful in the past, we witness the breakdown of the power relation. The effectiveness of power would seem to be so obvious a criterion for its presence as to preclude any need for further discussion.

The Latency of Power, or the Actual/Potential Problem

Power is often defined as a capacity to control or influence others. I have already briefly referred to some of the implications of so defining it: the capacity to perform acts of control and their actual performance are clearly not the same thing – power when thought of as a capacity is a dispositional concept. What Gilbert Ryle says about 'knowing' and 'aspiring' also applies to power conceived of as a capacity to control others:

> To say that a person knows something, is not to say that he is at a particular moment in process of doing or undergoing anything, but that he is able to do certain things, when the need arises, or that he is prone to do and feel certain things in situations of certain sorts.[14]

Ryle calls verbs such as 'to know', 'to aspire', and 'to possess' *dispositional* words that refer to recurrent tendencies of human beings to behave in certain ways, in contrast to the *episodic* words we employ to refer to specific behavioural events. The distinction between 'having power' and 'exercising power' reflects the difference between viewing power as a dispositional and as an episodic concept.[15] Unfortunately, power lacks a common verb form, which in part accounts for the frequent tendency to see it as a mysterious property or agency resident in the person or group to whom it is attributed. The use of such terms as 'influence' and 'control', which are both nouns and verbs, as virtual synonyms for power, represents an effort (not necessarily fully conscious) to avoid the suggestion that power is a property rather than a relation.[16]

The evidence that a person or group possesses the capacity to control others may be the frequency with which successful acts of control have been carried out in the past. Thus it makes perfect sense to say that the king or president still 'has' power even when he is asleep in his bed (though not if there has been a successful insurrection since he retired, and armed rebels are guarding the door to his bedroom). Or power may be imputed to an actor when the probability of his intending to achieve and effectively achieving control over another actor is rated high, even though he may not have previously exercised such control.

However, this sense in which power is latent or dispositional is sometimes confused with another, or at least the distinction between them is blurred. Power is sometimes said to be potential rather than actual, to be 'possessed' without being 'exercised', when others carry out the wishes or intentions of the power holder without his ever actually having issued a command to them or even having interacted with them at all to communicate his aims. Carl Friedrich has called such cases 'the rule of anticipated reactions'.[17] Obviously, they differ from a situation in which there may be a considerable time lag between the issuance of a command and compliance with it; to my knowledge, no one has ever regarded such a situation as anything other than an instance of actual, exercised power in view of man's 'time-binding' capacities enabling him to orient himself simultaneously to past, present and future events.

The ruler may be asleep in bed while his subjects are not merely engaged in carrying out directives he gave them before retiring but making decisions and taking actions based on their anticipations of what he would wish them to do in the relevant circumstances. It is this that is often called 'latent' or 'potential' power, as distinct from 'manifest' or 'actual' power where observable communications are transmitted and acted upon. Clearly, more is involved in such cases than the previously described situation where the ruler may be said to 'have' power while asleep in the sense that he has an unimpaired capacity to issue commands in the expectation that they will be obeyed. Both cases, however, seem to me to indicate essential attributes of all power relationships. In this sense Robert Bierstedt is entirely correct in maintaining that 'it may seem redundant to say so, but power is always potential'.[18]

But imputations of power based on the 'anticipated reactions' of the power subject confront a number of difficulties. For A's power over B to be real when it is not actually exercised, B must be convinced of A's capacity to control him and must modify his behaviour accordingly. Thus a mother has power over her child when the child refrains from doing something in anticipation of her displeasure even when the mother is not present to issue a specific prohibition. Similarly, the president has power over Congress when congressional leaders decide to shelve a bill in anticipation of a presidential veto. The consciousness of the power subject is a crucial consideration in imputations of power on the basis of anticipated reactions. Max Weber's conception of power as 'the probability that one actor in a social relationship will . . . carry out his own will'[19] may be interpreted as attributing the estimate of probability to the judgement of the power subject and not merely to that of the observer, say a social scientist. Otherwise, only overt acts of control or the subsequent imposition of a sanction after the performance of an act would validate an imputation of power made by an observer, and the distinction between latent and manifest power disappears.

When power is regarded as a capacity, therefore, and when it is understood to include B's acts based on his anticipations of A's reaction to them, the distinction between latent and manifest, or potential and actual, power is implicit in the very definition of power. Yet even when empirical students of power define it as a capacity, they frequently ignore the implications of such a definition in practice by treating power as identical with its actual exercise and confining themselves to its manifestations in drectly observable act-response sequences.[20] Other writers define power in such a way as to require the overt performance of an act by an imputed power holder that precedes the response of the power subject, thus excluding B's anticipatory responses from the realm of power relations. Actual participation in decision-making or observed 'initiation of interaction for others' becomes the criterion of power. Power is thus seen as a type of social behaviour that can be directly observed and unambiguously identified. (Frequently, of course, acts of power may have to be retrospectively reconstructed: the observer, at least where institutionalized power relations between groups are involved, is rarely right at the elbow of the decision-maker.)

Those who prefer to equate power with its exercise in a social relationship fear the subjectivity that appears to be implicit in the view that actors may 'have' power without exercising it so long as belief in the probability of their exercising it limits the choices of others. As I have already indicated, treating power as a capacity runs the initial risk of seeing it as vested too exclusively in the power holder 'from where it radiates to others'.[21] But once we correct this possible over-emphasis by insisting that power is always a relation between two actors, do we not then risk going to the opposite extreme of making it dependent entirely on what is in the mind of the power subject? Are we not in effect saying that someone's belief that someone else has power actually confers power on the latter?[22] Advocates of the so-called decisional method of studying community power structures have levelled this accusation at researchers who have used the reputational method.[23] Defenders of the reputational method have replied that the attribution of power to someone may indeed confer it on him. However, if this were always the case, popular beliefs about the distribution of power would never be false. Since it is doubtful that the users of the reputational method would themselves make so extreme a claim, it is obviuosly necessary to study the actual exercise of power to confirm or disprove the reputations for power revealed by opinion surveys. Supporters of the decisional method, however, have often recoiled so vigorously from the suggestion that reputation for power is equivalent to having power that they have fallen back on narrowly behaviouristic definitions equating power with its observable exercise.

Yet to avoid such a suggestion, one need only repeat the line of reasoning followed in correcting the opposite inference that power is a kind of force emanating from the power holder: if an actor is believed to be powerful, if he knows that others hold such a belief, and if he encourages it and resolves to make use of it by intervening in or punishing actions by others who do not comply with his wishes, then he truly has power and his power has indeed been conferred upon him by the attributions, perhaps initially without foundation, of others. But if he is unaware that others believe him powerful, or if he does not take their belief seriously in planning his own projects, then he has no power and the belief that he has is mistaken, a misperception of reality. We would not say that the residents of a street had power over a man with paranoid delusions who refused to leave his house because he feared attack by his neighbours. Nor would we say that the American Communist Party actually has great power because a certain segment of the public, influenced by right-wing ideologists, believes this to be the case and acts accordingly.

Raymond Aron has pointed out that the English and German languages employ the same terms, power and *Macht*, respectively, to refer both to the capacity to do something and to the actual exercise of the capacity.[24] In French, however, there are two distinct words: *puissance*, indicating potential or capacity, and *pouvoir*, indicating the act. While the prevailing usage of both terms, according to Aron, has tended to blur this distinction between them and to create new, less meaningful distinctions, Aron argues that *puissance* should be regarded as the more general concept of which *pouvoir* is a particular form. Unfortunately, this terminological distinction does not exist in English, but the idea of 'potential' should be regarded as implicit in all non-behaviouristic definitions that treat power as in some sense a capacity distinguishable from its overt exercise.

Asymmetry and Balance in Power Relations

Power relations are asymmetrical in that the power holder exercises greater control over the behaviour of the power subject than the reverse, but reciprocity of influence – the defining criterion of the social relation itself – is never entirely destroyed except in those forms of physical violence which, although directed against a human being, treat him as no more than a physical object.[24]

The asymmetry of power relations, however, is often stressed to a degree that would make it logically contradictory to speak of 'bilateral' power relations or of 'equality of power' in bargaining or conflict. Thus Gerth and Mills write: 'When everyone is equal there is no politics, for politics involves subordinates and superiors.'[26] And Peter Blau maintains that 'interdependence and mutual influence of equal strength indicate lack of power'.[27] Such assertions risk going too far in severing power relations from their roots in social interaction in its generic form, for the asymmetry of power relations is at least immanent in the give and take of dyadic interaction between equals in which the control of one actor over the other's behaviour is reciprocated by a responsive act of control by the other. Asymmetry exists in each individual act-response sequence, but the actors continually alternate the roles of power holder and power subject in the course of their interaction. In a stable social relation (where there is recurrent interaction between the parties rather than interaction confined to a single occasion) a pattern may emerge in which one actor controls the other with respect to particular situations and spheres of conduct – or 'scopes', as they have often been called – while the other actor is regularly dominant in other areas of activity. Thus a wife may rule in the kitchen, while her husband controls the disposition of the family income. Or a labour union, as in the unions of seamen and longshoremen, controls hiring, while the employer dictates the time and place of work.

Thus if we treat power relations as exclusively hierarchical and unilateral, we overlook an entire class of relations between persons or groups in which the control of one person or group over the other with reference to a particular scope is balanced by the control of the other in a different scope. The division of scopes between the parties is often the result of a bargaining process which may or may not have followed an open struggle for power – a separation in a marriage, a strike against an employer, a lawsuit in commercial rivalry, a war between nations.

The term 'intercursive power' has been suggested for relations characterized by a balance of power and a division of scopes between the parties.[28] It is contrasted with 'integral power', in which decision-making and initiatives to action are centralized and monopolized by one party. Intercursive power exists where the power of each party in a relationship is countervailed by that of the other, with procedures for bargaining or joint decision-making governing their relations when matters affecting the goals and interests of both are involved. Riesman's notion of a balance of veto groups, each able to prevent the others from acts threatening its interests, constitutes a negative system of intercursive power relations.[29] The various conceptions of 'pluralism' in contemporary sociology and political science are models of systems of intercursive power relations.

Integral power always raises the question *quis custodiet ipsos custodies*? – or who rules the rulers, guards the guardians, oversees the overseers? The assumption behind the query is that the rulers' power to decide at their own discretion cannot be entirely eliminated in human societies. 'Power cannot be dissolved into law,' as Franz Neumann observed,[30] and the liberal slogan, 'a government of laws, not of men', is, if taken literally, mere ideology expressing a mistrust of political power. Thus where integral power is established and recognized as unavoidable in at least some situations (or scopes), as in the case of the power of the state in modern times, attempts to limit it take a form other than that of transforming integral power into an intercursive power system. Integral power may be restricted without either reducing the decision-making autonomy of the power holder or countervailing it by giving others power over him with reference to particular scopes. Measures designed to limit integral power include periodic reviews of the acts of the power holder (legislative and judicial review), periodic reaffirmations of his power-holding status or his removal and replacement (rules of tenure and succession), the setting of limits to the scopes he can control or to the range of options available to him within each scope ('civil liberties'), and rights of appeal and petition concerning grievances.

If such measures are to be truly effective and not just window dressing, like the impressive constitutions created by so many absolute dictatorships in recent history, there must be sources of power independent of the integral power holder that can be mobilized to enforce them. The law must be a web that catches the lawmaker as well as his subjects. Conditions making this a reality may include the separation of executive, legislative and judicial powers within the government, the creation of different and independent levels of government as in federative states, divided rather than unified elites within society at large, and, ultimately, strong support for constitutional gaurantees or traditional 'unwritten' rights and liberties on the part of the power subjects. In other words, there must be real countervailing power centres able to enforce limits on the power of the integral power holder, and, insofar as this is required, the distinction between intercursive and integral power is not an absolute one. The checks on integral power, however, are largely negative. To quote Neumann again: 'All traditional legal conceptions are negative ones. They limit activities but do not shape them. It is this very character of law which grants to the citizen a minimum of protection.'[31]

There are four broad ways in which power subjects may attempt to combat or resist the power of an integral power holder: (1) they may strive to exercise countervailing power over him in order to transform his integral power into a system of intercursive power; (2) they may set limits to the extensiveness (the number of power subjects), comprehensiveness (the number of scopes), and intensity (the range of options within particular scopes) of his power; (3) they may destroy his integral power altogether, leaving the acts he formerly controlled open to free and self-determined choice; (4) they may seek to supplant him by acquiring and exercising his integral power themselves.

With reference to the integral power of modern states within their territorial jurisdictions, the first three choices correspond roughly to, respectively, efforts to establish democratic government, efforts to establish constitutional government, and the elimination of all government, or anarchy. The first two, of course, have frequently been combined as a political objective. The fourth way obviously corresponds to the different forms of political succession, such as putsch, revolution, or the legally regulated competition of electoral contests.

Such devices as the initiative, the referendum and impeachment by ballot, as well as the conception of elections as popular mandates, are established ways in which subjects exercise countervailing power over their rulers. The transformation of integral power into intercursive power, however, can never be complete in the case of modern states, in so far as there is an irreducibly integral element in political power that cannot be eliminated altogether.[32] Bills of rights, constitutional guarantees, jurisdictional restrictions, and statutory limits on the options available to the political decision-maker are ways of checking the integral power of the state without eliminating it altogether by depriving the ruler of any scopes in which he can decide and act according to his own discretion. The removal of certain substantive areas of choice by power subjects from any control by the state – such as the 'basic' freedoms of speech, religion, assembly, residence, etc. – has the effect of eliminating the integral power of the state in these areas, though the total elimination of state power – the third choice above – has never been permanently realized in any civilized society. (It has, of course, been the goal of anarchism as a political movement.)

It is misleading therefore to contend that 'all politics is a struggle for power'. The subjects or victims of power may seek to replace the power holder because they envy him and wish to use his power in the service of their own goals and interests, or because they are vengeful and wish to punish him as he may have punished them. But alternatively they may wish to free themselves from his control over them by limiting or abolishing his power and enlarging their own range of free choice. Politics includes both a struggle *for* power and a struggle to limit, resist and escape *from* power.

The Nature of the Effects Produced by Power

This issue does not strike me as an especially thorny one, so I shall discuss it very briefly. If A produces no change in B's actual behaviour but only a change in his feelings, attitudes, or beliefs, are we justified in imputing power to A?[33] The answer is implicit in the definition of power as the capacity of some person or persons to produce intended effects on other persons. If A's intention is to affect or alter B's attitudes rather than his behaviour and he succeeds in doing so in the desired direction, then he clearly has power over B to this extent in the relevant scope to which the attitudes refer. If, however, his intention is to produce a particular act by B and he fails to do so, his attempt to exercise power eliciting only an inner disposition on the part of B to comply that is not acted on, or a feeling of guilt, then he has not exercised power over B but rather unintended influence. The same would be true if he evoked B's bitter hostility and strong determination to resist compliance. Surely, in this latter case we would not wish to impute power to A at all but rather to speak of the failure of his effort to control B, though he may indeed have influenced B by arousing his antagonism. In many actual situations, A is likely to aim at influencing both B's sentiments and his behaviour. If he succeeds only in the former, then he has exercised power that is limited in comprehensiveness and intensity while failing in his more ambitious effort to control B's behaviour. But there are many situations where the aim of the power holder is no more than to maintain or strengthen an existing attitude or belief system of the power subject, an attitude or belief system, for example, that sustains inaction or 'non-decisions' in Bachrach and Baratz's sense.[34] One thinks of propaganda to reinforce uncritical loyalty to a political regime, or to rekindle the fires of hostility toward foreign enemies or domestic dissenters. Clearly, the controllers of the mass media often aim at this sort of power, whether they are an arm of the government or represent 'private' organizations engaged in 'public relations' or 'institutional advertising'.

Three Attributes of Power Relations

Bertrand de Jouvenel has distinguished three variable attributes of all power relations, which, when specified, greatly facilitate the comparison of different types of power relations and structures. 'Power or authority,' as de Jouvenel states,

> has three dimensions: it is *extensive* if the complying Bs [the power subjects] are many; it is *comprehensive* if the variety of actions to which A [the power holder] can move the Bs is considerable; finally it is *intensive* if the bidding of A can be pushed far without loss of compliance.[35]

The *extensiveness* of a power relation may be narrow or broad. The former is illustrated by an isolated dyadic relation in which a single person exercises power over a single other, the latter by political regimes in which one man rules over millions of subjects. De Jouvenel mentions only the number of subjects, but the power holder may of course also be plural – there may be many As as well as many Bs. The Aristotelian classification of forms of government is primarily based on whether sovereignty is 'in the hands of one, or the few, or of the many'.[36] Under kingship and tyranny, one man rules over many; under aristocracy and oligarchy, a few men rule over the many; and under polity and democracy, the majority of the community rule themselves. The direct democracy of the Athenian polis can be regarded as a differentiated, asymmetrical power structure with regard to the imposition of majority decisions on minorities and non-citizens (slaves and women). Much of classical and modern political theory, as well as a large literature in the fields of public administration and organization theory on the 'span of control', deals with the extensiveness of power relations. One might define extensiveness as the ratio of the number of persons who hold power to the number of the powerless. The major (and perhaps the only?) significant contention of the Italian neo-Machiavellian or élitist school to political theory (Pareto, Mosca, Michels) was to insist that in large societies or associations a minority of men inevitably come to wield power over the majority, or 'the masses'.

A serious limitation in the writings of the neo-Machiavellians is their readiness to assume that power wielded by a minority is likely to be unlimited, ideologies and rituals implying the contrary notwithstanding, and the more so the smaller the minority.[37] They failed to give independent consideration to the *comprehensiveness* of power: the number of scopes in which the power holder(s) controls the activities of the power subject(s). Robert Dahl employs the term 'scope' to refer chiefly to different institutional activities or 'issue-areas', such as education, political nominations, urban planning, and the like.[38] As a political scientist, he is primarily concerned with governmental decision-making. For a more general analysis of power relations, one may conceive of scopes as the different areas of choice and activity of the power subject. The comprehensiveness of a power relation, therefore, refers to the number of scopes over which the power holder holds power, or to the proportion or range of the power subject's total conduct and life-activity that is subject to control. At one extreme there is the power of a parent over an infant or young child, which is very nearly total in its comprehensiveness, extending to virtually everthing the child does. At the other extreme, there is the very limited and specific power of the incumbents of highly specialized 'situated roles',[39] such as those of a taxi dispatcher or a high-school student appointed to traffic safety patrol.

A third generic attribute of power relations is the *intensity* of the relation. If I understand correctly de Jouvenel's brief discussion of this attribute, he has in mind the range of effective options open to the power holder *within* each and every scope of the power subject's conduct over which he wields power. What limits are there to the actions which the power holder can influence the power subject to perform? Will the power subject commit suicide or murder under the power holder's influence? What intended effects sought by the power holder will be resisted, producing, at least initially, a breakdown of the power relation? Justice Holmes once wrote:

> I heard the original Agassiz (Louis) say that in some part of Germany there would be a revolution if you added a farthing to the cost of a glass of beer. If that was true, the current price was one of the rights of man at that place.[40]

Or, in the language employed here, the intensity of the power of tavern-owners to set the price of a glass of beer was severely limited with the prevailing price setting the upper limit.

I have previously noted that formal statutory guarantees of 'the rights of man', or civil liberties, set limits both to the comprehensiveness and the intensity of power. In the former case, certain scopes are specifically excluded from the control of power holders, such as the freedoms of speech, assembly, religious worship, travel, and so on. Statutory limits on the intensity of power curtail the range of options available to the power holder within those scopes where he does have control. Thus the courts may possess the power to impose punishments on lawbreakers, but not 'cruel and unusual punishments'; a trade union certified as a collective bargaining agent may require a union shop, but not, under the Taft-Hartley Act, a closed shop. These examples refer to formal legal limitations on the intensity of a power relation within a given scope, but obviously, as the remark of Justice Holmes reflecting his famous legal positivism suggests, *de facto* limits are likely to be present in even the most informal, interpersonal power relations. At the pole of maximum intensity one might locate the relationship between a lover and a loved one where the former declares 'your wish is my command' – and means it. At the opposite pole stands the 'decision-maker' whose choices are confined to a very narrow range: a tax assessor, for example, who by statute can raise or lower tax rates by no more than a few percentage points. The tendency in some social science writing to identify 'decision-making' with the exercise of power can be misleading if the intensity of the decision-maker's power to decide is not taken into account.

Herbert Simon's useful term 'zone of acceptance' can be understood as referring to the intensity of power.[41] P. H. Partridge, however, has adopted Simon's term to describe what I have called 'comprehensiveness' as a general attribute of power and also used it synonymously with the particular scopes, or areas of activity, that, taken together if there is more than one, constitute the comprehensiveness of a power relation. He writes:

> If I try to influence the views my students have about Marx, I may succeed; if I try to influence, still more to prescribe, their choice of wives, they will ignore me. Following Simon, we call this dimension the 'zone of acceptance' . . .[42]

Partridge then defines 'intensity' much as I have:

> . . . we find also that within the 'zone of acceptance', and with respect to *one* particular segment of a man's interests or activities, there is a limit to the extent that another can influence or control this segment . . . This dimension we call the 'intensity' of power . . .[43]

These differences of terminology are scarcely important, although I think that Simon's term comes closer to describing the intensity rather than the comprehensiveness of power. If a power holder tries to extend his power beyond a particular scope (or zone of acceptance in Partridge's sense) in which it is seen as legitimate, as in Partridge's example of a teacher trying to influence his students' choice of wives, he will arouse resistance. One may conclude that his power is limited to a specific scope, such as to the right to decide what will be covered in a lecture course, what reading will be required, what grades assigned on examinations, and a few details of classroom behaviour. But if a teacher assigns five times as much reading as is customary, fails every student registered in the course, or spends the entire lecture period gazing silently out of the window, his authority is also likely to be challenged. The first example of exceeding the 'limit within which authority will be accepted' (in Simon's phrase) reveals the comprehensiveness of the power relation; the second example indicates its intensity.

At a certain level of generality the distinction between com-

prehensiveness and intensity is of little significance because both
attributes or dimensions of power relations represent limits to the range
of effects that the power holder can produce on the power subject's
actions. I prefer to use 'scope' to refer to the segment or sphere of
conduct controlled by the power holder and 'zone of acceptance' to
indicate the range of compliant acts by the power subject within
particular scopes that the power holder is capable of producing.
Although there are empirical instances of power relations that are high
in comprehensiveness and low in intensity (which may itself vary within
the different scopes covered by a power relation) and *vice-versa*, there
are also power relations in which the two attributes vary together in the
same direction. 'Total' or 'absolute' power usually means power that is
high in both comprehensiveness and intensity. On the other hand,
limited scope-specific power relations are usually also low in intensity.

What interrelationships are there among these three attributes of
power relations? The most total and unlimited power, power that is
greatest in comprehensiveness and intensity, is likely to be least
extensive: namely, dyadic relations in which one person has power over
a single other. As far back as Aristotle, the power of a master over a
household slave has often served as the standard example of virtually
unrestricted power. The power of a parent over a small child – the *fons
et origo* of the human character structure – is another obvious example.
The power of the loved one over the lover in a passionate, 'romantic'
love relationship represents the most narrowly extensive and highly
individualized form of power relation, since the relation is based entirely
on the uniqueness of the particular individuals involved. As Philip Slater
has argued, an exclusive love relationship constitutes what he calls a
'dyadic withdrawal' from society and its obligations, in its most extreme
form the *Liebestod*, and has been subjected by all societies to normative
controls.[44] A love relationship, however, is often a relatively balanced,
or bilateral power relation between two individuals. A relationship
between a sadist and a masochist best exemplifies a narrowly extensive
but highly comprehensive and intensive interpersonal power relation.

A patriarch in the family, a tribal leader or a village despot may also
wield highly comprehensive and intensive power over a relatively small
number of subjects. The limited extensiveness of his power enables him
to dispense with intermediaries to whom power is delegated and who as
subordinate power holders may become potential rivals and
competitors. Where the power subjects are few in number, less power
has to be delegated from the top, and levels of power in a pyramidal or

scalar power structure are less likely to emerge. This is a special case of the well-known generalization of organization theory that the larger the group and the more differentiated the activities of its members the greater the number of supervisory levels required if it is successfully to achieve its goals.

The term 'totalitarianism' has come into use to describe tyrannical or oligarchical (in the Aristotelian sense) political regimes that wield more extensive, comprehensive and intensive power than any of the monarchies, tyrannies or oligarchies of the past. Totalitarian regimes exercise more extensive power in that they have flourished in large and populous nation-states rather than in small city-states or agrarian communities. Some writers indeed have argued that full totalitarian rule is possible *only* in large and populous societies.[45] Modern technology, especially new media of communications, permits more highly centralized bureaucratic control over the lives of the subjects, thus concentrating decision-making in few hands even though the power structure includes more intermediate levels between top and bottom. Yet the power of a totalitarian dictator over his subjects is scarcely as comprehensive as that of a parent over a child or a master over a slave. The difficulty of maintaining the *visibility* at all times of the behaviour of all the subjects sets limits to the comprehensiveness of totalitarian power. A Nazi once boasted that 'the only free man in Germany is a man who is asleep', but even in Nazi Germany at the time this was a considerable exaggeration. Negative utopian visions, such as those of Orwell and Zamiatin which describe societies even more totally controlled by small elites than the historical examples of totalitarianism in the present century, depend to a considerable extent on science-fiction solutions to the visibility problem, Orwell's two-way television screens being the best-known example.

In her great book, *The Origins of Totalitarianism*, Hannah Arendt regards the concentration camp as the ultimate and most significant expression of totalitarian rule. She calls the Nazi camps 'experiments in total domination'. But the camps were, of course, smaller communities than the wider totalitarian society in which they existed; so the total power their rulers exercised over the inmates does not invalidate the general rule that the comprehensiveness and intensity of power tend to vary inversely with its extensiveness.

New media of communication, techniques of observation and persuasion, and instruments of violence have also, it has often been argued, increased the intensity of power in totalitarian states.

Propaganda over centrally controlled mass media and psychological methods of 'thought reform' have allegedly enabled totalitarian power holders to indoctrinate their subjects more thoroughly with passionate and unconditional loyalties to the regime. At the same time deviance and noncompliance, let alone active resistance, have become more difficult with the use of new techniques of surveillance and extracting information, and new means of coercion. Even in the democracies, enormous anxieties have been aroused in recent years by electronic 'bugging' and wiretapping devices, subliminal advertising, and so-called 'brainwashing'. Events in Eastern Europe since 1945, and even in the Soviet Union and China, have somewhat reduced the plausibility of the assumption that control of the new technology has made totalitarian regimes virtually invulnerable to internal dissent and opposition. Political will and organization and the legitimacy of the regime in the eyes of its subjects remain, as in the past, crucial factors determining the efficacy of opposition, and these factors are by no means entirely subject to control by the ruling elite. Even though the new technology permits more centralized control and speedier response to incipient threats, it also requires the disciplined and dedicated cooperation of a larger number of men trained to wield its complex instruments, and this dilutes the total power of the ruling élite.

In summary, there are three main reasons why the greater extensiveness of a power relation sets limits to its comprehensiveness and intensity. First, the greater the number of power subjects, the greater the difficulty of supervising all of their activities. Second, the greater the number of power subjects, the more extended and differentiated the chain of command necessary to control them, creating new subordinate centres of power that can be played off against each other and that may themselves become foci of opposition to the integral power holder. Third, the greater the number of subjects, the greater the likelihood of wide variation in their attitudes toward the power-holder. The power-holder will not be able to wield power with equal comprehensiveness and intensity over all of his subjects. A few may be eager and pliant servants of his will, others will 'go along' less enthusiastically, still others will require constant supervision and threats to keep their performances in line, and there will be some against whom force must be used even to the extent of eliminating them from the ranks of the living.

CHAPTER TWO

The Forms of Power: Force, Manipulation, Persuasion

Many writers have defined power as the capacity to impose, or to threaten successfully to impose, penalties or deprivations for non-compliance. Perhaps the most influential definition of this kind is Max Weber's:

> In general, we understand by 'power' the chance of a man or a number of men to realize their own will in a social action even against the resistance of others who are participating in the action.[1]

The reference here to resistance clearly suggests a view of power as the capacity to impose penalties, or to coerce, and it has usually been so understood. Robert Bierstedt, recognizing the dispositional rather than the episodic nature of power, writes: 'Power is the ability to employ force, not its actual employment, the ability to apply sanctions, not their actual application.'[2] Similarly, Lasswell and Kaplan write:

> Power is a special case of the exercise of influence: it is the process of affecting policies of others with the help of (actual or threatened) severe deprivations for nonconformity with the policies intended.[3]

To define power, as I have, as the capacity to produce intended and foreseen effects on others avoids this equation of power with the ability to impose sanctions. The latter is certainly an important form of power, but I see no good reason for excluding from an initial definition situations in which someone, whether willingly or even unknowingly, complies with someone else's intention, whether or not the latter is able, or is believed by the former to be able, to impose sanctions. As J. A. A. Van Doorn has observed, this 'would not seem to be essential, since power is perfectly conceivable without any opposition on the part of the subject – notably when its exercise is accepted'.[4] Few writers on power hold as consistently to, or develop as fully the logical implications of their own definitions, as Bierstedt, who explicitly denies that persuasion and authority based on belief in competence (e.g. the authority of the physician over the patient) are forms of power at all rather than of influence.[5] I find it more useful to regard these as distinct forms of power, conceiving of power more broadly than Bierstedt.

Among more recent writers, Bachrach and Baratz, in their valuable critique of studies of power which identify the powerful with those participating in actual decision-making, follow Lasswell and Kaplan in equating power with the capacity to compel obedience in the face of opposition. However, unlike the writers previously mentioned, they do not treat voluntary compliance as 'institutionalized power' but reject it altogether as a form of power. They are quite clear on this, arguing that if a sentry orders an approaching soldier to halt or be shot and 'the soldier put obedience to a sentry's order at the top of his schedule of values' in complying with it, then 'the threat of severe deprivations had no bearing on his behaviour. In such circumstances it cannot be said that the guard exercised power'.[6]

Presumably, they would not regard persuasion either as a form of power on the same grounds, although they do not say so directly. Not only do Bachrach and Baratz reject voluntary obedience, traditionally labelled 'authority', as a form of power, but they also reject force and manipulation on the grounds that neither allows the individual any choice between compliance and non-compliance and both are therefore 'non-rational and tend to be non-relational'. ('Non-volitional' would be a better term than 'non-relational'.) Bachrach and Baratz are entirely correct in this contention, but I nevertheless find it more useful and in closer conformity with both popular and most scholarly discourse to define power more parsimoniously and broadly as simply the capacity to produce intended effects, regardless of the physical or psychological factors on which the capacity rests, and then to proceed to differentiate *force, manipulation, persuasion,* and *authority* as distinct forms of power.

I have the impression that a somewhat larger number of writers have defined power in this more general manner than have identified it with constraint or the overcoming of resistance. Goldhamer and Shils, for example, write: 'A person may be said to have *power* to the extent that he influences the behaviour of others in accordance with his own intentions.'[7] Gerth and Mills initially adopt the Weberian definition in stating 'we ascribe "power" to those who can influence the conduct of others even against their will', but two pages later they explicitly exclude constraint as the defining criterion of power: '*power* is simply the probability that men will act as another man wishes. The action may rest upon fear, rational calculation of advantage, lack of energy to do otherwise, loyal devotion, indifference, or a dozen other individual motives.'[9] Actually, Weber's discussion from which theirs derives places excessive weight on the word 'even': Weber writes of the actor's ability 'to carry out his own will even against resistance' and then adds 'regardless of the basis on which this probability rests'. The latter phrase suggests that there are multiple bases for the exercise of power going beyond the ability to coerce the subject by threatening him with deprivations. Weber goes on to observe: 'The concept of power is sociologically amorphous. All conceivable qualities of a person and all conceivable combinations of circumstances may put him in a position to impose his will in a given situation.'[10] This points to the existence of multiple and diverse bases on which someone may exercise power over another, including prestige considerations, persuasion, manipulation, a sense of duty, habit, and erotic and personal magnetism, as well as fear of physical or economic sanctions.

In common with many sociologists, Gerth and Mills define *authority* as 'legitimate power' involving the voluntary obedience of the subject based on the belief that obedience is his duty.[11] While I shall define authority somewhat differently in the next chapter, I accept authority as a special case of power, which remains the more general concept. I accept also Lasswell and Kaplan's view that power is a special case of influence, namely, intended as opposed to unintended influence as I have already argued.

The chart on page 24 shows the forms of influence and power and the relations among them. Power is intended and effective influence and there are four distinct forms of power, one of them, *authority*, itself divided into five subtypes.

Force, manipulation and *persuasion* are classified here as forms of power, but all three lack certain of the generic characteristics of power discussed in the previous chapter. Force and some forms of manipulation are not social relations at all involving reciprocal if asymmetrical interaction between self-conscious subjects, as I have already noted in connection with Bachrach and Baratz. Nor does the rule of anticipated reactions, so important a feature of the latent or

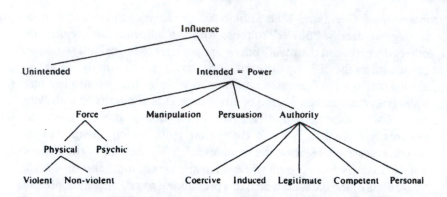

potential aspect of power, apply to either. Force and manipulation are either exercised to produce the intended effects of the power wielder or they are not, in which case they do not exist as forms of power. Persuasion, on the other hand, is unmistakably a social relation, but the rule of anticipated reactions can only be said to apply to it in a highly oblique sense. Like force and manipulation, persuasion, therefore, exists only in manifest form in its actual exercise, and lacks the latent or potential aspect of other forms of power.

Force

Force refers most commonly to physical or biological force: the creation of physical obstacles restricting the freedom of another, the infliction of bodily pain or injury including the destruction of life itself, and the frustration of basic biological needs which must be satisfied if the capacity for voluntary choice and action is to remain unimpaired. Force involves treating a human subject as if he were no more than a physical object, or at most a biological organism vulnerable to pain and the impairment of its life-processes. The ultimate form of force is *violence*: direct assault upon the body of another in order to inflict pain, injury or death. But the methods of *non-violence* adopted by some recent social movements, which proved so successful against the British in India and, more recently, against racial segregation laws in the American South, also exemplify force as a form of power. In non-violence, people use their own bodies as physical objects to prevent or restrict actions by others rather than acting directly on the bodies of others. By 'sitting-in' in a building or public place they make it impossible for the activities usually carried on there to take place. By lying down on railways or highways they confront the drivers of trains or cars with the choice of either stopping or running them over. Conversely, by declining to appear at a work-place or other site of customary co-operative activities, non-violent activists remove themselves from exposure to the commands, threats or appeals of the resident authorities and bring about a stoppage of the customary activities. The deprivation of basic biological needs is also a form of physical force. Obvious examples are the denial of food and of sleep or rest, as in the forcing of prisoners to stand for hours with lights flashing in their eyes or the long hours of exhausting physical labour in the German and Russian concentration camps. All destruction of valued property or imposition of economic sanctions amount to physical force in milder forms. Where the property destroyed or the economic benefits withheld are not necessary for subsistence or survival in the biological sense, one cannot say that the victim of force is being treated solely as a physical or biological object since his social and psychological needs are being taken into account. Yet the act of destruction or withholding need not be a social act involving minimally reciprocal interaction between two subjects.

The relation between the use of force and its threatened use is obviously an intimate one, but a forcible act is distinguishable from a threat to use force. A punch on the jaw is not the same thing as shaking a fist; a shot from a gun is distinct from pointing a gun and shouting 'Hands up!' or 'Your money or your life'. The crucial difference is that the latter examples are clearly social relations in which the threatener engages in communication with the other at the symbolic level; he does not, in short, treat the other as something less than a human being capable of understanding and choice. To be sure, he wishes to narrow drastically the range of the other's choices. Few have expressed the difference as well as Georg Simmel, who is worth quoting at length:

> Even in the most oppressive and cruel cases of subordination, there is still a considerable measure of personal freedom. We merely do not become aware of it, because its manifestation would entail sacrifices which we usually never think of taking upon ourselves. Actually, the 'absolute' coercion which even the most cruel tyrant imposes upon us is always distinctly relative. Its condition is our desire to escape from the threatened punishment or from other consequences of our disobedience. More precise analysis shows that the super-subordination relationship destroys the subordinate's freedom only in the case of direct physical violation. In every other case, this relationship only demands a price for the realization

of freedom – a price, to be sure, which we are not willing to pay. It can narrow down more and more the sphere of external conditions under which freedom is clearly realized, but, except for physical force, never to the point of the complete disappearance of freedom.[12]

The threat and the actual application of force are often collapsed together conceptually and labelled *coercion*, but the implications of the preceding analysis necessitate drawing a sharp distinction between them. Failure to distinguish between force and the threat of force leads to, as I shall argue more fully below, a tendency to minimize the role of coercion, defined as the threat of force, in human affairs. It is often stated that so-called 'naked power' (which invariably means power based on force) is inherently unstable and limited in what it can achieve. Such statements underplay the elements of coercion present in nearly all concrete power relations. They derive much of their plausibility from the fact that the intended effects on others which the actual use of force is capable of producing are strictly limited. Recognition of the larger range of effects that can be achieved by the threat of force and the fear it arouses in the subject is therefore blurred.

It is also frequently stated that the use of force or violence, far from being the fundamental manifestation of power, is evidence of the breakdown of power. Hannah Arendt, for example, writes: 'Power and violence are opposites; where the one rules absolutely, the other is absent. Violence appears where power is in jeopardy, but left to its own course it ends in power's disappearance.'[13] Such statements are elliptical. When an effort to exercise power by other means fails, force may be applied as the 'final persuader'. Or it may be applied as punishment for previous non-compliance. In both cases the resort to force is indeed the result of the prior failure of power, although its successful use represents the exercise of a new form of power in so far as it restricts the subject's freedom with respect to certain acts in accordance with the intention of the wielder of force. The use of force as punishment may also succeed in re-establishing the pre-existing power relation, whether it was based on the threat and fear of force, duty, self-interest, or some combination of these.

It should now be obvious why force as a form of power has reality only in its manifest form. Latent force is a separate form of power, social rather than physical. Someone who bases his conduct on the anticipation that force will be applied to him unless he performs, or refrains from performing, certain requisite actions is not subject to force but rather to the threat of force. David Easton is one of the few political scientists who has fully recognized the necessity of making this distinction conceptually:

I distinguish here between force and the threat of force. In the latter case we have an example of the exercise of authority. There is a significant difference between actually eliminating a person from the political system by jailing him and merely threatening him with incarceration. When only threats are made, the individual may be inclined to obey, thereby participating in an authority relationship, whereas in the case of pure force the individual continues to refuse to obey but is nevertheless compelled to conform to the decision of the authorities.[14]

Force is more effective in preventing or restricting people from acting than in causing them to act in a given way. 'The one thing you cannot do with bayonets is to sit on them,' as Talleyrand observed. Force can eliminate a man's freedom to act at all by killing him, starving or maiming him, confining him within four walls or otherwise removing him from the scene, or placing physical obstacles in his path. Force can achieve negative effects: the destruction, prevention or limitation of the possibility of action by others. But one cannot forcibly manipulate the limbs and bodies of others in order to achieve complex positive results: the fabrication or construction of something, the operation of a machine, the performance of a physical or mental skill. Force, however, is often employed not just to eliminate someone's capacity to act, but to establish in the mind of the power subject the future credibility of the power holder's willingness and capability to use force, or, in effect, to create, or recreate, a power relation based not on force but on the threat and fear of force. I shall postpone further discussion of the relation between force and coercion till the next chapter.

It is tempting to confine the use of the term force to *physical* force, as so many writers have done, including myself in the preceding discussion. But there is a form of conduct, often described as psychic, psychological or moral force or violence, which does not fit readily under the rubrics of any of the other forms of power. If physical violence involves inflicting damages on the body of a person, how is one to classify the deliberate effort to affect adversely a person's emotions or his feelings and ideas about himself by verbally, or in other symbolic ways, insulting or degrading him? If, as I argued in the previous chapter, power includes the production of purely mental or emotional effects and is not confined to the eliciting of overt acts, then the psychic assault of, say, a nagging, browbeating spouse or parent, the defamation of the character of a political foe or even of an entire social group, constitute exercises of power. There are, moreover, institutionalized forms of psychic violence: ritual degradation ceremonies, the practice of black magic or sorcery, the pronouncement of a curse.[15] Damage to the psyche is surely as real as damage to the body. But the former requires, as the latter does not, recognition of the human capacity of the subject to understand and respond, of his orientation to symbols. It is plainly not true that 'sticks and stones may break my bones but names can never hurt me'. Psychic violence, in which the intended effect of the perpetrator is to inflict mental or emotional harm, is continuous with physical violence and does not clearly fall under any of the other classifications of forms of power: manipulation, persuasion or authority.

Manipulation

When the power holder conceals his intent from the power subject — that is, the intended effect he wishes to produce, he is attempting to manipulate the latter. In Easton's words: 'When B is *not* aware of A's intention to influence him but A does in fact manage to get B to follow his wishes, we can say that we have an instance of *manipulation*.'[16] Such manipulation may occur within a social relation which may or may not be another form of power relation between the actors. If in persuading or commanding a power subject, the power holder fails to make explicit certain actions he induces the power subject to perform, even though he has made explicit other performed actions, he has manipulated the power subject in addition to exercising other forms of power over him.

Any deliberate and successful effort to influence the response of another where the desired response has not been explicitly communicated to the other constitutes manipulation. Dahl and Lindblom treat manipulation, or 'manipulated field control' as they call it in contrast to 'spontaneous field control' (which I have called 'unintended influence'), as one of the most widespread forms of influence: 'Deliberate manipulation of another's field by acting on information, rewards, and deprivations appears to be as universal, widespread and comprehensive as spontaneous field control . . .'[17] Such an exercise of power is unlikely to evoke resistance because the power subject is unaware of the effort to influence him; successful manipulation may even, as Dahl and Lindblom point out, 'simulate feelings of "free choice" and evoke enthusiasm and initiative'.[18] Clearly, much presenting of information to others, even where the information is accurate and intended to aid and encourage the recipient to pursue intelligently his own goals, constitutes manipulation in this sense.

Yet even such apparently benign uses of manipulation have not entirely escaped the suspicion and mistrust that cling to this form of power, a suspicion aroused by the subject's ignorance as to whether he has in fact been manipulated and the manipulator's concealed purpose. The idea of the calculated eliciting of responses from others suggests the con-man, the polished 'line', the rhetorician of *pseudo-Gemeinschaft*.[19] At best, he who is thought to practise it is likely to earn the reputation of being a 'cold fish.' The deliberate giving of signals to another in order to elicit a desired response implies a degree of calculation, affective detachment and 'playing on' another's feelings that is alien to norms of candour, emotional 'warmth', and the mutual disclosure of motives which govern personal relations in primary groups. Actually, as Erving Goffman has noted, it is surprising how rarely participants in informal social interaction plan their overtures and responses to one another more than a few conversational – or interactional – moves ahead. The apparent spontaneity and artlessness of most informal interaction depend on shared belief in the absence of manipulation by any of the actors, but much of the time the appearance is genuine. The reactions of the victims of Harold Garfinkel's students' experiments in the disruption of conventional expectations suggest as much.[20]

Manipulation may also occur where there is no social relation between the power holder and the power subject and the latter may not even be aware of the former's existence. This takes two main forms. First, the power holder may exercise concealed control over the power subject through symbolic communications designed to make veiled suggestions, to limit or determine selectively the power subject's information supply, or to inculcate without appearing to do so certain positive or negative attitudes. Much commercial advertising and many forms of political propaganda involve this kind of manipulation and they are probably what come first to the minds of most people when the term is used.

But an equally widespread kind of manipulation occurs where A alters B's environment in such a way as to evoke a desired response from B without interacting directly with B at all. One of the most common examples is the setting of prices by sellers in a market economy.[21]

Manipulation has a more sinister reputation than perhaps any other form of power, suggesting devilish cunning and malign purpose on the part of the manipulator. This is, as I have already indicated, because it is a form of power that cannot be openly resisted by the power subject, since he is unaware of the power holder's intent or even sometimes of his existence. There is no visible command for him to disobey, no identifiable adversary against whom to assert his freedom. Thus manipulation appears to be the most dehumanized form of power of all, more dehumanized even than physical force where the victim is at least likely to know himself to be the object of another's assault upon his body or frustration of his basic needs. Over a quarter of a century ago, Merton observed of contemporary city-dwellers:

> On every side, they feel themselves the object of manipulation. They see themselves as the target for ingenious methods of control, through advertising which cajoles, promises, terrorizes; through propagandas that, utilizing available techniques, guide the unwitting audience into opinions which may or may not coincide with the best interests of themselves or their affiliates; through cumulatively subtle methods of salesmanship which may simulate values common to both salesman and client for private and self-interested motives. In place of a sense of *Gemeinschaft* – genuine community of values – there intrudes *pseudo-Gemeinschaft* – the feigning of personal concern with the other fellow in order to manipulate him the better.[22]

Such attitudes have hardly decreased since Merton wrote.

The evil reputation of manipulation has, if anything, been enhanced by its association with new biological and psychological discoveries which arouse an already widespread fear of technological élites perceived as the masters of arcane specialized knowledge and gadgetry. The awareness since Freud of unconscious motivations and of the possibility of utilizing psychoanalytic knowledge to appeal to them has played a considerable role in inspiring fears of manipulation by mad or wicked practitioners of 'hidden persuasion'. Even before Freud, hypnotism held a snake-and-bird fascination for many as is revealed in popular superstititions, works of fiction and carnival sideshows. The stimulation of centres of the brain by electronic signals and the use of drugs to affect emotions and consciousness are more recent discoveries which have given currency to the belief that people can be psychologically influenced without their knowledge and against their will. Delusions of being influenced from a distance by mysterious rays or electric currents, by chemicals placed in one's food or by hypnotic suggestion have long been common symptoms of mental illness, so it is hardly surprising that new techniques and devices which seem to bring such things into the realm of possibility should arouse mass apprehension. Motivational research, subliminal advertising, the use of propaganda appeals based on sociological and psychological knowledge, even psychotherapy and some forms of pedagogy, are ways in which large numbers of people can allegedly be influenced that have incurred deep suspicion and often been labelled 'brainwashing'.[23] The forms of ideological indoctrination in Communist countries to which the term 'brainwashing' was originally applied, however, are more properly regarded as instances of what I have called psychic force or violence than of manipulation.

If one makes the assumption that the primary aim of power holders is always to establish and maintain their power for its own sake rather than to achieve a substantive goal, serve an ideal or fulfil a duty, then all forms of power other than force, the threat of force, and obedience induced by offering rewards are equivalent to manipulation. This is so because the securing of the power holder's power is not in and of itself a concern or interest of the power subject;[24] it is unexpressed in the legitimating arguments and appeals of the power holder designed to win the subject's acceptance of an obligation to obey. Thus all efforts by the power holder to legitimate his power are deceptive in intent and constitute 'fraud' as opposed to force or bribery. Force and fraud, or coercion and manipulation, are the only forms of power, to which all others can in the end be reduced. (The offering of rewards is the counterpart of force and the threat of force, the use of positive rather than negative sanctions to obtain compliance, but the subject's dependence on rewards in a stable relationship frequently converts the relationship into a form of economic coercion or exploitation.) There are, then, no truly consensual power relations. This is, of course, the viewpoint of cynical Machiavellianism (in the popular sense), which is assessed and, in the large, rejected in Chapter 5.[25]

In spite of the awesome repute of manipulation, the effects it is capable of producing seem to be fairly limited in extensiveness, comprehensiveness and intensity. Many of the claims made for the successful manipulation of masses of people are untested and the more plausible claims are largely confined to creating attitudes leading to rather limited actions such as buying a particular product or voting for a particular political candidate. True, fortunes have been made as a result of successful advertising campaigns and advertising in general may in contemporary capitalist societies have shaped men's 'felt needs' to a degree that makes obsolete the psychological assumptions of classical economics, as J. K. Galbraith has argued, or it may, as Herbert Marcuse has claimed, have distorted men's 'real' desires rooted in a universal human nature. But advertising depends only partly on manipulation as a form of influence. The same is true to an even greater extent of political propaganda. Manipulation by itself can achieve only limited results on a mass scale though it may effectively supplement persuasion, coercion and legitimate authority when employed in combination with these other forms of power.

Persuasion

Where A presents arguments, appeals or exhortations to B, and B, after independently evaluating their content in light of his own values and goals, accepts A's communication as the basis of his own behaviour, A has successfully *persuaded* B. Because B's choice of whether or not to accept A's arguments is in principle unconstrained by considerations of penalties, rewards or any felt obligation to do what A wants, and because, again in principle, B is free to present A with counter-arguments of his own and thus to reverse the roles of persuader and persuaded, persuasion is often not regarded as a form of power at all. Formally, it lacks the asymmetry of power relations. More than the other forms of power it resembles the spontaneous give-and-take, the reciprocity, that is the essential feature of communicative interaction in its generic form. As Arendt observes: 'Where arguments are used, authority is left in abeyance. Against the egalitarian order of persuasion stands the authoritarian order which is always hierarchical.'[26]

I have nevertheless classified persuasion as a form of power because it clearly represents a means by which an actor may achieve an intended effect on another's behaviour. Since individuals differ in their persuasive skills, the implicit equality inherent in persuasion may not in fact be realized through a continual interchange of roles between persuader and persuaded. Individuals everywhere vary in talents conducive to successful persuasion such as articulateness, oratorical ability or psychological intelligence and such individual variability is by no means irrelevant to power struggles on a large societal stage. Recall Hitler's extraordinary gift of demagogic oratory, virtually his only political talent in the view of most of his biographers. Reputation is also a 'persuasion resource' which some possess in greater degree than others.[27]

Inequality in the distribution of the means of persuasion is even more evident when we consider the mass media in modern societies. The owners or controllers of printing presses, radio and television transmitters, loudspeakers and amplifying equipment possess enormous persuasive advantages over the individual citizen. He cannot argue back but can only switch off the TV or radio, or refuse to buy a particular newspaper, and under conditions of modern urban life he cannot avoid completely becoming a member of a 'captive audience' exposed to the mass persuasions of those who control the ubiquitous communications media. The technological revolution in communications has created new and complex instruments of persuasion, access to which constitutes a vitally important power resource. Freedom of the press and the networks from government control is properly considered crucial to the maintenance of open political competition and the preservation of limits to governmental power in democratic polities. An amusing example of the importance of access to the means of persuasion is seen in the factional struggles within tiny political sects where the focus of conflict when an open split occurs is often over the control of the party press, the mimeograph machine, or even the office typewriter and mailing list, for these are usually the only resources possessed by ideological grouplets which enable them to maintain even the semblance of an active political existence beyond the limits of their own membership.[28]

Persuasion, therefore, depends like other forms of power on resources that are unequally distributed. But like force and manipulation persuasion exists only in its manifest form, although at the interpersonal level it conforms to the essential features of social interaction as such, whereas physical force is always a non-social relationship and manipulation may be non-social. Only in a highly attenuated sense is it possible to conceive of a person anticipating the arguments and appeals of another and guiding his subsequent conduct by them. Latent persuasion in accordance with the rule of anticipated reactions can therefore scarcely be said to exist.

Persuasion is probably capable of achieving greater extensiveness than most other forms of power. But it is limited in comprehensiveness and intensity since it depends entirely on the power subject's free acceptance of the persuader's communication. As distinct from legitimate authority, the power subject is not subjectively constrained by a sense of obligation to comply and he does not by definition run the risk, as in coercive authority, of deprivations inflicted by others should he fail to do so. Precisely for these reasons, however, successful persuasion is one of the most reliable forms of power from the standpoint of the power holder, requiring little expenditure of resources on his part and running the least risk of arousing the antagonism or opposition of the power subject.

CHAPTER THREE

The Forms of Power: Authority

If the essence of persuasion is the presentation of arguments, the essence of authority is the issuance of *commands*. Authority is, as L. Stein defined it long ago, 'the untested acceptance of another's judgment',[1] whereas persuasion is the *tested* acceptance of another's judgement. Even longer ago, Hobbes's distinction between *command* and *counsel* essentially corresponds to the difference between authority and persuasion:

> Command is where a man says *do this* or *do not this* without expecting other reason than the will of him that says it. . . . Counsel is where a man says *do* or *do not this*, and deduces his reasons from the benefit that arrives by it to him to whom he says it.[2]

In persuasion, B adopts A's communication as the basis of his own conduct because of the *content* of the communication, which he has independently evaluated and accepted. In authority, it is not the content of a communication but its *source*, that is, the perceived status, resources or personal attributes of the communicator, which induces compliance. Authority is a 'theirs not to reason why' affair even if the subordinate is convinced, as in Tennyson's poem, that 'someone had blundered' in giving a particular command. Authority, in short, is *successful ordering or forbidding*. Easton maintains: 'Anyone who is regularly obeyed is an authority.'[3] Any and all command-obedience relations between men are examples of authority.

To define authority in this way avoids any consideration of the particular grounds or motives for obeying on the part of the power subject. The varying motivations for obeying provide the basis for the classification of the five different forms of authority (see the chart on p. 24). De Jouvenel refers to 'naked authority', or what he also calls a 'pure relation of authority', as existing 'whenever B does A's bidding without

A's enjoyment of any endowment whereby he may bribe or threaten B
or any superadded prestige'.[4] Such cases are no doubt rare in reality and
are usually confined to interpersonal relations, but they highlight the
fact that ordering and complying are the *sine qua non* of authority, no
matter what the subject's reasons and motives for compliance based on
his perception of the resources, qualities, position or prestige of the
wielder of authority.

Max Weber defined authority, or domination as most of his
translators have rendered the German term *Herrschaft*, as any
command-obedience relationship, and he too regarded it as 'a special
case of power'.[5] 'Domination,' he wrote,

> will thus mean the situation in which the manifested will (*command*) of the
> *ruler* or rulers is meant to influence the conduct of one or more others (*the
> ruled*) and actually does influence it in such a way that their conduct to a
> socially relevant degree occurs as if the ruled had made the content of the
> command the maxim of their conduct for its very own sake. Looked upon
> from the other end, this situation will be called *obedience*.[6]

This definition does not exclude a relationship in which a subordinate
obeys a superior solely out of fear that he will suffer physical
punishment or economic deprivation should he resist. Weber's term
Herrschaft therefore cannot be identified with *legitimate* power, which
is a special case of *Herrschaft*, just as *Herrschaft* is a special case of
power in general. I have followed David Easton in using the term
'authority' as the equivalent of Weber's concept and then distinguishing
between *legitimate* and *coercive* authority. One might object to this on
the ground that 'coercive authority' sounds like a contradiction in terms
in view of the widespread tendency both in ordinary speech and in
sociological discourse to identify authority with a relationship in which
the subordinate obeys out of *consent* based on his acceptance of an
obligation to obey, or, in other words, out of a belief in the legitimacy of
the command-obedience relationship. The term used by most of
Weber's translators is 'domination', but, although adequately rendering
his meaning, it is not widely used in social science discourse in the
English language. Alone among Weber's translators, Talcott Parsons
has rendered *Herrschaft* as 'imperative control', and at a later date as
'authority', the latter to him connoting 'the integration of the
collectivity, in the interests of its effective functioning' rather than a
hierarchical command-obedience relationship.[7] But whether Weber
intended such an implication is precisely the point at issue: both a literal

reading of his definition and the emphasis of much of his substantive political analysis compel agreement with Reinhard Bendix that 'as a realist in the analysis of power he would have been critical of any translation that tended to obscure the 'threat of force' in all relations between superiors and subordinates'.[8]

Weber gives many illustrations of domination based on economic interests. In fact, he refers to 'domination by virtue of a constellation of interests' as one major type of domination, the other polar type being domination based on 'power to command and duty to obey'. He notes marginal cases on the borderline between these two types, observes that the former often develop into the latter, and cites a variety of relevant economic examples including the relationship between a central bank and its debtors and between breweries and tavern owners. He then states that he will use the term in the narrower second sense in which 'domination shall be identical with the authoritarian power of *command*' (italics in text).[9] He immediately offers the detailed definition already quoted.

In the more compressed treatment of domination in Chapter 3 of Part I of *Economy and Society* – written at a later date than the discussion in Part III reviewed in the preceding paragraph – Weber comments, after defining domination, that 'every genuine form of domination implies a minimum of voluntary compliance, that is, an *interest* (based on ulterior motives or genuine acceptance) in obedience'.[10] This statement could be interpreted as excluding a purely coercive power relationship from falling under the category of domination, especially since Weber in the next paragraph lists custom, affectual ties, material interests and ideal or *wertrationale* motives, *but not fear*, as possible motives binding an administrative staff 'to obedience to their superior'. He then observes that 'in addition there is normally a further element, the belief in legitimacy'. He argues that 'it is useful to classify the types of domination according to the kind of claim to legitimacy typically made by each', and mentions seven additional clarifying and qualifying considerations, each of them numbered, bearing on the nature of domination and legitimacy in general, before proceeding in a new section to present his well-known threefold classification of types of legitimacy.

It is easy to see how this presentation has led some readers virtually to equate *Herrschaft* or domination with legitimate authority and to minimize its coercive aspects. However, when Weber makes 'voluntary compliance' based on 'interest' a criterion of domination, he clearly does not mean to exclude a power subject's interest in avoiding the imposition of painful physical sanctions when confronted with a credible 'threat of force' from a power holder. The actual application of force to the body of the power subject is all that the criterion excludes. Like many other theorists of power and authority, Weber fails to differentiate explicitly between force and the threat of force, although elsewhere in *Economy and Society* he recognizes the relevance of the distinction: in a discussion of the relation between law and economic behaviour, he cites the Latin maxim *coactus tamen voluit* ('Although coerced, it was still his will') and observes 'this is true, without exception, of all coercion which does not treat the person to be coerced simply as an inanimate object'.[11]

Disagreement over the translation of *Herrschaft* in Weber's work bears on larger issues in sociological theory: on the opposition between so-called 'conflict' and 'consensus' theories of social structure, on whether prestige or status as opposed to wealth and power is the fundamental basis of social inequality, and, of greatest relevance in the present context, on differing judgements of the relative importance of coercion as opposed to voluntary submission in power relations in general. A great many sociologists, of whom Parsons is the most prominent, have defined authority as compliance based on the consent of the power subject and have contrasted it with 'naked power', or power based on force.[12] This dichotomy is misleadingly simple. In the first place, it fails to distinguish, as I have previously noted, between force and the threat of force, or coercion, and thus biases the issue of the relative importance of coercion and consent in human society in favour of the latter because the effects obtainable by the actual application of force are obviously restricted and largely negative. Moreover, in equating authority with the subordinate's acceptance of an obligation to obey it unduly directs attention to the motivation and consciousness of the subordinate rather than emphasizing the nature of the communicative relation – that of commanding and obeying – between superior and subordinate (or power holder and power subject in the terminology I have favoured).

It scarcely clarifies matters when authority is regarded as a special case of power, namely legitimate or institutionalized power characterized by the voluntary submission of the subject, and power itself is defined to include the capacity to impose sanctions or deprivations. Lasswell and Kaplan, Bierstedt, and Gerth and Mills are among the writers taking this line, as is Weber in so far as the reference to resistance in his definition of power implies a similar view. Now there is a genuine paradox, analysed by Bierstedt and Peter Blau,[13] which I shall discuss below, in the fact that submission to legitimate authority is voluntary and yet at the same time is experienced as mandatory or compulsory. But since power and authority are relations between actors, definitions that focus on the nature of the relation itself rather than only on one aspect of it – whether that is the resources of the power holder or the motivations of the power subject – are preferable and are more likely to avoid endless polemics on the coercion versus consent issue.

It cannot be claimed that Hannah Arendt, whose insights into the nature of politics and power are almost unequalled in acuteness and profundity, contributes much conceptual clarification to this question. In her essay, 'On Violence', she complains:

> It is, I think, a rather sad reflection on the present state of political science that our terminology does not distinguish among such key words as 'power', 'strength', 'force', 'authority', and, finally, 'violence' – all of which refer to distinct, different phenomena and would hardly exist unless they did.[14]

She simply ignores the many efforts, of which mine here is no more than the latest, to develop a taxonomy of the different forms of influence by carefully defining and distinguishing precisely the terms she mentions. She objects to de Jouvenel's equation of power with the effectiveness of command, arguing that to accept it means that Mao must be right, for 'there is no greater power than that which grows out of the barrel of a gun'.[15] She then argues that

> power corresponds to the human ability not just to act but to act in concert. Power is never the property of an individual; it belongs to a group and remains in existence only so long as the group keeps together.[16]

In effect, she equates power with legitimate authority and places it in stark contrast to violence without distinguishing between violence and the threat of violence.

Although Miss Arendt's observations on the attitudes of various contemporary thinkers and ideological movements towards power and violence are incomparably rich, this conceptual polarity is no improvement at all on the familiar dichotomy of 'naked' versus 'legitimate' or 'institutionalized' power, usually called 'authority', which has become such a commonplace in the sociological literature. Like the sociologists, with whom she shows, except for a footnote reference to MacIver, scant familiarity, Miss Arendt's definitions move away from the nature or structure of the power relation itself and direct attention to its origins, the wider social context in which it occurs, and the preceding dispositions or states of mind of the actors and the community to which they belong. These are undeniably central considerations in the analysis of power relations, but to stress them at the outset is to pass too quickly over the concrete, immediate relation itself. If a gun serves as a final and unanswerable 'persuader' in implementing a command, it does not follow that *all* commands are obeyed at gunpoint, or even that all commanders have access to guns as an ultimate resort. The right to command and the obligation to obey indeed often rest on the 'people's support' which has 'empowered' authorities 'to act in their name',[17] but a command-obedience relationship remains distinguishable from a violent, persuasive or manipulative relationship, whether it is based on threats and fear or on mutually acknowledged rights and duties. I fail to see why 'to think of power in terms of command and obedience' is 'to equate power with violence',[18] particularly when Miss Arendt herself, in defining authority, remarks: 'Its hallmark is unquestioning recognition by those who are asked to obey; neither coercion nor persuasion is needed.'[19] (She uses 'power' here to mean what I have called 'authority', and her 'authority' is identical with my 'legitimate authority'.) In an earlier discussion, Miss Arendt herself identified the command-obedience relationship, when grounded in mutual consent, with 'authority':

> The authoritarian relation between the one who commands and the one who obeys rests neither on common reason nor on the power of the one who commands: what they have in common is the hierarchy itself, whose rightness and legitimacy both recognize and where both have their predetermined stable place.[20]

But definitions are largely matters of convenience. If a thinker wishes for whatever reason to stress the contrast between obedience motivated by fear of punishment or the desire for reward on the one hand, and voluntary submission because of imputed 'intrinsic' social or psychological qualities of the giver of commands on the other, he or she is at liberty to reserve the word 'authority', which has long possessed consensual overtones, for the latter and to regard *coercion* and *inducement* (obedience exacted by threats and by the promise of rewards, respectively) as separate forms of power. I have chosen instead to stress the common features of command-obedience relationships by subsuming them under the generic term *authority* and then distinguishing subtypes on the basis of varying motivations for obeying.

Coercive Authority

For A to obtain B's compliance by threatening him with force, B must be convinced of both A's *capability* and *willingness* to use force against him. A may have succeeded in convincing B of both by advertising and displaying the means and instruments of force that he controls. States stage elaborate military reviews or publicized tests of nuclear weapons to impress foreign diplomats as well as their own citizens. In some countries policemen flourish nightsticks and wear highly visible revolvers on their hips. New political movements may adopt para-military forms of organization even when, as in the case of the S.A. before Hitler's coming to power, their arsenals are empty or virtually non-existent. Large property-owners electrify the fences surrounding their property and post signs stating that it is patrolled by armed guards. Small property-owners put up 'beware of the dog' notices on their lawns. Would-be 'tough guys' develop a swaggering walk and cultivate bulging biceps.

When such methods are unsuccessful in cowing others into compliance, an actual test of force may be necessary to establish in the mind of the power subject the credibility of the power holder's ability and readiness to apply force successfully. Force is often employed simply to eliminate people from the scene or to prevent them from acting at all, but it is more often used to establish credibility and thus to create a future power relation based on the threat of force that precludes the necessity of overt resort to it. Men are subjected to physical and psychic punishments to deter them from future repetitions of proscribed acts. Rebellions are brutally suppressed to discourage their surviving supporters from future attempts at rebellion. Prisoners are tortured to induce them to co-operate with their captors by providing desired information in the hope of avoiding further torture. Offenders may be removed by death or confinement to set an example to others – *pour encourager les autres* – and thus to reinforce a coercive relation between a power holder and power subjects who have yet to test his strength. In all these cases force is used less for the immediate effects on its victims than to establish or maintain a relation of coercive authority in the future between its wielder and either the victims or those who witness its use.

But a coercer may succeed without possessing either the capability or the intention of using force, so long as the power subjects believe he possesses both. Men have robbed banks by brandishing water pistols or even by cocking their fingers to resemble a hand-gun in their pockets. The rhetoric of violence sometimes succeeds even where the capacity to use it is lacking. On the other hand, superior force may be overcome where its possessor hesitates to use it. Gandhi's use of non-violent force against the British in India was successful because the British lacked the ruthlessness to massacre his followers, but, as has often been pointed out, it is doubtful that he would have prevailed against Nazis, Communists or even the pre-war Japanese.

What is unique about the introduction of nuclear weapons into world power politics, is that no power dares use them against another nuclear power in the absence of certainty that their use will destroy the enemy's nuclear arsenal, so immense are the destructive capacities of the weapons. Whether the nuclear 'balance of terror' might have been arrived at had atomic bombs not been used by the United States against Japan at the end of World War II is still subject to bitter debate. But with the balance of terror ruling out an actual test of the credibility of a nuclear power's force, such a power could, in theory at least, destroy its stockpile of bombs without altering the balance so long as its rivals continued to believe that it still possessed a formidable nuclear arsenal.

At least in the short-run, coercive authority is undoubtedly the most effective form of power in extensiveness, comprehensiveness and intensity: 'Out of the barrel of a gun grows the most effective command, resulting in the most instant and perfect obedience.'[21] With the exception of the actual use of force, coercion is potentially the most extensive form of power of all because it requires a bare minimum of communication and mutual understanding between the power holder and power subject to compel the latter's obedience. The brandishing of a weapon is easily understood by men of utterly diverse cultural backgrounds. The military conquest and subsequent rule of alien peoples make up a large part of the historical record. Many past civilizations have based their economies on the forced labour of slaves. Since most men value life and health, more often than not they prefer submission even to the point of slavery to the injury, starvation or death risked by forcible resistance to a stronger adversary.

Because of its potential universal effectiveness and the wide range of conduct it can dictate and control, coercion is, with legitimate authority, one of the two major forms of *political power* – that is, of the most extensive kind of power at all, a power that rules over a larger and more inclusive constituency than the constituencies subject to the social controls of families, local communities, churches, voluntary associations and the many other groups composing the social order. Political institutions are, in fact, most clearly differentiated from other institutions by virtue of their monopolistic control of the means of coercion. A leading tradition in Western political and social thought that goes back at least to the Greeks and includes Machiavelli and Hobbes, the Social Darwinists of the nineteenth century and the Italian neo-Machiavellian school of the early part of the present century, has regarded coercion as both the ultimate and the only 'real' form of power, seeing it as the very foundation of social order itself in all but the smallest communities.[22]

The rival tradition stresses, of course, the primacy of *consensus*, the bond of shared values uniting ruler and ruled which enjoin the latter's submission. I shall review this classic debate in greater detail in a later chapter and attempt a synthesis of the two perspectives. Here let it only be noted that the consensualist critique lays stress on the limitations of coercive authority. Coercion, in the first place, requires costly expenditures of material and human resources on the instruments of coercion and the social organization needed to wield them, even when the threat of force is rarely put to a test. Moreover, usually, as Kenneth Boulding observes:

> . . . the credibility of threats depreciates with time if threats are not carried out. Hence threats occasionally need to be carried out in order to re-establish the credibility. Another reason is that threat capability declines if threats are not occasionally carried out, particularly where this capability is enshrined in complex social organizations and in apparatus such as armed forces.[23]

Coercion also has to face the visibility problem in especially acute form: if rebels and deviants are restrained primarily by the fear of punishment, the power holder must be constantly vigilant in overseeing and keeping informed about their activities. Otherwise, 'when the cat is away, the mice will play'. Students of crime have long argued that it is not so much the severity of punishment that deters potential criminals – when indeed they *are* deterred by fear of the law – but the *certainty* of punishment, or a high probability of being caught and punished. The reliability of anticipated reactions is low for the coercive power holder unless the power subject is convinced that he is under constant surveillance. Thus efficient information-gathering and espionage organizations must be added to the power holder's investment in the means of violence and the social organization trained in their use.

Finally, power based on coercion both presupposes and creates a conflict of interest between power holder and power subject; the ensuing hostility and antagonism on the part of the latter require over time an ever-greater vigilance and investment in the means of coercion by the power holder. For these reasons, Boulding argues, 'the unilateral threat system, or the threat-submission system, which may be fairly successful for a time, almost inevitably degenerates into the bi-lateral threat system, or deterrence'.[24] Or, in the language employed in Chapter 1, the integral power of a coercive power holder is successfully countervailed and transformed into a system of intercursive power.

Authority by Inducement

The counterpart of coercive authority is authority based on inducement, or the offering of *rewards* for compliance with a command rather than threatening deprivations. Authority by inducement employs positive sanctions to bring about obedience on the part of the power subject rather than the threat of negative sanctions. Superficially, authority by inducement resembles a reciprocal, implicitly egalitarian, exchange relationship in which A promises B a reward or service in return for B's performance of an action desired by A. Such a relation is clearly not a power relation at all.

At the other extreme, where one party controls the means of subsistence necessary for the very survival of the other party, he having nothing to offer but his labour power, the relationship easily becomes one of economic exploitation, as was pointed out long ago by Marx. Authority by inducement falls between two poles on a continuum: the classical relationship of economic exchange between equals in the market on the one hand, and coercive authority based on 'wage slavery' on the other. It is difficult to draw a sharp line between the various points along the continuum. Authority by inducement can properly be said only to characterize relationships in which one party submits 'voluntarily' to the employer's commands in return for economic rewards well above sheer subsistence needs.

This relationship, however, when a recurring one, is subject to change over time in the direction of coercive authority. Just as the application of force may make its continued application unnecessary by transforming a power relation initially based on force into one based on the threat of force or coercive authority, so may the power subject's repeated acceptance of rewards result in the threat of their withdrawal being experienced as coercion rather than as inducement, thus transforming the original relation into another form of power – namely, coercive authority. Men become accustomed to, or enslaved by, a standard of living well above sheer subsistence level so that a threat to the maintenance of this standard is felt to be as coercive as a threat to destroy their material possessions. Peter Blau has lucidly described how this consideration may transform a power relation originally based on the receipt of rewards:

> Regular rewards make recipients dependent on the supplier and subject to his power, since they engender expectations that make their discontinuation a punishment . . . Regular rewards create expectations that redefine the baseline in terms of which positive sanctions are distinguished from negative ones. The air we breathe is not conceived by us to be a special reward, nor is the freedom to move about the streets as we please, but being suffocated or imprisoned is experienced as a punishment. Correspondingly, a man who has reason to expect to remain in his job does not think of his regular earnings as distinctive rewards, and the loss of his income is a punishment for him. Only a raise in income is a specific reward, although even raises that occur regularly come to be expected, and in these cases failure to receive a raise tends to be experienced as a punishment and may be so intended by the employer.[25]

If coercive authority is the distinctive basis of *political* power, authority by inducement is characteristic of *economic* power, or at least of those forms of it that fall short of crude economic exploitation. It is, therefore, an almost universal type of power, existing in all societies where some men exercise greater control over the means of subsistence than others – usually as a result of greater control over the means of production. In virtually all societies that have attained a level of productivity above subsistence, the division of labour gives rise to inequalities of access to productive resources, enabling some men to exercise authority over others. Human material wants beyond sheer subsistence needs are sufficiently varied and insistent to ensure that such authority is capable of a high degree of comprehensiveness and intensity. There are things that money cannot buy, but it can surely buy a great deal.

The extensiveness of authority by inducement, or economic power, varies more widely according to the level of technological development than its comprehensiveness and intensity. The Industrial Revolution freed the majority of men from nearly total dependence on local feudal landowners by making them dependent instead on an impersonal market in which their relations to others assumed the legal form of a reciprocal exchange relation that was the antithesis of any form of power relation at all. Marx's analysis of the fetishism of commodities and the reified, depersonalized power of money was an effort to reveal the hidden power relations existing in a capitalist economy in which control of the means of production was in the hands of an owning class whose collective power was far more extensive than that of the agrarian landowner over the peasants and serfs within his limited domain. With the growth in size of the productive enterprise (foreseen, of course, by Marx) the extensiveness of economic power has enormously increased in the advanced industrial, or 'post-industrial', societies at the same time that the comprehensiveness and intensity of the power of any single employer has been limited by constitutional democracy, welfare legislation and the rise of trade unions. Nevertheless, the Jeffersonian ideal of a society of small producers – yeoman farmers and artisans – in which differences in power derived from economic inequalities are minimal has become ever more remote from reality.

The concentration of economic power possible in a commercial money economy in which the bulk of the population is landless and propertyless and depends on the market for the satisfaction of most material wants is very great indeed. It parallels the greater concentration of political power made possible by modern, technically advanced means of coercion and persuasion. It makes the line between compliance with authority based on the expectation of economic rewards and compliance dictated by fear of deprivation more difficult to draw than in predominantly agricultural societies. The combination of concentrated economic power and centralized political power in state socialist societies is the basis of rule by a dictator, a single party or a 'new class' of administrators. In democratic capitalist societies the power of 'private' corporate élites to exercise influence over the agencies of the state is often perceived as a threat to democracy. The possibility of a single élite monopolizing control over technically advanced means of production, coercion and persuasion amounts virtually to a definition of totalitarianism. Although there have been precursors of modern totalitarian rule in pre-industrial societies in the past, the extensiveness of such rule, and to a lesser degree its comprehensiveness and intensity as well, were limited in the absence of modern techniques.[26]

Authority based on the capacity to offer economic rewards is in one obvious sense less efficient than authority based on coercive threats. To be effective and stable over time, authority by inducement must actually provide the promised benefits, thus depleting the economic resources of the power holder and requiring continuous effort on his part to produce or obtain a regular supply of economic goods with which to maintain his control over others. Coercive authority, on the other hand, relies on the relatively inexpensive communication of threats. Yet, as I have previously noted, investment in the instruments of coercion and the social organization required to wield them, as well as their occasional use, and in the means and organization of surveillance, are necessary if coercive authority is to perpetuate its credibility. Authority by inducement arouses less resistance and antagonism on the part of the power subjects. Moreover, since those who possess the greatest capacity to confer economic benefits typically control the means of production and not merely consumption goods, they can utilize the promise of economic rewards to provide an incentive to power subjects to increase their productivity in augmenting and continuously replenishing the supply of economic rewards. Free labour systems are notoriously more productive than forced labour systems. Nevertheless, the managerial and supervisory costs of labour systems that strive for maximum productivity may also be far from inconsiderable: as William J. Goode observes,

> . . . had the feudal lord of the manor tried to elicit maximum productivity from his serfs, he would also have had to spend far more time and energy in management. He would have had to plan more, and he could not have devoted as much time to falconry, stag hunting, and other courtly pleasures.[27]

Authority by inducement alone is capable of achieving great extensiveness, especially in a non-agrarian money economy employing modern techniques of machine production. Its comprehensiveness and intensity, however, are not as great as those of some of the other forms of power. No profound sense of common purpose or moral community unites power holder and power subject where the latter's compliance is based solely on expectations of benefits conferred by the former. Disagreement and conflict over the terms of the bargain, or the ratio of the exchange, are very likely to arise. When the benefits anticipated are not seen as essential to the continuation of life itself, they can be foregone if the power holder attempts to extend his power too far, or to push his commands to a point where other interests and values of the power subjects are threatened by compliance with them. Authority by inducement stands between coercive and legitimate authority on a scale ranging from the most to the least likelihood of arousing antagonism and resistance on the part of the power subject.[28]

I have discussed authority by inducement primarily in the form of economic relationships in which one party controls greater material resources than the other. However, the unequal distribution of anything that human beings desire or seek can in principle become the basis for authority by inducement. The so-called 'exchange' theorists generalize the model of exchange in the market to include all social relations, those involving the exchange of services, and of psychic benefits such as emotional support, friendship, approval, prestige and love, as well as money or material goods.

In stressing the element of exchange or reciprocity in all social relations, the exchange theorists underline the point developed in Chapter 1 that power relations, in so far as they are a form of social interaction, are never totally unilateral but always involve a minimal counter-influence exercised by the power subject on the power holder. Yet the implication of equality and symmetry in the very notion of exchange, with its overtones of the 'free market' of classical economics, has led the major exchange theorists to deal at length those apparent exceptions in which there is so great a disproportion in the resources controlled by the parties to an exchange that unequal and even 'exploitative' power relations may result.[29]

Possession of superior knowledge or skill, high status, and the love of others all may be bases for exercising power. The advantaged party's conferral of non-material benefits on the other, however, does not necessarily deplete his supply of benefits as in the case of economic goods. To the extent that this is so, authority based on the conferring of non-material rewards is more efficient than that conferring only material rewards in requiring less depletion of the power holder's resources and less subsequent expenditure of effort to replenish them in order to maintain the power relation. The principle of diminishing marginal utility, however, undoubtedly applies to some psychic rewards: repeatedly granted requests for love or sexual favours are apt to reduce the fascination and magnetism exercised by the loved one over the lover.[30]

Exchange theorists have employed considerable intellectual ingenuity in 'deriving' the various forms of power relation from the combination of inequality of resources and the generic exchange or reciprocity model of social interaction, whether the model is seen as reflecting a universal cultural norm or fundamental psychological tendencies inherent in social behaviour itself.[31] Power relations based on coercion and inducement – punishments and rewards – are readily interpreted as intrinsic to social relations in which the parties control unequal resources. Both Blau and Homans, however, recognize that *legitimate authority* (or what they tend to call simply 'authority') necessarily implies a wider, 'extrinsic' social context in which the two parties to the authority relation are involved.[32]

Legitimate Authority

Legitimate authority is a power relation in which the power holder possesses an acknowledged *right to command* and the power subject an acknowledged *obligation to obey*. The *source* rather than the *content* of any particular command endows it with legitimacy and induces willing compliance on the part of the person to whom it is addressed. Legitimate authority is thus distinct from persuasion where the persuaded adopts as the basis of his conduct the directives or suggestions of the persuader after having independently assessed them in the light of his own goals.

Legitimate authority presupposes shared norms. These norms do not prescribe the content of the commands issued by an authority – they prescribe, rather, obedience within limits irrespective of content. 'Theirs not to reason why, theirs but to do and die, though someone had blundered', as Tennyson described the doomed hussars of the Light Brigade. Tennyson's example refers to military duty where the intensity of the power relation is very high: soldiers are expected even to obey orders that oblige them to risk their lives. Most relations of legitimate authority are of lesser intensity; commanded actions that fall outside certain recognized limits, though these limits may be imprecise and ambiguous, are likely to be defined as illegitimate and thus to nullify the authority relation. Compliance with a command because it is seen as issuing from a legitimate command giver is a special case of conformity to a social norm. Obedience to authority as normatively prescribed is, however, clearly distinguishable from conduct guided by accepted norms, which obviously embraces a far wider range of human actions.

The shared norms that constitute a legitimate authority relation are not shared exclusively by the two parties to the relation. They are shared within a larger group or community to which both belong. Although not directly implicated in a particular legitimate authority relation, this larger community provides the background for such a relation, which cannot be understood in isolation from it. Two friends or lovers may create a set of reciprocal expectations in which one comes to take for granted a right to command and the other an obligation to obey, but such an interpersonal relationship is not one of legitimate authority although it may be properly described as one of *personal authority* (see below). The authority of a parent over a child or a master over a servant, however, although it is dyadic in form, is a relation of legitimate authority because the norms of the larger society uphold it and may indeed prescribe it. (I am assuming, of course, instances where the child or servant obeys out of felt obligation rather than out of fear or anticipated reward.) Many sociologists would say that legitimate authority is a relation between actors filling, or 'playing', social roles rather than between individuals, as in a love affair in which one person is dominant. The line between such 'institutionalized' relations, as they are often called, on the one hand, and interpersonal or informal small group relations, on the other, is often much too sharply drawn in definitions of authority and legitimacy, but I shall postpone discussion of this issue until my consideration of personal authority.

There is an apparent paradox in the fact that submission to legitimate authority is widely regarded as 'voluntary' and based on 'consent' rather than on coercion and yet at the same time is felt to be 'mandatory' or 'obligatory' in contrast to persuasion and 'mere' personal influence. As Robert Bierstedt has written:

> . . . authority which may or may not be accepted hardly qualifies as authority in accordance with the ordinary connotation of the term. There is something mandatory, not merely arbitrary, about the acceptance of authority and no analysis can quite rationalize this mandatory element away and retain the full significance of the phenomenon.[33]

Both Bierstedt and Blau succeed in explaining and resolving the paradox instead of contenting themselves with the conventional definitional distinction between authority as the normatively sanctioned (or 'legitimated') exercise of power in contrast to power based on coercion, inducement or persuasion. Blau's summation can scarely be improved upon:

> Authority entails voluntary compliance, in contrast to coercion, since the influence of the superior on subordinates rests on their own social norms. But authority entails imperative control, in contrast to persuasion and personal influence, since social norms and group sanctions exert compelling pressures on individual subordinates to follow the superior's directives. Compliance is voluntary from the perspective of the collectivity of subordinates, but it is compulsory from the perspective of its individual members.[34]

(Bierstedt and Blau, of course, equate 'authority' with what I have here called 'legitimate authority'.)

The imperative or compulsory nature of legitimate authority has two main features. First, the subordinate feels obliged to obey even though he may dislike or disagree with a particular command. Second, he is aware of the norms of the larger 'collectivity of subordinates' which prescribe obedience and of the disapproval he will incur if he fails to comply with them. These two constraints are present even in 'private' or voluntary associations with an established hierarchy of authority, for, as Bierstedt observes, 'even in what we have called voluntary associations a member who refuses to submit to constituted authority is ordinarily required, in an exercise of authority, to resign'.[35] Bierstedt concludes that 'the consent in these cases applies to membership in the association and not to the acceptance of the particular commands of constituted authority. Membership may be voluntary, but acceptance of authority is mandatory. It is one of the conditions of membership.'[36] One might contend that the larger group to which both power holder and power subject belong exercises psychic coercion over the latter in the form of what is often called 'social pressure'. But this is, of course, true to some degree in the case of *all* social norms other than those that have been thoroughly internalized, and, as we noted in Chapter 1, to equate power with the generalized power of the group over the individual is to collapse the concept of power into that of social control and to evade the necessity of considering power relations as a special class of social relations.

Because legitimate authority presupposes shared values among those subject to it, its extensiveness is inherently more limited than that of coercive authority or authority by inducement. Different legitimate authority structures vary across the entire range of comprehensiveness and intensity from 'greedy institutions' which 'make total claims on their members and which attempt to encompass within their circle the whole personality',[37] including on occasion demanding the sacrifice of life itself, to the strictly limited, scope-specific obligations imposed by specialized bureaucracies. There are also authority structures that are highly comprehensive but fairly low in intensity, such as modern, relatively 'permissive' boarding schools, company towns where the labour force is unionized, and modern armies of drafted soldiers with rights even during their period of military service that are protected by civilian courts.

Legitimate authority creates far greater reliability of anticipated reactions than the other forms of authority, just as internalized social norms ensure more reliable conformity than norms the observance of which is more dependent on situational sanctions or *ad hoc* negotiation over their meaning and applicability. Legitimate authority is more efficient than coercive or induced authority in that it minimizes the need for maintaining means of coercion in constant readiness, continual surveillance of the power subjects and regular supplies of economic or non-economic rewards. For these reasons, naked (that is, coercive) power always seeks to clothe itself in the garments of legitimacy. Or, as Franz Neumann puts it even more strongly: 'Those who wield political power are compelled to create emotional and rational responses in those whom they rule, inducing them to accept, implicitly or explicitly, the commands of the rulers.'[38] That legitimation or acceptance is never complete, at least where *political* power in large communities is concerned, is a subject to be discussed in a later chapter.

Competent Authority

I have been struck by the fact that one finds little or no discussion of authority based on specialized knowledge or skill in most analyses by social scientists of the various forms of influence, power and authority. If it is mentioned at all, it is commonly regarded as a form of persuasion or sometimes as a form of authority by inducement in which compliance is obtained in return for the promise of some non-material benefit such as the performance of a service. The authority of the expert or *competent authority*, however, cannot be equated with persuasion, and, although it is possible to treat many instances as special cases of authority by inducement, there are other cases that do not fit the usual conception of this type of authority. More important than issues of definition and taxonomy, the neglect of competent authority is somewhat surprising in view of the fact that it is presented as an ideal exemplar of all authority at the very beginnings of Western political thought. At the same time, contemporary debates over 'technocracy' or 'post-industrial society' clearly presuppose and see as problematical the existence of social power derived from knowledge and skill.

Competent authority is a power relation in which the subject obeys the directives of the authority out of belief in the authority's superior competence or expertise to decide which actions will best serve the subject's interests and goals. At least as far back as Socrates, the most common illustrations of competent authority have been the physician-patient relationship and the responsibility of a helmsman or pilot for the navigation of a ship. The phrase 'competent authority' is often used, however, to refer to authority that is exercised in accordance with public or private statutory law. Such a usage makes it merely a special case of legitimate authority, notably Weber's rational-legal type. But, as Talcott Parsons has pointed out, 'competent authority' in this sense is not at all the same thing as authority based on 'technical' competence – that is, on knowledge or skill. In Parsons's example, the treasurer of a corporation authorized to sign cheques is not necessarily a better cheque signer than the secretaries and clerks who work in his office.[39] I mean here by 'competent authority' authority that rests solely on the subject's belief in the superior knowledge or skill of the exerciser rather than on formal position in a recognized hierarchy of authority.

The authority of 'doctor's orders' may be taken as the prototype of competent authority. The doctor who says 'stop drinking or you will be dead within a year' is not threatening to kill the patient should the patient refuse to comply; the doctor's authority does not rest on the ability to impose any coercive sanctions. Nor is the doctor appealing to a duty or moral obligation to obey that is incumbent upon the patient; he may greet the patient's refusal with a shrugged 'do what you want, it's your life'. Legitimate authority is not therefore involved. Competent authority resembles persuasion, which is why it has often been seen as the most benign and desirable form of authority.

In common speech the term 'authority' is used as a synonym for the possessor of special knowledge or expertise, as when we describe someone as an authority on tax law or the philosophy of Hegel. Such a usage does not refer to a social relationship at all, let alone a power relation, but it implies at least that we are disposed to act on the advice of such authorities in practical matters, recognizing that their directives possess, in Carl Friedrich's phrase, the 'potentiality of reasoned elaboration'.[40] But there is nothing compulsory or morally mandatory about such influence, which is why it appears to be identical with persuasion. Yet we are not speaking loosely or obliquely when we refer to doctor's *orders* rather than 'suggestions' or 'arguments'. If successful persuasion involves the acceptance by the subject of the *content* of the persuader's communications on the basis of his or her independent assessment of them, whereas authority involves the subject's compliance with a directive because of its *source* rather than its content, then the subject's belief in the superior competence of another provides a basis for authority that is not reducible to, or a special case of, persuasion. The patient may understand nothing of the rationale for the doctor's directives; he complies with them out of trust in the doctor's superior competence to judge what will cure him of his ailment. The doctor may even become annoyed if the patient presses for a detailed explanation of the connection between the symptoms and the proposed cure, thereby attempting to convert a relationship of competent authority into one of persuasion. The difference is especially clear in the case of competence that has been granted professionalized status, as has been pointed out by Eliot Freidson:

> [What] is desired – even demanded – by the profession is that the client obeys because he has faith in the competence of his consultant without evaluating the grounds of the consultant's advice. Indeed, members of consulting occupations attempt to avoid persuading their client to follow their advice. In medicine, such persuasion is invidiously labelled 'selling oneself'. Stress is on the necessity of faith or trust in the practitioner – in short, on *imputed* rather than demonstrated competence. A professional's advice should be obeyed because it is a professional who gives it, not because the advice is or can be evaluated on its evidential merits. Here we find the special source of the authority of the profession – incumbency in an expert status.[41]

Aristotle noted that the rule of a master over a slave is 'exercised primarily with a view to the interest of the master' in contrast to authority that 'is exercised in the first instance for the good of the governed or for the common good of both parties, but essentially for the good of the governed, as we see to be the case in medicine, gymnastic, and the arts in general, which are only accidentally concerned with the good of the artists themselves'.[42] Aristotle's examples suggest as a salient characteristic of competent authority the subject's subordination to another in the belief that his own self-interest is thus served rather than the aims of the power holder or a 'higher' collective interest or ideal purpose. Utilitarian rather than normative or coercive resources are the basis of the power relation, in Etzioni's terminology.[43] In this respect, competent authority resembles most closely authority by inducement. The main difference is that the competent authority provides services, which his knowledge or skill enable him to make available to others, rather than material goods. (This distinction has been the basis for often overdrawn contrasts between 'industrial' and allegedly 'post-industrial' or 'knowledgeable' societies.) Typically, the relation takes the form, as in the sale of goods, of an exchange relation, with expert advice exchanged for a fee.

The doctor-patient relationship in solo private practice is the most obvious illustration of competent authority, but other familiar examples, such as the navigator of a ship or the pilot of an airliner, show that it is not confined to dyadic relationships. Indeed the provision of electricity, water, communications media and other services to populations in the millions provides examples of competent authority possessing high extensiveness. Both the comprehensiveness and intensity of competent authority, however, are typically low, confined to the often strictly delimited scopes in which the authority possesses acknowledged competence and to actions promoting particular aims and interests of the subject. The quality of the service the subject receives in return for compliance with a competent authority may be less tangible and measurable than material benefits, but minimum levels of service must be met if the subject's faith in the authority and his or her continued compliance are to be maintained.

Knowledge is a resource that is not depleted or impaired when it is applied in the service of a goal, but, of course, the time, effort and material equipment required to obtain it in the first place may be considerable. Moreover, scientific expertise may require heavy investment in technical instruments and paraphernalia. The separation of the applied scientist from the means of practice – from the application of his expertise – is often under modern conditions as marked as the separation of the 'pure' scientist from the means of research. Again, modern medical practice provides one of the best examples.

Despite the apparent specificity of competent authority with respect to comprehensiveness and intensity, it tends to shade into legitimate authority when it is vested in professional roles. Freidson's previously cited paper is entitled 'The Impurity of Professional Authority' and his major conclusion is that 'the authority of the professional is . . . in everyday practice, more like that of an officeholder than conventional characterizations would have us believe'.[44] The professional practitioner possesses no sanctions over the client, but he has achieved through state recognition a virtual monopoly of the service he supplies. His formal credentials function like insignia of office in permitting him to avoid the burden of having to persuade the client to follow his advice. The client, moreover, is not free to prescribe drugs for himself or to decide which academic courses should entitle him to a degree, in two of Freidson's examples. In addition, a large part of professional work does not consist of applied technical and objective knowledge but of moral judgements and often self-serving occupational custom. In a later work, Freidson concludes that 'the professional has gained a status which protects him more than other experts from outside scrutiny and criticism and which grants him extraordinary autonomy in controlling both the definition of the problems he works on and the way he performs his work'.[45]

Renford Bambrough has correctly pointed out that there is a fallacy in the Platonic analogy between the navigator and the statesman in that the former only directs his vehicle to a destination, and often along a route, that he has not himself chosen, whereas the political ruler is responsible for the ends of policy as well as the means of achieving them.[46] Bambrough, however, fails to note that there is a significant difference between a ship captain or navigator and a doctor as examples of competent authority, although he also rejects the doctor-statesman analogy on other grounds. The doctor's interest in serving his patient's interest in a cure is far less urgent and direct than that of the navigator in safely completing his journey. Nor is the difference merely that the navigator-captain's authority over his passengers and crew is more extensive than that of the doctor or of other professionals who advise single clients in a dyadic relationship.

The crucial distinction is that the pilot or navigator risks his own physical safety as well as that of those subject to his authority if he endangers his craft, whereas a faulty medical diagnosis affects only the patient's health. At most, the doctor may lose his patient to another practitioner or run the even more remote risk of lowering his professional reputation or facing a malpractice suit. What is true of the doctor is true of other professionals and experts who provide skilled services to clients, with the car mechanic or shoemaker (one of Socrates' preferred examples), whose skills are easily testable, standing at one extreme. But even they, unlike the navigator, are not exposed to the same risk as those who receive their services. Their own lives, safety or comfort are not dependent on the practice of their skills.

There is therefore a genuine and intrinsic community of interest between the navigator as an expert and those subject to his authority that is absent in the case of the physician. The greater popularity of the helmsman metaphor and the prevalence of expressions like 'we're all in the same boat' suggest that the difference is widely if tacitly recognized.[47] The common interest of the entire group of power holders and power subjects also accounts for the virtual merging of competent and legitimate authority in the case of pilots and ship captains, whose authority often possesses quasi-legal backing and who even have the right to impose negative sanctions, at least of a preventive sort, when defiance of their orders is seen as placing the group and its enterprise in jeopardy. The potential for absolutism and even of the degeneration of authority into brutal coercion in this situation, especially when the group is isolated for a long time from outside contacts as in the era of the great sailing ships, is part of the perennial fascination of sea stories – recall Captains Ahab, Bligh, and Jack London's Wolf Larsen. Such great writers as Melville and Conrad were drawn to the theme. More recently, the tension between the elements of competence and of legitimacy in the authority of a ship captain was the central theme of Herman Wouk's popular World War II novel *The Caine Mutiny*, although the issue there was complicated by the fact that the legitimacy of the military chain of command was also involved since the ship was a naval vessel.

When competent authority is exercised by a hierarchically organized group, the distinction between competent and legitimate authority also becomes blurred. The result may be the emergence of 'figurehead' roles at the top symbolizing ultimate authority and assuming responsibility to outsiders, often superiors in a larger hierarchical organization, while leaving the direction of actual operations under the control of immediate subordinates. The captain of a ship has long served as a standard example of competent authority, yet in the modern merchant marine the captain who is most popular with his crew is he who remains almost invisible, delegating the operation of the ship at sea to his subordinate officers. He carries the burden of responsibility to the shipping company for the success of the voyage, but withdraws from the exercise of day-to-day operational authority.[48]

If competent authorities sometimes take on some of the attributes of legitimate and even coercive authorities, it is also true that the latter may lay claim to certifiable competence in leadership and administration. This is typically the case in modern bureaucratic organization, as was recognized by Max Weber. 'Bureaucratic administration,' he wrote in a famous statement, 'means fundamentally the exercise of control on the basis of knowledge. . . . The decisive reason for the advance of bureaucratic organization has always been its purely technical superiority over any other form of organization.'[49] Weber's stress on the *expertise* of the bureaucrat, an expertise based not only on administrative experience but on educational certification as well, has been insufficiently recognized, according to Charles Perrow, by contemporary sociologists, who have exaggerated the difference between professionals and administrators, or between 'staff' and 'line' positions within formal organizations.[50] Increasingly, administrators present themselves as experts in management and exhibit graduate degrees from schools of business or public administration. Perrow, however, overlooks that these very fields of applied knowledge, or would-be 'professions', presuppose that the practitioner has the power to impose sanctions and to enjoin compliance as a duty. His control over both coercive and normative resources, in Etzioni's terminology,[51] derives from his incumbency in office. The bureaucratic manager may lay claim to special competence in management, and the possession of educational credentials may even be a requirement for, or a mode of access to, holding office. But in contrast to the expert or professional whose authority rests primarily on his certified competence, the manager has other resources at his disposal to obtain compliance and these are clearly the chief basis of his authority. His claim to superior competence in administration amounts to an additional legitimating argument invoked to buttress the authority of his office, although his academic knowledge may indeed help him to exercise authority more efficiently.

In summary, the professional, who possesses power based on knowledge, also possesses, according to Freidson, some of the attributes of power based on legally ratified status, and this status depends on the power of the collective organization of his fellow experts. The bureaucrat with degrees in management has acquired knowledge that supplements the authority of office and the sanctions and resources it controls. Both, though not to the same degree, represent adulterations of an ideal typically 'pure' competent authority.

The extraordinary prestige and high degree of organization of professionals in modern society carries the risk that 'expertise is more and more in danger of being used as a mask for privilege and power rather than, as it claims, as a mode of advancing the public interest'.[52] If this is true of professionals who possess a real, if specialized, competence, claims to superior knowledge and expertise have long been advanced by other power holders to legitimate their rule. For centuries competent authority has served as a model, or idealized exemplar, for authority in general. Competent authority has frequently been invoked metaphorically to legitimate power relations in which neither the superior competence or knowledgeability of the power holder nor priority of concern for the interests of the subjects are, to put it mildly, unambiguously present. Characterizations of the ruler as the 'helmsman' of his people, or of the statesman as 'physician' to the 'body politic',[53] are almost as common in ancient political texts as analogies between political rule and parenthood.

One might, in fact, regard the parent who urges her child to obey because 'mother knows best' as appealing to a rational and consensual model of competent authority as opposed to the mother who asserts 'you should obey me because I am your mother', which is an appeal to an absolutist, traditionalist legitimation. That one is inclined to suspect the mother who makes the first claim of hypocrisy, detecting a ring of sanctimoniousness in it, suggests the ambiguity of the claim to superior knowledge or competence beyond limited and specifiable scopes. Yet there are parents who see their task as the exercise of authority solely in order to equip the child so that he or she is able eventually to dispense with the need for dependence on authority. R. G. Collingwood wrote:

> The parents are able to exercise *transeunt rule* over their children because they are capable of *immanent rule* over themselves. And so there is a self-ruling community, or society, upon which the children are dependent; and into this society the children are drawn as they grow up. . . .[54]

Carl Friedrich has noted in a similar vein that

> as the child grows. . . a wise parent will increasingly prefer to explain what needs to be done and to be believed, to give reasons, thus replacing subjection by understanding. . . By coming to understand these regulations and beliefs, the child is helped, so to speak, to shape them into proper possessions, to make them his own. Thus discipline is transformed into self-discipline.[55]

Extending this model of the family to the larger polity, Collingwood argued:

> In a well-ruled body politic the rulers never forget that the ruled are in training to become rulers; and in the meantime . . . must be treated as partaking in their degree of the moral freedom or will-power . . . which in an eminent degree is peculiar to the rulers.[56]

This is a description of authority that aims at its own liquidation over time, authority exemplifying the liberal ideal of a government that seeks to replace as much as possible the authority of persons with the authority of self-regulating consciences. A better example of such self-liquidating competent authority than parenthood, where, at least in traditional societies, elements of absolutism are usually not eliminated, would be the teacher-pupil or master-apprentice relationship.

The *claim* that special knowledge and competence, as distinct from their demonstrable reality, underlie the exercise of authority is an ideological claim, a legitimating rationale. Venerable though it is, such a claim is especially prevalent in an age when science has become the supreme cognitive arbiter. This endows competent authority with significance as a model transcending its very real importance as an actual form of power relation.

Personal Authority

In a relationship of personal authority the subject obeys out of a desire to please or serve another person solely because of the latter's personal qualities. Personal authority might be considered a 'pure' type of authority in which commands are issued and obeyed without the command giver possessing any coercive powers, transferable resources, special competence or legitimacy conferred by a community. His or her personal significance to the subject constitutes the sole grounds of the latter's compliance. The prototype of personal authority is the power of the loved one over the lover who declares 'your wish is my command' and acts accordingly.

But this example suggests some ambiguities, for love can be thought of as a reward and an asymmetrical love relationship may be assimilated to, as Blau has argued, an unequal exchange relation.[57] A purer, if idiosyncratic, example would be a sado-masochistic love relationship in which the domination of one and the submission of the other are desired entirely for their own sakes. Personal authority has the double implication of being based, on the one hand, on particular traits and capacities of the power holder rather than on his or her social role or generalized normative qualities, and, on the other, of deriving from the subject's perception and valuation of unique personal qualities rather than the power holder's resources to coerce, reward or provide expert advice. But these two attributes can obviously exist independently of one another. An armed robber exercises coercive authority over his victim outside of an institutionalized role relationship; so may a person who rewards another to comply with his or her wishes. Competent authority may also be exercised on a purely personal basis if someone places a high value on another's knowledge and judgement and follows unquestioningly his or her practical advice. Only legitimate authority, which is grounded in the consensus of a group, excludes by definition a personal, non-institutionalized authority relationship.

Many writers, as we have seen, identify authority *per se* with legitimate authority and contrast it with all non-institutionalized power relations. I have chosen, however, to define authority as *any* command-obedience relation and have distinguished different forms of authority that may (with the exception of legitimate authority) appear in non-institutionalized or 'personal' as well as institutionalized relations. Following this definition, *personal authority*, in addition to referring to a non-institutionalized relation between persons as such rather than roles, acquires a residual character in covering all command-obedience relations that do not rest on the subject's fear of coercion or expectation of reward or expert advice. Love, admiration, friendship or the presence of psychological dispositions towards dominance and submissiveness, are the basis of personal authority relations.

I have chosen not to limit the term authority to legitimate, institutionalized relations in order to avoid the strong consensual, not to say conservative, bias that characterizes the more restricted definition. The definitions of forms of authority that I have offered therefore – again with the exception of legitimate authority itself – cut across the division between 'personal' and institutionalized relationships that has been so crucial to the theorizing of some sociologists.

If personal authority were limited in extensiveness to dyadic or small group relations, the difference between the two definitions would be of little significance. But there is one form of personal authority characterized by considerable extensiveness that has been the subject of much social and political analysis: Max Weber's conception of charismatic authority. Bierstedt has objected to the conventional understanding of this conception on the grounds that it confuses 'leadership', which 'depends upon the personal qualities of the leader in the situations in which he leads', with 'authority', in which 'the relationship ceases to be personal and, if the legitimacy of the authority is recognized, the subordinate must obey the command even when he is unacquainted with the person who issues it'.[58] Bierstedt here brings out what is implicit in a good many sociological conceptualizations: the drawing of a sharp line between the sociological, viewed as referring to interaction that is institutionalized or controlled by generalized norms, and 'merely' social psychological or interpersonal interaction. Although they do not specifically discuss relations of power and authority, Talcott Parsons, Edward Shils and Robert Nisbet have broadened Weber's concept of charisma by treating it not only as an attribute of persons but also of positions or roles, associations, and institutions.[59] In effect, they virtually equate charisma with Durkheim's concept of the sacred. Such an approach, however, ends up making charismatic legitimation or authority scarcely distinguishable from Weber's concept of traditional authority, for he frequently referred to the 'sacredness of tradition' and the 'sanctity of age-old rules and powers'.[60] This is not the place to discuss at length the concept of charisma, but, although Weber did see it as partially transferable from persons to offices in undergoing what he called 'routinization', his prototype of charismatic legitimacy was the prophet who declared to his followers, 'It is written, but I say unto you', thereby pitting his own sense of mission against the demands of tradition or positive law.

There is an important difference in the time-span relevant to much general sociological theory, especially theory in the Durkheimian tradition, on the one hand, and to students of politics and political history, on the other. Theorists in the former tradition are concerned primarily with *institutionalized* social relations that are transmitted inter-generationally and are the basis of the historical continuity of a society. Political scientists and political sociologists, however, are often interested in political movements and regimes that may not even survive for a generation and which frequently do not outlive their charismatic founders or leaders. Clearly, such movements have been of immense historical significance. National Socialism lasted barely a quarter of a century, disintegrating with the death of Hitler. Italian fascism, though in power for a longer period, was also short-lived and did not outlast the death of Mussolini. Both of these movements won exclusive state power and the regimes they established were overthrown only as a result of defeat in a world war. In Latin America, the 'caudillo' pattern, the formation of a party, movement or power-seeking clique or junta on the basis of the following of a strong man, has become virtually a tradition. Religious and political movements organized and led by particular magnetic individuals have waxed and waned in all countries without ever having achieved either the status of denominations or churches in religion, or state power in politics; they often linger on after the death or discrediting of their founder-leaders as no more than isolated sects looking back nostalgically to a more radiant past.

One reason, though certainly not the only one, for the decline of such movements, is their failure to solve the 'problem of succession' that Weber saw as critical to the survival of charismatic movements and organizations. More generally, politics is the arena in which the struggle for power to *impose* institutionalization and the legitimations under-girding it takes place. The sociologist who is not primarily concerned with political conflict may confine himself to gradual, developmental change that takes place within established institutions over a long period of time and thus may treat personal authority, deriving from the appeal of a particular individual, as a marginal social psychological phenomenon. But the student of politics cannot afford to ignore the personal authority of prophets and political leaders when their followings become sufficiently extensive to challenge existing establishments. Charismatic movements centred on an individual to whom extraordinary gifts and powers are imputed are not, as Weber recognized, confined to politics and religion but also appear in the arts, intellectual life, morals, and even in economic enterprise. Charismatic political and religious movements, however, exhibit personal authority in its most extensive form.

Genuine charismatic authority is based on the followers' faith and belief in the mission of the leader, who usually demands unconditional devotion and obedience. Charismatic authority, therefore, typically exceeds the other forms of non-coercive power and authority in comprehensiveness and intensity. In particular, it is not restrained by the limits of tradition or legal statute as are Weber's other two types of legitimation, the traditional and the rational-legal. Yet in resting solely on the followers' belief in an individual leader, charismatic authority is also more unstable than other forms of authority, for it is vulnerable to total collapse not only when the leader dies but if he suffers setbacks or defeats that create doubts about his charismatic gifts.[61]

Weber's concept of charisma has suffered the fate of becoming a popular journalistic term and is indiscriminately used as a pretentious synonym for the personal appeal of any political figure. Such a usage is remote from that of Weber, who regarded charisma as a relatively rare attribute of leaders – more accurately, an attribute imputed by followers – giving rise to tension and conflict between charismatic movements and the *status quo*.

Nor is charismatic leadership to be equated with personal authority, although it is perhaps the most pronounced and pure form of it. Personal authority is the most diffuse form of authority in that elements of it are present in nearly all authority relations because authority is always exercised by concrete persons with distinctive personal qualities. The personal popularity of incumbents of head roles – monarchs, presidents, party leaders, commanding generals – buttresses their legitimate authority. Doctors cultivate the famous 'bedside manner' and other professionals adopt equivalent modes of 'presentation of self'. The legitimate authority of parents gives them great power over their children, but their personalities rather than this authority *per se* have greatest impact in shaping the children's characters.

CHAPTER FOUR

The Forms of Power: Combinations and Interrelations

In the two preceding chapters I have followed the fairly traditional procedure of presenting a classification of the forms of influence and power. My particular classification has a few novel features and the descriptions of the various forms are more detailed than is customary, but the general practice of setting forth such a taxonomy is scarcely new. The usual justification for distinguishing carefully between the various forms of power is that they are habitually confused and confounded in everyday language and scholarly discourse and even in the reflections of great thinkers.

Yet the formal definitions and distinctions made by different writers scarcely succeed in dispelling this confusion, for they reveal at least as much diversity as uniformity. Power is regarded as a form of influence, or influence as a form of power, or they are treated as entirely distinct phenomena. Power is held to rest always on consent, or it must always confront and overcome resistance. Authority is a subtype of power, or power and authority are distinct and opposite. Persuasion is a form of power; it is not a form of power at all. Force is a form of power; it is not power but a sign of the breakdown or failure of power. Manipulation is or is not a form of power. Personal leadership is or is not a form of authority. Competence is a basis for persuasion and has nothing to do with power or authority, or it is the fundamental implicit ground of all legitimate authority. All power is reducible to the unequal exchange of goods and services, or the offering of benefits in return for compliance is simply one form of power.[1]

Confronting this definitional chaos, it is small wonder that some recent writers have been moved to assay new conceptual approaches to the understanding of power and have even counselled abandonment of the slippery concept altogether.[2] However, the discrepancies in the definitions of influence, power, authority *et al.*, offered by different writers (including, of course, myself), are not primarily the result of mere semantic idiosyncrasies, of the vanity of academic men who, as Weber once remarked, feel as proprietary of their preferred vocabularies as of their toothbrushes. Differences in definition sometimes result from different resolutions of the larger conceptual problems of defining power discussed in Chapter 1. But they also stem from the fact that in reality the forms of influence and power shade into one another along several axes or continua from the non-social uses of force and manipulation to a near-complete fusion of will and purpose between power holder and power subject. The axes can, of course, be extended to include the give-and-take of mutual influence present in all social interaction, as was noted in Chapter 1. Different writers have cut into the axes at different places and have chosen to stress particular contrasts between points along them in elaborating their definitions: whether a power relation is coercive or consensual, for example; or whether or not a relationship implicates the larger community to which its partners belong; or whether the content or the source of a communication induces compliance.

The purely taxonomic and definitional character of a typology of forms of power – a feature, of course, of all classifications – can be overcome by showing how the various forms intergrade in reality, combine and coexist in particular power relations, and exhibit regular 'tendential laws' of transition from one form to another. Such an effort aims to reduce the apparently nominal and arbitrary nature of a set of definitions by using it to formulate propositions about real social processes, however limited in scope or abstract these propositions may be.[3] I am certainly not disposed to argue that my own classification in the two previous chapters is better in itself than earlier ones; only that I attempt in the present chapter to *use* the classification to elucidate what – for want of a better word – might be called the 'dynamics' of power relations and to formulate a few general propositions, rather than merely applying the classification illustratively as a set of verbal labels.

The Forms of Power as Ideal Types

Classifications of the forms of power are 'ideal typical' or 'analytical' and by no means imply that any and all actual power relations can be neatly subsumed under under one or another of the labelled forms. Despite familiar warnings against 'reification' or the attribution of 'misplaced concreteness' to concepts, one still often finds, even among supposedly sophisticated social scientists, a tendency to assume naïvely that there must be a one-to-one correspondence between observed phenomena and definitional categories. On the other hand, taxonomies of the forms of power are often criticized and rejected on the grounds that in reality most power relations are mixed, exhibiting qualities of contrasted types interwoven into an apparently inseparable blend. The analytical status of such classifications was fully recognized by Max Weber, whose definitions of the types of domination and legitimation have been so influential, in each of the different sections of *Economy and Society* where he elaborated his typology.[4] The value of any classification depends not on how literally it encompasses the inexhaustible variety of the world, but on the subtlety and discernment with which it is 'fitted' to reality and on whether or not it can be employed to generate illuminating propositions.

Not, to be sure, that there are not pure examples of the types in reality. *Force* and *manipulation*, in fact, can be said to exist only in their pure forms because the attitudes or motivations of the power subject towards the power holder are by definition irrelevant in both forms of power. Force involves treating the power subject as a physical or at most a biological object, and manipulation presupposes the power subject's ignorance of the intent of the power holder. Whether or not physical force is applied can be unambiguously determined. In the case of manipulation it may be more difficult to determine whether the power holder does or does not communicate his intent to the power subject, or whether the latter in fact perceives his intent even when it is concealed. In principle, however, it is possible. This difficulty, moreover, does not arise in those cases of manipulation where the power holder does not interact at all with the power subject but arranges the latter's environment in such a way as to elicit a desired response. The non-volitional, non-interactional nature of both force and manipulation was discussed in Chapter 2.

Persuasion and the five types of *authority*, unlike force and manipulation, assume the presence of particular motives for compliance on the part of the power subject. It is possible to find in reality clear-cut examples of each, but the ambivalent, overdetermined and multi-layered nature of most human motivation ensures that many – probably most – actual instances of apparent persuasion or authority will turn out to be mixed or border-line cases. The same applies to *psychic* as distinct from physical force, where the extent to which a power subject retains even a minimal freedom to choose when subject to sustained emotional assault may be a highly moot point.[5] Empirically, the distinctions between psychic force, persuasion, the five forms of authority, and the subtler kinds of manipulation are matters of degree rather than of kind, which is to say that they represent variations along a continuum.

A host of concrete examples of the mixed motives underlying compliance with the directives of a power holder comes to mind.[6] Someone believes – persuades himself? – that he has been persuaded by the arguments of another, but the other's impressive, overbearing personality (personal authority) or apparent mastery of the issue at hand (competent authority) may have played the major part in inducing the subject's compliance. A doctor's charm and air of confidence (personal authority) may, far more than his credentials and professional reputation (competent authority), inspire a patient's trust in his competence to diagnose and cure. The law-abiding citizen may piously affirm the value of obeying the law (legitimate authority), although he actually conforms partly out of fear of being caught and punished should he fail to do so (coercive authority). In the United States, it has long been a cliché for people to claim that they work hard and obey the boss because they 'like to eat' or 'for the wife and kids' (authority by inducement), a claim that often masks a strong achievement motive or a sense of obligation (legitimate authority). David Riesman has noted the tendency of Americans to adduce self-interested motives for conduct that they actually pursue for moral, even idealistic, reasons. On the other hand, the hidden aggressiveness and even sadism of stern moralists were noted by novelists, and by Nietzsche, long before psychoanalysis explored the link between the superego and aggression. Such considerations obviously may apply to professed and consciously sincere motives for obedience to authorities.

The point is not merely that people often produce rationalizations for their actions that conceal or deny their 'real' motives. It is, rather, that their real motivations are often – some would say always – a complex mixture of duty, fear, love, status seeking and utilitarian self-interest. This is true, of course, of the motivations of both power holder and power subject. The motivations of the former are ultimately just as important as those of the latter in understanding the nature of stable power relations, but classifications of the different forms of power (including my own) stress the differing motivations of the power subject in complying with the *intention*, whatever the motives underlying it, of the power holder.[7] Submission to the power of another is generally seen as psychologically more problematical than the disposition to exercise power over others.

In short, the analytical status of any typology of the forms of power results from the multiplicity of meanings and motivations involved in all human actions, including those constrained by the superior power of others, except, of course, for manipulation and brute force that treats the human subject as no more than a physical or biological object.

Different Links in the Chain of Interaction

Analysts of power have treated single 'power acts' as the basic units of stable power relations. With reference to human action in general, Talcott Parsons has argued that a 'unit act', consisting of a single end pursued by an actor availing himself of chosen means under given conditions, is the smallest isolatable component of more complex systems of action in which previous unit acts become means or constraining conditions for later ones.[4] In the case of social interaction, Parsons has treated as its basic element an 'ego-alter' relation in which two persons guide their conduct by their perceptions of the other's expectations in relation to their own 'need dispositions'.[9] It is not necessary to accept Parsons' view that consensus, or what he calls 'complementarity of expectations', is the fundamental form of social interaction. Conflicting or misunderstood expectations may be regarded as equally possible, as well as a range of intermediate possibilities.[10] But some notion of a single mutual act-response sequence as the basic unit of social interaction is indispensable and applies as much to the asymmetrical interaction involved in power relations as to other forms of interaction.

Social interaction, however, builds up complex chains or networks composed of many distinct 'ego-alter' interactions as links. A single interaction, when examined apart from its total context, may possess clear-cut attributes which are blurred or modified when it is viewed as part of the entire sequence or network to which it belongs. This was brought home to me with blinding clarity as it applies to acts of power by a not especially noteworthy experience of a good many years ago.

One October afternoon I was watching a World Series baseball game on television in the student lounge of the university at which I taught. Later that afternoon our department had invited a visiting sociologist to address a colloquium of faculty and students. The chairman of the department had made it a fixed rule that all faculty members should

attend these colloquia; he was a somewhat authoritarian person of
European background with absolutely no interest in baseball. The game
was exciting, but as the hour of the colloquium approached I got up and
headed for the lecture hall, grumbling inwardly yet mindful of my status
as a junior faculty member without tenure, my future heavily dependent
on the chairman's judgement. After the talk, it was the custom to
entertain the visiting speaker at a cocktail party at the faculty club. I
found myself engaged in a discussion with the visiting speaker, as we
sipped martinis, on the perennial question of the role of values in
sociology. He maintained vehemently that sociologists should not
restrict themselves to supposedly value-free statements, since they knew
with certainty what the good society was: it was a society lacking any
coercion, in which individuals always acted voluntarily 'just as you and
I have freely chosen to stand here talking'. I smiled with what I hoped
was a touch of irony, but refrained out of politeness from pointing out
that had it not been for my untenured status I would gladly have
foregone both his talk and the cocktail party in order to continue
watching the baseball game.

   It would be pedantic to overanalyse this trival experience, but clearly
the various links in the interactional sequence differed in the degree to
which coercion or voluntary choice was present. Having felt compelled
to attend a lecture in which I was not much interested, I scarcely needed
any external pressure or encouragement to imbibe cocktails afterwards
in an informal social setting, an 'entitlement' contingent on my having
dutifully been present at the colloquium. Yet the chairman's power over
my future career was a sufficient condition to initiate the entire sequence
from my dragging myself away from the television set to engaging in a
discussion lubricated with alcohol of the philosophy of the social
sciences a couple of hours later. Was my part in the entire sequence
coerced, or should one separate out the coercive and voluntary links in
the chain while recognizing that the entire chain was in some sense an
experiential whole (or 'totality')? I would opt for the latter, but the point
of the example is to indicate the difficulty of applying neat conceptual
distinctions between forms of power to the contextual subtlety of actual
experience.

Combinations of the Forms of Power

In the discussion of the forms of power in previous chapters, I tried to
assess the potential of each of them with respect to the extensiveness,
comprehensiveness and intensity of a power relation. Some permit

relations of wide extensiveness but limited comprehensiveness and intensity, e.g. competent authority, persuasion, manipulation; some tend to be confined to relations of limited extensiveness but high comprehensiveness and intensity, e.g. personal authority; others are capable of great extensiveness and comprehensiveness but are limited in intensity, e.g. force. Coercion, inducement and legitimate authority, based respectively on control over instruments of force, economic resources and normative symbols,[11] are the forms generally capable of creating relations of the widest extensiveness, comprehensiveness and intensity. A future chapter will deal with the interrelations between coercive and legitimate authority, since these are the two distinctive bases of political power and have long been a major subject of political theory and philosophy, both ancient and modern. I also briefly reviewed in previous chapters the relative costs to the power holder in energy, time and resources of maintaining a power relation based on the various forms of power, emphasizing in particular their unequal potentialities in sustaining reliability of anticipated reactions.

Each of the forms of power shows a somewhat different profile with regard to these several variables. Each is also subject to distinctive instabilities, which will be discussed at greater length later in this chapter. *It is therefore to the advantage of a power holder to extend and diversify the forms of power he exercises over a given power subject.* This generalization holds subject to two conditions: (1) The power holder seeks to maintain stable, long-term control over the power subject; and (2) the power holder seeks a control of some generality, one that is not confined to a few limited scopes or a narrow range of options, that is, he seeks a relation of at least moderate comprehensiveness and intensity.

A persuader saves time and effort if he can get some of his suggestions acted on immediately out of a belief in his competence or by establishing his personal authority. As Freidson pointed out in a passage quoted in the previous chapter, it is often a point of pride on the part of doctors to reduce to a minimum the need for explanations to the patient designed to persuade him of the wisdom of a course of treatment. The idiom that force serves as a 'final persuader' suggests that a power holder may sometimes have to climb a 'ladder of escalation' from the mildest and most consensual to the most punitive forms of power in order to obtain compliance. For this to be possible, the power holder must, of course, possess the capability of exercising more than a single form of power. I suggested in Chapter 1 that the power of a parent over a child was the most comprehensive and intensive form of power in human experience. Imagine a parent, modern, educated, with a firm belief in the superiority of reason, trying to persuade an unwilling child to undertake some task. Argument fails, so the parent promises a future treat (inducement) if the child will do what he or she wants right now. The child remains unmoved, so the parent says in the imperative mode 'Do it, you'll be grateful to me afterwards', an appeal to competent authority. The child is still obdurate, so the parent finally asserts his or her legitimate authority: 'Do it, that's an order!' – perhaps preceding this with a moral appeal to the child's duty to obey, an attempt at what Parsons has called 'the activation of commitments'. The child's continued resistance inspires a threat of punishment (coercive authority) and finally the carrying out of the threat – the child is denied supper (force). (By this time, the child's defiance of parental authority may itself have become an issue overshadowing the original disagreement.) Parent and child in this example have climbed the ladder of escalation from persuasion to force, conceivably in the course of no more than a few minutes.

To take an example at the macro-social level, several recent American presidents have resorted to 'jawboning' to fight inflation, attempting to persuade corporations and unions not to raise prices or make new wage demands. In doing so, they were appealing to the prestige and legitimate authority of their office and to the presumed competence of their expert economic advisers in warning of the dangers of inflation. Yet the implicit threat of compulsory wage and price controls lay behind the presidential exhortations should they fail to be heeded. Also, the memory of President Kennedy's successful threat of sanctions against the steel companies that had broken administration price guidelines in 1962 has added new 'persuasiveness' to the jawboning of later presidents. President Nixon, of course, did eventually introduce wage and price controls for a period.

These examples show rather obviously the advantage to a power holder of being able to resort to alternative forms of power should those initially tried fail. They also underline the complexity of human motivations previously stressed, for the child and the corporations and unions would hardly be unaware that if they refused to be persuaded they could be commanded and ultimately coerced into compliance; they would certainly know of the full panoply of powers possessed by parents and presidents.

The very capacity and readiness of the power holder to muster

several different forms of power, however, are likely to reduce the
effectiveness of the milder, more consensual forms, those, that is, that
least arouse opposition and hostile sentiments on the part of the power
subject. As Etzioni has argued, there is an inherent incongruence in
combining persuasive and moral appeals with the implicit threat, let
alone the actual use, of force, which tends to neutralize the effectiveness
of the former.[12] A lesser incongruence also exists in the combination of
utilitarian appeals to self-interest with normative appeals to duty or
ideals, as Merton's well-known study of a World War II war bond drive,
cited by Etzioni in this connection, indicates.[13] Etzioni's examples of
incongruent combinations of forms of power are largely drawn from
impersonal, macro-level, inter-organizational relations. Yet whatever
psychic dissonance may be evoked in the power subject by awareness
of the power holder's capacity to back up non-coercive appeals with
ultimate resort to force, such a combination obviously characterizes
many stable power relations, especially those, such as parents and
children, of low extensiveness and high comprehensiveness and
intensity. When a power holder has actually escalated from persuasion
to force, the difficulty of restoring a relation based on persuasion or
legitimate authority may be considerable, although even this occurs
often enough in domestic and small group contexts.

Etzioni qualifies his assertion of the incongruence of different forms
of power by observing that they 'seem to be incompatible if relied upon
in the same control relation'.[14] In other words, when the power relation
is least extensive, as in a parent-child dyad, or when the power subject,
though plural, is assumed to respond uniformly, as in the example of
presidential anti-inflation campaigns, incongruence and incompatibility
are most likely to be perceived and to have effects. But in extensive
power relations, the assumption that the many power subjects will all
respond in the same way and can be treated as if they were a single
power subject is an unrealistic one. Some may be persuaded by appeals
to their self-interest, others by normative appeals; some may comply
out of firm belief in the legitimacy of the power holder; others may fear
that non-compliance will expose them to the risk of negative sanctions; a
few may actually have to be coerced into compliance or subjected to
force, rendering them incapable of further non-compliance.[15] Thus, *it is
to the advantage of the power holder confronting a heterogenous and
differentiated aggregate of power subjects (individuals or groups) to be
capable of exercising multiple forms of power to control them.*
Obviously, this situation prevails in inter-organizational or inter-

institutional power relations and constitutes an important difference between such macro-level relations and most micro-level relations.[16] Organizations build up great accumulations of power to cajole, reward, convert or coerce the many power subjects with which they deal in diverse situations or scopes. And none more so, of course, than states.

Incongruence in combining different forms of power is not totally eliminated in highly extensive power relations, although its neutralizing effects are likely to be greatly reduced. The pious, law-abiding citizen knows, after all, that the law presents a less benign face to those who are merely suspected of inclinations to break it – the poor, the underemployed, certain minority groups. He is subject to what might be called the 'there but for the grace of God go I' syndrome. The power holder has an interest in insulating from one another groups subject to different forms of power, hence the disposition to secrecy concerning certain practices of the police and conditions in prisons, not to speak of concentration camps in totalitarian countries. The need to buy off other groups with material rewards also inspires secrecy as smacking of 'bribery', 'corruption', and pandering to 'special interests' in the eyes of ordinary, loyal citizens.

Yet total insulation of convinced supporters, self-seeking opportunists, and those subjected to punishment may not be necessary to maximize the security of the power holder's position in view of the complexity and subtlety of human awareness and motivation with their capacity to synthesize apparent opposites. One recalls Durkheim's famous discussion of punishment as a ritual serving not so much to frighten the law-abiding as to dramatize and reaffirm in their eyes the sanctity of the law. Machiavelli argued from a purely instrumental standpoint that the prince 'ought to be both feared and loved, but as it is difficult for the two to go together, it is much safer to be feared than loved, if one of the two has to be wanting'.[17] Later in the same paragraph, he seems partially to identify 'love' with the receipt of material benefits and doubts the security of 'friendship which is gained by purchase'. Machiavelli, in effect, sees love, fear and material reward as distinguishable bases of the prince's power which can be used in combination to secure support, whether of one or many subjects, although he regarded fear as the most reliable. Writers who have viewed the union of 'terror and propaganda' as the *differentia specifica* of modern totalitarian rule[18] have not meant to suggest by the phrase that some citizens are targets of propaganda while others, distinct from the first, are victims of terror. For, as many accounts testify, the shadowy, nameless fears spread by the very incompleteness of the secrecy with which the use of terror was shrouded in Hitler's Germany and Stalin's Russia served to strengthen the unconditional loyalty to the regime of subjects who were not themselves members of oppositional or proscribed groups. Terror and propaganda, apparent opposites in that one is coercive and the other persuasive, nevertheless reinforced each other under conditions of total power. These considerations suggest that it is difficult to determine the exact balance most optimal to a power holder between insulating the groups subject to different forms of power, on the one hand, and ensuring, on the other, at least limited awareness by each group of the treatment of the others.

The generalizations advanced in this section that it is to the advantage of the power holder to possess the capacity to wield different forms of power, and the more so the more extensive the power relation, do not contradict the emphasis on the motivations of the power subject in defining the forms of power (excepting, as always, force and manipulation). These generalizations simply state what would most effectively, from a rational, instrumental standpoint, secure and stabilize the power holder's control. They do not depend on any assumptions about the substantive interests, let alone the psychology, of actual power holders, topics to be discussed in later chapters.

Tendential Laws

Each of the forms of power has a built-in tendency to metamorphose over time into a different form when the power relation recurs often enough. Obviously, this is once again a special case of what is a general human tendency. Love deteriorates into habit. Prisoners become attached to their bars. An occupation chosen for financial gain is maintained out of a pride of craft. The mask of a chosen role grows into and becomes the real face of its wearer.

The instability of the particular forms of power is likely to manifest itself only in power relations that are not narrowly limited in comprehensiveness and intensity, such as those confined to stable but highly segmental social relations like night watchman, hotel manager or train conductor. More comprehensive and intensive power relations, far from exhibiting any inherent tendency towards stability or equilibrium, are prone to change as a result of their very recurrence.[19] I have already described several examples of such transitions in discussing the different forms of power in the two previous chapters. I shall now try to enumerate them more systematically.

Persuasion that is repeatedly successful is likely fairly quickly to become personal or competent authority. If someone is persuaded a number of times, the outcomes presumably turned out satisfactorily or else he or she would not have listened again to the persuader's arguments. But after x cases of successful persuasion, the persuaded will probably on the next, $x + 1$, occasion have acquired sufficient trust in the persuader's suggestions to act on them without independently evaluating them. The persuader has become a personal or competent authority.

But there is another much more significant route from persuasion to authority that may be followed and bears on central issues in the understanding of legitimate authority. Persuasion and authority are often used interchangeably by writers who nevertheless formally distinguish between them. The reason for this, presumably, is that both are seen as consensual in that both involve voluntary acceptance by the subject of the communications of another person as the basis for his own subsequent conduct. It would be pedantic to object to such entirely understandable, and sometimes even unavoidable, verbal looseness, but an important distinction is involved that should not be left implicit. One may persuade someone to submit to one's own or to another's authority in the future, as when a person insists that his directives should be followed in a course of action because of his superior experience or knowledge, or when a parent planning to be absent urges a child to obey an older sibling chosen temporarily to stand *in loco parentis*. The presentation of arguments as to why A should be obeyed constitutes persuasion (or attempted persuasion); if B is persuaded and proceeds to obey A's orders, his compliance with them constitutes an exercise of authority on A's part. B has been persuaded to submit to authority, but the persuasion and the authority relation it has created are different forms of power manifest in separate interactions that stand in a temporal sequence. Of course, an authority may also delegate his authority to someone else: in my previous example, the parent may *command* the child to obey an older sibling. In this event, instead of persuasion leading to authority, we have one relation of authority producing another new relation of authority.

The process of legitimation exemplifies persuasion passing into authority. The presentation of arguments, appeals or exhortations as to why one *should* obey an authority is distinct from actual compliance with the orders of an authority independently of the particular content of those orders (within, of course, the scopes and zones of acceptance embraced by the authority relation). Carl Friedrich's succinct statement that legitimate authority involves 'the potentiality of reasoned elaboration' is entirely consistent with this view.[20] The actual elaboration of reasons for compliance amounts to attempted persuasion, but when commands are obeyed because the subject is aware of the *potentiality* of their justification by rational argument we are dealing with authority. Friedrich's phrase is most obviously applicable to competent authority, although he uses the generic term 'authority' to include both the competent and legitimate subtypes. In short, legitimations, including Weber's famous threefold typology of them, are 'reasoned elaborations' invoked to persuade someone that he ought to obey an authority, but they are not equivalent to the fact of obedience itself. Authority may revert back to attempted persuasion either when a particular order is questioned, or when the authority's right to control the subject over an entire range of scopes and zones of acceptance that may have been accepted in the past becomes subject to questioning or challenge. Weber's types of legitimacy, of course, referred to the latter rather than to the attempt to justify obedience only to a particular command.

One might argue that the overtones of rationality in Friedrich's 'reasoned elaboration' are scarcely applicable to Weber's traditional and charismatic types of legitimacy. 'That's the way we have always done things', 'What was good enough for my father is good enough for me', 'When in Rome, do as the Romans do', or, more broadly, 'What is, is right' represent typical traditionalist legitimations of norms or authority relations, but only in a very broad sense can they be regarded as 'rational'. Weber's conception of traditional legitimacy was related to purely habitual action in his more general typology of social action and the unthinking automatism of habit – or custom when it is collective – is essentially non-rational. Conservative thought and ideology represent an effort to rationalize tradition – traditionalism become conscious of itself, as Mannheim put it – which occurs in response to the rise of counter-ideologies challenging the traditional order.[21] Weber's charismatic legitimacy is an expression of affectual action, of action stemming from emotional commitment or faith, in his typology of social action and is unmistakably non-rational.

Friedrich's phrase, then, suggests a link not only between authority and persuasion, but between authority and that old hero of classical and

German idealistic thought, Reason. He shares this emphasis with a number of other quite disparate thinkers who have in common a German origin, such as Hannah Arendt and the philosophers of the Frankfurt School, including Erich Fromm, Herbert Marcuse and, more recently, Jürgen Habermas. The interconnections of persuasion, authority and reason can, of course, be traced back to Platonic and Aristotelian models. Talcott Parsons's consensual view of power may even owe something to his graduate education in Germany.

Persuasion is an implicitly egalitarian relationship that leaves intact the free choice and 'substantive rationality' of the persuaded, which is why many writers have refused to consider it a power relation at all. Authority eliminates by definition argument and exchange of opinions about the communications in the form of commands issued by the superior; it curtails, accordingly, the subject's opportunity to exercise his rational faculties and freedom of choice. There is a disposition therefore to regard all forms of authority as non-rational and even coercive. To Hannah Arendt, as we saw at the beginning of Chapter 3, any form of command-obedience relationship is at best 'a kind of mitigated violence'.[22] On the other hand, authority — which she calls 'power' — is based on the prior consensus of a group acting freely in concert to create new institutions that thereafter derive their authority from the original act of foundation.[23] Despite its classical roots, her approach converges, at least in this respect, with that of so utterly different a thinker as Talcott Parsons.[24] Jürgen Habermas's conception of 'emancipation from domination', as fully realized in an 'ideal speech situation' in which all propositional statements and practical decisions are subject to rational assessment of their 'truth claims' in debate and argument leading to eventual intersubjective agreement, goes even further in suggesting the possibility of eliminating altogether any command-obedience relationships.[25]

The view that authority grows out of an uncoerced consensus, or that it can be supported by persuasion if questioned, can obviously lead to a highly idealized justification of existing institutions. But if existing institutions are regarded as 'irrational' or 'repressive', they are open to criticism by comparison with a model of 'rational' authority of which the craftsman, the expert or the teacher have long been exemplars.[26] The conviction that *all* command-obedience relations are non-rational, coercive, and even amount to a form of violence may also lead, however, to the extreme anti-authoritarianism of many New Left student radicals in the late 1960s who, heavily influenced by Marcuse, embraced a utopian anarchism that envisaged the abolition of all authority; many of them even denounced as 'élitism' the ideal of competent authority – the ideal and not merely the tarnished realities of contemporary professionalism – which goes back to Plato and Aristotle.[27] Even the authority of parents over small children came under attack.

Legitimations of authority amount to successful arguments for obedience, but authority cannot be collapsed into persuasion, nor into a consensus achieved through persuasion, nor does it follow that persuasion can necessarily be substituted for authority in all situations, even in many where superior competence cannot be reliably ascertained. Legitimations are claimed by authorities who also have coercive and utilitarian resources at their disposal, a fact rarely unknown to the targets of persuasion. Indeed, at the macro-social level of political power, legitimate authority usually grows out of and partially supplants coercion rather than persuasion. This is the subject of the next chapter in which I also argue that a minimal element of at least psychic coercion is present in even the most benign or paternalistic authority relations. But to recognize this does not mean that command-obedience relations – or authority – can be equated with violence any more than with persuasion and a consensus forged by it. Still less does it suggest the utopian possibility of dispensing with all power relations, whether in the form of the anarchistic communalism upheld by the 'counter-culture' of the 1960s or in the more rarefied vision of world history as a seminar capable of arriving discursively at a universalist ethics that is implicit in Jürgen Habermas's recent writings.[28]

As was argued in previous chapters, force may be used simply to remove people from the scene or to prevent them from acting at all. But it is often used to establish the credibility of the power holder's will and capacity to use it so that he may exercise coercive authority over the subject and dispense with the necessity of resorting to force in the future. There is, it follows, an inherently self-liquidating character in such a use of force. I have previously argued at length for the importance of distinguishing sharply between force and the threat of force, or coercive authority when it is successful. Yet there is sometimes a close interplay between them with one giving way to the other and then reversing the sequence: force is used to create a credible threat of force and then resorted to again if that credibility is challenged or is in danger of being challenged by the power subject.

A power relation based on inducement tends over time to be

increasingly experienced as coercive by the power subject. The subject becomes dependent on the goods or services provided by the power holder to the point where the threat of their withdrawal is felt as a punishment or deprivation rather than as a reward. I quoted Peter Blau to this effect in Chapter 3. Anthony Giddens has also observed that

> inducements offering some definite rewards in exchange for compliance, always offer the possibility of being transformed into negative sanctions; the *withholding* of a reward represents a punishment and represents a definite form of coercion.[29]

The tendential laws stating the transformation of persuasion into competent or personal authority, inducement into coercion and the interplay between force and the threat of force require no very complex interpretation to elucidate them. They are evident enough at the level of common sense understanding. Dynamic tendencies in competent authority are less obvious and are fully manifest only when it is institutionalized in expert roles. Competent authority, when supported by the collective organization of experts and legally recognized by the state, tends, as the discussion of Freidson's analysis of the medical profession in the previous chapter indicated, to acquire some of the characteristics of legitimate and even coercive authority. When competent authority is exercised over a group in circumstances of considerable risk to the authorities and their subordinates and clients or customers, it tends both to merge with legitimate authority and to create an especially strong identity of interest within the entire group. This situation, even more commonly than the expert-client or professional model, has long been invoked as a legitimating ideal and exemplar for more comprehensive and intensive power relations ranging from the family to the state.[30]

The interaction between persuasion and legitimate authority is more problematical. Persuasion may succeed in creating legitimate authority which then dispenses with the need for it by substituting commands for arguments. Challenges to authority, however, may result in a reversion back to a relation of persuasion. Yet these are too simple linear notions: the legitimation of authority is a ceaseless process of persuasion designed continually to evoke and rekindle in its subjects the loyalties and obligations to obey and to ensure reliability of control through anticipated reactions.

At the level of large-scale political power, coercion also interacts with legitimation and the authority it affirms. Stable coercive power relations usually show a tendency to evolve in the direction of legitimate authority for a variety of reasons of which the instrumental interest of the power holder in reducing his costs, increasing the reliability of anticipated reactions and coping with a plurality of differently situated and motivated power subjects is only one. There is also, however, a counter-tendency, epitomized in Hegel's famous master-servant dialectic, for legitimate authority to become 'demystified' over time and increasingly experienced as coercive. But I shall discuss these rival tendencies and their interrelations more fully in the next chapter.

With regard to inducement, Machiavelli was no doubt right in observing that

> it may be said of men in general that they are ungrateful, voluble, dissemblers, anxious to avoid danger, and covetous of gain; as long as you benefit them, they are entirely yours; they offer you their blood, their goods, their life, and their children . . . when the necessity is remote; but when it approaches, they revolt.[31]

We might call this the 'but what have you done for me lately?' syndrome.[32] Yet it is also true that people sometimes grow to love the hand that feeds them, that compliance originally based on the desire for benefits evolves into acceptance of a duty to obey, or legitimate authority.

That personal authority is likely to be transitory under conditions of sustained intimate association is expressed in a number of maxims such as 'familiarity breeds contempt' or 'no man is a hero to his valet'. The sad wisdom that romantic love is often incompatible with the humdrum realities of married life is a well-known special case of this.[33] Another example is the 'clay feet' experience of adolescents when they discover that their parents are not the moral paragons they have previously appeared to be but themselves possess the very foibles and human weaknesses against which they have so often preached. Even where personal contact is absent, adults often recall with amusement the shocked surprise with which they reacted to the realization that such lofty figures as monarchs or presidents have to go to the bathroom. These examples suggest the dissolution altogether of a power relation based on personal authority, but personal authority may be supplanted by coercion, inducement or legitimate authority – submission out of fear, self-interest or duty – as often occurs in parental or marital relationships when the power subject's intensely personal attachment to the power holder becomes attenuated. A certain social distance warding off or setting up barriers to regular intimate association seems to be almost a prerequisite for the preservation of personal authority.[34]

Charismatic movements, the most extensive manifestations of personal authority, often elaborately ritualize the social distance between the leader and his adoring followers, although his closest lieutenants may be cynically aware that he too is 'human, all too human'. But the personal authority of the charismatic leader, apart from its general fragility, is subject to the long-term dissolution that Weber called the 'routinization of charisma'. Since the leader is mortal, his death requires that he be replaced by a more impersonal legitimate authority, whether traditional or rational-legal in Weber's terms, in which obedience to the incumbent of an office or head role supplants obedience to an individual person.

Some of the 'tendential laws' I have described in this section represent highly probable or even inevitable transitions from one form of power to another as a result of the inherent instability of the initial form: from persuasion to competent or personal authority, from inducement to coercion, and the interaction between force and coercive authority where the former is employed to establish credibility. Other tendencies to change, however, amount to no more than possibilities which may or may not be realized: the various transitions and interactions between persuasion, coercion, inducement, and competent and legitimate authority, and the instability of personal authority. The transitional tendency inherent in each form of power makes it to the advantage of a power holder to acquire the capacity to employ more than a single form of power in addition to the considerations mentioned in the preceding section.

Summary

This chapter has attempted to show several ways in which the forms of power blend, intergrade and overlap in reality. Four kinds of combination and interrelation of the various forms have been discussed.

(1) The forms of power are conceptually distinct, but this does not mean that all observable power relations can be neatly classified as exemplifying a particular form. A fairly obvious epistemological point is at issue here, for *all* concepts are abstractions from reality and do not describe it in its plenitude. Max Weber's argument that the construction

of 'ideal types', simplifying models of the real world, is peculiar to the social sciences need not be accepted,[35] but he was right in seeing that the dependence of the social sciences on assumptions about the subjective meanings and motivations of human actors removes their conceptualizations a step further from raw experience than those of the natural sciences, an argument later developed more fully by Alfred Schutz.

Although it is possible to find 'pure' examples of each of the forms of power, most power relations are inevitably mixtures since the taxonomy of forms is largely based on assumptions about the motives of the power subjects and human motivation is almost always an impure and heterogeneous blend of different, often conflicting, impulses and affects. This, of course, is a substantive rather than an epistemological point.

(2) Particular acts of power are usually part of wider networks of interaction that include acts or interactions which, viewed in isolation from their context, manifest different forms of power.

(3) A stable power relation of some comprehensiveness and intensity is rarely based on a single form of power. It is to the interest of the power holder to be capable of exercising multiple forms of power to ensure the maintenance of his control. This is especially true of extensive power relations involving control over a plurality of power subjects some of whom will yield to one form of power, others to a different form.

(4) Most of the forms of power exhibit tendencies of different degrees of strength to change over time into a different form. The process of legitimation of an authority relation involves a continuous interaction between persuasion and the command-obedience relation that is the essence of authority. The complex interactions and transitions between coercion and legitimation are discussed at length in the next chapter.

CHAPTER FIVE

The Forms of Power: The Interaction of Coercion and Legitimation

Declarations that force is the main, or only, or ultimate form of power have a long history in social thought. 'Might is right' is an ancient proverb in several European languages. Some dictionaries of quotations attribute it to Plato, equating it with Thrasymachus' 'justice is the interest of the stronger' in the first book of *The Republic*, although the actual phrase does not appear there, at least in the Jowett translation. Machiavelli argued that 'all armed prophets have conquered and unarmed ones failed' and that for rulers 'it is much safer to be feared than loved'. Hobbes wrote that 'covenants without the sword are but words and of no strength to secure a man at all'. Perhaps the best-known contemporary assertion of the primacy of force is Mao's aphorism that 'political power grows out of the barrel of a gun'.

The claim that only force – meaning, of course, essentially the threat of force – is 'real' and that other forms of power are mere appearances or illusions is found in many nineteenth- and twentieth-century secular ideologies and theories of history, including Social Darwinism, vulgar Nietzscheanism, neo-Machiavellian élitism, some brands of Marxism and various doctrines that can loosely be labelled 'fascist'. Such views usually also recognize material inducements – 'bread and circuses' – as an additional foundation for the exercise of power. As George Orwell pungently summed up the more cynically realist versions of this outlook:

In effect . . . humanity is divided into two classes: the self-seeking, hypocritical minority, and the brainless mob whose destiny is always to be led or driven, as one gets a pig back to the sty by kicking it in the bottom or rattling a stick inside a swill-bucket, according to the needs of the moment.[1]

Yet crisp and succinct though they are, the statements proclaiming the priority of force that I have cited are full of ambiguities. Rousseau maintained in *The Social Contract* that phrases like 'might is right' or 'the right of the strongest' are tautologies. He did not use that term, but his argument is worth quoting for it could scarcely be improved upon by a contemporary analytic philosopher:

> If force compels obedience, there is no need to invoke a duty to obey, and if force ceases to compel obedience, there is no longer any obligation. Thus the word 'right' adds nothing to what is said by 'force'; it is meaningless.[2]

From Force to Legitimacy

'Might is right' is often rendered as 'might makes right' which is susceptible to a different interpretation. It can be understood as asserting the undeniable fact that coercive power holders, having won their power by superior strength in overt physical conflict, succeed (at least partially) in inducing the defeated to acknowledge the legitimacy of their rule, the moral validity of their laws and institutions. Most large states since ancient times have been created by military conquest; indeed it has often been held that centralized political institutions, or the state itself, originated out of the necessity of governing conquered and still hostile subjects. The maxim, then, means only that power is initially won by might, not that it is everywhere and always maintained primarily by the threat of force and the obedience out of fear the threat imposes. Machiavelli, to be sure, does claim the latter (although he does not deny that 'love' may also play a role), as does Hobbes in a more qualified way. Mao, on the other hand, as well as Machiavelli on armed prophets, says no more than that political power is first won in military struggle, not necessarily that it is maintained by force alone. These views suggest a temporal sequence from victory in a test of force, to the establishment of coercive authority over the losers, to the successful conversion of the latter to a belief in the rightness of the power holder's rule.

Once again, Rousseau summarizes cogently the limitations of rule by force alone: 'The strongest man is never strong enough to be master all the time, unless he transforms force into right and obedience into duty.'[3] Coercion, as we saw in Chapter 3, is a highly effective form of power but a costly one. It requires large investments in the instruments of force, the social organization trained to wield them and in means of surveillance of the subject population – required because the reliability of anticipated reactions is low unless the activities of the subjects are, or are believed to be, visible to the rulers. The hostility of the subjects, maintained and even increased by coercive rule, creates the risk of a renewed outbreak of violent struggle, the outcome of which is uncertain when chance and luck continue to play a large part in war even though modern weaponry has reduced both the risk of rebellion and the uncertainty of its outcome. Yet in the absence of occasional tests of strength the credibility of the power holder's willingness to use force diminishes. Moreover, the deterioration of weapons and armies through inactivity may also reduce the power holder's capabilities and increase the risk of successful rebellion. Thus every stable political order 'impresses the mores of the ruling group upon the population',[4] that is, strives to convert coercive into legitimate authority.

The Legitimacy of Force

The attempted transformation of coercive into legitimate authority is a special case of the generalization advanced in the previous chapter that it is to the advantage of a power holder to extend and diversify the forms of power he can exercise over a given power subject. Since coercion and legitimate authority are the pre-eminent forms of political power, which typically and even by definition possesses high extensiveness, our second generalization, that it is to the advantage of the power holder with a plurality of power subjects to be able to exercise multiple forms of power to control them, also applies to the legitimation of power initially established by force. Some subjects continue to be controlled by threats of force whereas others come to accept the power holder's right to command them.

Max Weber's famous definition of the state as a 'human community that successfully claims the monopoly of the legitimate use of physical force within a given territory'[5] implies that the state exercises more than a single form of power. The definition is often interpreted, whether critically or approvingly, as insisting on the primacy of force in politics, echoing Thrasymachus, Hobbes and Machiavelli, the last of whom Weber praised as an intellectual ancestor. Yet Weber's definition refers to *both* force and legitimacy as attributes of the state's authority. He can hardly have meant to suggest that those who were coerced by the state also acknowledged its right to coerce them (although this may, of course, be true of remorseful criminals). Clearly, the state's use of physical force is seen as legitimate by those subjects who do not themselves have to be coerced in order to obtain their compliance.[6] Such law-abiding subjects confer legitimacy on the state's coercion of other subjects who break its laws. Weber's definition thus presupposes a plurality of power subjects, some of whom obey the state out of duty while others have to be forced to comply or forcibly prevented from persistent non-compliance. Weber does not even regard force as the state's primary means of obtaining compliance: he immediately adds 'of course force is not the normal or the only means of the state – nobody says that – but force is a means specific to the state'.[7] The state also relies on persuasion, inducement and other forms of power, but Weber sees its distinctiveness in comparison with all other social structures as lying in its monopoly over the use of force, a monopoly which emerged only gradually in modern history and received its most famous normative justification from Hobbes.[8] If Weber's definition implies that both force and legitimate authority are the basis of political power, a major aim of his famous essay 'Politics as a Vocation' was to emphasize the tension between ethics and politics resulting from the acceptance by the politician of violence as a necessary means in a world where no universal consensus on values prevails:

> He who lets himself in for politics, that is, for power and force as means, contracts with diabolical powers . . . he who seeks the salvation of his soul, of his own and of others, should not seek it along the avenue of politics, for the quite different tasks of politics can only be solved by violence.[9]

Weber praises Machiavelli in this connection for having recognized these painful truths.[10]

From Legitimacy to Force

The idea that force is the ultimate form of political power implies a different sequence from the evolution of military conquest into stable political domination in which force and the threat of force come first but eventually are supplanted by legitimate authority exercised over at least some subjects. When force is described as the ultimate form of power, it is seen as coming *last* in another sequence: it is the final resort, the last court of appeal, of the power holder who has failed to obtain compliance by first employing the milder, more consensual forms of power. Machiavelli's recommendation that the prince be sure he is feared and Hobbes's insistence that covenants without the sword are worthless share this perspective, as do contemporary writers who make such statements as 'all politics is a struggle for power: the ultimate kind of power is violence'.[11] Only the power holder who can resort to force is able to climb to the top of the 'ladder of escalation' when confronted with a recalcitrant power subject. Student radicals of the 1960s adopted a kind of practice (or 'praxis') based on this conception when they engaged in 'confrontation politics' designed to provoke the authorities – usually university administrations – into using force against them. Their assumption was that the resort to force would antagonize passive observers and destroy the remaining legitimacy of the authorities by exhibiting the incongruence of combining force with persuasion and appeals to legitimacy.[12]

Yet the view that the power holder is able to apply force as a last resort – or, prescriptively, that he should 'speak softly but carry a big stick' – is not really at odds with the frequent claim that resort to violence is evidence of the 'failure of power'.[13] Insistence that force is the final recourse of the power holder is often described as a Thrasymachean, Machiavellian or *realpolitische* view of politics and history, implying a 'conflict' or 'coercion' theory of society, whereas the claim that the use of force reveals the breakdown of power is seen as indicative of a 'consensus' or 'integrationist' social theory.[14] A Machiavelli or a Hobbes doubted that most men will habitually restrain their selfish and aggressive impulses in the absence of the relative certainty that they will be subject to negative sanctions should they fail to do so. A Socrates or a Rousseau, without denying that force is an effective constraint, contended that persuasion and legitimate authority are far superior in sustaining the social solidarity necessary to maintain the co-operation that is the essence of the social order itself. The difference between them, however, is largely a matter of tone and emphasis even if the contrast between so-called 'conflict' and 'consensus' theories of society involves genuine disagreements on other issues.

One can readily agree, therefore, with E. V. Walter's conclusion that 'the most useful concept of power would not exclude from its domain either persuasion or coercion, nor would it consider either authority or violence to be more essential or ultimate'.[15] Why writers insisting on the importance of force have so often, as far back as Thrasymachus, adopted a debunking, cynical tone, one that anticipates disbelief and sometimes seems designed to shock their intellectual adversaries, is a separate question that I shall discuss at a later point. It requires consideration of the underlying motivations of both power holders and power subjects.

Consensus versus Coercion Theories of Society

Ralf Dahrendorf has been chiefly responsible for the by now exceedingly influential interpretation of sociological theory that sees it as divided between proponents of a 'consensus' and of a 'conflict' model of society, or, as Dahrendorf later called the two views, an 'integration' and a 'coercion theory of society'.[16] As the last label suggests, with reference to power the consensus approach emphasizes the predominance of legitimate authority while the conflict approach insists on an irreducible element of coercion in all power relations. Dahrendorf's formulation of the two approaches was dualistic, for he regarded them as opposites each of which was valid if confined to its own appropriate range of empirical problems, although the polemical thrust of his argument was directed against the consensual bias of theories dominant in the 1950s, notably Talcott Parsons's 'normative functionalism'.

Dahrendorf's dualism led him to neglect the interaction and mutual influence between legitimacy and coercion in *stable* power relations. He limited himself to contending that structures of legitimate authority in and of themselves generate opposition and antagonism on the part of subordinates who, coming to feel coerced, are drawn into conflict with their superiors the outcome of which is a new, altered structure of authority from which the whole cycle begins again. The conflict or coercion model, therefore, is adapted to understanding social change, whereas the consensus model is static, accounting only for 'equilibrium'. Although Dahrendorf is primarily interested in change, he does not differ from Parsons in wanting to keep one set of books for the analysis of change and another for the investigation of stability.[17] As Dahrendorf's critics have pointed out,[18] he begins by assuming an existing structure of legitimate authority which is postulated as given, just as norms and 'value-consensus' are the unexplained starting-points of Parsonian theory.[19] This is a most 'undialectical' approach in failing to show how pressures towards *both* the legitimation of power and resistance to its coercive face are present in *all* power relations, whether the interaction of these pressures leads to change or persistence.

Hobbes as well as Marx, whose model Dahrendorf is explicitly seeking to generalize at a more abstract level, was more subtle. Hobbes wrote that 'war consists not in battle only, or the act of fighting, but in a tract of time wherein the will to contend by battle is sufficiently known'.[20] To Marx, the class struggle was always *latent* in societies based on economic exploitation, but specific changes, many of them technological and economic rather than rooted in the internal dynamics of the power relation itself,[21] had to take place before the subordinate class rejected the ideological hegemony of the dominant class.

In later writings Dahrendorf changed his mind about the equal importance of consensus and conflict models and announced that he now considered the latter to be manifestly superior:

> There is no problem that can be described in equilibrium terms that cannot be described at least as well in constraint terms, and there are many problems that Thrasymachus can tackle but Socrates cannot.[22]

Yet Dahrendorf fails to overcome the dualism of his earlier view, as is especially evident in an essay devoted primarily to explaining the universality of inequality in human societies.[23] Norms or shared rules of conduct, he argues in Durkheimian fashion, are constitutive of society itself. Since norms are enforced by positive and negative sanctions, enforcement means the power to impose these sanctions:

> . . . we have to assume that a third fundamental category of sociological analysis belongs alongside the two concepts of norm and sanction: that of institutionalized power. Society *means* that norms regulate human conduct; this regulation is guaranteed by the incentive or threat of sanctions; the possibility of imposing sanctions is the abstract core of all power.[24]

Dahrendorf goes on to assert that 'in the last analysis, established norms are nothing but ruling norms, i.e. norms defended by the sanctioning agencies of society and those who control them'.[25] This comes close to saying that law is essentially the 'command of the sovereign' (Hobbes), or that norms are dictated and enforced by the ruling class (Marxism). But Dahrendorf also claims in a footnote that 'norm has to be understood as anterior to power',[26] a statement surely implying that norms are initially the products of consensus or 'social contract' even though punishments and rewards may be required afterwards to enforce them. Dahrendorf slurs over this implication in his readiness to see coercive power and the inequality and conflict it creates as the fundamental social reality. As in his earlier writings, the existence of consensus – here in the form of norms, there as legitimate authority – is taken as a given which ultimately generates coercion and ensuing resistance and conflict.

Dahrendorf's desire to argue that coercive power, inequality and conflict are inherent in society as such compels him to dismiss as 'fantasies' the claims made by some anthropologists and sociologists that there are 'societies without rulers . . . that regulate themselves without power or authority'.[27] But there is no good reason to doubt the testimony of anthropologists who have reported on 'stateless' or 'acephalous' societies, lacking both centralized political leadership and formal legal institutions.[28] Dahrendorf appears to mean merely that in such societies, as in all others, the Many exercise power over the One by imposing sanctions for nonconformity. But this collapses the concept of power into that of social control. The power of the group over the individual, as I argued in Chapter 1, is a basic datum of sociology which should not be equated with the idea of power as a particular kind of asymmetrical relation between individuals or groups, although, of course, the socialization process is largely mediated through the power exercised by adults over the young.

If it is misleading – and undialectical – to regard consensus and conflict as equally valid alternative organizing concepts for viewing society, each suited to different problems, it is no less so to see consensus as merely 'a special case of constraint', as in Dahrendorf's more recent formulation.[29] Dahrendorf became chiefly responsible for the label 'conflict theory' because, more starkly than other writers, he proclaimed the conceptual polarity of consensus and conflict. The conflict theorists of the 1950s and 1960s, although they worked more or less independently of one another, were mainly concerned with rectifying the neglect of group conflict and the historical change it often sets in motion in the consensual models dominant in that period. At the 'macro-sociological' level, a conception of the institutional order as the outcome of past and on-going political conflict is certainly much preferable to system theories postulating an underlying consensus or tendency towards integration. Insistence on the importance of political power and its inherently coercive aspect (often influenced by Weber) was also a justified corrective to the over-emphasis on legitimate authority in consensus and system theories.[30] But whatever the superiority of a perspective stressing conflict at the level of the total society, for there to be conflict between groups there clearly has to be consensus *within* groups.[31] That the latter is by no means non-problematical has long been recognized in Marxist discussions of the genesis of class consciousness. In any society other than a Hobbesian state of nature (which is not a society but the negation of one) *both* consensus and conflict are necessarily present. The most significant and challenging questions about them, in fact, have to do with the proportions in which they coexist and combine and with the dynamics of their interaction. A conflict or coercion theory, therefore, is just as one-sided as its opposite.[32]

The same applies with minor qualifications to coercion and legitimacy within the more limited sphere of power relations. In real life one can find pure types of coercive and legitimate authority, although there are no purely consensual or purely conflict-ridden societies. But elements of coercion and legitimacy usually coexist and are interwoven in particular power relations, whether because a single power subject's motives for compliance are 'over-determined' or because the power holder in command of both forms of power wields each to control different power subjects. To adapt Machiavelli's language, the 'fear-love' mix in most concrete power relations varies, which is what differentiates them from one another and gives each compound its distinctive volatility under changing historical circumstances. I am using 'love', of course, to stand for the consensual forms of power in general, although Machiavelli in the politically unstable world of Rennaissance Italy intended it more literally as an attribute of the personal authority of princes who lacked secure legitimate authority derived from position or office. However, 'love' and 'fear' can also be understood – if anachronistically in the case of Machiavelli, who lived several centuries before Freud – as referring back to the matrix of human character structure itself out of which all social relations, including structures of legitimate authority, develop. The fear-love mix, then, reflects Freud's 'law of primal ambivalence'[33] as a psychological universal. From a standpoint quite different from both Freud's and Dahrendorf's, a recent critic of sociologists' over-emphasis on 'values and value consensus' suggests that

> the methodological problem is . . . how to measure *the variance accounted for by force and force-threat*, in an action or set of actions in which the participant may not have an accurate idea of its impact . . .[34]

The Praetorian Guard Argument

A common argument against the possibility of a society entirely ruled by coercion or 'naked power' is that the wielders of the instruments of force, even though they may succeed in instilling fear in the rest of the population, must be united among themselves and obedient to their leaders on grounds other than fear.[35] Since both the actual use of force and the display of its instruments for purposes of threat require a social organization, it is argued that the wielders of force themselves must submit to the direction of their leader out of motives other than the fear of force. For they cannot reasonably be afraid of themselves; hence it must be concluded that material rewards, or belief in the legitimacy of their collective task, or devotion to the personal authority of a leader must be the basis of their compliance. Thus even under the most ruthless military dictatorships or police states, the army or the police are not coerced by their own leaders but obey them for reasons other than fear. The political system may be based on a fear-love mix in which fear is by far the largest component, but non-coercive bonds prevail at the very least among the controllers of the means of violence even though they may be a small minority. Indeed, the solidarity of the coercers is likely to be based on ties stronger than those of material interests alone in any relatively stable political system. Machiavelli himself warned princes against reliance on mercenaries:

> The mercenaries and auxiliaries are useless and dangerous, and if any one supports his state by the arms of mercenaries, he will never stand firm or sure, as they are disunited, ambitious, without discipline, faithless, bold amongst friends, cowardly amongst enemies, they have no fear of God, and keep no faith with men . . . The cause of this is that they have no love or other motive to keep them in the field beyond a trifling wage, which is not enough to make them ready to die for you.[36]

This argument is generally a valid and compelling one, but Michael Polanyi, with the last years of Stalin's rule in mind, has suggested an exception to it:

> It is commonly assumed that power cannot be exercised without some voluntary support, as for example by a faithful praetorian guard. I do not think this is true, for it seems that some dictators were feared by everybody; for example, towards the end of his rule everyone feared Stalin. It is, in fact, easy to see that a single individual might well exercise

command over a multitude of men without appreciable voluntary support on the part of any of them. If a group of men each believes that all the others will obey the commands of a person claiming to be their common superior, all will obey this person as their superior. For each will fear that if he disobeyed him, the others would punish his disobedience at the superior's command, and so all are forced to obey by the mere supposition of the others' continued obedience, without any voluntary support being given to the superior by any member of the group. Each member of the group would even feel compelled to report any signs of dissatisfaction among his comrades, for he would fear that any complaint made in his presence might be a test applied to him by an *agent provocateur* and that he would be punished if he failed to report such subversive utterances. Thus the members of a group might be kept so distrustful of each other, that they would express even in private only sentiments of loyalty towards a superior whom they all hated in secret. The stability of such naked power increases with the size of the group under its control, for a disaffected nucleus which might be formed locally by a lucky crystallization of mutual trust among a small number of personal associates, would be overawed and paralyzed by the vast surrounding masses of people whom they would assume to be still loyal to the dictator. Hence it is easier to keep control of a vast country than of the crew of a single ship in mid-ocean.[37]

Polanyi's example depends on the widespread existence of what social psychologists have called 'pluralistic ignorance': each individual member of the group fails to communicate his real feelings and beliefs to others out of a conviction they they are not shared and that he would be punished for even expressing them. Yet in fact there is a consensus within the group, although it remains unknown and concealed. Thus all group members actually share a secret hatred for their leader. By requiring frequent public manifestations of deference, ritual flattery, head-bowing and foot-scraping, and the equivalent of *Heil Hitler* salutes, the ruler helps to create this situation and exploits it to his advantage. His insistence on compulsory public displays of obeisance therefore has a function in helping to strengthen and maintain his power in addition to that of merely feeding his vanity. Yet, well aware of his power to compel the *appearance* of deference and willing compliance, the ruler can never be certain that genuine loyalty motivates the obedience of his followers rather than fear or calculated self-interest. Hence the frequent paranoia of absolute rulers – why, in Shakespeare's words, 'uneasy lies the head that wears the crown'.

An incident that allegedly occurred at the famous Twentieth

Congress of the Communist Party of the Soviet Union, when Khrushchev delivered his 'secret speech' denouncing Stalin, is consistent with Polanyi's argument. As Khrushchev was describing the indignities to which Stalin forced even his closest associates to submit, someone in the audience shouted out 'Why didn't you kill him?' After a stunned pause, Khrushchev bellowed back 'Who said that?' but no one answered. Then Khrushchev added '*That's* where I was', recognizing that the veteran delegates in the audience knew only too well that the man addressing them had not only been one of Stalin's confederates but had recently emerged as his successor.[38]

Polanyi's example suggests an exception to two earlier generalizations: first, that the more extensive the power relation, the less comprehensive and intensive it is likely to be; and second, that its greater extensiveness leads to greater diversification of the forms of power exercised by the power holder. Polanyi, however, restricts his argument to the closing years of Stalin's rule and doubts its wider relevance, observing that 'no dictator will fail to use his coercive powers for inculcating loyalty to himself in his subjects' and that 'a claim to legitimacy is a most formidable instrument of power'.[39] Nevertheless, conditions broadly similar to those described in Polanyi's example have been widely seen as typical of totalitarianism as such. The 'atomization of man', the destruction of spontaneous trust rooted in an autonomous group life, and the practice of terror to achieve these effects have been regarded as features of totalitarian rule differentiating it markedly from even the most cruel traditional despotisms.[40] Brutally coercive though the latter have often been, they have usually confined the use of extreme violence to political enemies, slaves and prisoners of war.

E. V. Walter, however, has attempted to define an ideal type of 'terroristic despotism' which has flourished also in primitive societies, notably in East African kingdoms, and bears many resemblances to modern totalitarianism. Walter insists against the consensualist tradition of Western political thought that terrorism can be a relatively stable basis of political rule; also that, as in the case of the early nineteenth-century Zulu kingdom, it may be the only effective way of creating and maintaining a centralized polity by overcoming centrifugal tendencies in the underlying social structure. He is in addition concerned to emphasize, in opposition to writers who have seen the new technological means of coercion as constituting the essence of totalitarianism as a uniquely modern phenomenon, that 'a system of terror depends not on the instruments of violence, but on the technique of social control. The secret of a terroristic regime is its social organization'.[41]

As the reference to social organization suggests, Walter refuses to treat terrorism and consensus or legitimacy as opposing principles: he wishes rather to 'challenge prevailing assumptions about the relation between violence and authority because there are systems of terror that were supported by authority, consent, and tradition' which are 'unintelligible to the conventional political mind and demonstrate the need for a new theoretical approach.'[42] His account of the rule of Shaka, the most powerful and terroristic of the Zulu kings, reports that Shaka's victims often sang his praises even as they were being dragged off to be put to death. Although Walter does not draw the parallel, one is inescapably reminded of the public confessions of Arthur Koestler's Old Bolsheviks in *Darkness at Noon*, despite the vastly cruder 'ideology' of the Zulu tribesmen in the name of which they acquiesced in their own destruction. (Koestler's interpretation has, of course, been widely criticized on the grounds that extreme fatigue, physical torture and threats to relatives are sufficient to account for the behaviour of most of the victims of Stalin's purge trials.) Although he delineates the unrestrained terroristic violence practised by several Zulu rulers, Walter ends by accepting a version of the praetorian guard argument:

> In terroristic despotism, groups of persons pursuing their common interests and supported by ideology worked to uphold the absolute, unchecked power of the sovereign. The secondary powers in such a state *wanted* the ruler to be omnipotent – sometimes against the will of the despot himself.[43]

Analysts of totalitarianism have contended that the boundless and indiscriminate use of violence creates a mood of terror in the population that paralyses resistance and induces a semi-automatic compliance with the demands of the regime. Like Polanyi, many have noted that this mood affects even the dictator's chief lieutenants, the very members of his 'praetorian guard' – indeed this result has been seen as a deliberate aim of the ruler, especially in the case of Stalin. Yet the combination of terror with 'propaganda' and 'ideology' has also been regarded as peculiarly characteristic of totalitarian rule even if in practice the ideology is reduced to worship of the dictator and the organizational weapon of the party or its élite cadres, while the normative content of the ideology becomes no more than a ritual incantation invoked to justify the 'will of the *Fuehrer*' or the 'party line' whatever they may momentarily happen to be. This feature of totalitarian regimes is brilliantly summed up in Raymond Aron's description of them as 'orthodoxies without doctrines'.[44] Yet totalitarian leaders lay claim to a legitimacy based on popular support and create vast networks of mass communications subjecting the populace to a constant barrage of 'propaganda and public enlightenment'[45] in order to give real, or at least apparent, substance to the claim. More than anything else, this has seemed to differentiate totalitarianism from previous despotisms which were content to leave their subjects alone so long as they refrained from overt resistance. In claiming to be mere agents of the real will of the people, totalitarian leaders have often echoed familiar populistic and plebiscitarian legitimations, but the claim also has provided justification for overriding all legal and traditional limitations on the exercise of power. Even Zulu terror grew out of the king's traditional right to kill his subjects whenever he chose, a right that became a bone of contention with the British and Boer colonial authorities long after the period of maximum reliance on terror as a technique of rule.[46]

A fear-love mix, then, albeit in new and shifting blends and compounds, is present in totalitarian regimes as well as in others. In the Soviet Union and its Eastern European satellites the terroristic ingredients have obviously declined since the death of Stalin and the chief wielders of violence, the secret police, have lost power to the party. The mix, which contained different proportions at the outset, has also changed in China since the death of Mao, or perhaps since the end of the Cultural Revolution of the late 1960s. The degree to which these changes have reduced the distinctiveness of these regimes which had led them to be called totalitarian in the first place, and have even cast doubt on the usefulness of that label itself, continue to be a matter of debate among scholars.[47] My concern here, however, is no more than to stress that even the most far-reaching claims for the potency and ubiquity of terror under Hitler and Stalin did not deny the presence of a fear-love mix undergirding the authority of their regimes. Hitler, of course, was always the beneficiary of considerable popular support for most of the duration of his regime. Nor has the loyalty of a 'praetorian guard' up to the very end in the Berlin bunker ever been seriously doubted.

'The significance of persuasion grows with the growing complexity of society.'[48] The greater technical and organizational complexity of advanced industrial societies has increased the importance of 'love' over 'fear' in the fear-love mix on which power and authority rest. A latter-day Machiavelli would certainly qualify the Florentine's conclusion that fear was by far the most important foundation for political power. An overseer's whip may suffice to keep galley oarsmen, cotton-pickers or ditch-diggers adequately performing their tasks, but complex skills, including the operation of machinery, are more vulnerable to 'conscientious withdrawal of efficiency', in Veblen's phrase, and even to covert forms of sabotage. Bureaucratic organization makes possible much more extensive centralized power structures, but at the same time the power holder at the centre becomes more dependent on subordinate officials in a lengthened and dispersed chain of command. Expert knowledge and technical skills also become more important instruments and accessories of power. In short, the size of the praetorian guard on whose reliability and loyalty the ruler depends is much larger in modern societies. Solzhenitsyn's *The First Circle* shows that Stalin found it necessary to offer special privileges and material inducements to imprisoned scientists whose skills he nevertheless needed to devise new means of surveillance and espionage. The invention of nuclear weapons suddenly made atomic physicists, the possessors of highly arcane specialized knowledge, a national resource and gave rise to the doubts, fears and phobias about their loyalty that the names of J. Robert Oppenheimer and Andrei Sakharov bring to mind.[49] More recently, the vulnerability to disruption of the technical services on which modern populations depend has been underlined by the bombings and hi-jackings carried out by small groups of terrorists, not to speak of the 'acts of God' which caused electric power blackouts in New York City in 1965 and 1977.

The greater need for loyalty, or at least reliable co-operation, by a much larger proportion of the population accounts to a considerable degree for the far-reaching efforts at ideological indoctrination made by totalitarian regimes in contrast to earlier despotisms in agrarian civilizations or small city-states. It also helps explain the abandonment of widespread reliance on terror in the Soviet Union and its satellite states after the death of Stalin.[50] Although the Chinese Communists never made use of terror on anything like the same scale as the Soviet regime, the 'de-Maoization' taking place since Mao's death can also be seen as an effort to protect existing administrative hierachies from the sort of disruption to which they were subjected during the Cultural Revolution. More conventional delimited forms of legitimate authority and greater use of material incentives have supplanted the 'permanent purge' in the Soviet Union[51] and the mobilization of egalitarian enthusiasm in China. It should be noted, however, that in neither case do the changes necessarily represent even incipient democratization or greater tolerance of political opposition to the party-state regimes.

'Machiavellian' Cynicism

Writers who have insisted on the primacy of force have often tended to adopt a tone of heavy cynicism, of debunking with obvious relish what they see as the illusions and hypocrisies of others, of irreverently tearing off the fig leaves of legitimacy that scantily conceal the nakedness of power. Thrasymachus 'roared like a wild beast' in his eagerness to pour scorn upon the 'nonsense' of Socrates and his companions. In *The Prince*, if less so in his other writings, Machiavelli leaves himself open to the charge of wishing to shock his readers by dwelling on the cruelties and deceits of the leaders who best exemplify his rules for political success. Hobbes anticipated that his readers, not having 'well weighed these things', might question his argument that 'nature should thus dissociate and render men apt to invade and destroy one another'; after pointing out that a doubter is himself likely to go armed when travelling and to lock his doors and chests when at home, he asks with obvious irony the rhetorical question 'Does he not there as much accuse mankind by his actions as I do by my words?'[52] More recently, Pareto's sarcasm and mordant witticisms at the expense of sentimental humanitarians and idealistic democrats are well-known. Even liberal and radical writers whose declared purpose is to show up and condemn the coercive nature of power rather than to justify it have often adopted a tone of cynical realism or ironical exposé that contrasts with and even undercuts their righteous indignation. Perhaps the most acute perception of how a note of acceptance and even admiration for power at its most brutally coercive may be combined with a proclaimed stance of either dispassionate analysis or moral outrage is to be found in George Orwell's essay on James Burnham from which I quoted at the beginning of this chapter.[53]

To locate these arguments for the pre-eminence of force in their proper social context, we must ask to whom they are addressed. What exactly is their intended audience? Whose illusions are being attacked? Whose hypocrisies are being unmasked? Where force alone is at issue, the answer cannot be the subjects or victims of coercion, for they must be fully aware that they obey out of fear rather than consent. Conflict theorists, in fact, up to the present time have always been inclined to argue that the perspective on politics of the oppressed and exploited is a more realistic one than that of their rulers. The sufferer may be presumed to know how and where the shoe pinches and is not fooled by claims that it is really a perfect fit. The naïveté and credulity of power holders, or at least of their hangers-on and beneficiaries, are therefore major targets of the iconoclastic onslaughts of cynical realists about power. Members or allies of the ruling élite are often misled by the overt respect and cap-in-hand deference accorded them by the powerless, as in the case of those upper-class Southerners who sincerely believed that 'their' Negroes were entirely happy and even grateful despite their condition of servitude and subordination. The relative invisibility of the apparatus of coercion also encourages the wishful belief that authority rests on voluntary support. This is especially true of modern societies with their high organizational differentiation where the essence of legitimate authority is, as Arthur Stinchcombe has argued, the right to call upon other organized groups to back up – by force if necessary – one's own will or interests.[54]

Force, however, has invariably been linked with 'fraud' in the arguments of Machiavellian thinkers. The Jowett translation of *The Republic* attributes the words 'fraud and force' to Thrasymachus, describing the means used by successful tyrants. Perhaps Jowett was echoing Hobbes's use of the phrase 'force and fraud' in *Leviathan*. Machiavelli's advice to rulers to cultivate the qualities of both the lion and the fox also coupled them together. Pareto defined 'lions' and 'foxes' more elaborately as distinctive political-psychological types and saw them succeeding one another as governing élites in recurring cycles of change. That Machiavelli thought princes needed to have the qualities of both lions and foxes and that Pareto saw leonine élites as vulnerable to displacement by new men in whom cunning and shrewdness rather than the martial virtues prevailed (and *vice-versa*) attest to the recognition by both men of the limitations of force and of fraud when political rule relies primarily on only one of them.

To Machiavellians, all forms of power other than force are reducible to fraud. All attempts by power holders to claim a legitimacy grounded in the divine or natural order or in the requirements of the common good or the general welfare are necessarily fraudulent. *Cui bono?* is the only relevant question when such claims are made, for they always amount to rationalizations of the power holder's primary interest in retaining power. Specific promises, such as to reduce taxes, bring peace or confer concrete benefits, can be tested against performance – the element of truth in Lincoln's statement that you can't fool all of the people all of the time – but the broader and vaguer legitimations advanced by power holders can only be accepted on faith. Hence the tendency of Machiavellians to see the people, the power subjects, either as virtuous dupes potentially capable of being liberated from their sentimental illusions or as mindless beasts of burden worthy only of contempt.

Fraud is identical therefore with *manipulation* as a form of power. Power holders conceal their real aim – to keep themselves in power – from their subjects because 'the masses would not co-operate if they knew they were simply serving the purposes of a minority'.[55] At least where political power is concerned, manipulation is the only relevant form of power other than coercion and inducement (which, let it be recalled, is readily transformed into economic coercion or exploitation). All persuasion and legitimate authority are reducible to manipulation. Machiavellians assert their 'realism' against the hypocrisy of the élites and the gullibility of the masses. Sometimes, as in the case of the Italian élitists of the early twentieth century, they appeal, implicitly at least, to leonine counter-élites: men of strong principles and firm discipline who will not shrink from the use of violence to seize power from the reigning bourgeois foxes who rely primarily on manipulation. This emphasis is what links the neo-Machiavellians to the ethos of fascism, whether or not Mussolini was actually influenced by them and whatever the still-disputed attitudes of Pareto, Mosca and Michels to the regime he created.

I insisted in Chapter 1 on the intentionality of power: power always involves the production of a particular effect on others that was consciously aimed at (or foreseen) by the wielder of power. The various forms of power, however, are distinguished from one another by the different reasons or motives for the power subject's compliance: fear in the case of coercion, voluntary submission enjoined by the norms of a group in the case of legitimate authority, belief in the superior knowledge and expertise of another in the case of competent authority, and so on. Chapter 4 argued that it is to the instrumental advantage of the power holder to be able to exercise multiple forms of power, especially when he confronts a plurality of power subjects. This conclusion presupposes the power holder's interest in retaining his power but makes no assumptions whatever about his reasons, motives or particular purposes for wanting to do so. In this sense, typologies of

the forms of power, including my own, are asymmetrical in focusing on
the motives of the power subject for complying rather than on those of
the power holder for seeking and retaining power. Perhaps this reflects a
tendency in Western culture to regard the former as psychologically
more problematical.

Machiavellians see power holders as employing the most effective
means – force and fraud – to the end of securing themselves in power.
The power holder's strategy consists of devising a force-fraud mix that
creates and sustains the fear-love mix motivating the power subject's
compliance. In this perspective,

> if political leaders who promise their followers an ideal end do not believe
> in their own doctrine, they are logical [in the sense of Pareto]; if they do
> believe in it, they are not logical. It is the hypocrite who acts logically, not
> the believer.[56]

The unmasking of such deceptions, whether directed at the naïveté of
the masses or the hypocrisy of élites, is undertaken in tones of fury,
scorn or disillusionment, or with the self-congratulatory presumption of
superior realism on the part of the unmasker.

Some eighteenth-century writers denounced religious beliefs as a
pack of lies dreamed up and promulgated by the priests for the purpose
of winning power for themselves as self-appointed intermediaries with
the deity. Marx's famous statement that 'religion is the opium of the
people' is often similarly – and vulgarly – so understood. Such views
aim to expose the conscious intention to deceive or conceal implicit in
fraud and manipulation. Later interpretations, however, take a much
more complex and subtle view of the consciousness and motivation of
the powerful. The Marxist theory of ideology, neo-Machiavellian
élitism, Freud's conception of religion as both an individual consolation
and an instrument of social control, the sociology of knowledge and a
host of other intellectual movements and tendencies in the late
nineteenth and early twentieth centuries were intended as critiques of
Enlightenment rationalism. All of them explicitly reject the simplistic
claim that legitimating beliefs are designed and put forward by the
powerful for the express purpose of inducing the acquiescence and
compliance of the powerless. The Marxist notion of 'false
consciousness' (a term never actually used by Marx himself), Freud's
'unconscious', Pareto's 'residues' and Mannheim's 'total conception of
ideology' refer to cognitive or motivational expressions that are not

rationally chosen by their human agents and of which they may not even be aware. Karl Mannheim's distinction between 'unmasking a lie' and 'unmasking an ideology' is applicable to all such versions of the non-rational sources of human conduct advanced by modern social and psychological thinkers.[57]

Such theories themselves represent rational attempts to account for the non-rational, although there are, of course, 'irrationalist' versions of them as well. They reject the implication of Enlightenment rationalists that the powerful are consciously conspiratorial. Power holders at the very least deceive themselves as well as their subjects when they offer legitimations of their power. Moreover, the powerless too are driven by a need for faith and are not merely ignorant and stupid. The contrast between the amoral intelligence of the élites and the credulous innocence of the masses dissolves. This is even true in the case of the Italian writers despite their tendency to psychologize the differences between the active minority and the passive majority; even Pareto, who retained strong affinities with Voltairean scepticism, recognized that élites needed to cherish illusions about their role and proclaimed that he would not have written his own sociological opus had he expected it to find many readers.[58]

I shall postpone until a later chapter on 'the uses of power' discussion of whether a 'power drive' or 'lust for power' accounts for the motivation of at least the powerful minority, a notion that has loomed large in the Machiavellian tradition. But even the most cynical modern representatives of that tradition do not in the end treat legitimating ideologies as ultimately reducible to conscious fraud or manipulation practised by the powerful at the expense of the powerless. Both power holders and power subjects possess a genuine will to believe, although its psychological dynamics differ in accordance with their different situations.

The Need for Legitimation

The powerful are — usually, at least — neither psychopaths nor ruthless egoists; they have been socialized, they have superegos. They experience, accordingly, a need to believe that the power they possess is morally justified, that they are servants of a larger collective goal or system of values surpassing mere determination to perpetuate themselves in power, that their exercise of power is not inescapably at odds with hallowed standards of morality. This need is enhanced by their uneasy awareness of the half-truth expressed in Lord Acton's famous dictum that power corrupts, not to speak of the inevitable complicity of political power with what Max Weber called the 'diabolical forces lurking in all violence'. Thus power holders are driven to legitimate themselves in their own eyes, making legitimation far more than a mere strategem to secure more effective control over their subjects. Weber regarded claims to legitimacy as arising out of

> the generally observable need of any power, or even of any advantage of life, to justify itself . . . he who is more favoured feels the never ceasing need to look upon his position as in some way 'legitimate', upon his advantage as 'deserved', and the other's disadvantage as being brought about by the latter's 'fault'.[59]

Gaetano Mosca's term for legitimating claims or rationales was 'political formula', which certainly has the ring of something artfully devised by rulers to deceive their subjects. But in a significant passage Mosca denies that 'political formulas are mere quackeries aptly invented to trick the masses into obedience' and goes on to observe that

> anyone who viewed them in that light would fall into grave error. The truth is that they answer a real need in man's social nature; and this need, so universally felt, of governing and knowing that one is governed not on the basis of mere material or intellectual force, but on the basis of a moral principle has beyond any doubt a practical and a real importance.[60]

Note that Mosca attributes to *both* rulers and ruled the need to believe that they act – whether in commanding or in obeying – on the basis of a moral principle. I shall discuss rather briefly at a later point the will to believe of the powerless that predisposes them to accept the legitimating rationales of the powerful after first examining more fully the power holders' need for self-legitimation.

Dostoevsky's 'The Legend of the Grand Inquisitor' presents the most subtle and profound case for absolute power that those who exercise it might conceivably make. As Philip Rahv observed, 'thus would the inquisitor's counterparts in real life speak if they had candour and were capable of making independent forays into the philosophy of history.'[61] The legend, along with Ivan's 'negation of God' in the preceding chapter of *The Brothers Karamazov*, strongly influenced Max Weber's formulation of the tension between the ethics of brotherhood and the 'demon' of politics. My use of it here is a highly selective one that draws on it primarily to illustrate the psychology of power and in particular the need for legitimation integral to that psychology. The legend includes, of course, a great deal more than this: many critics have seen it as the summation of Dostoevsky's deepest beliefs about God, man, good and evil, and human society.

As Ivan Karamazov tells the story to his saintly brother, Alyosha, Christ once returned to earth, to Seville at the height of the Spanish Inquisition. He was instantly recognized and surrounded by adoring crowds. The cardinal, the Grand Inquisitor who has the day before directed a successful *auto-de-fé* at which almost a hundred heretics have been burned to death, passes by and orders Christ arrested and imprisoned. That night the Inquisitor, 'an old man, almost ninety, tall and erect, with a withered face and sunken eyes in which there is still a gleam of light', visits Jesus in his dungeon and addresses him in a long monologue.[62] Although urged to speak, Christ remains silent; at the end of the Inquisitor's speech he 'softly kissed him on his bloodless aged lips'. Although the Inquisitor has declared his intention to burn Jesus at the stake as a heretic, he now opens the door of the cell and says 'Go, and come no more . . . come not at all, never, never!' The prisoner leaves. (Critics have devoted as much effort to deciphering the meaning of Christ's kiss as to the symbolism of the white whale in *Moby Dick*.)

The Inquisitor asserts that he and the earthly rulers of the church have altered and improved upon Christ's original teaching, although they have done so in his name. Possessed of a far truer understanding of the weakness and corruptibility of human nature, they have vanquished the moral freedom for which Christ stood and in doing so have made mankind happy, for 'man is tormented by no greater anxiety than to find some one quickly to whom he can hand over that gift of freedom with which the ill-fated creature is born'. Although 'Man was created a rebel', he will readily exchange his freedom for subjection and obedience to those who satisfy his basic needs for bread, a fixed purpose in life and participation in a community of worship maintained by 'miracle, mystery, and authority'.[63] Men are not strong enough to shoulder the 'fearful burden of free choice' that Christ imposed upon them. Indeed, the ecclesiastical powers, including the Inquisition, are the true lovers of mankind because they love man in his weak and fallen state whereas Jesus cares only for the elect, the few strong ones who are capable of receiving the 'terrible gift' of free moral choice. 'Did we not love mankind', the Inquisitor asks, 'so meekly acknowledging their feebleness, lovingly lightening their burden, and permitting their weak nature even sin with our sanction? Why hast Thou come now to hinder us?'

The Grand Inquisitor's doctrine has often been regarded as a subtle and sinister Machiavellianism, reflecting a 'cynical-satanical pose' adopted by Dostoevsky, as D. H. Lawrence described his first reaction to the legend, one which he later modified.[64] But it seems to me that there is ample internal evidence that this is a misreading. Such a view indeed is more or less identical with that of Alyosha in the novel, who bursts out that the Inquisitor's ideas are nothing more than the ideal of the Jesuits with

> no sort of mystery or lofty melancholy about it . . . It's simple lust of power, of filthy earthly gain, of domination – something like a universal serfdom with them as masters – that's all they stand for.

He denies that the Inquisitor can truly be a suffering man and declares this 'a mere fantasy'. Ivan replies:

> Why can there not be among them [the Jesuits] one martyr oppressed by great sorrow and loving humanity? You see, only suppose that there was one such man among all those who desire nothing but filthy material gain – if there's only one like my old Inquisitor, who had himself eaten roots in the desert and made frenzied efforts to subdue his flesh to make himself free and perfect. But yet all his life he loved humanity, and suddenly his eyes were opened, and he saw that it is no great moral blessedness to attain perfection and freedom, if at the same time one gains the conviction that millions of God's creatures have been created as a mockery, that these poor rebels can never turn into giants to complete the tower, that it was not for such geese that the great idealist dreamed his dream of harmony. Seeing all that he turned back and joined – the clever people. Surely that could have happened?

Critics have often pointed out that Dostoevsky's saintly men embodying Christian love are not very bright (Prince Mishkin is 'the idiot' in the title of that novel). Dostoevsky was in this sense 'anti-intellectual', sensitive to the sin of 'intellectual pride' and deeply suspicious of 'the clever people' – nowhere more so, for that matter, than in the portrait of Ivan in *The Brothers Karamazov*. Yet it is clear (to me at least) from the exchange I have just cited that Dostoevsky accepts Ivan's view of the Inquisitor, seeing him as a tragic figure with a nature tinged with nobility who has chosen to assume great moral burdens in order to serve humanity according to his unillusioned view of it. Nor after years of correcting and reversing Christ's teachings has he become indifferent to them: unlike Pontius Pilate, he spares Christ and 'the kiss glows in his heart'. Nor is the Inquisitor pictured in any way as a sleek, self-satisfied man of power, let alone as a gross sensualist bloated from indulgence in 'filthy material gain'. He is, rather, dignified, careworn, and even ascetic in appearance and bearing.

Yet the Inquisitor states unambiguously that he and the other lords of the church practise deception and consciously manipulate the emotions of the masses in order to keep them satisfied and to restrain their rebellious tendencies which are also inherent in human nature. The inquisitors rule in Christ's name although they themselves repudiate his original message; they burn people at the stake for heresy to a doctrine in which they themselves do not believe; they take the bread the people themselves have made (in an echo of the theory of surplus value) and return it to them as if they had performed a miracle; they 'allure them with the reward of heaven and eternity' in full knowledge that 'beyond the grave they will find nothing but death'. They do not, in short, believe for a moment in the legitimations they present in support of their rule.

The Inquisitor, however, is not a Machiavellian power seeker in the vulgar sense, for he sees himself as serving a 'higher purpose' consistent with the nature of man, although this is a secret understood only by the rulers themselves who have assumed the burden of 'guarding the mystery . . . from the weak and the unhappy, so as to make them happy'. We confront here a version of Plato's 'noble lie', although Plato, a pagan lacking Christian belief in the infinite worth of every human soul, did not agonize like the Inquisitor (or like Dostoevsky) over the inequality of human endowments. What the Inquisitor reveals to Christ is the esoteric legitimation accepted by the rulers themselves as opposed to the exoteric legitimation they preach to the masses. The Inquisitor's doctrine is that of a double truth: a private, sophisticated 'higher truth' for the ruling élite and a public 'lower truth', crude and manifestly false, but answering nevertheless to the needs of human nature as defined by the higher truth. The former is the self-legitimation of the rulers, yet it imposes its own demands and burdens which can be seen, as I think Dostoevsky intended, as ennobling. (The half of the truth about power ignored in Acton's aphorism is that power can ennoble as well as corrupt.)

There can be little doubt that Dostoevsky himself chose Christ over the Inquisitor, although critics who have accepted the sad wisdom of the latter's credo have often tried to argue that Dostoevsky shared it and that Christ's kiss was meant to express the impossibility of answering the Inquisitor's argument. But Dostoevsky as a man of religious faith was committed to an ethics of intention or of ultimate ends in Weber's terms which transcend the tragic and morally corrupting necessities imposed by the exercise of worldly power, necessities that must be confronted by all who opt for Weber's ethics of responsibility.

The dialogue in Orwell's *Nineteen Eighty-Four* between O'Brien, the Prosecutor, and Winston Smith, stretched on a rack wired to give painful electric shocks at the touch of a lever, reads like a darkened echo or sinister parody of the Grand Inquisitor's encounter with Christ. Philip Rahv thought that Orwell intended the scene to be one 'which simultaneously recalls and refutes the ideas of Dostoevsky's Grand Inquisitor' in order to divest 'the dialectic of power' of 'surviving elements of the idealistic rationalization of power in the ideology of the Grand Inquisitor'.[65] O'Brien says to Winston Smith: 'You understand well enough *how* the Party maintains itself in power. Now tell me *why* we cling to power. What is our motive? Why should we want power?'[66] Winston's answer reproduces the self-legitimation of the Grand Inquisitor:

> The Party did not seek power for its own ends, but only for the good of the majority. It sought power because men in the mass were frail, cowardly creatures who could not endure liberty or face the truth, and must be ruled over and systematically deceived by others who were stronger than themselves. The choice for mankind lay between freedom and happiness, and for the great bulk of mankind, happiness was better. The Party was the eternal guardian of the weak, a dedicated sect doing evil that good might come, sacrificing its own happiness to that of others.

O'Brien responds to this by administering a painful electric shock, exclaiming 'That was stupid, Winston, stupid! You should know better than to say a thing like that.' He then presents the true rationale for the Party's power, one far more brutal and free of moral pretension than that of the Grand Inquisitor:

> The Party seeks power entirely for its own sake. We are not interested in the good of others; we are interested solely in power. Not wealth or luxury or long life or happiness; only power, pure power. What pure power means you will understand presently. We are different from all the oligarchies of the past in that we know what we are doing. All the others,

even those who resembled ourselves, were cowards and hypocrites. The German Nazis and the Russian Communists came very close to us in their methods, but they never had the courage to recognize their own motives. They pretended, perhaps they even believed, that they had seized power unwillingly and for a limited time, and that just around the corner there lay a paradise where human beings would be free and equal. We are not like that. We know that no one ever seizes power with the intention of relinquishing it. Power is not a means; it is an end. One does not establish a dictatorship in order to safeguard a revolution; one makes the revolution in order to establish the dictatorship. The object of persecution is persecution. The object of torture is torture. The object of power is power. Now do you begin to understand me?

Orwell's concept of 'doublethink' –

to know and not to know, to be conscious of complete truthfulness while telling carefully constructed lies ... consciously to induce unconsciousness, and then, once again, to become unconscious of the act of hypnosis you had just performed[67]

– also reads like a further refinement of the Grand Inquisitor's conception of two truths. Doublethink is not, as Orwell makes clear, a technique for consciously deceiving and manipulating others; it is, rather, a form of disciplined self-deception quite distinct from mere lying. In several essays written not long before *Nineteen Eight-Four* Orwell described as 'schizophrenic' the mental atmosphere created by totalitarian ideologies, writing, for example, that 'totalitarianism ... does not so much promise an age of faith as an age of schizophrenia'.[68] Doublethink is his imaginative realization of the fullest development of this tendency. The craftiness and guile of the Machiavellian prince are here exercised primarily upon the self and have become an habitual mental reflex, a form of semiautomatic self-manipulation.

Yet O'Brien and his fellow members of the Inner Party are the inventors of doublethink and are not themselves bound or crippled by it. The icily brutal passage I have quoted from O'Brien's instruction of Winston Smith is not an exercise in doublethink. And this passage is intended to convey the chief message of the book. Philip Rahv's criticism is convincing:

But there is one aspect of the psychology of power in which Dostoevsky's insight strikes me as being more viable than Orwell's strict realism. It seems to me that Orwell fails to distinguish, in the behaviour of O'Brien, between psychological and objective truth. Undoubtedly it is O'Brien, rather than Dostoevsky's Grand Inquisitor, who reveals the real nature of total power; yet that does not settle the question of O'Brien's personal psychology, the question, that is, of his ability to live with this naked truth as his sole support; nor is it conceivable that the party-élite to which he belongs could live with this truth for very long. Evil, far more than good, is in need of the pseudo-religious justifications so readily provided by the ideologies of world-salvation and compulsory happiness, ideologies generated both by the Left and the Right. Power is its own end, to be sure, but even the Grand Inquisitors are compelled, now as always, to believe in the fiction that their power is a means to some other end, gratifyingly noble and supernal.[69]

Rahv fails to note that in the novel Winston Smith comes close to recognizing this very objection to O'Brien's claims for the self-sufficiency of power-seeking as a motive, at least in so far as power is regarded as the gratification of an *individual* drive. Winston is struck by O'Brien's tired and aging face. Reading his thoughts, O'Brien says:

> You are thinking that I talk of power, and yet I am not even able to prevent the decay of my own body. Can you not understand, Winston, that the individual is only a cell? The weariness of the cell is the vigour of the organism ... The first thing you must realize is that power is collective. The individual only has power in so far as he ceases to be an individual ... Alone – free – the human being is always defeated. It must be so, because every human being is doomed to die, which is the greatest of all failures. But if he can make complete, utter submission, if he can escape from his identity, if he can merge himself in the Party so that he *is* the Party, then he is all-powerful and immortal.

It is clear from this passage that just as fully as the servant of a transcendent God or a lofty ideal O'Brien sees himself as the agent of a purpose that reaches beyond his own individual existence with its self-centred needs and lusts and its finitude. The larger purpose to which he is dedicated – the perpetuation of the collective power of the Party – is a bare and inhuman one promoted by monstrous means, but is a larger purpose nonethless. O'Brien may be a fanatic, but he is not a psychopath, or an undersocialized brute, or even an example of Freud's 'narcissistic' ego-oriented (as distinct from superego or id-oriented) character type.[70] No more than the Grand Inquisitor is he driven by desire for 'filthy material gain' or merely *personal* power. Whatever

Orwell's beliefs on the matter may have been, his portrait of O'Brien does not exemplify the 'lust for power' as a quasi-biological drive.[71] It exhibits, rather, an extreme version of 'moral man, immoral society', or the furthest extension of the power of the sanction of a group to legitimate any form of behaviour whatever against the declared enemies of the group. O'Brien too experiences the need for legitimation. What is legitimated, however, is unrestrained coercion and manipulation of the powerless and this behaviour is coldly defended as maintaining and even magnifying the *collective* power of the ruling élite.

Dedication to the service of this collective power is not psychologically reducible to the mere sum of individual satisfactions, even those intrinsic to the exercise of power, of those who wield it. Yet one must in the end agree that even a group possessing power is likely to claim legitimations going beyond the sheer fact of its possession, to insist that in some ultimate sense this must be the best of all possible worlds. Dostoevsky's insight into the psychology of total power remains therefore unequalled.

Less space is required to discuss the need for legitimation experienced by the powerless because it is widely recognized. Helpless to resist coercion, fearful of punishment, dependent on the powerful for satisfaction of basic needs and for any opportunities for autonomous choice and activity, the powerless are inescapably subject to a will to believe in the ultimate benevolence of the power holder, in his acceptance in the last analysis of some limits to what he will demand of or inflict upon them, grounded in at least a residual concern for their interests. The more absolute the power, the greater the need to believe that the power holder observes self-imposed restraints, or that his power, however apparently arbitrary and capricious, is part of a larger cosmos in which the power subject also has a secure place and from which he derives actual or prospective benefits.

One of the cornerstones of psychoanalytic theory is awareness of the child's disposition to see his parents as omnipotent yet kindly loving figures and to regard the deprivations he suffers at their hands as ultimately just and deserved, even in particular cases that to an outside observer would appear to provide ample evidence to the contrary. Human character is formed in infancy and, as we saw in Chapter 1, the power of a parent over a small child is the most comprehensive and intensive of all power relations. Anna Freud's discussion of 'identification with the aggressor'[72] is the *locus classicus* for analysis of the specific psychological mechanism exhibiting the child's need to accept the treatment he receives as both inevitable and just. She describes this as 'a preliminary phase of superego development' that is outgrown by the 'normal' person as he or she becomes capable of the 'internalized criticism' that constitutes the superego. The superego, of course, is the result of the transformation into self-discipline of what was formerly imposed by the external power of the parent. It reflects the permanent effects of past subjection to power, but at the same time succeeds in freeing the individual from the need to justify present authorities on whom he may be dependent or to accept a moral obligation to obey them.

Whether or not one chooses to label it as 'regression', identification with the power holder and his image as a stern but beneficial parental figure whose protection is needed, has frequently been observed in situations where adults are subject to arbitrary coercive power. Bruno Bettelheim's famous account of 'behaviour in extreme situations', describing the emulation of the SS and partial adoption of their values by long-term prisoners in Dachau and Buchenwald, is a well-known example.[73] Stanley M. Elkins' 'Sambo' slave personality type and Eugene Genovese's 'paternalistic ethos' influencing the slaves as well as the slaveholders are other cases in point.[74] Both concepts have given rise to impassioned polemics over the nature of American slavery and of the culture, or lack of it, of the blacks who were enslaved. Bettelheim's views on the psychological adaptation of concentration camp prisoners have also been criticized, especially by Jews in connection with the heated controversy in the 1960s over Hannah Arendt's *Eichmann in Jerusalem*. Elkins has recently observed that the slavery debate largely centred on the different emphasis placed by rival interpreters either on the degrading and demoralizing effects of slavery or on the integrity and inner strength of its victims which, even if overt resistance was rare, enabled them to preserve an autonomous culture with its own distinctive values.[75] Curiously, Elkins does not mention the similarities between the slavery debate and the controversy over the Bettelheim-Arendt depiction of the victims of the Holocaust as passive and fatalistic, although he himself compared the Sambo slave personality type to the responses of inmates of the Nazi camps as described by Bettelheim and others. He does note the resemblance of the slavery debate to disputes among British historians over the relative weight to be given to 'immiseration' and resistance to exploitation in the case of the working class during the Industrial Revolution.

These debates, all of which have mobilized strong sentiments of group pride and ideological commitment, deal with a variety of issues of which the tendency of the powerless to develop legitimations of their subordinate position that also serve as apologias for the power holders is only one. For the most part, disagreements bear on the *frequency* in particular historical situations of this and other responses producing passive accommodation to a brutal and exploitative power relation. The existence of the underlying psychological mechanism or disposition is not itself at issue. I am concerned here only to make the point that power subjects do exhibit a tendency to accept and legitimate their inferior status in the most coercive and exploitative power relations, whether or not this tendency becomes dominant over others in any single individual, let alone characterizes a majority in a given historical situation. Both Dostoevsky and Orwell recognized this in their fictional examples. The need of men to bow down and worship a Master clothed in 'miracle, mystery and authority' is central to the Grand Inquisitor's rationale for absolute power. The horrific ending of *Nineteen Eighty-Four* is the final capitulation after prolonged subjection to physical and psychic coercion of Winston Smith when he acknowledges at last that 'he loved Big Brother', a scene anticipated earlier in the book when he reflects that he loves O'Brien even though O'Brien has tortured him and will eventually have him killed.

It is rationally expedient for the power holder to try to transform might into right, coercive into legitimate authority. The dependence and helplessness of the power subject motivates him to come half-way to meet the power holder in achieving this conversion, even – or especially – when the power subject has been cruelly coerced and exploited and is almost entirely at the power holder's mercy. But the power holder too is driven to legitimate his power, to see it as predicated by the very nature of things, in order to assuage the guilt created by the use of violence against other human beings. This need is independent of the instrumental advantages gained from inducing the power subject to obey willingly. We may conclude that *there are psychological pressures from both sides of the power relation to convert coercive into legitimate authority.*

The Irreducibility of Coercion

I have already argued that the compliance of the subordinate in all concrete relations of authority rests on what I have called, adapting from Machiavelli, a 'fear-love mix'. Thus the passage from coercive to legitimate authority is never complete, never succeeds in totally purifying the relation of all fear and hostility, however repressed, on the part of the power subject. It is worth stressing this point again in view of the prevalence of heated debates 'over the predominance of fear or acceptance of legitimacy, of coercion or consent, whether in relatively comprehensive and intensive authority relations in general or in particular 'extreme situations' such as those mentioned in the previous section; also, because I have throughout this chapter tended to discuss the movement from coercion to legitimacy although in reality the reverse movement occurs as well. What Eugene Genovese concludes about Stanley Elkins' slavish personality type is generally true:

> Sambo, in short, was Sambo only up to the moment that the psychological balance was jarred from within or without; he might then well have become Nat Turner, for every element antithetical to his being as Sambo resided in his nature[76]

Freud maintained that no personal relationships were entirely free of ambivalence. How much more obviously true this must be of asymmetrical relationships involving inequalities of power! Freud also argued that observance of the superego's injunctions and prohibitions intensifies both the wish to violate them and the frustrated aggressiveness that is turned back upon the hapless ego augmenting the severity of its demands. Thus the most virtuous and self-denying men are more wracked with guilt and inner conflict than those with less strict superegos.[77] If this is true of conformity with general norms or moral commandments that have become self-imposed, it is obviously much more so when an internalized norm enjoins obedience to another person (whether as an individual or as a role-incumbent) regardless – within limits – of the content of that person's directives. Finally, if separate persons subject to the authority of others experience such psychic tensions, there are bound to be wide variations among individuals in the psychological balance they strike between fear and love, inner resistance and sense of duty, where extensive authority relations involve a collectivity of subjects.

It is not that conflict between the interests and goals of power holder and power subject is inevitable, as is at least implied by the widely accepted Weberian definition of power with its stress on resistance. Of course, this occurs often enough; in one version, the power holder's interest in maintaining his power deforms or displaces the goals affirmed by both power holder and power subject that originally legitimated their relationship, as in Michels' famous 'iron law of oligarchy'. Nor is it primarily that power holders receive more prestige than their subordinates whose self-respect is lowered as a result, although this too commonly happens. Still less is it a question of power itself being a sought-after prize for its own sake, for the power subject may wish only to evade control by the power holder rather than seek to assume his power or to change positions with him.

The conclusion is unavoidable that there is something intrinsically unsatisfying and even painful in subjection to the authority of another. The very need of the subjected to legitimate the authority relation when they cannot escape it springs from this circumstance. Theorists who insist on the positive value of power as a 'social resource' for the implementation of collective goals often overlook the inherent tension present even in consensual authority relations, at least in those with some degree of comprehensiveness and intensity. The highly scope-specific nature of competent authority, its restriction to the limited sphere of the expert's or technical specialist's particular knowledge and skill, is what makes it the apparently most benign and acceptable form of authority; that is why it has played so large a role as a legitimating model for more comprehensive power relations, where claims to privileged knowledge by the power holder and the unambiguous need or interest of the power subject are not easily judged.

The Grand Inquisitor maintained that rebelliousness was as much a part of human nature as the wish to be ruled by a master. The younger Dostoevsky argued in *Notes from the Underground* that there was a wilfulness in man's nature that drove him to chafe against and resist all external restraints, even those dictated by rational concern for his own interests. The ultimate horror in Orwell's imagined anti-utopia is that men are deprived of the very capacity for cherishing private thoughts and feelings opposed to the regime, let alone acting on them. But even writers who have drawn pictures of true utopias, imaginary societies in which peace, happiness and abundance universally prevail, have been criticized for eliminating the tension between rulers and ruled which is seen as inalienably human.[78] Among sociological theorists, Ralf Dahrendorf has attacked the idea of a utopia that eliminates conflict between those with power and those lacking it and has proclaimed such conflict to be the guarantor of both freedom and social progress.[79]

If subjection to authority is painful and creates a need for legitimation where resistance or evasion are out of the question, when these become real possibilities this need may suddenly disappear or lose much of its urgency. Tocqueville's 'law' holds that established power becomes more offensive to its subjects and more vulnerable to resistance when it relaxes its hold by moderating its demands, in striking contrast to its apparently greater legitimacy when it was more oppressive, dominating the lives of its subjects. Lesser restrictions are now experienced as intolerable precisely because their perpetuation after more exacting controls have been abandoned seems more contingent and arbitrary than when authority appeared absolute and unassailable. The increasing irksomeness of subjection to power under such conditions is, of course, only a special case of what has come to be called the 'law of rising expectations'.

Revolutionary situations exhibit a sudden 'collapse of all the hierarchies'[80] that is attended by a great sense of euphoria and liberation, an explosive release from restraints imposed by authorities who shortly before had appeared to be accepted as entirely legitimate. This phenomenon has been repeatedly noted by observers of the early period of popular revolutions as well as of more limited rebellions that have won initial successes (such as some of the campus revolts of the 1960s). One of the best-known and most vivid accounts is that of George Orwell in *Homage to Catalonia* of Barcelona in the early months of the Spanish Civil War. Steven Lukes attaches considerable symptomatic significance to such occurrences in his self-described 'radical view' of power.[81] Unquestionably, they reveal in a flash, as it were, that subjection to authority is experienced as burdensome, even under 'normal' and stable conditions. (Such situations are, however, of short duration: revolutions are always 'betrayed'.)

In all of these concrete historical situations it is difficult to disentangle the inherent unpleasantness of subjection to authority from conflicts over substantive interests dividing power holder and power subject, the lesser prestige associated with subordinate status, and the aspirations of the power subject to acquire the power holder's power (although this is by no means invariably present in all authority relations). Perhaps inner resistance to authority *per se* is more rarely visible in pure form than those motives and attitudes that provide the basis for classifying the different forms of power, although these too, as was argued in Chapter 4, appear most frequently in blends and compounds. Or perhaps the assumption that subjection and dependence are painful is so widely taken for granted that it has scarcely seemed to require separate discussion. According to psychoanalysis the infant's loss of his original feeling of omnipotence and his discovery that the world is indifferent or resistant to his desires – the 'reality principle' – are crucial traumatic experiences. And central to them is the awareness of dependence on the parent and the ensuing fear of frustrations or punishment of which 'loss of love' becomes the most anxiety-provoking. Psychoanalysis, however, has often – and not without justification – been regarded by social scientists as too obsessed with what Erikson has called 'originology', with tracing back later motivations to their infantile sources in 'reductive' fashion, to be of much help in understanding politics or institutionalized power relations. The assumption that power relations inevitably create resistance by subordinates is central to Dahrendorf's conflict sociology. But he never fully elucidates just *why* this should be so, largely, one suspects, because of the traditional sociological bias favouring so-called 'structural' explanations and the allied suspicion of excursions into psychology.[82]

Yet there are social psychological attempts to go somewhat further. In his influential early book *Escape from Freedom*, Erich Fromm postulates an inherent 'desire for freedom' which he roots in a more generalized 'striving to live, to expand and to express the potentialities that have developed in him [man] in the process of historical evolution'.[83] He distinguishes between 'rational authority' that is not inimical to the subject's individual growth and 'irrational authority' that arouses resentment because it inhibits such growth; since in the latter situation the expression of hostility may be dangerous, as in Fromm's example of a master-slave relationship, it is repressed and the need for legitimation (in my terms) replaces it.[84] Fromm's concept of rational authority is almost identical with what I have called competent authority. His chief example is the teacher-pupil relationship, which is – ideally – grounded in the pupil's interest in learning and is self-liquidating in so far as he succeeds in learning and 'becomes more and more like the teacher himself'.[85] Fromm recognizes, of course, many gradations between the two extreme cases he presents. His discussion does not fully distinguish between a person's authority in a power relation and the authority of internalized norms constituting the superego. Indeed one of his major aims is to argue that the latter is often as repressive as the former of individual growth and self-fulfilment in contemporary democratic societies which have eliminated tyrannical external authorities. John Schaar, however, is probably correct in concluding that

In Fromm's view . . . the dictates of authority are wrong even when they
may be good for the subject, because the authority always has his own
interests foremost in mind. The interests of the subject are secondary . . .
In addition, submission to authority is also always wrong, because any
act of submission means a crippling of one's human powers. Fromm's
view on this comes close to saying that might is always wrong, that there
can be no right in an authoritarian-inegalitarian relationship between two
men. Where there is a superior-inferior relationship there is evil.[86]

Presumably, this judgment would hold even of authority relations
where 'might', in the sense of the availability to the power holder of
physical force as a last resort, is lacking.

More recently, Jürgen Habermas has argued that emancipation from
domination is one of three universally human 'knowledge-constitutive
interests.'[87] Habermas, of course, is a philosopher-sociologist rather
than a psychoanalyst, like Fromm, and his primary concern is with
epistemology rather than with human motivation as such. But he shares
with Fromm intellectual origins in the Freudo-Marxist ambience of the
Frankfurt School with its 'critical' and libertarian perspective.
Habermas, moreover, gives psychoanalytic therapy as his major
illustration of a dialogue in which the 'emancipatory' interest is primary
(although he has been criticized for idealizing the therapeutic
relationship)[88]. Habermas's concern, however, with grounding all
knowledge in interest leads him away from distinguishing between the
domination of men by other men and their domination by unknown
causal laws, both of which he sees as giving rise to an emancipatory
interest in attaining knowledge.[89] His focus on the goals of cognition
results in his conceiving of domination in an even more generalized way
than Fromm's irrational authority which embraces both the power of
actual persons and of repressive internalized norms.

These thinkers as well as others who might be cited do not distinguish
between, on the one hand, the latent threat of force and the presence of
conflicts of interest and, on the other hand, inner psychic resistance felt
by the power subject, even where the power holder's concern for the
subject's own good is scarcely to be doubted. The subject's aspirations
to autonomy, self-determination and freedom to act in accordance with
his own rhythms, to express his own will however frivolous or even self-
destructive (viz., Dostoevsky), are frustrated even when authority is
genuinely paternalistic in its regard for the subject. Thus a degree of
psychic coercion – to use one of the more vague, catch-all categories in

my typology of the forms of power – is inherent in all authority. A cogent, if rather too stark, example of Orwell's is relevant:

> There are families in which the father will say to his child, 'You'll get a thick ear if you do that again,' while the mother, her eyes brimming over with tears, will take the child in her arms and murmur lovingly, 'Now, darling, *is* it kind to Mummy to do that?' And who would maintain that the second method is less tyrannous than the first?[90]

The presence of an irreducible element of coercion in all power relations is at least implicit in the opposition to 'domination' of the Frankfurt School tradition. Undoubtedly, its philosophical roots derive in part from Hegel's master-servant model in which the servant becomes conscious of himself as an autonomous subject equal to his master as a result of acquiring awareness of his own powers in dealing with objects and of his master's dependence on these powers for satisfaction of his needs. The subject's consciousness of the minimal reciprocity and mutual dependence that are present in the asymmetrical interaction of a power relation may increase to the point where it 'demystifies' and explodes the power relation itself.

But what of the Grand Inquisitor's claim that man derives positive satisfaction from abasing himself to a master and willingly surrendering 'that gift of freedom with which the ill-fated creature is born'? What of Fromm's drive to 'escape from freedom', of the alleged existence of a desire to be ruled by a strong man? Machiavellians who have made so much of the 'lust for power' have also had to postulate a correlative desire to be dominated on the part of the vast majority of mankind, for their major contention is that the rulers are always a small minority. The élite may be divided into lions and foxes, but most men are sheep. To Freud, a fundamental constituent of human nature is the child's dependent love of the parent. 'The credulity of love [becomes] the most fundamental source of *authority*.'[91] But Freud's view is more complex: dependent love is only one side of the 'primal ambivalence' and Freud places as much emphasis upon, in Rieff's words, 'the implicitness of the coercion that defines the political relation as such – between leaders and led.'[92]

Fromm, in accord with his affirmative, even Rousseauian, view of human nature as opposed to Freud's pessimism, saw *both* the will to dominate and to be dominated as central to a particular, historically specific social character type, the product of early capitalism, which he called the 'sado-masochistic character'. This type was later more fully defined and empirically identified in *The Authoritarian Personality*, perhaps the single most influential piece of social research in the early post-World War II years. The assumption that the psychological roots of fascism were to be found in the 'petty bourgeois' character structure under stress was less salient in this study than in *Escape from Freedom*, but it was part of the early Frankfurt School legacy shared by Fromm and by Theodore Adorno and Max Horkheimer who were the major theoretical influence on the later study and others in the series of which it was a part.

One may disagree, as many have, with the purported psychological affinities between fascism and the lower-middle class under 'late capitalism', as well as with the historical relativization of dominant and submissive, or sado-masochistic, drives in human nature especially pronounced in the work of Fromm. But the insight that a will to power and a will to submission are likely to coexist in the same personality is undoubtedly valid. It represents a marked improvement over ancient distinctions between those 'born' to rule or to obey which survive in the thought of latter-day Machiavellians. Hannah Arendt, who can scarcely be accused of any sympathy with psychoanalysis, has observed that

> The old adage 'How fit he is to sway/That can so well obey', some version of which seems to have been known to all centuries and all nations, may point to a psychological truth: namely, that the will to power and the will to submission are interconnected . . . Conversely, a strong disinclination to obey is often accompanied by an equally strong disinclination to dominate and command.[93]

Apart from the vicissitudes of a particular character type, however, one may doubt that submission in itself is generally desired and experienced as gratifying. Is it not, rather, accepted as the price that is seen as having to be paid for protection, material security, and an orderly world in which everything is arranged for one by powerful others and one is spared the painful agonies and uncertainties of choice and responsibility? This, it seems to me, is the gist of the Grand Inquisitor's doctrine, not that men find some intrinsic pleasure in obeying the commands of superiors and deferring humbly to them. Men accept these as necessary evils in order to secure their bread, enhance their sense of the miraculous, participate with their fellows in a community of worship and, most of all, to escape from the burden of freedom and, in an echo of Hobbes, the anarchy and chaos that the universal reign of freedom appears to threaten. If the behavioural core of the authority relation is command and obedience, the giving and taking of orders, it does not come into existence or survive because compliance with the orders of a superior is pleasurable to the subordinate.[94] Where authority is seen as legitimate, it rests on belief in a tacit contract in which the subjects have bartered their freedom for security.[95] In this sense it can be assimilated to an exchange relationship, or be seen as merging into authority by inducement, although the idea of exchange has too many overtones of shrewd and calculating market behaviour to do justice to the intense reciprocal emotions of power holder and power subject in a comprehensive authority relation. But willingness to give up the costs and risks of freedom need in no way imply that subjection as such is a welcome condition. Even in its milder forms it is apt to be experienced as coercive and demeaning.

Summary

This has been a long chapter in which I have not always resisted the temptation to digress. The temptation arises because its subject has been a central problem, probably *the* central problem, of Western political philosophy long before the birth of modern social science and of the totalitarian regimes of the twentieth century which have given the problem new and fearsome dimensions. I shall try to summarize the main points made in the chapter schematically and in numbered order so that the reader can more easily grasp them in the context of the book as a whole.

(1) Those who win power by coercive means (such as military conquest) strive, usually with at least partial success, to convert might into right by establishing a claim to legitimacy in the eyes of their subjects.

(2) Political power rests on a monopoly of physical force, but the use of this force against those who challenge the state's legitimacy is itself seen as legitimate by other subjects who accept the legitimacy of the state's laws and directives in general.

(3) Force is often described as the 'ultimate' form of power in a way that seems to suggest that it is somehow more important or more 'real' than other forms. But this need mean only that the power holder who is

able to wield multiple forms of power can be compelled to resort to force as a last resort if attempts to exercise the milder forms of power prove unsuccessful. The reality and importance of the non-coercive forms of power is not thereby denied.

(4) The familiar dichotomy between consensus and constraint theories of society, and between legitimate and coercive authority, is usually drawn much too sharply, for both are present and interact to form different 'mixes' or compounds in virtually all power relations. The motivation for compliance even of single individuals combines constraint and duty – 'fear' and 'love' – and the relative predominance of one or the other of these varies widely in a population subject to extensive authority.

(5) The example of a cohesive 'praetorian guard' using their collective control over the means of violence to coerce a much larger population is often seen as a limiting case in which consent is minimal and political rule maximizes coercion. Modern totalitarian dictatorships raise the possibility of an almost total reliance on terror and its mass psychological consequences as a basis of rule. Such regimes, although they may be more durable than theorists who stress the primacy of consent and legitimacy have acknowledged, appear to be transitory in the long run.

(6) A long tradition of political analysis, often called 'Machiavellian', has tended to regard legitimation as merely a ruse on the part of rulers to secure the convenient acquiescence of their subjects. Such an approach treats coercion and manipulation, or 'force' and 'fraud', as the only significant forms of political power. However, more recent thinkers, including the so-called neo-Machiavellians, have recognized that conscious deception by the rulers plays a lesser role than genuine ideological conviction of their mission to rule, which springs from a will or need to believe that is shared by both rulers and ruled.

(7) The rulers' need for legitimation is recognized by Dostoevsky in his famous analysis of the psychology of absolute power in 'The Legend of the Grand Inquisitor'. It is even acknowledged, though in highly truncated form, by George Orwell in *Nineteen Eighty-Four*, possibly despite Orwell's intention to deny it. The disposition of the powerless to believe that those who dominate them are really benevolent figures has also been widely recognized, even – especially? – in situations such as the Nazi camps and American slavery where power has been both brutal and nearly total. The need for legitimation has roots in the infantile experience of dependence as understood by psychoanalysis.

(8) Yet successful legitimation never entirely eliminates an element of coercion from authority relations, however attenuated or psychic rather than physical. Subjection to authority is in itself unpleasant even where there is no threat of force or conflict of interest. An exception perhaps exists in the case of so-called 'sado-masochistic' or 'authoritarian' personality types which have been much discussed in connection with fascist or proto-fascist attitudes. In general, submission to a master may be sought for the security it brings in what can be seen as an implicit kind of contract between power holder and power subject, but this does not imply that the actual taking of orders from another is itself a gratifying experience free of tension. In power relations, fear is rarely if ever completely dissolved into love.

CHAPTER SIX

The Bases of Power: Individual and Collective Resources

A common approach to power is to enumerate the bases or resources that make possible its exercise. 'Assets' and 'values' or 'value-bases' are terms often used synonymously with 'resources'. Some writers have grouped the different kinds of resources, control over which permits the exercise of power, under a few broad rubrics. One of the most influential classifications has been Etzioni's distinction between coercive, utilitarian and normative assets, corresponding, respectively, to instruments of force, material rewards such as goods and services and symbols of legitimacy, prestige or love.[1] William Gamson has developed a similar threefold typology of constraint, inducement and persuasion resources.[2] The wide appeal of these typologies is presumably the result of their breadth and parsimony and of the obvious links they suggest between different resources as bases of power and different forms of realized or enacted power such as coercion, inducement and persuasion.

Lists of power resources are not necessarily more economical and elegant than lists of the actual forms of power as exercised. Lasswell and Kaplan, for instance, listed eight 'base values' of power corresponding to eight 'forms of power and influence'.[3] Robert Dahl has advanced an even more comprehensive and particularized list of 'resources available to political man for influencing others' which includes

an individual's own time; access to money, credit, and wealth; control over information; esteem or social standing; the possession of charisma, popularity, legitimacy, legality; ... the rights pertaining to public office ... ; solidarity: the capacity of a member of one segment of society to evoke support from others who identify him as like themselves because of similarities in occupation, social standing, religion, ethnic origin, or racial stock . . . , the right to vote, intelligence, education, and perhaps even one's energy level.[4]

Dahl pares down this initial list to make it 'short enough to be manageable' and considers in detail only social standing, access to cash, credit and wealth, access to 'certain resources at the disposal of elected leaders, such as the legal powers of public office, popularity, and jobs', and control over information.[5] Obviously, even this shorter list can readily be converted into more familiar sociological categories such as prestige, wealth, legitimate authority derived from office, personal appeal and skill or specialized knowledge.

As we have seen, the *forms* of power and authority are differentiated according to the various reasons and motives for compliance by the power subject (with the exception of physical force and manipulation where by definition the power subject's consciousness is irrelevant). By contrast, the *bases* of power focus on the power holder, although not on his reasons and motives for exercising power but rather on the various resources he brings to the power relation that enable him to do so. Power is always relational, so the neglect of one side of the relation is relative and not absolute. Although the forms of power direct attention to the grounds of the power subject's compliance, they presuppose that the power holder intends to obtain compliance and also that he presents arguments, makes threats or issues commands as the case may be. Similarly, concentration on the resources the power holder brings to the power relation presupposes that the power subject lacks these resources and that the inequality in control over resources is the basis of the power relation.

Resources and the Actual-Potential Problem

The stress on resources is reminiscent of Hobbes's definition of power as 'man's present means to any future apparent good'. Possession of means or resources that may be employed to wield power over others is not, however, any guarantee that they will in fact be so employed. A wealthy miser who chooses to live in poverty and conceal his fortune from the world is obviously not using his economic resources even minimally to control the activities of a few suppliers of goods and services. Nor is someone with a secret arsenal in his cupboard making any use of his coercive resources. These examples are, if idiosyncratic, painfully obvious and indicate the essential grounds for making the distinction between *bases* and *forms* of power.

Yet it makes perfect sense to describe the miser and the owner of hidden weapons as possessing a *capacity* or *potential* for power even if it is never exercised and no one other than themselves knows of it. The miser and the gun-owner may derive an inner sense of security, of superiority to their neighbours, even of megalomania, in contemplating or fantasizing about the possible uses to which they might put their economic and coercive resources. But this is a matter of total indifference to everyone else unless and until the miser goes on a spending spree, buys a controlling interest in a business, or finances a political campaign, and the gun-owner, like the taxi-driver in Martin Scorsese's movie of that name, goes on a shooting spree to right what he sees as the wrongs of his world. Otherwise, their possession of secret resources does not even illustrate the sense in which, as I argued in Chapter 1, power should always be treated as a dispositional concept with the idea of 'capacity' or 'potential' regarded as inherent in its definition.

I mentioned in Chapter 1 two senses in which power is always potential. The first, a trivial one, is that it is meaningful to assert that someone 'has' power even when not engaged in exercising it if there is no reason to doubt his ability and disposition to exercise it on future occasions as he has in the past, e.g. the king asleep at night. The second, far more significant and complex sense in which power is potential is summed up by Friedrich's well-known phrase 'the rule of anticipated reactions'. People may react to the possessor or controller of resources by anticipating the effective use of these resources to control their own actions. For this anticipatory reaction to take place, however, they must know or believe that someone actually posseses the relevant resources and that there is a reasonable probability of his using them to wield power should their own actions or inactions fail to accord with what they take to be his wishes. These conditions are not met in the examples of the secret miser and the possessor of hidden weapons even though it is meaningful from their own standpoint, or from that of an omniscient 'objective observer', to regard them as possessing a capacity or potential to exercise power. *It is preferable therefore to use the term 'latent' rather than 'potential' to indicate the double sense of power as a dispositional concept, for 'latent' suggests the covert presence of something actually affecting a situation in contrast to the weaker implication of 'potential' that something may assert its presence under purely hypothetical or counter-factual conditions.*

Robert Dahl's 'slack resources' and William Gamson's 'influence in repose', useful though these concepts are in other connections, should not be confused with the latent aspect of all realized power – the sense in which power may be *possessed* even when not being actually exercised.[6] Dahl and Gamson are, rather, referring to resources not presently employed to wield power, but which could and might be so employed at some time in the future if their possessors chose to do so. This amounts only to the *possibility* of power, whereas latency is an aspect of actual, realized power. The distinction is an especially important one, as we shall see below, when *collective* rather than individual resources are under consideration.

To impute latent power to someone, it is not enough, as I argued in Chapter 1, to point to the anticipatory reactions of others if the alleged power holder is utterly ignorant of and oblivious to his capacity to elicit these reactions. To justify an imputation of power to him, it needs to be shown that he *knows* that others, aware of his resources, consider him powerful and guide their actions by what they believe to be his wishes and intentions. He need issue no commands, nor even communicate with those who think him powerful, so long as he does nothing to refute their beliefs and allows his own interests and goals to be furthered as a result of his reputation for power. Obviously, we must have access to the consciousness of the imputed power holder (as well as, of course, to that of the imputed power subjects) in order to determine whether these conditions exist and this may in practice be impossible or difficult to obtain. But its difficulty is not a sufficient reason for falling back on behaviouristic or decisional definitions of power and making a methodological absolute of them.

This argument is worth illustrating concretely for it goes to the heart of recent debates over reputational as opposed to decisional approaches to the study of power. Insisting that an imputation of power is justified only when there is evidence of actual, overt participation in decision-making, Nelson Polsby remarks that those who conclude that 'Banker Sly' must be powerful when no such evidence exists 'to support the supposition that millionaires or bums are running the community' apparently possess 'some human equivalent to inaudible dog whistles'.[7] Polsby proceeds to doubt Matthew Crenson's contention that the fact that U.S. Steel was both the major employer and the major air polluter in Gary, Indiana, accounts for the inaction of the city government on legislation to control air pollution resembling that passed in cities with a more diversified industrial base.[8] In an earlier book, Polsby criticized – though less sardonically – Robert Schulze on similar grounds for attributing a 'power potential' to large corporations in Ypsilanti, Michigan, when Schulze's own research revealed that these 'economic dominants' sedulously avoided any involvement in community politics.[9] Polsby's argument strikes me, to put it mildly, as disingenuous. Banks and large corporations are scarcely invisible in communities and are likely to elicit anticipatory reactions both from local political leaders and from the citizenry in general, which is not apt to happen in the case of bums, however visible they may be. This fact alone, as we have seen, is, however, insufficient to justify an imputation of latent power to bankers and corporate managers. But it is implausible that Banker Sly, in Polsby's example, will be unaware of how he is regarded and that he will fail to encourage tacitly, or at least take no action to prove false, his reputation for power, even if Polsby's 'presumption' that 'if a man's work is banking . . . he will spend his time at the bank, and not in manipulating community decisions'[10] holds true.

In contrast to Polsby, his teacher, Robert Dahl, has acknowledged the importance of 'anticipatory influence' as a real constraint on people's actions.[11] Dahl's examples of anticipatory influence, however, are largely confined to that exercised over community leaders by 'persons or groups who are not leaders'. His major example is the anticipatory influence of voters on elected office-holders who decline to raise taxes out of fear of being defeated at the next election. In *Who Governs?*, Dahl uses the term 'indirect influence', which is vaguer than anticipatory influence in that he appears to mean by it both the eliciting of anticipatory reactions and influence that is indirect because it is mediated through others.[12] Again, his major examples are the influence of voters on office-holders, although at several points he does take note of the anticipatory influence of economic élites, or social and economic 'notables', on elected political leaders.[13] But Dahl most frequently refers to anticipatory or indirect influence for the purpose of emphasizing the reality of political democracy even when participation in governmental decision-making by the bulk of the population is confined to exercising the right to vote at scheduled elections. Yet the concept of anticipatory influence is clearly double-edged: it can also be employed to refer to the anticipatory reactions of politicians or of the mass electorate itself to such economic elites as the directors of banks and corporations, as critics of the Dahl-Polsby approach have contended.[14] There is no reason to limit it to the influence of subordinates on leaders; it can work the other way around and include the influence of inactive persons and groups controlling major resources. The concept of anticipatory influence is therefore neutral with regard to the longstanding controversy between 'élitist' and 'pluralist' views on the distribution of power.

If, of course, anticipatory reactions are based on *incorrect* anticipations of the wishes and intentions of the persons or groups eliciting them, we are not entitled to impute latent power to the latter – at most no more than latent unintended influence. Such mistaken anticipations are certainly common.[15] Dahl and Raymond Wolfinger both mention that at the time of their study it was widely believed in New Haven that Yale University covertly dominated the city.[16] They rejected this conclusion on the basis of their research, but the implications of my preceding argument would require them in addition to ascertain whether political leaders and citizens in New Haven acted on a belief in Yale's power and whether Yale knew of its reputation and profited from it, before they would be justified in concluding that Yale's reputation for power was simply a collective misperception (a case of 'false consciousness'?).

Inaction as well as action may be the effect of power. The most forceful criticism of the attribution of power only to actual participants in decision-making is Bachrach and Baratz's now-famous argument that what they call *nondecisions* must also be taken into account if we are to understand how power works.[17] Dahl and his colleagues insist that the study of power must focus on how particular, readily identifiable issues are resolved. But, as Bachrach and Baratz contend, issues do not fall like manna from the heavens nor spring full-blown like Athena from the head of Zeus. Issues have to be *raised* or *made* by someone; they are not merely given. The failure of an issue to be publicly raised and debated in community politics may indicate a negative exercise of power which has succeeded in suppressing that issue. Latent power based on anticipated reactions is obviously one way in which the raising of issues that pose a challenge to the interests and goals of the power holder can be prevented.

Nondecisions leading to inaction therefore may be real events which can in principle be identified in the minds, if not the overt behaviour, both of the actor who negatively influences the anticipations of others and of the others whose choices and actions are thereby constrained.

This conception of nondecisions as negative anticipatory reactions is a version of what Steven Lukes calls a 'two-dimensional' view of power as distinct from a 'one-dimensional' view limited to overt or positive decision-making. Both Lukes and Frederick Frey criticize Bachrach and Baratz for sharing the view of their adversaries – Dahl, Polsby, Wolfinger – that *conflict* between the goals and interests of power holder and power subject is essential to justify an imputation of power, whether decisions or nondecisions are involved.[18] As we saw in Chapter 2, Bachrach and Baratz adopt a version of the Weberian view of power as necessarily involving resistance on the part of the power subject and therefore implying conflict.[19] To define power more broadly as the capacity to produce intended effects does not make resistance by the power subject a part of the definition.[20]

All of the major participants in the recent debate over nondecisions – Polsby, Wolfinger, Bachrach and Baratz, Frey, Crenson, Lukes – have recognized that it raises complex and important theoretical questions about imputations of 'false consciousness' and the existence of 'real' or 'objective' interests as distinct from perceived or subjective interests. Lukes' proposed 'three-dimensional' view of power is an explicit attempt to confront these questions. I shall postpone discussion of them, however, until a later point, for my concern here is primarily with the role of anticipated reactions in producing nondecisions and the bearing of such reactions on the concept of political or power resources.

Individual and Collective Resources

Individuals may possess power resources without using them at all or, more commonly, using them only to pursue non-political goals. The secret miser and gun-owner are idiosyncratic examples of the former. Robert Dahl's remark that 'one wealthy man may collect paintings; another may collect politicians'[21] illustrates the latter. William Gamson distinguishes between resources according to their 'liquidity': highly liquid resources are those requiring 'little or no redeployment to be put to immediate use in the exercise of influence', whereas resources of low liquidity 'can only be used to influence after they have been redeployed or mobilized in some fashion'.[22] Gamson distinguishes somewhat confusingly between 'potential resources' of low liquidity and 'resources without modifier', although resources by themselves, no matter what their liquidity, provide their possessors with no more than potential or possible power. Gamson's conception of resources varying in liquidity along a continuum is nevertheless a useful one.

Money possessed by individuals is obviously a highly liquid resource – in fact, the very concept of liquidity is borrowed from economics. To redeploy his bank account to political uses, Dahl's wealthy man need do no more than start writing cheques to campaign committees instead of to art dealers. A celebrity from the entertainment world can convert his or her resource of reputation to political use by endorsing candidates for office instead of soft drinks or shaving cream. In short, an individual need only change his mind and decide to use his resources politically for them to cease to be 'slack resources' (Dahl) or 'influence in repose' (Gamson). In this sense, most resources that can be possessed by individuals – free time, money, reputation, personal appeal, manipulative or persuasive skills, some kinds of knowledge or information – have relatively high liquidity, that is, are easily convertible to political uses.

Bachrach and Baratz's claim for the importance of nondecisions drew heavily on E. E. Schattschneider's well-known statement that

all forms of political organization have a bias in favour of the exploitation of some kinds of conflict and the suppression of others because *organization is the mobilization of bias*. Some issues are organized into politics while others are organized out.[23]

As the reference to organization suggests, Schattschneider was not talking about individuals and their resources at all but about *groups*. His entire argument, in fact, was put forward in a critique of the so-called 'group theory of politics' favoured by many American political scientists in the 1940s and 1950s. He pointed out, among other things, that only a very small proportion of the population is organized into political pressure groups, which gives the organized considerable advantages in promoting their interests over the unorganized. Consequently, as Schattschneider concluded in his most-quoted lines:

The vice of the groupist theory is that it conceals the most significant aspects of the system. The flaw in the pluralist heaven is that the heavenly chorus sings with a strong upper-class accent. Probably about 90 percent of the people cannot get into the pressure system.[24]

Organization, then, is a collective political resource that is at least as unequally distributed in the population as are the individual resources of wealth, prestige, expertise *et al*. Robert Dahl, in *Who Governs?* as well as elsewhere, often recognizes the distinction between individual and collective resources and has, as we shall see, some acute and valuable things to say about the latter. Yet, invariably, he, as well as his colleagues Polsby and Wolfinger, fall back on examples of individual resources to illustrate their views of power and influence.

Polsby facetiously equates bankers and bums as equally plausible candidates for power in the absence of definite evidence that either participates in community decision-making. But bankers direct large organizations that are highly visible in the community and vital to its commercial and economic life, whereas bums tend to be isolated persons with minimal social ties of any kind.

As an example of potential rather than actual influence, Dahl invents the fictional case of Rodney Brown, 'the richest man in town . . . [who] made a small fortune on the stock market', but who 'pours his money prodigiously into support for eternally bankrupt ballet companies' and 'is considerably less interested in politics than in the coddled egg he eats for breakfast every morning'.[25] Rodney's brother yearns to be a power in local politics, but is forced to work for a modest living in one of Rodney's radio stations. Rodney's chauffeur, on the other hand, is the local Democratic precinct leader, although Rodney doesn't even know this. When Rodney dies, he leaves all his money to his brother who is suddenly able to realize his political ambitions by mobilizing resources that were politically inactive when in Rodney's hands.

Rodney, the luxury-loving balletomane, would be a bit more plausible if Dahl had depicted him as having inherited his wealth rather than having made it himself. He must, after all, at one time have been interested in more than the ballet to have struck it rich on the stock market. Whatever his apparent lack of interest, one suspects that he has kept a shrewd eye on the management of his enterprises and how they are affected by local politics. Dahl ignores the fact that Rodney, like Polsby's Banker Sly, stands at the head of large organizations that are themselves powerful collective actors. Moreover, both Dahl and Polsby are exclusively interested in who influences public policy – in how governmental decisions are arrived at. This is certainly a legitimate and even primary concern for political scientists, but 'private' organizations like banks and corporations obviously also make decisions that deeply affect the community and have therefore been treated by other students of community power as major power centres, even if individual bankers and businessmen remain aloof from local government.

One would expect the political leaders in small or middle-sized cities at least to know the names of the top officials of the larger private organizations in the community, although the ordinary citizen may not. But in big cities and in the nation at large the names of those individuals who, in C. Wright Mill's phrase, 'man the command posts of the corporate world' are likely to be known only to a small number of people outside their own organizations. The frequent ignorance of one another by reputedly influential men in the community has been invoked as an argument against the reputational method of studying community power by Dahl's fellow-researcher and 'pluralist', Raymond Wolfinger.[26] Andrew Hacker, on the other hand, has stressed the anonymity and interchangeability of 'men at the top' at the national level in criticizing 'élitist' and Marxist writers who, unable 'to visualize power as exercised administratively . . . instead of the edifice of Chase Manhattan, seek out Rockefellers in the flesh'.[27] In short, reputationists and decisionists, elitists and pluralists, are all prone to locate power in the resources of individuals rather than in impersonal organizations. Even Bachrach and Baratz, the nondecisionists whose starting-point is Shattschneider's conception of organization as the mobilization of bias, are criticized by Lukes for 'follow[ing] the pluralists in adopting too methodologically individualist a view of power'.[28]

The lengths to which Robert Dahl goes to represent resources as possessions of individuals can be seen from the list that I reproduced from *Who Governs?* on pp. 125–126. He includes 'solidarity' on the list but defines it cumbersomely as

the capacity of a member of one segment of society to evoke support from others who identify him as like themselves because of similarities in occupation, social standing, religion, ethnic origin, or racial stock.

Yet 'solidarity' is almost by definition a non-reducible property of *groups* – of occupational associations, social classes, and religious, ethnic or racial communities – rather than an attribute of the individual members of these groups. Gamson, by contrast, although he does not distinguish explicitly between individual and group resources, gives as an example of a resource with low liquidity 'a solidary group with little organization for political action'.[29]

Yet Dahl, with his customary lucidity, recognizes later in *Who Governs?* the importance of collective as distinct from individual influence, noting the weight of 'the *aggregate* resources of a group'. He makes the obvious point that 'the aggregate outlay of a hundred million-aires who spent $10,000 apiece on politics would be equalled by the total contributions of a hundred thousand persons who spent $10 apiece'. He then notes that the likelihood of whether 'a group of individuals will in fact combine their resources to support a common strategy' is a crucial variable in political analysis.[30] He does not follow up on this, however, but reverts to a discussion of factors affecting the disposition of individuals to make political use of their resources.

I have chosen to dwell on Dahl's discussion because he himself sees clearly that 'the idea of potential influence, which seems transparently clear, proves on examination to be one of the most troublesome topics in social theory'.[31] Moreover, this idea is, as he also sees, intimately linked to the notion of political or power resources. Yet it is hard not to conclude that Dahl's concentration on individual resources with their high liquidity, that is, their easy convertibility to political use, is related to his desire to reaffirm the reality of pluralistic democracy in face of his own finding in New Haven that a very small group – he calls it 'the political stratum' – participates regularly in community politics while the majority of citizens are at best only intermittently active, most of them not even exercising their right to vote in local elections. As Robert Presthus has written of the debate between elitists and pluralists: 'To some extent, where sociologists found monopoly and called it élitism, political scientists found oligopoly but defined it in more honorific terms as pluralism'.[32]

Collective resources are far more variable in their liquidity than individual resources, ranging from the actual power exercised by fully organized and mobilized groups and institutions to the relatively remote possibility of power attributable to categories of persons who, though sharing some common fate or plight, lack any social organization or even a consciousness of collective identity. Social organization and collective identity are clearly matters of degree with respect to which groups or social categories vary widely. But organization and identity (or solidarity) are themselves the fundamental collective resources underlying and making possible the mobilization of all others.

The most obvious collective resources are those created by *the pooling of individual resources* for employment in the service of a common aim. Small financial contributions from many people can, as in Dahl's example, match or outstrip the donations of a few wealthy individuals, as laws regulating campaign expenditures have recognized. Individual reputational resources are pooled when prominent people jointly sign petitions supporting public causes or candidates for office. The free labour time of many individuals is pooled when volunteers unite to demonstrate for or against something or to work in a political campaign. Students have often been a politically influential group because, although they lack most other resources, they have enough free time available to constitute a formidable volunteer force if they are fired with sufficient enthusiasm for a cause or a candidate. This has not happened very often in the United States, but it did in 1968 when student volunteers – dubbed a 'children's crusade' – campaigned for Senator Eugene McCarthy in New Hampshire and helped to discourage President Johnson from running for re-election.

A small group, the members of which are able to pool large amounts of individual resources, can wield greater power than larger groups with members who are poorer in resources. Small groups committed to using violence are the most obvious example. Companies of knights owning their own weapons and armour in the Middle Ages, and mercenary soldiers at a later date, are cases in point. More complex and expensive weaponry increases the chances for small armed and disciplined groups to prevail over unarmed or unorganized multitudes, as suggested by the British imperialist jingle 'Whatever happens, we have got/the Maxim gun, and they have not'. Nuclear bombs represent the polar development in this direction and fears are widely expressed today over the possibility of a small nation ruled by a mad dictator obtaining a bomb, or even of the invention of a compact, portable bomb which might be used by tiny groups of fanatical terrorists.

Reputational resources and legitimacies are pooled in the creation of *ad hoc* 'blue-ribbon' commissions, whose pronouncements are expected to restore public confidence in times of crisis. The 'persuasion resources' of eloquence and information are combined when teams of speechwriters and public relations men are assembled by a candidate for office, or when new journals of opinion committed to a particular cause or ideology are founded. Associations of experts speaking with one voice may be listened to where no one of them alone could gain a hearing.

The size of a group, the sheer numbers of people composing it, is a crucial collective resource. A group's size often determines the total amount of resources of wealth, reputation, strength *et al.* it controls, because this depends considerably on the number of persons contributing their quanta of individually owned or controlled resources to the common pool. For this reason, one may regard *size* or *numbers* as a non-reducible collective attribute or property of a group in contrast to the collective resources previously mentioned which represent simply the aggregation of individual resources or the summation of the attributes of individual persons. But, it might be argued, why is the size of a group any the less an aggregated or additive property than a sum of money raised from individual contributions, since size is merely the sum of the individuals constituting the group just as the money is no more than the sum of the contributions of individuals? This issue is mentioned by Paul Lazarsfeld and Herbert Menzel in a discussion that, in contrast to the present one, is primarily concerned with the measurement rather than the conceptualization of non-reducible, or what they call 'global', properties of a group as distinct from aggregated, or in their terms analytical', properties.[33] Lazarsfeld and Menzel conclude:

> At some point arbitrary decisions have to be made. On an intuitive basis we decided to consider the numbers of members in a collective (e.g. population size) as a global property, although one might argue that it is analytical, obtained by counting the 'existence' of each member.[34]

My own intuition leads me to the same conclusion.

The relevance of size as a collective resource to the exercise of power is variable, as we shall see in greater detail in the next chapter. Obviously, it helps determine in the first instance the weight of aggregated individual resources: the more people who contribute their holdings to a common pool the greater the aggregate resources to pursue a group's goals and enhance its power are likely to be. Larger numbers are especially advantageous in the cases of money, labour time and the more rudimentary forms of violent and nonviolent force where the massed strength of individuals makes a difference, as in strikes, sit-ins, rioting mobs storming buildings or destroying property, and armies with fairly simple weapons wielded by individuals. But in the examples of pooled reputations, persuasive skills and legitimate and competent authority derived from offices and professions that I gave above, the effectiveness of the group depends upon its relative exclusiveness which limits its size. (One is reminded of Groucho Marx's famous crack that any club that would admit him as a member wasn't exclusive enough to be worth joining.) Large groups also face greater difficulties in maintaining a high level of contributions of individual resources from their members and in efficiently coordinating their members' actions. A notorious case in point is the ineffectiveness of large committees or collegial bodies and the consequent reliance of such bodies on delegating their decision-making authority to much smaller subcommittees or even to single persons.[35]

Another global or non-reducible resource is *monopoly of jobs or skills* that are in demand by the larger community. Again, one might argue that such a monopoly is not different from the aggregated resources of individuals, for it is no more than the sum of all the jobs or skills possessed by an aggregate of individuals. Yet it is because no one possessing the job or skill is excluded from the group that the monopoly becomes an attribute of all the group's members taken together. One could for this reason, I believe, make an even stronger case for job or skill monopoly as a global, non-reducible property of a group than for the size of the group. I shall not bother to argue such a case in detail, however, and, as in the case of group size, shall arbitrarily and intuitively (in the words of Lazarsfeld and Menzel) classify it as a non-reducible group property.

Job or skill monopoly is a crucial condition for the exercise of power by trade unions. The threat of a withdrawal of services or the cessation of activities on which others depend defines the strike as a weapon. In short, job or skill monopoly is a collective resource that may be employed to wield a form of nonviolent force. It is essentially this resource that writers have in mind when they refer to the 'functional indispensability' of an activity or skill as providing a basis or opportunity for the exercise of collective power. Gerth and Mills have stated it with exemplary clarity:

New York harbor pilots or Manhattan elevator boys – not to mention miners, steel workers, and railroad workers – hold in hand more crucial links in the multiple chains of interdependent functions that constitute modern society than do musicians, barbers, textile workers, or small-scale farmers. Obviously, the functional place of workers is not simply a question of skill: to push the button of an elevator and count the floors requires less skill than to play the violin or to operate a barbershop. The question is: What links in the interlocking chains of activity are broken by the group's withdrawal of effort?[36]

The most important collective resources are unambiguously classifiable as non-reducible or global properties of groups: namely, *solidarity* and *organization*. They constitute, in fact, the major defining attributes of a group itself in the sociological sense as distinct from a mere population or statistical category. Collective resources resulting from the aggregation of individual resources, as well as group size and job or skill monopoly which I have chosen to consider non-reducible collective resources, can only be mobilized for political uses, or even acquire existence *as* collective resources, because of the prior achievement of a degree of minimal solidarity and organization by a plurality of individuals. The contributions by individuals of money, labour time, skill *et al.* to a common pool for employment in the service of a shared aim imply a consensus among them about the aim and a resulting solidarity based on a sense of collective identity. The same applies to group size and monopoly as collective resources. In addition, if aggregated individual resources, group size and monopoly, once they have been created, are to be used effectively to exercise power, at least some social organization, or co-ordination of the activities of members of the group, is also necessary. The same holds true for the maintenance of a level of resource contribution from individuals, including their continued membership in the group, sufficient to keep the group in existence. For these reasons, solidarity and organization are the basic collective resources presupposed by the others that I have enumerated.

Solidarity and social organization are, of course, matters of degree. Groups vary from ephemeral, haphazardly assembled audiences or crowds, sharing only a temporary mood or focus of attention, to relatively permanent, highly organized, associational structures which make provision for their own perpetuation. Sociologists have classified groups closest to the first pole under the rubric of 'collective behaviour' and those closest to the second as 'formal organizations'. Both solidarity and social organization can be subdivided into a number of variable aspects which might also be regarded as distinct collective resources. Solidarity includes the degree of awareness of boundaries between group members and non-members (the familiar Sumnerian 'in-group–out-group' distinction), the intensity of mutual emotional identifications with one another based on a sense of similarity or 'consciousness of kind', rituals symbolizing belonging and collective identity, and so on. Social organization comprises the degree and complexity of division of labour, the presence of leadership or a power structure, rules governing interactions between members and between members and outsiders, and much else. These different aspects of solidarity and social organization amount, of course, to well-known variable characteristics of what sociologists call 'social structure'.

I have been considering organized groups as collective actors controlling resources which give the group the capacity to exercise power over non-members: the general public, particular clienteles, the local community, political leaders. But the group itself may develop an internal power structure directing the activities of its own members. This necessitates qualification of my earlier account which seemed to suggest that consensus on common goals brings the group into being and remains the foundation of its solidarity. Such a view would mean that the group's own leaders primarily exercise legitimate, competent, or personal – including charismatic – authority over subordinate members, that is, only the consensual forms of power. Yet the other forms of power discussed in Chapters 2 and 3 may also be used to obtain the obedience of subordinates. Groups may function as collective actors wielding power over outsiders and yet be held together by fear or material incentives, that is, by coercion or inducement. Wars have been won by armies of mercenaries. Governments have been overthrown in the contemporary Middle East by paid mobs. Bought votes have decided the outcome of elections. Huge enterprises have exploited the forced labour of slaves or prisoners. The notion of a 'collective goal' need not carry the implication that such a goal is necessarily established by consensus among the members of the group organized to achieve it. Although imposed through coercion by the group's leaders, it may still be a collective goal in the sense that the activities of the group's members are directed and co-ordinated toward realizing it.

Organized groups are themselves arenas in which individuals and subgroups engage in conflicts over status, material rewards and power just as the groups themselves contend for power in the larger society.[37] Group leaders may control resources enabling them to exercise power over subordinate members at the same time that their control of these members is itself a resource enhancing the power of the group as a collective actor *vis-à-vis* outsiders, including other organized groups. In the case of hierarchical organizations controlled from the top, it would be misleading to regard organization itself as a collective resource used to advance the goals and interests or enhance the power of all members rather than merely of the leaders considered either individually or collectively. The builders of the pyramids or of the White Sea-Baltic

Canal, to take two extreme examples, were hardly the beneficiaries of their own efforts: as Randall Collins notes, 'throughout most of history, large-scale organizations have operated principally by coercion'.[38] If organization is, in Schattschneider's phrase, the 'mobilization of bias', then the bias often favours the goals and interests of the leaders who control the group rather than of the members who are controlled.

The large bureaucratic structures of the modern world suggest a different possibility. Organizations may be collective or corporate actors *sui generis*, wielding and accumulating power that serves neither the goals and interests of their members, nor of a minority of organizational leaders, nor, for that matter, of outside individuals or groups to which the leaders are accountable. The efforts and energies of individuals in such cases are resources utilized by the organization for its own self-aggrandizement; the organization is not an actualization of the power of individuals using and combining their resources to create new collective resources mobilized to advance a common goal.[39] The prevailing mood of pathos about bureaucracy, which found its earliest and still most forceful expression in the writings of Max Weber, assumes this to be the case. It is true that 'corporate actors', as James Coleman says, 'ultimately . . . derive their resources from natural persons', including 'natural persons' who in order to pursue a common end aggregate their individual resources and in so doing create new collective resources of solidarity and organization.[40] But, as Coleman recognizes, the distance travelled from these beginnings is a long one in the case of the massive organizational actors confronting us today.

Organized groups differ in the forms of power that constitute the primary basis of their control structures as well as in their modes of combining the different forms.[41] It follows that they differ in the degree to which they are perceived by their members as a collective resource to advance common ends, as the instrument of their leaders, or as a 'living machine' (Weber) dominating their human cogs. When its members regard the organization as serving their own goals and values, their solidarity will be much greater and the more consensual forms of power are likely to be the basis of the organization's power structure. Solidarity will be lower in organizations relying on inducements and is apt to be negative in coercive organizations where covert resistance to the organization's goals and its leaders becomes a bond uniting its subordinate members. Solidarity and social organization, therefore, may be negatively correlated in coercive and, though to a lesser degree, in utilitarian organizations, reducing the comprehensiveness and intensity of the power they wield beyond the specific tasks they are organized to carry out. By contrast, groups that achieve *both* high solidarity and rigorously disciplined hierarchical organization, such as the Society of Jesus and Leninist revolutionary parties,[42] are the most effective 'organizational weapons'.[43]

Solidarity is crucial to the survival and effectiveness of power-seeking groups that are formed by the voluntary association of their members. Contemporary analysts of group politics usually have such nominally membership-controlled groups in mind rather than hierarchical groups, whether coercive or utilitarian, organized from the top down to perform particular economic and administrative tasks. They presuppose the relatively permissive, more or less democratic, context of those modern societies which grant the 'right of free assembly' to their members and encourage the proliferation of what sociologists call 'voluntary associations'. Parties, pressure groups and social movements are the politically relevant examples of primary concern to political scientists and political sociologists.

Yet it must be emphasized that *any* group by virtue of its sheer existence *as a group* constitutes a collective resource – actual, potential or possible. Legal restrictions placed on the political activities of business corporations, government bureaucracies, and a variety of other large organizations such as churches, hospitals, schools and universities, and foundations are based on a recognition of this fact. Laws prohibiting campaign donations by corporations, the Hatch Act outlawing political activity by civil servants, and the conditional granting of freedom from taxation to charitable, educational and cultural organizations are cases in point. That even small informal groups of kin, neighbours, and co-workers play an important role in shaping, transmitting and crystallizing political preferences was the major finding of Lazarsfeld's *The People's Choice* and later voting studies modelled on it.[44] The enactment of the secret ballot by all modern constitutional democracies prevents possible coercion or inducement (bribery) of the individual voter by any of the groups to which he belongs, whether by his superiors in specialized organizations, such as priests and employers, or by his peers in primary groups.[45]

The previous discussion has dealt with the power potential of any established group commanding collective resources. One must distinguish, however, between two different senses in which collective resources may be described as potential or possible with regard to their political use. First, unorganized aggregates of people with a nonexistent

or highly attenuated awareness of collective identity may constitute a
target for political mobilization aimed at forging a new group out of
previously isolated individuals, at creating a new collective political
actor where none previously existed. Such terms as 'latent group',
'quasi-group' or 'social category' have often been employed to describe
such aggregates and to distinguish them from mere statistical
categories (such as all blue-eyed persons) which have little or no
potential for unity.[46] The literature on class and 'class consciousness'
going back to Marx himself abounds in such distinctions.

This sense in which collective resources may be seen as potential
rather than actual differs from the second sense implied by Gamson's
reference to 'a solidary group with little organization for collective
action' as an instance of 'potential resources' or 'resources with low
liquidity'.[47] Any organized group that is not currently engaged in
exercising political power possesses at least *some* potential for such
exercise. But this is not the same thing as the case of an aggregate of
persons possessing *the potential to become a group* because their
common circumstances suggest the possibility of mobilizing them for
collective action. Groups that are already organized differ widely, of
course, in the relative liquidity of their collective resources with respect
to political action. Groups with relatively limited specific goals are
likely to rank low in liquidity even though they may be highly organized
and stable. As we have seen, specialized large-scale organizations are
often subject to legal restrictions on their political activity in
contemporary advanced societies. Moreover, their internal power
structure is often utilitarian or even coercive rather than normative,
which severely limits their flexibility in redeploying their collective
resources for broad political purposes. Collectivities united by diffuse
bonds of solidarity but lacking organization, such as ethnic or religious
groups, are more promising candidates for political mobilization, as
vote-seeking politicians well know.

Conclusions and Implications

There are significant differences in the liquidity of individual and
collective resources. Individual resources that lie idle or are used for
nonpolitical purposes can be politically mobilized if their possessors
decide to use them for political ends. An individual's determination to
withhold his resources from political use may, of course, be
unshakeable, but death or other contingencies can lead to their transfer

to other persons of different inclination, as in Dahl's example of Rodney whose politically ambitious brother became his heir. Unused individual resources provide no more than a basis for possible power, but either a decision to redeploy them or their transfer to other persons amount to fairly straightforward occurrences. Thus the political liquidity of individual resources is generally high.

Collective resources, on the other hand, provide a basis for possible power in a much more qualified and ambiguous sense. Frequently, collective resources must first be *created*, not just diverted from other uses, by the achievement of solidarity in support of common goals, social organization and leadership resulting from the mobilization of previously disunited individuals. Or the members and/or leaders of existing groups must decide to redeploy their collective resources to political uses. In particular instances of both of these processes, the liquidity of collective resources may be so low as to be virtually nonexistent. Thus the sense in which collective resources may be regarded as slack', 'in repose', or 'potential' with regard to their mobilization for the exercise of power is different, more variable and considerably more complex than in the case of individual resources. This is obscured when individual and collective resources are not differentiated in discussions of potential power.

Failure to recognize the highly variable liquidity of collective resources is a classic error of political analysis evident both in crude 'conspiracy theories of history' and in scholarly élitist interpretations of the social order. Its essence is to attribute power to Jews, bankers, interlocking corporate directorates, bureaucrats, labour bosses or even intellectuals, because it can be plausibly argued that these groups could exercise great power if they were cohesive and their members shared a common political aim. That this is often not the case, or is true only to a limited degree, is passed over or suppressed. ('If only the bankers *would* conspire!' Keynes is alleged to have once remarked.) The widespread belief that a group, say, bankers or government bureaucrats, is powerful cannot possibly by itself confer power on the group if it is in fact unorganized and lacking common goals and perceived interests. The reputed power of an individual, on the other hand, may in itself suffice to endow him with the real thing, especially at the community level.

Yet imputed power may also sometimes lead to actual power in the case of groups, though scarcely on the society-wide, history-making scale that is implied in sweeping conspiratorial and élitist theories. Since the existence of a group, for whatever purpose it is organized, in itself constitutes a formidable potential political resource, a group is more likely to arouse anticipatory reactions than an individual whose resources are not in political use. If the group (or its leaders) becomes aware of this and acquiesces in or tacitly encourages the anticipatory reactions it has aroused, it then acquires latent power as in the examples (real and hypothetical) of Yale in New Haven, the bank headed by Banker Sly in Mudville, and the managers of branch-plant corporations in Ypsilanti. If collective resources are more likely than individual resources to arouse anticipatory reactions, they can be said at least in this respect to possess higher liquidity. In addition, groups already mobilized for non-political purposes can be expected to attract the attention of politicians and public administrators as possible targets for political mobilization.

Robert Dahl, in an influential article published before *Who Governs?*,[48] has clearly distinguished between a group's 'potential for control' and its 'potential for unity'. His argument that the latter may vary independently of the former is a persuasive critique of the assumptions about collective power made by many élitist writers. Yet the factors affecting a group's potential for unity are not random, nor are they entirely independent of the individual resources possessed by the group's members. These factors need to be systematically taken into account, as Dahl fails to do in *Who Governs?*, in any assessment of the equality or inequality of the distribution of political resources in a community or larger society. If this were done, Dahl's conclusion that the different resources are 'dispersed' rather than 'cumulative' in contemporary communities would require serious qualification.

Groups, not individuals, are the major political actors, the collective makers of history. Collective resources are superior to individual resources and also more enduring when possessed by relatively stable groups and organizations. Tasks that are clearly beyond the powers of individuals, no matter how rich in resources, can be carried out by organized groups. These are sociological commonplaces. They imply nevertheless that the creation and maintenance of collective resources is vastly more significant than the distribution of individual resources in determining the structure of power in a society. Hannah Arendt acknowledges the primacy of collective resources in her definition of power when she writes that

> power corresponds to the human ability not just to act but to act in concert. Power is never the property of an individual; it belongs to a group and remains in existence only so long as the group keeps together.[49]

The question of political mobilization, of *which* groups or potential groups become mobilized for political action, is a crucial one, if not *the* crucial one, for political sociology. In a famous definition, Harold Lasswell once equated politics with 'who gets what, when, and how'.[50] From a collective rather than an individualistic perspective, politics might more appropriately be defined as 'who gets mobilized, for what collective goals, when, and how'. We turn to this question in the next chapter.

CHAPTER SEVEN

The Bases of Power: Who Gets Mobilized?

Much theorizing about politics is an attempt to answer the question 'Who gets mobilized?' Or who, that is, what groups, communities or social categories, succeed in creating and maintaining collective resources used for political ends? Who become the major contenders in the arena of political competition and conflict? Conversely, which potential or possible groups do not become contenders because they fail to create and maintain collective resources or to make political use of existing collective resources? Which groups or social categories that are not politically mobilized nevertheless exercise anticipatory influence because of the possibility of their mobilization?

My primary purpose in this chapter is less to try to answer these questions with reference to actual societies than to show that an exceedingly wide and disparate range of theorizing about politics, both old and new, can be interpreted as an effort to answer them. From Machiavelli to research on power in local communities, from Tocqueville to theories of mass society and totalitarianism, from Marx to studies of voting behaviour, from Weber and Michels to studies of collective behaviour and the rise of new social movements, generalizations about politics focus to a considerable degree on the problem of actual and potential mobilization, of the creation and maintenance of collective resources. Even the routine conduct of politicians and power-seeking groups illustrates the centrality of the problem.

The question 'Who gets mobilized?' can be broken down into a number of separate questions about the actual, latent or merely possible existence of collective resources and their role, whether direct or anticipatory, in influencing others. (1) Which organized groups are fully mobilized to seek power? (2) Which groups, though organized, are not mobilized politically, but confine their activities to the pursuit of non-political goals? (3) Which groups (or, more exactly, quasi-groups or social categories) are unorganized, but are potentially mobilizable, whether temporarily or permanently, because of diffuse solidary bonds or latent interests shared by their members? Perhaps one should restate this question to ask which groups *are perceived as* potentially mobilizable, for even if potentials are not realized, such groups may nevertheless exercise at least anticipatory influence on others, including power holders and power seekers. (4) Which groups are likely to remain mobilized on a more or less permanent basis? (5) What accounts for the differences in actual and potential mobilization?

The creation and maintenance of collective resources is a central concern of all sociology. All groups and organizations are mobilizations of aggregated and global collective resources; such a description is simply another way of defining a group. Except for relatively undifferentiated small groups and ephemeral crowds, all groups possess a formal or informal leadership hierarchy that wields power over the membership. This is as true of sports clubs and fraternal associations that are in no way concerned with seeking control over others or even with maintaining patterned interaction with non-members as it is of state structures or political parties. The enduring (though not necessarily unchanging) institutional structures of society engaged in economic, educational, religious, child-rearing, military and therapeutic activities constitute mobilizations of collective resources as much as primarily political structures and organizations.

Thus to ask 'who gets mobilized?' is in one sense to ask about the conditions conducive to solidarity and organization as such, about how society itself is possible, rather than to attend only to the political realm. Not surprisingly, political sociologists have made use of the notions of 'political culture' and 'political socialization'. Culture, socialization, social structure and consensus on collective goals are to be found wherever human beings sustain a permanent group life. The formation of groups, how they perpetuate or reproduce themselves, often inter-generationally, and the motivation of individuals who devote their limited resources, including time and energy, to serving collective goals are generic social phenomena. So – at least at the level of total societies – are counter-cultures, deviant motivations and resistance to socialization, group conflict, and dissensus on collective goals. The latter are the salient concerns of political analysis.

It is scarcely my aim in this chapter to apply general sociological theory to the problem of political mobilization,[1] nor even to advance a particular theory of the formation of conflict or power-seeking groups.

Such projects would lead far beyond a focus on collective resources as a basis of power, although, of course, power itself is a ubiquitous reality inherent in virtually all social relations. My intention is no more than to indicate that the conditions under which collective political resources are produced and maintained is the central concern of a number of diverse perspectives in political thought as well as of political practice (or 'praxis').

The Nature of Political Mobilization

The term 'mobilization' is of military origin, referring to the assembling and organizing by governments of men and materials for purposes of war or preparedness for war. People and material resources are withdrawn from 'private' or non-military uses and re-allocated to the armed forces or weapons production. The term has been extended to apply to any effort to co-ordinate people and material resources in the service of a collective goal. As one writer defines it: 'Mobilization refers to the process of forming crowds, groups, associations and organizations for the pursuit of collective goals.'[2] In the case of political mobilization, the collective goals involve influencing, controlling or gaining access to government. They presuppose therefore the existence of the state as the central decision-making agency in society, monpolizing the means of coercion and making the legitimating claim to represent the general interests of the entire population subject to its rule.

Solidarity and organization, as we saw in the previous chapter, are the fundamental collective resources, fundamental in the sense that they are prerequisites for the mobilization of all the others. The presence of at least a minimal diffuse solidarity tends to be a prerequisite for initial efforts to achieve organization. As this consideration suggests, solidarity and organization are matters of degree; they differ in this respect from the size of a group and from the many aggregated collective resources that can be summarized by a single discrete measure, such as a budget. Nevertheless, it may be useful to present at least a schematic model or ideal type of a group that is fully mobilized. Such a group possesses the following characteristics:

(1) Solidarity or social cohesion based on an awareness by the members of their collective identity as a group and of their common commitment to a goal, interest or set of values. The survival of the group itself may be a far from unimportant shared interest. A fully

developed sense of collective identity implies consciousness of clearly marked boundaries that separate members of the group from non-members, or of an in-group – out-group awareness.

(2) Perception by the members of shared goals, interests and values that are in conflict with those of other groups or established power holders. Awareness of conflict rather than of mere difference is what distinguishes this characteristic from the first one.[3]

(3) Perception by the members of the relevance of state action or public policy to promote or consolidate the interests and values they share as a group.

(4) Some social organization specifically designed to promulgate and promote the goals, interests and values of the group in competition or conflict with rival groups and power holders perceived as antagonistic. Some degree of division of labour and of differentiated leadership is implied by this criterion.

These criteria of political mobilization are admittedly too general to be terribly illuminating and they even verge on the tautological. The first and the fourth – if the reference in the latter to competition and conflict with other groups is omitted – are virtually defining criteria of a group itself in sociological terms. Enumerating them in the present connection at least serves to underline the point that the sheer existence of a group, of any group, in itself constitutes a potential collective resource for political use. The second and third criteria simply specify what makes a group political or politically-oriented. The conventional political scientist's label 'parties and pressure groups' refers to groups that fully meet these four criteria of political mobilization. They are also met by those large voluntary organizations, often calling themselves 'movements', that are devoted to promoting a single issue or set of issues, such as environmental conservation or women's rights.

Since solidarity and organization are themselves collective resources and also prerequisites for the mobilization of all other collective resources, the opportunity to create with their help other formidable collective resources often determines whether an effort at mobilization is undertaken. The potential size of a mobilized group is an obvious consideration. The difference between a political party or movement and a pressure group is essentially a difference in the limits to the size of the constituencies to which each can appeal with some prospect of success. Even though a group may be small, the dependence of others – whether the general public or policymaking élites – on its skills and activities may encourage efforts to mobilize it to take advantage of its functional indispensability in order to further its interests or values. The efforts of atomic physicists to win a voice in the determination of nuclear military policy and of harbour pilots or air traffic-controllers to wield economic power by organizing trade unions are two quite different cases in point.

The existence of diffuse solidarity also stimulates efforts to mobilize groups sharing what John Torrance has called 'primary similitudes'.[4] Groups with common values, beliefs and customs derived from ethnic origin or religious affiliation are the most obvious examples. It has often been noted that in the United States ethnic loyalties have sometimes been created among immigrants where they did not previously exist by the appeals of vote-seeking politicians to national bonds based on country of origin that transcend those of region or locality which may have been all that the immigrants were conscious of in the beginning.[5] Democratic politicians survey the population with electoral divining rods designed to seek out hidden sources of solidarity that are potentially convertible into at least bloc support at the polls. Ethnic and religious groups are particularly promising targets for political mobilization because, in addition to the facts that they are often large and geographically concentrated, their members, even if unorganized and unaware of any collective political interest, already share some norms and values in common, which indeed is what constitutes their ethnic or religious identity. As Daniel Bell has put it, ethnicity already 'combine[s] an interest with an affective tie'.[6]

Ethnic and religious groups differ in this respect from classes and are therefore more attractive candidates, at least in the short run, for efforts at political mobilization.[7] In some contemporary societies, including the United States, ethnic groups can be regarded as versions of what Max Weber called 'status groups', which he distinguished from classes on the basis of their subjective awareness of solidarity and collective identity.[8] Neither Marx nor Weber regarded class as necessarily characterized by such subjective awareness since classes are objectively determined by 'production relations' or impersonal market forces. Subjective awareness leading to political mobilization may or may not develop depending on the social and historical context. To Marx, the proletariat but not the peasantry was capable of overcoming the objective condition of being a 'class-in-itself' by becoming a 'class-for-itself' possessed of full class consciousness. To Weber, whose definition of class was equally objective although different from that of Marx, whether a common class situation gives rise to 'communal action' by its members depends on a number of conditions that he specified very broadly.[9] The diffuse solidarity that provides a possible basis for the collective organization of economic classes is based on latent interests which are less salient – though often more permanent and shared by larger numbers of people – than the norms and values to which people of the same ethnic or religious background are committed. The possibility of 'like' interests developing into 'common' interests (in MacIver's terms[10]) applies to many groups or population aggregates other than classes, but it has been far more widely discussed with reference to classes because of Marxist influence. The most famous single statement is Marx's analysis of why the mid-nineteenth-century French peasantry was incapable of achieving political mobilization. It has been quoted countless times, but I cannot resist citing it fully once more so succinctly does it summarize, suggesting the possibility of wider generalization, the conditions deterring mobilization of the peasantry:

The small peasants form a vast mass, the members of which live in similar conditions, but without entering into manifold relations with one another. Their mode of production isolates them from one another, instead of bringing them into mutal intercourse. The isolation is increased by France's bad means of communication and by the poverty of the peasants. Their field of production the small holding, admits of no division of labour in its cultivation, no application of science and, therefore, no multiplicity of development, no diversity of talents, no wealth of social relationships. Each individual peasant family is almost self-sufficient; it itself directly produces the major part of its consumption and thus acquires its means of life more through exchange with nature than in intercource with society. The small holding, the peasant and his family; alongside them another small holding, another peasant and another family. . . In this way, the great mass of the French nation is formed by simple addition of homologous magnitudes, much as potatoes in a sack form a sackful of potatoes. In so far as millions of families live under conditions of existence that divide their mode of life, their interests and their culture from those of the other classes, and put them in hostile contrast to the latter, they form a class. In so far as there is merely a local interconnection among these small peasants, and the identity of their interests begets no unity, no national union and no political organization, they do not form a class. They are consequently incapable of enforcing their class interest in their own name, whether through a parliament or through a convention. They cannot represent themselves, they must be represented.[11]

The conditions of peasant life that negatively affected their opportunities for political mobilization were reversed in the case of the proletariat, as Marx argued in other writings.[12] Since these variable conditions are relevant to the prospects for mobilization of a large number of groups, including some that are not classes, it is worth making explicit what is left implicit in Marx's rich but condensed analysis:

(1) The territorial dispersion of the peasants diminishes their sense of collective identity as a nation-wide class. The lack of spatial concentration or density leads to an absence of what Durkheim called 'moral density', or of frequent interactions among similarly situated persons causing an intensified and constantly rekindled awareness of the traits they possess in common.[13] France's 'bad means of communication' ensure that geographical scattering will mean relative social isolation, and the poverty of the peasants both makes it impossible for them to afford existing means of communication and transport and reduces the time they can take off from work to engage in travel and social intercourse. These last limitations obviously apply in some degree to all materially disadvantaged groups, including the industrial working class.[14]

(2) The peasants' struggle for subsistence pits them against nature rather than against powerful human authorities who directly command, coerce or exploit them. Their self-sufficiency makes their dependence on people outside the family, on society itself, less visible. This consideration bears directly on the second characteristic of full political mobilization listed above and also on the third. Peasants are unlikely to develop more than a sporadic sense of negative solidarity or conflict-consciousness resulting from perceptions of another class or of more personalized authority figures as opponents to be collectively resisted.[15] Nor are they prone to envisage actions by the state as vitally relevant to their lot, especially to its improvement. The entire world beyond the horizon of their immediate locality may appear alien and mysteriously threatening; like Carlo Levi's peasants of Lucania, they feel 'cut off from History and the State' and may express their sense of isolation in a symbolic phrase like 'Christ stopped at Eboli'.

(3) The heavy and monotonous nature of the peasant's work of cultivation involves little division of labour or application of skills and knowledge derived from education. The peasantry therefore is unlikely to produce orators and intellectuals who might supply political leadership and construct ideologies which express its collective interests

and goals. The paucity of social contacts in work means the absence of political skills and information based on understanding the diversity of men and their ways. The lack of any complex social organization of labour results in lack of preparation for the organization required to sustain political mobilization.

Marx recognized that his description applied mainly to the conservative peasants in the more economically backward and isolated regions of France such as the Vendée. The alleged political passivity of the peasantry, however, became something of a staple of Marxist historiography and sociology at least until the Chinese Revolution of 1949. Yet, as Barrington Moore, Jr., opens the last chapter of his immensely valuable *Social Origins of Dictatorship and Democracy*:

> The process of modernization begins with peasant revolutions that fail. It culminates during the twentieth century with peasant revolutions that succeed. No longer is it possible to take seriously the view that the peasant is an 'object of history', a form of social life over which historical changes pass but which contributes nothing to the impetus of these changes.[16]

Moore later notes that the peasants of the Vendée stood at an extreme in their isolation that is 'rather atypical for peasants in civilized societies',[17] although he concedes that Marxists are correct in holding that 'the peasants have to have leaders from other classes'.[18] Often enough this has been true of the proletariat as well, a subject that, to put it mildly, has hardly escaped notice and controversy by both scholars and Marxist political leaders since Marx's death.

The three major factors stressed in Marx's analysis of the French peasantry can be generalized to apply to other groups: the effects of spatial density on 'moral' or social density, the degree to which an occupation is perceived as part of a division of labour giving rise to conflicts among its component groups, and the degree to which an occupation requires social skills, understanding and a range of human types all of which facilitate political mobilization. At an even more general level, the preconditions for political mobilization can be subsumed under two broad headings: conditions promoting solidarity based on a consciousness of similarities extending beyond local territorial limits;[19] and conditions revealing what Weber called 'the *transparency* of the connection between the causes and the consequences of the "class situation"'.[20]

Marx's purpose in his account of the French peasantry was to explain why the peasants had overwhelmingly supported Louis Napoleon in 1848–1852. He saw it as the result of their incapacity to 'represent themselves', making them vulnerable to enchantment by a political adventurer laying claim to a great name from the past. In addition to the prerequisites for political mobilization in general, their example also raises the issue of the nature of representation itself, of the relationship between a political organization – including an ambitious or charismatic individual and his entourage – and the larger constituency the organization claims to represent. Marx's view that the peasantry could not organize but would always depend on self-selected outsiders to represent it does not mean that, like many in the anarcho-syndicalist tradition, he believed the proletariat to be capable of spontaneous mass action, merely that it would, in contrast to the peasantry, in time create its own organization with leaders recruited from its ranks. But even this eventuality does not dispose of the representation problem around which the issue of 'party-class' relations posed by Leninism and the interminable discussions of Michels' 'iron law of oligarchy' have revolved.

The ideal type of a politically mobilized group includes the political scientists' parties and pressure groups but can be understood more broadly as equivalent to Weber's concept of 'party' which he did not restrict to organized groups seeking to capture state power whether by force or by winning elections.[21] Politically mobilized groups are what one writer has called 'demand-bearing' groups, another 'challenging' groups.[22] I prefer the simpler label 'power-seeking' groups. The type of group commonly called a 'social' or 'mass' movement refers to newly mobilized or mobilizing collectivities that have recently acquired a heightened sense of solidarity focused on a political demand without yet having produced a specialized permanent leadership and organization claiming to represent a larger following through routine channels and institutionalized procedures.[23] Social movements are transitional formations emerging at the boundary where, in a phrase of the poet, John Berryman's, 'political life issues from social life like a somatic dream'. They arise at the point of intersection between the spheres of public and 'private' life, between the associational life of society and formal political organizations such as parties, established interest groups, and the multiple structures of government itself. For this reason, political sociologists, and not only those in the 'collective behaviour' tradition, have always been particularly interested in social movements, often tending to leave parties and established interest groups to political scientists or theorists of formal organization.

Politically mobilized groups are distinguishable from the larger collectivities they claim to represent, although social movements, as we have seen, emerge at the borderline between diffusely solidary and more organized groups. An authoritarian demagogue like Louis Napoleon or a totalitarian party may effectively substitute themselves for 'the people' or the class in whose name they act both at the level of ideology and by institutionalizing a *Fuehrerprinzip* or the practice of 'democratic centralism'. But interaction between leader or organized power-seeking group and the followings they claim to represent is rarely so unilateral, even in the case of those nominally membership-controlled groups to which Michels' 'law' is most applicable. Classes, of course, are the relevant larger constituencies to Marxists. Lehman has coined the more inclusive term 'macro-solidary groups' for the largest political constituencies into which modern societies are divided.[24] Routine journalistic commentary on national politics identifies 'blue-collar workers', 'blacks', 'the business community', 'suburbia' and the like as broad constituencies sharing common political sentiments. These labels are not intended to refer merely to demographic or statistical aggregates; although political outlook is related to age, sex and educational level as attributes of individuals, 'women' or 'old people' are also seen as political constituencies oriented to special issues affecting them though their numbers fall far short of the total demographic or social category to which they belong.

Voting blocs are the least solidary and organized politically mobilized units in constitutional democracies which hold regular elections based on universal suffrage. Electoral support registered by the total vote received by a party or candidate is a collective resource based on the aggregation of the individual votes of many citizens. Dahl included the right to vote on his list of individual political resources. The right to vote is exclusively a political resource in that, unlike money or free time, it cannot be used for other than political ends; votes can be bought, but the secret ballot makes it impossible for the buyer to know with certainty that he has received what he purchased. The right to vote by secret ballot extended to all adult citizens was, of course, itself the object of intense political struggle in Western democracies over the past century and a half.

The act of voting requires a minimum of effort and sacrifice once the electoral machinery has been established. It is usually regarded as the most elementary form of political participation by writers concerned with classifying and measuring different degrees of individual participation in politics.[25] Research on voting has fully demonstrated that voters for the same party or candidate often perceive their programmes very differently, even as standing for diametrically opposed policies. Thus the beliefs and values shared by the members of a voting bloc may be quite limited in number. Nor do voters require much organization; what little is needed may be supplied by election officials or by the campaign staffs of parties, which engage in activities ranging from publicizing their candidate to driving voters to the polls on election day.

Yet even Marx's scattered and isolated French peasants showed sufficient solidarity to vote by large majorities for Louis Bonaparte on three separate occasions between 1848 and 1852, however misguided they may have been in seeing him as the embodiment of their interests and values. High electoral turnout and high rates of voting by members of classes and status groups for the party or candidate claiming to represent their interests amount to a minimal form of political mobilization. The conditions favouring high turnout and class or status-based voting can be seen as special cases of the conditions conducive to more demanding and intensive political mobilization. Indeed they largely reflect the effects of other primarily non-political forms of mobilization: union membership in the case of workers, networks of formal and informal social ties in the case of the middle and upper classes, and the degree of homogeneity of their social environments in both cases. Workers who form relatively isolated occupational communities such as miners or sailors, and farmers who grow a single cash crop subject to sharp price fluctuations, are particularly likely to achieve negative solidarity in opposition to employers and commercial middlemen which is expressed in high rates of voting for parties appealing to their interests as well as in other ways.[26] The visible power of employers over wages and working conditions – and living conditions in company towns – of distributors and processors over the price of agricultural produce, and the obvious possibility of government regulation to limit these powers, encourage solidarity and organization. Marx's peasants of the Vendée were isolated from regular contacts with each other as well as with other groups; the relative social and geographical isolation of some occupational communities of workers and commercial farmers,[27] however, may increase their interactions with each other while reducing their contacts with outsiders and conflicting communications that expose them to political 'cross-pressures', thereby favouring rather than deterring political mobilization.

Lipset lists the following social traits as correlates of high turnout and high rates of interest-group voting: high income, high education, occupations that form relatively bounded communities, middle and old age, long-time residence in a community, marriage, membership in organizations, minority group status and residence in a relatively advanced economic region.[28] All of these traits can be interpreted as reflecting one or more of the conditions promoting political mobilization in general: wider contacts and communications; more leisure; higher levels of information, education and skill in human relations favourable to political awareness and organization; the transparency of the connection between the exercise of power by others and a given group or 'class situation'; the obvious relevance of government policy to group interests; greater awareness of the size of the group—of the power of numbers and of occupational monopoly; and high social density combined with limited interaction with non-members of the group. The obvious advantages in nearly all of these respects of middle and upper class urbanites are also evident from Lipset's account, as are those of ethnic and religious communities which he stresses in a later publication.[29] Voting blocs are the least solidary and least organized politically mobilized collectivities, but they conform nevertheless to wider generalizations about the creation and maintenance of collective resources.

Political mobilization ranges from fully mobilized power-seeking groups to the larger, relatively unorganized constituencies, including voting blocs, that they claim to represent. Classes, status groups, ethnic and religious groups, regional and local communities, and ascriptive groups based on bonds of sex, age, generation or race are all targets for mobilization and constrain the decisions and actions of power holders and power seekers. The relationship between the fully mobilized and the diffusely solidary larger groups, whether phrased as the problem of party-class relations or, more broadly, as the problem of representation in general, is a crucial focus of political analysis.[30] But the non-political group structure of society is also relevant in a variety of ways to the possibilities of politics and the uses of political power.

Mediation Between State and Society

Groups mobilize politically in order to gain access to the decision-making agencies of the state. In the ideal model of representative democracy, the political process is pictured somewhat as follows. The people articulate their diverse demands through parties and interest groups which mediate between them and the state. These mediating organizations compete for public or official support – by appealing for votes in state-regulated electoral contests in the case of parties. The winner is awarded temporary control of the powers of the state and forms a government or administration to carry out the mandate received from the people. If parties are organizational vehicles for translating the desires of their supporters into political demands, governments possess the integral powers of the state enabling them to act autonomously in many scopes and within wide zones of acceptance, although their performance is eventually subject to the electoral test. On assuming office, the party politician becomes a statesman, literally a 'state's man', although the tension between his role as party leader continuously engaged in 'politics' in anticipation of the next election and as national leader provides much of the ammunition for attacks on his administration by the opposition parties. Since he is now leader of 'all the people', not merely of those who voted him into office, he is expected to strive to serve the interests of the entire public or the 'national interest'. Parties represent the sectional constituencies from which they draw support; governments try to strike a balance between the claims of party, the voters who elected them, and the 'public interest'; both act within the framework of the state structure as laid down by the legal order, often partially embodied in a written constitution.

The proverbial bright schoolchild would dismiss this description of representative democracy as partly mythical (especially since the Watergate scandal). Yet it correctly pictures politics as involving three levels even if it misconceives or grossly oversimplifies the interactions between them. As a skeletal model of the polity, it identifies the triad of the state shaped by the legal and constitutional order, political organizations that compete for access to or control over it, and an underlying substratum of politics consisting of diffusely solidary political constituencies, organized groups engaged in non-political activities including local communities, small informal groups and families, and loose aggregates lacking solidarity and organization that are at least possible targets for mobilization (see figure p. 159). A great

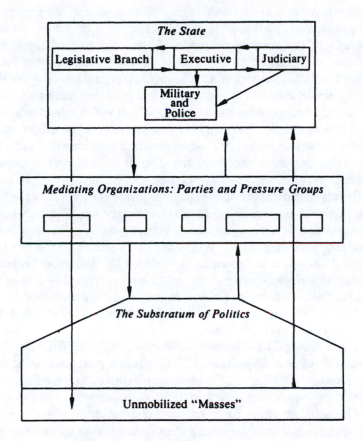

deal of what happens in politics and various ways of conceptualizing the political process can be interpreted in terms of the interactions and interdependences between state, mediating political organizations and the substratum of politics – that is, the social order as distinct from the political order. Since this book is not intended to be a complete treatise in political sociology, I shall confine myself to suggesting that this three-tiered model provides a useful perspective on the generation and distribution of collective resources and on a variety of contrasting theoretical and ideological views of the political process.

The three levels are fully visible in constitutional democracies which allow for the formation of rival political organizations that compete for votes, both as a means of selecting governments (in Schumpeter's well-known formulation[31]) and as a consequence of basic freedoms of speech, the press, and assembly. Yet in all democracies the proportion of the population participating in politics remains far below the ideal standards of the democratic credo. Little over half of the eligible electorate may choose to vote, as in recent American presidential elections; the political parties may be *de facto* oligarchies controlled by small groups of eternally incumbent leaders; and the state bureaucracy may use its administrative expertise and security of tenure to modify or defeat policies that are initiated by elected governments. 'Élitist' critics of representative democracy have endlessly documented and stressed such deviations from the democratic ideal of widespread popular participation, whether they have chosen to condone or deplore them. Yet there is considerable evidence that the forms of democracy continue to be cherished even by citizens who rarely make use of them, whether because of limited aspirations, complacency with things as they are or despairing 'alienation'. Since World War II democratic regimes have collapsed or been overthrown to be replaced by military or one-party dictatorships in many 'new nations' of the underdeveloped world as well as in such older nations as Chile, Uruguay and the Philippines. On the other hand, 'temporary' dictatorships have proved unstable and have been overwhelmingly repudiated at the polls in Greece and India, and Spain and Portugal have witnessed the surprisingly rapid restoration of democracy after long periods of authoritarian rule. Democracy has been a spectre haunting the Communist regimes of Eastern Europe, as revealed by events in Hungary in 1956, Czechoslovakia in 1968, and more localized revolts in East Germany and Poland.

By definition, non-democratic rulers do not permit themselves to be voted out of office and deny or severely curtail political freedoms. Yet even under authoritarian regimes – short of the (largely hypothetical) complete totalitarian atomization discussed in Chapter 5 – covert politically-oriented groups engage in backstairs plotting, court intrigues and veiled efforts to win advancement for their members or to promote favoured policies. The assumption that such groups flourished even under Stalin's dictatorial rule was central to the art of 'Kremlinology' developed by analysts of the Soviet regime to try to determine which men and whose policies were winning or losing in a hidden struggle for power.[32] More recently, China-watchers have devised similar techniques. Such political cliques and factions within the ruling party constitute at least a distorted version of a party system in contemporary Communist societies. Although hardly to be regarded as performing a regular representative function, they do on occasion serve to 'mediate' covertly between the party-state regime and larger social groups which in industrial and industrializing societies are inescapably subject to the impact of political decisions, especially when decision-making is as centralized as it is under Communist rule.[33] Centre and periphery, state and economy, the political and the social, although more sharply differentiated structurally, are more closely interwoven in industrial than in non-industrial societies.

The large-scale agrarian societies of the past can be ranged, as Lenski has contended, along an 'autocracy-oligarchy continuum' according to the degree to which the ruler is able to assert his power over the landowning nobility and the bureaucracy on which he depends or is checked by these groups to the point where he becomes little more than *primus inter pares*, the status to which they constantly endeavour to reduce him.[34] Struggle between the ruler and the 'governing class' of nobles and officials is a constant in agrarian civilizatiqns. Rulers have sought to check their power by a variety of means, including choosing aliens, eunuchs, or members of unpopular minorities such as Court Jews as their chief administrators or by seeking political advice only from their mistresses of humble origin rather than from those with aristocratic connections.[35] One might regard the cliques and cabals jostling for access to the ruler or for preferments that restrict his power over them as rough equivalents of mediating politically organized groups; the landowning nobility, the class of retainers, the priesthood, and to a lesser extent the merchant class are then equivalent to larger politically-oriented constituencies. Lenski describes the class of retainers as performing 'the crucial task of mediating relations between the governing class and the common people'. But he means that the retainers 'deflected much of the hostility and resentment which otherwise would have been directed at the political élite' rather than that they served as an upward channel for communicating to their rulers the wishes and discontents of the lower classes.[36] Moreover, all the classes and groups involved in politics amounted to no more than 10 per cent of the population, the vast majority consisting of peasants who were the passive victims of domination and exploitation.[37] The only forms of resistance available to the peasantry were banditry or sporadic, usually hopeless, violent rebellion.

Pre-industrial rulers sometimes made allies of the lower classes against the nobility or the plutocracy. Such 'caesaristic dictatorships', in Franz Neumann's term,[38] largely arose in republican city states or, as in the case of the Roman emperors, the alliance was with the urban plebs in the capital city. Our most ancient images of politically mobilized masses are of the Roman mobs rallied by demagogues who promised them 'bread and circuses'. But these examples, like the plebiscitarian dictatorships of modern times, occurred in societies where democratic beliefs and representative institutions, however decayed, existed, the term 'democracy' itself being, of course, of classical origin. Urban plebs in such settings were obviously more available for political mobilization than the peasantry of vast agrarian empires ruled by hereditary dynasties. To be sure, a disposition on the part of the lower classes to see the ruler as their father and protector against the governing class was present under Oriental despotisms and was doubtless encouraged by the rulers themselves; the many legends of rulers disguising themselves to mingle with the crowds in the bazaar to find out the needs of their subjects, of which the tale of Harun-al-Rashid is the best known, suggest as much. But these tales also attest to the isolation of the ruler from the masses and their non-involvement in his political struggles with the governing classes. There was little or no substratum of politics in which these struggles were even shallowly rooted.

The three-tiered model represented diagramatically on page 159 exists, then, only in distorted form in totalitarian or semi-totalitarian industrial societies and in thoroughly truncated form in the agrarian societies of the past. Before the French Revolution, the three levels were visible and partly institutionalized only in the city states of classical Greece and Rome and Medieval Europe. Since the 'age of the democratic revolution', in R. R. Palmer's phrase, both theories of politics and political ideologies – always, of course, closely intertwined – have been largely preoccupied with the relations between the three levels, both with what they are in reality and with what they ought to be in a properly ordered society. The state by definition exercises ultimate power in society and is placed at the top of the figure viewed vertically. The mediating power-seeking groups of the second level, each possessing its own internal power structure, mobilize supporters at the third level. The arrows running downward indicate these power relations between the levels. But where representative institutions exist, the two higher levels are responsive to the demands of the people at the third level – the groups, strata, and publics forming the political substratum. Thus the figure also includes arrows running in the reverse direction. William Gamson would label as 'social control' the arrows running downward from the state, which alone possesses the legitimate power to make decisions that are binding upon the whole population.

The arrows running upward he would call 'influence', indicating the process by which classes and groups compete in an effort to obtain state decisions that accord with their interests and values.[39]

Each level is itself divided and interaction takes place *within* as well as between levels; hence the horizontal arrows connecting the various divisions at each level. In constitutional democracies, the executive, legislative and judicial branches of the state are structurally distinct and their relations are legally regulated.Within the executive branch, the subordination of the army and the police, the actual wielders of the state's coercive powers, to the civil authorities is also a criterion of constitutional government. Political power is further subdivided in federal states. Civil freedom encourages the existence of a plurality of parties and interest groups at the second level. The number of parties, partly shaped by the electoral laws establishing the terms of their competition, form party systems, coherent entities capable of being studied by political scientists.[40] The third level is not that of a homogeneous 'people' or 'public' as in simplistic versions of the democratic creed but contains all the stratifications, differentiations and cleavages that comprise the diversity of complex societies. There is a 'pluralism', in short, at each level: constitutional pluralism affirmed by doctrines of checks and balances in the structure of the state; party pluralism at the mediating level; and societal or group pluralism at the level of the underlying social structure. Since all societies are pluralistic in that they are not undifferentiated hordes, the pluralism relevant to modern politics implies more than sheer social heterogeneity: it requires the existence of classes and groups in which membership is not ascriptive and which do not fully enclose the individual, completely determining his outlook and his life-chances.[41]

Only a minority of the population participate in politics at any of the three levels except for voting, and occasionally little more than half of the eligible electorate bothers even to vote (fewer still in local or subnational elections). Participants and non-participants are not randomly distributed among the various classes and groups composing the social order. Wealthier, more educated, higher-status citizens – those possessing greater individual resources – are more active at all levels and more disposed to aggregate their resources to produce politically effective concentrations of collective resources. For this reason, the arrows showing upward influence in Figure 2 do not begin at the base of the trapezoid representing the substratum of politics. The apathetic and unorganized – 'the mute, voiceless masses' – are nevertheless included in the diagram because in democracies with universal suffrage they exercise at least anticipatory influence on the state and on politicians at the second level in contrast to the lower classes in traditional agrarian societies.[42] Whether this anticipatory influence constrains political élites to take their interests into account or whether it leads to élite manipulation and the inculcation of 'false consciousness' is a major point of contention between 'pluralist' and 'élitist' theorists of democracy, as is the related argument over whether the apathy of the majority reflects relative contentment or hopelessness induced by a felt lack of opportunity to exercise significant political power.[43]

The relations of different groups in the substratum to the political process is a major focus of controversy in political thought. A sociological approach is inherently inclined to seek for the social bases of politics and to regard both power-seeking groups and the state itself as shaped by 'deeper' social forces. 'In the history of ideas,' as Aron has written, 'sociology can almost be defined by the primacy of the concept of society over the concept of politics (or the state)'.[44] The classical nineteenth-century sociological perspective might be summed up as asserting the historical, causal and moral priority of society over the state. *Historical* in that it repudiated the idea of a state of nature that was pre-social as well as pre-political, as maintained most starkly by Hobbes; *causal* in that society was seen as shaped not by the statecraft of rulers or the content of laws but by impersonal collective forces of which men in the past were largely unaware but which social science was now bringing to light; *moral* in that political leaders were urged to accommodate themselves to these forces rather than futilely obstruct them, for progress and social harmony lay in accepting the necessities of man's nature, of social evolution and of the conditions of social organization as revealed by the new sociology.[45] Sociology had affinities with both socialism and conservatism in insisting that the pattern of collective life established the opportunities and limits to what might be achieved through the exercise of political power.[46] Socialists wished to abolish the distinction between private and public itself in order to eliminate inequalities arising from the unequal distribution of private property; Marxist socialists saw the emerging proletariat as the collective actor destined to forge a fully socialized humanity. Conservatives in the aftermath of the French Revolution switched their allegiance from the state to society when confronted with a partially democratized political order open to pressures for reform and with the birth of the idea of revolution as a political means of achieving thoroughgoing social change.[47]

Both socialism and conservatism were collectivist in their opposition to bourgeois liberalism and the doctrines of classical economics and utilitarian philosophy in which it found expression. In addition to articulating the separation of state and society, sociology also arose as a challenge to the primacy claimed for relations of economic exchange among men. The 'discovery of society'[48] involved recognition of social relations as an autonomous realm, on the one hand distinct from narrow political and economic relations, and, on the other, including the latter as special cases of the more inclusive category of the 'social'. Economic individualism from Hobbes and Locke to Adam Smith and Jeremy Bentham lacked an adequate conception of society and of human nature as the product of social life; hence the 'revolt against individualism' shared by sociology, socialism and conservatism. Yet the notion of a self-regulating market governed by the famous 'invisible hand' contributed to the view of society and the social process as independent of the state.[49] Hegel's idea of 'civil society' was directly influenced by Smith, and Marx's reversal of the Hegelian subordination of civil society to the state represented a distinctively sociological viewpoint shared with Saint-Simon, Comte, Spencer, Sumner and the other 'founding fathers' of sociology. As the last two names suggest, economic individualism was capable of being reconstituted as a sociology. The kinship between the radical Karl Marx's view that the economic base shaped the political and legal superstructure and the pro-capitalist William Graham Sumner's dictum that 'stateways cannot change folkways' is surely obvious despite their different conceptions of the fundamental nature of the dominant social reality.

This excursion into the history of ideas is only apparently remote from our subject, for the intellectual bias of classical sociology has often been perpetuated in the approach of contemporary political sociologists to the empirical study of politics. They have tended to stress the arrows running upward in the figure, particularly in treating the mediating political organizations as instruments or expressions of the groups in the substratum that support them or from which their leaders are recruited. Parties are seen as 'reflecting' the interests of the groups, usually classes, that they claim to represent. The party system therefore is a mirror of the cleavages in the social structure rather than in part the result of the form of balloting prescribed by election laws. In some of the most influential voting studies, the voter's decision is treated as essentially an expression of his non-political ties and allegiances, especially of the informal networks of kin, neighbours, and friendship cliques in which he participates. At the community level, the elected government has been considered subservient to the informal control of 'economic dominants', usually successful local businessmen. Some studies of community power have almost seemed to be mini-versions of the orthodox Marxist view of the state as the 'executive organ of the ruling class' – that is, the bourgeoisie.

Sociological emphasis on the interaction between society and the state has long since transformed political scholarship, replacing detailed exegeses of statutory and constitutional law and descriptive accounts of the formal structure and functioning of government which minimized or ignored the social content of politics. But more recently, students of politics, not all of them political scientists rather than sociologists, have criticized the reductionism and unilateralism of a variety of sociological approaches to politics. At the theoretical level, the subordination of the state and politics to society has been challenged by both Marxist and non-Marxist thinkers.[50] These challenges have been evoked by such twentieth-century experiences as the rise of totalitarianism, the greater intervention of the state in the market economy, and the increasing penetration of welfare and of warfare states into the daily lives of their citizens. But even at the level of more circumscribed areas of empirical research, the one-sidedness of recently dominant sociological approaches to politics has been criticized.

Political parties have been recognized as not merely articulating the demands of their followers, but as aggregating into a coherent programme the multiple, sometimes conflicting demands of the diverse groups to which they appeal for support.[51] They may indeed *mediate* between the social structure and political decision-making, between society and the state, but in a more creative, synthesizing fashion than that word has often been taken to imply. Parties are even more autonomous in so far as they succeed over time in mobilizing the unmobilized, organizing the unorganized, giving a voice to the voiceless: they may raise demands, create issues and mount appeals which do not just reflect the established outlook and sentiments of their constituencies but which succeed in mobilizing previously latent groups, creating solidarity and consensus on collective goals where none before existed. I have already noted that this may happen in the case of ethnic groups which, although sharing elements of a common culture, lack any sense of collective identity. Of classes, defined by common objective economic conditions, Giovanni Sartori has observed:

> To put it bluntly, it is not the 'objective' class (class condition) that creates the 'subjective' class (class consciousness). More carefully put, whenever parties reflect social classes, this signifies *more* about the party end than about the class end of the interaction. The party is not a 'consequence' of the class. Rather, and before, it is the class that receives its identity from the party. Hence class behaviour presupposes a party that not only feeds, incessantly, the 'class image', but also a party that provides the structural cement of 'class reality'. . . . In sum, large collectivities become class structured only it they are class persuaded; and the most likely and apt 'persuader' is the party (or the union) playing on class-appeal.[52]

Nor are party systems reducible to the 'cleavage structure' of the societies in which they exist. To begin with, they are to some extent shaped by the election laws, that is, at the level of the state rather than of the substratum in the figure, although Maurice Duverger's argument that proportional representation promotes a multi-party system and single-member plurality district voting a two-party system was grossly overstated.[53] Of greater significance, a party system once it has been established possesses an inertia and durability of its own independently of changes in the underlying social structure. As Lipset and Rokkan have contended, party systems reflect *past* cleavages in the society which achieved political expression at historical transitional points when nation-building was completed and/or when the franchise was first universalized or when the working classes first achieved political mobilization.[54] The party systems of most Western democracies (not including the United States) became established and 'frozen', as Lipset and Rokkan put it, in the 1920s. This freezing process and inertia mean that new cleavages and group conflicts may develop outside the system of party competition and may pose a threat to the democratic regime or even to the survival of the nation itself. The most obvious and venerable example is the conflict between Northern and Southern states over slavery which fragmented the American party system in the late 1850s and led to civil war.

The conditions under which the political stability sustained by the partial autonomy of parties and party systems becomes a dangerous rigidity are bound to be debatable. Theodore Lowi regards parties and interest groups — the mediating political organizations — as subject to what he calls, in a variation of Michels, an 'iron law of decadence'. He looks to social movements, nascent rather than fully organized groups, to revitalize democracy by freeing it from the restraints and deadlocks of the balance of power among established groups who represent only a small minority of the population. Lowi argues that

> Governments in the United States – federal, state, and local – have never moved with greater certainty or with greater effectiveness than when pushed by movements. And governments never move more vaguely and ineffectively, and never resist change so adroitly, than when guided by needs as defined by groups in a group bargaining process.[55]

Social movements springing up out of the substratum of politics upset stasis at the levels of the mediating groups and the governmental structure. Lowi's polemic is against the blurring of the distinction between the two levels of the state, the creator and enforcer of the legal order, and the groups striving for access to it. The interpenetration of interest groups and governmental agencies constitutes what Lowi called in an earlier book 'interest-group liberalism' and 'policy without law' is one of its consequences.[56] Lowi is essentially concerned with interest groups rather than political parties, but he regards both American parties as having embraced interest-group liberalism, thus partially abdicating their proper representative role in Congress.

As a political scientist, Lowi focuses on the relinquishment of the distinctive legitimate and coercive power of the state to make public policy to a bargaining process with interest groups that both 'privatizes' and at the same time gives governmental legitimation to administrative policy-making bypassing public law. His first book largely consisted of detailed illustrations of this in the areas of agriculture, the urban crisis, anti-poverty programmes, the federal regulatory commissions and even military and foreign economic policy. Social movements surging upward from below, he argued in his second book, can alone be expected to revive the centralized authority of democratic government by reactivating the *formal* procedures of legislative and executive decision-making in place of informal arrangements that consolidate and give quasi-legal status to established interest groups. If successful, social movements are subject to the iron law of decadence and become incorporated into the system of institutionalized log-rolling; for this reason, 'the good democrat should try to foster new groups and should distrust old groups'.[57]

Lowi's quarrel is partly with his fellow political scientists whom he sees as having provided, though largely unwittingly, ideological legitimation for interest-group liberalism. And to remedy the latter condition, he invokes social movements, which, as we have seen, have always been an object of study particularly attractive to sociologists who have treated them as spontaneous eruptions of popular discontent in response to deep-seated strains and dysfunctions produced by social change. Even sociologists like Smelser, who have been primarily concerned with the structural preconditions for the rise of social movements, have relied heavily on mass social psychological concepts such as 'anxiety', 'hostile outburst', 'mood of protest', 'generalized wish-fulfilment fantasy' and the like.[58] But social movements have no more than parties and party systems escaped the recent tendency of sociologists to give greater attention to the partial autonomy of politics, that is to the creative and independent role played by mobilizing individuals and organizations often from outside the collectivity they seek to lead and represent. Far from spontaneously overflowing into action, '. . . grievances and discontents may be defined, created, and manipulated by issue entrepreneurs and organizations.'[59] This approach has been aptly described as a 'resource mobilization' theory of movements in contrast to the traditional 'collective behaviour' perspective favoured by earlier sociologists.[60]

Advocates of this approach have taken very seriously the 'Olson problem' that 'rational, self-interested individuals will not act to achieve their common or group interests'.[61] This is so, argues the economist, Mancur Olson, Jr., because individuals will benefit from the collective good (in the economist's language) that is achieved as a result of organization whether or not they contribute their own mite of individual resources to the joint effort. 'Let George do it' is the most rational maxim to follow, at least where the group formed to realize a common goal is a large one. Only those who have 'selective incentives' to contribute to collective action are sufficiently motivated to do so — such incentives as the personal power, prestige and gain to be won by assuming a leadership role in organizing and directing the group effort. Rather than relying on voluntary pooling of resources in the service of a collective goal, coercion or special inducements are often necessary to mobilize collective resources, as in the examples of compulsory trade union membership or taxation for services provided by governments. I shall return to the Olson problem at a later point; suffice it to note here that it suggests that the obstacles to collective mobilization are greater than they are often thought to be and that more weight must be given to the part played by leaders and organizers who benefit or expect to benefit from selective rewards.

In opposition to the treatment of the voting decision as a reflection of the voter's non-political group ties, it has been argued that, though often poorly informed about the issues in a campaign, the voter nevertheless makes an essentially *political* judgement rooted in specifically political attitudes, even if his decision is based on a rational assessment of his informants on politics rather than directly of the candidates, their parties and programmes.[62] I have already reviewed in the previous chapter the debate over community power studies initiated by Dahl and his fellow-researchers who have insisted on the relative independence of the actual political decision-makers as opposed to the behind-the-scenes influence of individuals and groups rich in resources who do not hold official positions. If Dahl and his associates challenged the readiness of some sociological researchers to see politicians as mere front-men for socially dominant groups, their most effective critics, such as Peter Bachrach, Robert Presthus and Matthew Crenson, have also been political scientists; scarcely inclined to depreciate the importance of political power, these critics have objected primarily to the too narrow behaviouristic conception of it adopted by the New Haven team.

The newer recognition of the relative autonomy of political action, of politics as a partially 'independent variable', does not imply a retreat to a pre-sociological view of society as a mere given,[63] passive material to be shaped and transformed by individual and collective political actors. No serious scholars have entertained new versions of 'great man' or 'conspiracy' theories of history (except perhaps with strictly limited reference to Nazism and Stalinism), or even nineteenth-century German idealist views that the state is the quintessential expression and fulfilment of a people's culture and destiny. In the words of George Lichtheim:

> The distinction between state and society lies at the root of modern political thought. Every theorist who defines the subject of politics – and *a fortiori* every practitioner who concerns himself with the exercise of power – makes the primary assumption that the two spheres are separable, react upon each other, and are definable in ways that are immediately obvious to everyone. Indeed the very notion of politics depends upon the ability to make such a distinction.[64]

Reference to Lichtheim serves to remind us that even Marxism, in some ways the example *par excellence* of the nineteenth-century view of politics as epiphenomenal shared with 'bourgeois' sociologists, has increasingly abandoned this standpoint. Central to the thought of the most influential recent thinkers in the Marxist tradition (excluding, of course, what passes for thought in the Communist countries) has been a revisionist emphasis on the independent role of the state under capitalism, an insistence that it is more than a mere instrument in the hands of the dominant class, the owners of the means of production. The names of Habermas, Offe, Althusser, Poulantzas and O'Connor suffice to indicate the salience of 'state theory', as it has been called, in contemporary Marxist or neo-Marxist thought. The virtual canonization of Gramsci as an intellectual ancestor is also notable, Gramsci having always moved in the Machiavellian ambience of Italian thought which was never disposed to minimize the importance of political power. There is also the immense prestige of the original Frankfurt School theorists who, although not specifically concerned with the role of the state as such, abandoned in their cultural studies and critique of ideology the crude determinism of the doctrine that the economy was 'base' and all else 'superstructure'. The existential phenomenological Marxism of Merleau-Ponty and Sartre deserves mention as well for its emphasis on freedom of choice and the will to individual or collective action as historically crucial. These names and schools suggest the range, diversity and even discord within the universe of thinkers who still claim derivation from Marxism, although all of them have clearly rejected the 'orthodox' Maxism of the old Second International and the official Soviet creed.

Yet at the level of practice, Marxists have always renounced the view that politics is secondary by giving priority, in opposition to anarchists, syndicalists and trade union 'economism', to political action directed towards the capture of state power.[65] Only after the revolution and the achievement of socialism is the state expected to 'wither away' and in the meantime it remains the prime instrument for the reorganization of society. Yet reorganization does not have to start from scratch, for the new society has already formed itself in the womb of the old before the revolution as the 'midwife of history' brings it to birth. Marxism thus provides warrant for both the orthodox German Social Democratic ideology of inevitable transition to socialism, even in the absence of continuous militant political action, and Leninism with its voluntaristic insistence on the party as the agent of revolution imposing its long-term goals on the working class in whose name it acts.[66] The split between

Lenin's inevitabilist theory and his voluntaristic practice paved the way for Stalin's 'revolution from above' which in reality totally reversed the subordination of state to economy and society in the traditional doctrine still enshrined as the official ideology of the Soviet regime.[67] Trotsky was one of the first to grasp the totalitarian essence of Stalinism in concluding his biography of Stalin with the penetrating remark that

> '*L'État, c'est moi*' is almost a liberal formula by comparison with the actualities of Stalin's totalitarian regime. . . . The totalitarian state goes far beyond Caesaro-Papism, for it has encompassed the entire economy of the country as well. Stalin can justly say, unlike the Sun King, '*La societé, c'est moi*'.[68]

Yet Trotsky resisted the full implications of his own insight in insisting up to the day of his murder by the GPU that the Soviet regime was a 'degenerated workers' state' subject to 'bureaucratic deformation'.

An emphasis on the indirect political effects of the non-political group structure of society is central to the so-called 'theory of mass society' that was popular in the 1940s and 1950s. As the historical experiences that evoked it have receded into the past, namely, the interwar 'fascist era' in Europe that culminated in World War II, this theory has been widely criticized along with various conceptions of politics in contemporary industrial societies with which it seemed to be closely linked. As so often happens in social thought (Hegel's Owl of Minerva principle), the most systematic, 'academic' formulation of the theory, William Kornhauser's *The Politics of Mass Society*,[69] appeared just before the political winds changed in the 1960s, as was also true of the related notion of 'the end of ideology'. The terrible events of the 1930s and the 1940s began to fade into memory, becoming cautionary tales addressed by the middle-aged to their fidgety juniors which invariably took the form of Santayana's admonition, inscribed at the exit from the museum on the site of the Dachau concentration camp, that 'those who forget the past are condemned to repeat it'.

To a later generation, the image of mobilized masses rallying behind hate-ridden demagogues seemed to reflect a conservative fear of *any* movements of protest demanding reforms, and the mass society theory was plausibly linked to the older nineteenth-century 'psychology of crowds' that expressed a reaction against the French Revolution and its successors with explicit anti-democratic overtones. Yet mass society theory was essentially an appalled response to the fascist movements, especially to National Socialism and the dictatorial regime it created, as well as, though to a much lesser extent, to Stalinism.[70] This background needs to be mentioned because later critics have tended to ignore it in assimilating the theory to more conventional brands of conservatism that stress the need for stability and the dangers of widespread popular participation in politics.[71]

Mass society has been a peculiarly protean notion which has assumed many different forms, some of which are still widely accepted.[72] I am concerned here solely with the version of mass society theory which attempts to account for the rise of militant political movements threatening to substitute themselves for both state and society as independent structures – with what might be called the 'demonic theory of the masses'. This theory can be regarded as an attempt to revise without abandoning the classical nineteenth-century view of the ascendancy of the social over the political in light of twentieth-century experience, in particular the emergence of totalitarianism. It did this by arguing that the weakening of the underlying social fabric by rapid, often convulsive social change made it possible for political movements to move into the resulting vacuum by mobilizing 'uprooted' masses in support of their bid for state power. The absence of a stable 'intermediate structure' – a phrase borrowed from Durkheim – encouraged large numbers of people to seek to overcome anomie by fervently attaching themselves to political movements promising individual and collective regeneration.

The notion of 'intermediate' groups or relations as a barrier to political mobilization is *not* equivalent to what I have called 'mediating organizations'. Intermediate groups are not conceived in this perspective as power-seeking organizations mediating in some more or less representative fashion between state and society, but rather as part of the realm of 'society' itself, of the substratum of politics, that mediates between the state and individual persons or, in Kornhauser's formulation, between the state and the primary groups, including families, that exist in all societies. The intermediate structure of larger groups such as voluntary associations, professional guilds and semi-autonomous local communities constitutes, in the language I have been employing, collective resources deployed for essentially non-political uses that make them unavailable for political mobilization. They are, in Gamson's terms, solidary groups with low political liquidity. Unlike a 'pluralist society' possessing intermediate groups, mass society does not keep men's sentiments from fastening on remote objects, precisely because it fails to absorb enough of the interests and emotions of its members into a variety of proximate concerns.[73]

The suggestion is that participation in intermediate groups channels people's time, energy and other individual resources away from politics. In a well-known pluralist argument, multiple group memberships are also held to breed a spirit of moderation and compromise by reducing the likelihood of intense commitments to the political expression of the interests and values of any single group. Socially unattached 'masses' are not so restrained.

The view that supporters of Nazi and fascist movements, as well as less successful versions of them in Western democracies, were drawn from the ranks of previously apolitical and socially isolated persons has been questioned on solidly empirical grounds. Criticism of the pluralist argument about the political effects of multiple group membership has become as conventional as the original argument. It is primarily based on the fact that only small middle- and upper-class minorities belong to more than one extra-familial association. I am not concerned here to review this familiar debate, but simply to note that the stress on the role of intermediate groups recognizes that they at least constitute collective resources with a potential for political use, as is routinely acknowledged by vote-seeking politicians who are eager to accept invitations to make 'non-partisan' speeches at Rotary Club luncheons, bar association banquets and even academic conventions. Any group is in this minimal sense a political resource. The social order is always a 'para-political' structure,[74] restraining or facilitating direct efforts at political mobilization.

One of the most telling criticisms of mass society theory is that intermediate groups can *facilitate* as well as deter support for new political movements. As Maurice Pinard showed in his study of the sudden success of the Social Credit Party in rural Quebec in the early 1960s, a movement can acquire almost instantaneous respectability and political momentum by winning the allegiance of the leaders of voluntary associations in the community.[75] The intermediate group structure can serve as a conveyor belt or channel for mobilization by a new movement rather than as a source of resistance to its spread.

Mass society theorists have not always clearly distinguished between a mass society and a totalitarian society.[76] Successful totalitarian movements are able to destroy remaining autonomous groups of all kinds in the society; by eliminating alternative sources of social attachment, they increase the psychic dependence on them that attracted supporters seeking to overcome anomie and alienation before they came to power. In this sense they carry even further the process of 'massification' allegedly initiated by urbanization, industrialization, secularization, the diffusion of a commercially produced 'mass culture' and the disruptions of war and economic depression. Thus totalitarianism is even more of a mass society than a weak, conflict-ridden democracy. This view possesses an attractive theoretical coherence, but the trouble is that it does not accurately describe conditions in any of the countries in which totalitarian movements have triumphed. An historian of Hitler's rise to power remarks that 'if there ever was a "mass society" in Germany it was a product of, not the cause for, the Third Reich'.[77] The demonic theory of the masses is largely based on the example of Weimar Germany. Pre-fascist Italy and Spain before Franco's military victory were scarcely mass societies. Russia before 1917 was the most politically and socially backward nation in Europe – 'communal' rather than 'mass' in Kornhauser's terminology – a fact not unconnected with its becoming, at least under Stalin, the most fully realized totalitarian society yet to exist.

The view that totalitarianism creates rather than grows out of a mass society is expressed in an apt 'dialectical' formulation by Leszek Kolakowski, describing Stalinism:

Its integration was identical with its disintegration; it was perfectly integrated in that all forms of collective life were entirely subordinated to, and imposed by, one ruling center; and it was perfectly disintegrated for the same reason: civil society was virtually destroyed, and the citizens, in all their relations with the state, faced the omnipotent apparatus as isolated and powerless individuals.[78]

The conception of a mass society that precedes and makes possible the success of a totalitarian movement shares with Kolakowski's portrait of Stalinism an emphasis on the isolation and powerlessness of the individual. But there is obviously an important difference: totalitarian regimes exercise centralized bureaucratic control over the lives of their subjects whereas an antecedent mass society is seen as tending towards an amorphous, undifferentiated social structure in which individuals are vulnerable to mass persuasion and the emotional contagions of crowd psychology. Totalitarian regimes may make use of techniques of persuasion and manipulate the mechanisms of crowd psychology in order to keep their subjects in a state of constant enthusiastic mobilization, but their subjects, though powerless, are not socially isolated in the sense of forming a 'mass' of footloose, 'privatized', anomic persons bereft of social attachments and leadership. For in addition to destroying all independent groups and subcultures, totalitarianism replaces them with its own co-ordinated structure of intermediate groups thoroughly penetrated and controlled from the centre – the process of *Gleichschaltung*, as the Nazis called it.[79] Totalitarianism creates, in effect, its own intermediate structure to serve as a protection against the possible opposition of independent groups and as a channel for mobilization in support of the regime; individuals are integrated into this structure.

The destruction of all independent groups, or their penetration and reconstitution as agencies of the party or dictator, evinces a recognition that all groups are para-political in consisting of concentrations of collective resources capable of being diverted to oppositional political uses, however limited and innocent their present employment. As Hannah Arendt put it, even chess clubs presumably committed to a belief in 'chess for chess' sake' are perceived as an implicit threat to the regime and must be destroyed, absorbed into a network of party-controlled associations or at the very least subjected to constant surveillance.[80] Even family loyalties are suspect. Totalitarian regimes have not confined their attention to 'secondary groups' or Kornhauser's 'intermediate relations' but have attempted to weaken or reshape the family as well. A tendency to move towards the complete elimination of the family and its replacement by bureaucratically regulated mating and collective childrearing institutions has often been imputed to totalitarianism. The 'breeding camps' allegedly conducted by the SS and official Nazi encouragement of illegitimate births have been interpreted in this light, as have Soviet policies in the 1920s, although in both cases these practices aimed at short-run objectives or were transitory. The family policies of the Communists and the Nazis did involve enrolling young people in party organizations – the Hitler Youth and the Komsomols – in order to reduce the authority over them of parents who had grown up in pre-revolutionary times, and children were encouraged to report evidence of political opposition on their parents' part. Yet the Nazis extolled ties of blood and kinship as part of their ideology and were fully sensitive to the usefulness of the family as the surrogate of the larger society in inculcating support of the regime once a reliable post-revolutionary generation had been produced.[81]

A stable family may be either a rival of the state for the loyalties of its members or a conservative bulwark of popular support for an established regime. Soviet family policy has in the sixty years since 1917 shifted from the first to the second attitude.[82] The institutions of marriage and the family themselves constitute a form of social control over dispositions to withdraw from obligations to the larger society.[83] Highly communal or collectivistic societies, of which totalitarianism is only one species, have tended to go even further in trying to prevent development of the intense personal attachments bred by sexual and parental bonds.[84] Yet the family as the major agency of socialization may also be a microcosm of the larger society serving to reinforce its controls. The earlier mass society theorists overemphasized the erosion of the family and of primary group ties in general in their stress on the 'isolation' and 'atomization' of the individual as a precondition for thoroughgoing mobilization by new political movements. They also overemphasized the actual or apparent anti-familial policies of the Nazis and Communists in the early years of their rule. As in the case of the larger 'secondary' groups, they overlooked the extent to which the family once the new regime is securely in power can function as a channel rather than an obstacle to political mobilization. One can even detect a certain nostalgic exaggeration of the autonomy and psychic self-sufficiency of the patriarchal or bourgeois family in the writings of some mass society theorists.[85]

If one moves from primarily interpretive theories about politics to more directly prescriptive statements, it is possible to identify the major ideological tendencies of modern history with different conceptions of the proper or ideal relation among the three levels of state, mediating organizations and substratum of politics. *Anarchism*, of course, stands for the abolition of the two top levels and regards the community as capable of governing itself without differentiated political structures by functioning when necessary as a kind of 'committee of the whole', as it were. Traditional *authoritarianism* dispenses with representative mediating organizations and strives to rule its subjects directly but without penetrating or interfering in many areas of their lives. *Totalitarianism* is a term that has for the most part been adopted by its opponents or analysts rather than a self-chosen label favoured by its supporters, although it was first used by Mussolini and his party ideologists to describe the goals of fascism in the 1920s. The Nazis occasionally spoke of the 'total state' as their goal, but the term did not figure prominently in their rhetoric. In practice, however, if not in the ideological discourse of the various movements and regimes to which the totalitarian label has been applied, their kinship has been seen as stemming from their common tendency to extol the supremacy of party, movement or leader over *both* state and society. What is formally a mediating organization, or began as one, becomes the final source of authority and, if successful, subordinates both state and society to its control. Hence the dual 'party-state' of totalitarian regimes and the duplication – even multiplication – of agencies at all three levels, the party, however, always remaining the real locus of power.[86]

The hallmark of *populism* is a deep distrust of all mediating organizations for which it wishes to substitute the direct expression of the 'will of the people'. Thus it is attracted both to direct democracy and to versions of corporatism that give formal political powers to classes and interest groups, eliminating altogether parties based on territorial representation.[87] Populist sentiments may be found from right to left across the full political spectrum, giving support, on the one hand, to plebiscitarian dictators of which Louis Napoleon was the first in a long line and at the other extreme favouring anarcho-syndicalist ideas or direct 'participatory' forms of democracy. In the older European societies, populism has had its roots in the peasantry, or, more broadly, the petty-bourgeoisie. While it has in the past often had an agrarian base in North America, the lack of highly developed class consciousness has given it wider appeal and populist attitudes expressing a distrust of 'élitism' in general and of party politicians and government bureaucrats in particular are frequently expressed by ambitious 'outsider' politicians such as George Wallace and, more recently in milder form, Jimmy Carter. Populist rhetoric indeed is something of a staple ingredient of all American political discourse.

Marxist socialism affirms the priority in the political process of one feature of the substratum: the class divisions resulting from the forces and relations of production. The capture of state power by the proletariat mobilized behind the mediating organization of a revolutionary party eliminates the autonomy of and the tension between all three levels of the polity. Since class conflict is seen as the essence of politics itself, the eventual achievement of a classless society after the revolution will also result in a stateless society when the state withers away with the attainment of the final phase of true communism. Such a doctrine, interpreted and vulgarized in a particular direction, is not inconsistent with Soviet ideology in which party, state and people are regarded as a unity and coercion by the state can by definition no longer be defined as oppressive.[88]

Pluralist democracy sees the substratum as the seedbed of a multitude of groups raising political demands in the defence and promotion of their interests and values which find expression in mediating organizations competing for access to state power. The competition is regulated by a constitutional and legal order which is itself regarded as the product of past consensus on the 'rules of the game'. As critics of pluralism have not failed to point out, the formal equality of rights of citizenship in the legal-political sphere is not inconsistent with the existence of marked social and economic inequalities rooted in private property and bureaucratic hierarchies, giving decisive advantages in the market economy to those with the most resources, which are transmitted to the next generation through the family. Yet those with few resources remain free to mobilize politically for the purpose of modifying prevailing inequalities in their favour; the use of the powers of government to regulate the market economy and to create the modern welfare state has been the major focus of domestic political struggle in Western democratic capitalist societies for over a century. Pluralist democracy as an ideal presupposes the participation of all individuals and groups in protecting and promoting their interests and values, but the inequality of resources creates formidable obstacles to the participation of the lower classes which are often overlooked by upholders of the ideal and minimized by academic theorists of pluralism. All persons sharing a common situation may be considered 'potential groups' capable of mobilizing to exercise political power,[89] but, as we have seen, there is a considerable gap between this potential and its realization. Nor is the attribution of at least anticipatory influence to the enfranchised lower classes by sophisticated pluralists such as Robert Dahl entirely satisfactory, for, as indicated in Chapter 6, anticipatory influence is a two-edged sword that can be used by minorities with ample resources as well as by relatively resourceless majorities possessing little more than the right to vote.

The Problem of Latent or Objective Collective Interests

People who share a common situation often have like interests which are capable of transformation into common interests. If they achieve successful mobilization by developing a sense of collective identity and finding or creating an organization to defend and promote their interests, the interests of all then become the interests of each. The maintenance of the organization and of the solidarity that helps sustain it becomes vitally relevant to the fulfilment of individual interests previously pursued in isolation or in competition with other members of the collectivity. The organization and the solidarity its existence symbolizes may even become a value in itself rather than being perceived merely as a useful instrument for protecting and advancing the individual interests of its members, although the degree to which this occurs is highly variable. (Compare, for example, American business unionism with the socialist working-class subculture of the SPD in Imperial Germany.[90].)

Religious and ethnic communities, as we have already seen, possess shared supra-individual beliefs and values that give them at least a diffuse solidarity. Religious believers already have organizations in the form of churches, sects, cults or denominations. Ethnic groups, as Randall Collins has pointed out, are simply former territorial communities that have been transported to another location where they come into closer contact with outsiders.[91] People who have only, or primarily, a shared social and economic situation in common lack even the minimal solidarity of unorganized religious and ethnic communities. In addition, their like interests tend to be secular and self-centred rather than sacred or normative. They face therefore much greater obstacles to mobilization even though the sheer numbers of people inescapably constrained by the situation that mobilization promises to improve may be vastly greater than the size of religious or ethnic groups. Religious and ethnic heterogeneity may, of course, itself be an additional obstacle.

Mobilization under such conditions is not likely to be instantaneous: it is a process more readily measured in decades than in years. Moreover, it may be achieved only temporarily in transitory crisis situations and show little staying power. Permanent mobilization and organizational consolidation are likely to require constant effort and collective discipline as well as tangible gains at the expense of dominant groups and power holders. It is no accident that working-class movements have so often adopted the very word 'solidarity' as a cherished and evocative slogan.[92] Despite the greater territorial and social density of the working class, their large numbers, lack of individual resources and engagement in physical rather than mental work are barriers to effective mobilization that differ only in degree from those confronted by the French peasants discussed by Marx in *The Eighteenth Brumaire*. The difficulties of sustaining solidarity, at least in the formative stages of labour movements, make it seem more than a mere means to the exercise of collective power but almost a moral achievement of intrinsic worth. As George Lichtheim put it,

> 'Solidarity' is for the worker what 'honor' was to the feudal order and 'honesty' for the bourgeois: a claim which is felt as absolute because the existence of the individual depends on it.[93]

One may speak of the 'latent interests' of collectivities subject to the relatively unlimited power of others over their means of subsistence and conditions of labour even when they have yet to mount any organized resistance to the demands of the power holders. Their interests are latent in that they have not become focused on articulated collective goals, let alone an organization, and their only overt manifestations are diffuse grumbling, covert expressions of protest and what Veblen called 'the conscientious withdrawal of efficiency'.[94] Slaves, prisoners and all inmates of coercive total institutions achieve such diffuse negative solidarity based on common interests in evading or passively resisting the demands of those who dominate them. Where domination is more restricted in scope, there are more favourable prospects for mobilization to convert latent interests into coherent collective goals and to organize to further them.

So understood, latent interests are obviously subjective psychological states, however inchoate, in the collective consciousness of groups subject to the power of others and cannot be equated with the 'objective interests' that have played so large a role in the Marxist tradition. Objective interests to Kautsky, Lenin and Lukács were by definition interests that are independent of the actual consciousness of the subordinate class; they are communicated to it by leaders from outside its ranks who lay claim to a superior understanding of the future course of history and the part the proletariat is destined to play in it, whether understood in positivist or Hegelian terms. The élitism of such a view and the rationale it provides for oligarchical, even totalitarian, rule by parties and regimes claiming Marxist inspiration have been pointed out often enough. An apotheosis of sorts was achieved in 1956 when in the streets of Budapest Russian tanks shot down 'in the interests of the Hungarian working class' flesh and blood workers who were defending a popular government of which György Lukács himself was a member.

Yet the issues raised by the notion of objective interests and the related concept of 'false consciousness' are not so easily dismissed. Versions of these ideas have recurred in the writings of social theorists who are in no sense apologists for the deeds of Communist states, nor Hegelians, nor even necessarily Marxists. False consciousness, in particular, is frequently used, if vaguely, by contemporary sociologists. Often it connotes no more than that people are ignorant and misinformed about the society in which they live and that their incorrect view of it is the result of control over their information supply and indoctrination in favour of the *status quo* practised by the dominant groups who are its chief beneficiaries. Marx's famous statement that the ideas of an epoch are the ideas of its ruling class and serve as ideological legitimations of its rule is often cited in this connection. Although Marx's view was actually more subtle and modulated, false consciousness – a term first used by Engels after Marx's death – is equivalent to 'ideology', the promulgation of which constitutes manipulation by collective power holders of their subjects.[95] There is nothing conceptually opaque about this use of false consciousness whatever its empirical merits.

But later Marxists, especially Lukács, have meant a good deal more than this and have linked the term to the notion of 'interests', which would seem on the face of it to be a concept referring to motivation rather than to cognition. Motivations are psychological dispositions to act, although they need not be conscious and may be expressed in action only in distorted, veiled and indirect form as in the classic Freudian account. In such a conception, interests are essentially wants or desires, however unconscious, and are clearly 'subjective' (even if collective rather than individual) as opposed to 'objective'. Objective interests are conceived of as non-psychological: they do not refer to any element present even latently, and therefore in principle subject to empirical confirmation, in the human psyche. To Lukács, they signify the total transformation of the psyche itself that will emerge in the moving 'totality' of history propelled by class conflict and/or in a post-revolutionary society that is the outcome of proletarian victory if and when the proletariat makes its revolution, i.e. becomes the 'subject-object' of history.[96] The party, the vanguard organization of Marxist intellectuals, must spur the proletariat to engage in revolutionary struggle since actual proletarian consciousness does not contain within it the disposition to embark upon such struggle in the absence of outside leadership. The revolutionary intellectual's understanding of the objective interests of the proletariat is not grounded in empirical knowledge as ordinarily understood but presupposes privileged insight into the historical future, insight derived in Lukács's case from a Hegelian interpretation of Marxism.

Without relying on such a claim to privileged insight, other writers have insisted nevertheless that a collectivity can be said to possess 'real' or 'objective' interests even if its members do not acknowledge such interests and profess to be satisfied with a *status quo* that fails to fulfil them. Though disguised as an empirical assessment, this often amounts to little more than the judgment that the group under consideration *ought to* give priority to those interests which the observer would prefer them to pursue – an outlook prevalent among radical intellectuals discouraged by the lack of revolutionary temper on the part of the masses and 'the damned wantlessness of the poor' – a phrase variously said to have been uttered in mock exasperation by Engels, Ferdinand Lassalle or George Bernard Shaw. (This might be called the 'let's you and him fight' syndrome.) The arrogance and implicit authoritarianism of such an outlook, which claims to know better than other people themselves what is good for them, are unmistakable.

Some sociologists, however, not all of them professed Marxists, have striven manfully to formulate a definition of objective interests that is at least in principle empirically supportable. They have argued that one can validly regard some interests as inherent in the positions or roles of a social structure in so far as the incumbents of these positions are constrained to act in certain ways if they are to retain their positions even if they hold subjective beliefs, sentiments and self-definitions discrepant with the required actions.[97] Marxists are likely to invoke in this connection the dictum that 'social being determines consciousness; consciousness does not determine social being'. There is, however, nothing specifically Marxist about this assertion – it might as readily have been made by Durkheim or by a host of later sociologists. The Marxist's classic example would presumably be the capitalist full of benevolent feelings who is compelled nevertheless by the system to exploit his workers if he is to survive the competition of his fellow-capitalists, but the shaping of actions (and also motives and beliefs) by the constraints and demands imposed by group pressures or a social role is much more broadly applicable as a sociological principle.

Ralf Dahrendorf, for example, has attempted to justify in conventional sociological language the imputation to the subordinates in a power relation of a latent or objective interest in resisting their superiors, although it should be noted that he always puts quotation marks around 'objective'. Dahrendorf argues that these interests are emphatically 'non-psychological', in no sense present in the 'consciousness and articulate orientations' of subordinates, although they may, of course, become so and emerge as 'manifest interests'.[98] The analogy Dahrendorf draws between such 'objective interests' and 'role expectations' of the incumbents of a position to which they may or may not conform is hardly persuasive. What Dahrendorf seems to mean is that it is possible, even probable, that over time subordinates will develop a subjective or manifest interest in resisting their superiors and act on it but that whether or when this happens depends on 'structural' or non-psychological realities. It remains obscure, however, as to *why* this latent possibility should exist in the first place. Surely, there is an implication that subjection to authority is inherently unpleasant even if its unpleasantness is denied or repressed, as I argued in Chapter 5. Yet Dahrendorf explicitly rejects even so broad a psychological assumption as the 'pleasure principle', arguing that it is not a 'required assumption' to support the claim that power relations inevitably involve a conflict of interests.[99] Collective mobilization and the articulation of counter-ideologies challenging the legitimations of those in authority, as in the Marxist model of the development of class consciousness, may be necessary before subordinates express and even become fully aware of their interest in opposing established authority; whether or not this happens depends considerably on changing historical and structural conditions external to the authority relation itself. But it is hard to see why the original latent and diffuse discontents of the subordinates should be characterized as non-psychological. Dahrendorf is not so much concerned with upholding a radical vision of a new society transcending the present consciousness of those who are deprived in the existing one as with defending a traditional Durkheimian line of separation between the realms of sociology and psychology. At times he seems to mean no more than that actions have objective consequences conducive to the 'maintenance or modification of a status quo' and that these consequences rather than psychic events in the minds of the actors are the proper concern of the sociologist trying to understand group conflict and social change. This can be conceded without denying that the covert dissatisfactions of power subjects are a necessary though not sufficient condition for the occurrence of conflict and change.

Steven Lukes adopts a somewhat different tack in defence of the idea of 'real' as distinct from 'subjective' interests.[100] He is concerned less with conceptual distinctions than with trying to show that real interests can be empirically testable – or at least arguable – on the basis of certain counter-factual assumptions. If the exercise of power produces effects on the conduct of the power subject that would otherwise not occur, then what the latter would do in the absence of subjection to power reveals his real interests. The empirical check is provided by examples of what happens when the exercise of power is non-existent, is relaxed or is eliminated altogether. Lukes gives several examples. His first is Matthew Crenson's contention that Gary, Indiana would have passed legislation controlling air pollution at least as early as the neighbouring city of East Chicago had it not been for the anticipatory power exercised by United States Steel, the major employer and air polluter in the city.[101] Lukes also mentions the sudden emergence of an alternative world-view held by the formerly powerless in revolutionary situations when the old order has been repudiated, citing Gramsci in support. Another example given is the process of sanskritization in which the lower Hindu castes collectively adopt Brahminic practices in order to improve their status in the caste system; the periodic mass conversions of low-caste Hindus to religions that do not make a doctrinal principle of caste are also mentioned. In effect, the real interests of the citizens of Gary were to avoid being poisoned by dirty air, of the supporters of revolution to free themselves from the worldview imposed on them by a hegemonic class or institution, and of low-caste Hindus to escape from the inferior status assigned them in the caste system. Lukes goes so far as to define power as A affecting B 'in a manner contrary to B's interests' even if B is not aware of the interests imputed to him by 'the radical' who

> maintains that men's wants may themselves be a product of a system which works against their interests, and, in such cases, relates the latter to what they would want and prefer, were they able to make the choice.[102]

Power to Lukes is coercive by definition in contrast to what he calls 'influence', even if it is not acknowledged as such by the power subject. The imputation of real as opposed to perceived interests reveals the exercise of power in the latter circumstance.

Let us examine Lukes' examples more closely. Gary's citizens unquestionably did not like breathing polluted air even if they thought that nothing could be done about it without running the risk that U.S. Steel might move its plant elsewhere or lose markets to low-cost competitors who had not installed anti-pollution equipment, resulting in each case in local unemployment. Revolutionaries undeniably experience a sense of liberation from the restraints of the old order. Even the promise of social mobility through rebirth does not prevent low-caste Hindus from finding their low status painful and engaging in collective efforts to improve it by emulating the Brahmins. There need be nothing unperceived or non-subjective about the sentiments present in all these cases. What the citizens of Gary may have failed initially to realize is that U.S. Steel would bow to political pressure and control pollution without leaving town or cutting production. Low-caste Hindus sometimes reject the caste system altogether by converting to more egalitarian religions, although caste distinctions have proved sufficiently entrenched to have survived even among Christian and Muslim converts. The victors of revolution in the first flush of enthusiasm anticipate a new order in which liberty and equality will prevail, but they are, alas, usually disappointed.

In other words, even in the case of so limited and obvious an interest as the wish not to be poisoned by air pollution there is a gap between the power subject's desire to avoid or mitigate some of the effects of the power exercised over him and his assurance that alternative social arrangements are available that will guarantee the removal of these effects without damage to other interests. A notion of real interests that embraces both the felt discontent and measures or policies designed to alleviate it conceals this gap. Low status and subjection to the unrestricted power of others may be experienced as unpleasant and yet be accepted as necessary evils, given the real situations in which individuals and groups suffering them find themselves. To argue that they can be reduced or removed by government policies, popular revolution or the establishment of 'socialism' is to express a hope and a faith in the improvement of man's condition. Steven Lukes recognizes this in claiming that both the concepts of power and of interests are ultimately normative and thus 'essentially contested', but he passes too lightly over the abuses to which the concept of real or objective interests not only might be but actually has been put by states claiming a legitimacy derived from Marxism. He does mention the possibility that power might be exercised over someone in his real interests which would be 'open to misuse by seeming to provide a paternalist license for tyranny'.[103] He argues, however, that such a power relation is bound to end when the subject becomes aware of his interests; if it persists, then a conflict of interests comes into existence. Power holders try to legitimate their power by claiming to serve the real interests of their subjects, as we have seen. In our secular age, the scientific aura that clings to such notions as 'real interests' and 'false consciousness' makes them particularly attractive as legitimating symbols; both the tyrannies created and justified in the name of Marxism and the invocation of science and technology to provide technocratic legitimations amply attest to this.[104] They also provide an ever-present temptation to radicals frustrated by the lack of response to their appeals to embrace the idea of a temporary 'educational' dictatorship in order to enlighten the masses as to their real interests without the interference of the competing voices, including those of conservative élites, permitted by democracy. The trouble, of course, is that temporary dictatorships have a way of becoming permanent. These seem to me to be sufficient reasons for being chary of the concept of real interests that are not perceived by those to whom they are imputed, but there are further theoretical difficulties with the concept as well.

Lukes does not use the term 'objective interests' and concedes that he 'continue[s] to tie interests to subjective preferences under conditions of relative autonomy'.[105] His approach is essentially a version of what Max Weber called 'the method of objective possibility', which was taken over by Lukács in developing his notion of objective interests. But trying to assess what would have happened – or might have with a strong degree of probability – if certain events had not taken place, e.g. if the Greeks had lost the Battle of Marathon, Weber presupposed a relative constancy of the goals, values and subjective preferences of the historical actors. Lukes wants to question not just the outcome of a sequence of events shaped by the power subject's submission to the decisions of the powerful but the autonomy of the power subject's underlying motivations themselves:

> To put the matter sharply, A may exercise power over B by getting him to do what he does not want to do, but he also exercises power over him by influencing, shaping or determining his very wants. Indeed, is it not the supreme exercise of power to get another or others to have the desires you want them to have – that is, to secure their compliance by controlling their thoughts and desires?[106]

A critic of Lukes has argued that it is impossible to estimate reliably what someone might do if the power exercised by someone else over his actions is removed or 'thought away' in a mental experiment because his actions may be the overdeterimined result of the power exercised by others as well, as Lukes himself has noted.[107] Lukes replies rather weakly that

> unless Bradshaw seriously maintains that *all* our preferences are heteronomous, and the products of some exercise of power, then he must allow that some of A's (actual or hypothetical) preferences and choices are authentically A's.[108]

But human character itself is in part precisely the product of past exercises of power – namely, the power of the parent over the child which eventually destroys the infant's illusions of omnipotence. The capacity for moral judgment of self and others is the result of the child's internalization and generalization of the initially external constraints imposed upon him by the parent. Antinomian left Freudians from Otto Gross before the First World War[109] to Wilhelm Reich to Erich Fromm, Herbert Marcuse and Norman Brown more recently have argued that only the abolition of psychological repression and the dissolution of the superego will make men truly autonomous and liberated. However, the left Freudians disagree among themselves both about the content of what is repressed and how the realization of autonomy is to be achieved. To some of them, changes in social institutions are not enough – human nature itself must be transformed radically by new ways of socializing children. Other left Freudians equate the coerciveness of political and economic institutions with the psychological repressions that are the foundation of individual character; thus, under the influence of Marcuse, the term 'repression' is today widely used to connote the coercive powers of states and ruling classes which were formerly described as 'oppressive' without the psychoanalytical resonances of 'repression'.[110] The sociological – more accurately, the macrosocial – and the psychological are collapsed into one another – illegitimately, because not only are they independently variable but they often vary inversely. Societies with considerable social and political freedom and equality may produce and even require individuals with strong superegos capable of repressing some instinctual impulses and controlling others, whereas authoritarian social orders imposing strong constraints may refrain from efforts to shape from within the psyches of their subjects. (The instinctual freedom of the proles in Orwell's *Nineteen Eighty-Four* is a hypothetical case in point.) Lukes implicitly recognizes the difference between the intra-psychic and the social environment in distinguishing between relative and absolute autonomy, but it remains unclear as to where he draws the line between them. In any case, short of the total instinctual liberation envisaged by left Freudian utopianism, most human motivations leading to social action have been shaped by previous subjection at least to parental power in infancy and childhood.

The recurring appeal of the idea of objective interests lies not only in its ideological uses – or misuses – but in the fact that it conflates two important distinctions and therefore carries richly suggestive overtones. Most obviously, there is the distinction between the subjective wants of individuals and groups and the situation, often misperceived by them, in which these wants seek satisfaction. Objective interests, however, are often taken to refer to the contrast between the like interests of separate individuals viewed additively and common interests resulting from their achieving identity as a group and combining their individual resources to wield collective power to increase their share of material and psychic resources in competition and conflict with other groups. This is, of course, precisely the problem of mobilization and the conditions under which it is more or less likely to occur. Apathy, hopelessness, and individual self-seeking may diminish or eliminate entirely possibilities of solidarity and organization which could transform the situation of the members of a collectivity if only they could unite and mobilize their resources in a common effort.[111] I have already noted the extent to which 'solidarity' and 'unity' themselves become potent value symbols for nascent ('latent' or 'quasi' in Dahrendorf's terms) groups dominated by organized minorities. Those who violate the precarious unity that is a prerequisite for the exercise of collective power are likely to be sharply condemned; the anathema attached to 'scabs' in the labour movement is a case in point.

Yet the call for sacrifice and effort in the service of a common cause often falls on deaf ears. There is first of all the Olson problem that from a strictly rational calculation of personal advantage it is not in the interests of any particular individual to contribute his resources when his contribution will be too small to have much effect on the outcome and he will benefit in any case from whatever collective gains are achieved by mobilization. Olson, of course, explicitly confines this principle to large collectivities in which individual resources are more or less equally distributed.

But there is also an important difference in the time-scale involved in assessing the interests of individuals considered separately and that of the collectivity viewed as a whole. The mobilization of large and dispersed aggregates of individually powerless persons is likely to be, as I have already noted, a long and slow process involving initial defeats and uncompensated sacrifices. When an early socialist labour leader (Eugene V. Debs) declared 'I want to rise with the ranks, not from the ranks', his statement was widely recognized as essentially 'idealistic' and even heroic. Much of the concern of sociologists with rates of social mobility and prevailing beliefs about its incidence has been based on a recognition that aspirations to mobility for oneself or one's children have often been obstacles to collective action by American workers even at the level of trade unionism, let alone the formation of class-conscious socialist parties on the European model. As Hannah Arendt observes: 'Nothing, unfortunately, has so constantly been refuted by reality as the credo of 'enlightened self-interest', in its liberal version as well as in its more sophisticated Marxism variant.'[112] Taking the conflict between landlords and tenants as an illustration, she goes on to remark in terms that apply generally to the relation between individual and collective interest:

> Self-interest is interested in the self, and the self dies or moves on or sells the house; because of its changing condition, that is, ultimately because of the human condition of mortality, the self *qua* self cannot reckon in terms of long-range interest, i.e. the interest of a world that survives its inhabitants. Deterioration of the building is a matter of years; a rent increase or a temporarily lower profit rate are for today or tomorrow. And something similar, *mutatis mutandis*, is of course true for labor-management conflicts and the like. Self-interest, when asked to yield to 'true' interest – that is, the interest of the world as distinguished from that of the self – will always reply, Near is my shirt, but nearer is my skin. That may not be particularly reasonable, but it is quite realistic; it is the not very noble but adequate response to the time discrepancy between men's private lives and the altogether different life expectancy of the public world.[113]

The power of numbers or of monopoly over the provision of vital goods and services as a base for the exercise of force or its threat can often produce an immediate 'pay-off' to the members of the mobilized group. This is far less likely to be the case where more complex collective goals such as making and securing a revolution or 'building socialism' are at issue. Lenin is reputed to have said shortly after the Bolshevik seizure of power that fifty years of toil, sacrifice and discipline would be necessary before the rewards of abundance, social peace and personal fulfilment promised by socialism would begin to be enjoyed. Given human life-expectancy, it is understandable that men might not greet joyously such a prospect. People do respond enthusiastically to short-term demands for sacrifice and even heroism when the goal is tangible and clear-cut (Churchill's 'blood, sweat, and tears') and no enduring society could be organized primarily on the principle of *carpe diem*, neglecting any provision for future generations. Otherwise, at the very least the birth rate would fall below replacement levels. The conservative effects of religious beliefs in reinforcing the norms of the established order with supernatural sanctions including reward or punishment in an after-life have often been noted. Yet the decline of belief in immortality in modern society has also reduced the readiness of people who know they have only one short life to live to make great sacrifices for the primary benefit of their successors. Their attitude is more likely to be 'I don't want it when I'm dead. I want it now.'[114]

It is hardly surprising therefore that revolutionary consciousness as opposed to conflict consciousness has been more pronounced among workers in the early stages of industrialization whose lives have been sharply disrupted and who stand closer to a traditional religious world-view.[115] Nor perhaps that revolutionary Marxism is still more successful in the Catholic countries of Southern Europe and Latin America than in Northwestern Europe and North America.[116] Nor that bourgeois intellectuals prepared to lose their souls rather than their chains have so often been more militant than the workers and peasants they aspire to lead, as Lenin himself, of course, recognized.[117] The superiority of Marx's vision to that of the utopian socialists lay in his awareness that people would not be readily inspired to try to realize attractive blueprints of a future society; for socialism to become a reality there must be a combination of unplanned social and economic change bringing a socialist society to the verge of actual existence and the development of political solidarity and organization by the class that stood to benefit most from the new order. Marx's historical forecasts have proved wide of the mark, but they were more realistic than those of his opponents on the left. The failure of his forecasts as early as the first decade of the present century gave rise to the rival social democratic and Leninist forms of revisionism which are still debated today by parties, movements and political sects unwilling to abandon their claims to the heritage of Marx by treating him as an historical figure.

It can certainly be validly argued on empirical grounds that mobilization will often bring tangible benefits to individuals (overlooking for the moment the Olson problem of whether it is in the interests of particular individuals to contribute to a collective effort). It is also evident that, in contradistinction to their felt deprivations and resentments against the exactions of powerful others, the members of a collectivity may be oblivious to, or at most only dimly aware of, the advantages to be gained by co-operating to resist those who exercise power over them. In this sense, they can be said to have an objective interest in forging bonds of solidarity in order to aggregate their individual resources and build an organization capable of waging conflict. But even an imputation of objective interest in these terms may pose difficulties in particular cases. A student at a doctoral oral examination rejected the notion of false consciousness because he considered it presumptuously élitist. He later mentioned that rivalry between blacks and Puerto Ricans was so intense in the Harlem neighbourhood where he taught elementary school that it erupted among the small children in his classroom. His earlier questioner remarked triumphantly, 'See, an obvious case of false conscious-ness!' The student denied that it could properly be called this, but one sees his critic's rationale for thinking so. If blacks and Puerto Ricans were to form even a limited electoral alliance they could wield much greater political power in New York City: in 1977 each group ran their own candidates for mayor who finished fifth and sixth in a seven-man field in the Democratic primary. But how can the satisfactions of individual ego-enhancement and group pride fulfilled by competition with the other group on a variety of fronts be 'objectively' measured against the benefits to be won from City Hall as the result of forming an effective voting bloc?

If such doubts arise concerning limited political mobilization for realistic goals by blacks and Puerto Ricans in New York, they obviously have much greater force when the possibilty of revolutionary class consciousness is at issue. The victims of extreme coercion and exploitation clearly have an interest in ending their suffering, but their interest is apt to be both conscious, shared and directed towards a collective goal that is immediate and concrete, if negative and often unattainable through their own efforts independently of outside support. Traditional Marxism anticipated the collapse of capitalism under the weight of its cumulative contradictions, with the progressively greater immiseration of the working class providing the spur to its mobilization for the revolutionary conquest of power. The concept of objective interests is essentially a pale surviving echo of these once radiant expectations. It is related to the Leninist practice of judging political actions by their presumptive consequences rather than according to the actor's intentions. Thus the victory of the Communist Party that stands for the working class is inevitable and criticism of the party line from within its ranks can be branded as 'objectively' providing support for the bourgeoisie. Although he remained a Leninist, Lukács' use of the term was, to put it mildly, richer and more subtle: it expressed to him the contrast between the consciousness of the isolated individual confronting an external social world that he never made and the role of the proletariat as a collective historical actor destined to shatter the reified social structures produced by earlier collective actors. Despite their indebtedness to the Lukács of *History and Class Consciousness*, contemporary voluntaristic or humanist schools of Marxism are disinclined to use the term ' objective interests' without in any way abandoning their conviction that socialist transformation is both desirable and possible if sufficient numbers of people, not necessarily confined to the working class proper, can be mobilized to support it as a goal taking precedence over their short-run interests and concerns. Apart from the sinister uses to which it has been put at the level of action (or praxis), the concept of objective interests has inescapably positivistic and 'objectivistic' overtones despite Lukács' ingenious equation of it with the contrast between the limited capacities of the individual and the history-making potential of the class as a collective actor. One need not be a dogmatic methodological individualist to agree with Weber's observation, advanced in criticism of none other than Lukács himself, that the concept of 'class interests' is

ambiguous as soon as one understands by it something other than the factual direction of interests following with a certain probability for a certain 'average' of those people subjected to the class situation.[118]

There are ambiguities in the rarely analysed concept of interests itself apart from what adjectives may be used to qualify it. On the one hand, it carries an unmistakably subjective reference to what interests a person,[119] what desires or goals guide his orientation to the world.

Interests are also used, however, to refer to definite courses of action or
policies that individuals may pursue. The first sense equates interests with
wants or impulses seeking satisfaction, but "if wishes were horses,
beggars would ride' and wants are not necessarily converted into
actions designed to satisfy them but may reveal themselves only in
distorted, symptomatic behaviour in the form of dreams, fantasies and
the 'psychopathology of everyday life'. To speak of 'latent interests' is
altogether meaningful in this connection and fully congruent with
Freud's concept of latent dream contents which reflect repressed wishes
from which the latent-manifest distinction itself was originally borrowed. Fantasies and myths of liberation are undeniably important
components of the consciousness of individuals and groups. Latent
interests understood in this way, however, can hardly be characterized
as objective in the sense of being identifiable independently of anyone's
psyche even though they may be unconscious rather than conscious.

But the concept of interests suggests not only wants and desires but
actions or policies designed to fulfil them. This implication is clearly the
source of the view that interests in the sense of courses of action can be
imputed to actors who remain unaware of what they might do to
advance their interests in the sense of subjective wants and desires.
Collective action represents just such a course of action for people
facing the common situation of subjection to the power of others. It is
easy to see how the subjective-objective and individual-collective
distinctions thus become conflated in the concept of objective interests
imputed to a group. The claim that the victims of power have much to
gain by overcoming their quarrels among themselves and pooling their
resources to resist an oppressor – in short, by mobilizing – has a *prima
facie* plausibility, especially when the victims actually have little to lose
but their chains: 'if we don't hang together, we'll all hang separately'.
But a much longer time-scale and vastly greater uncertainty of
outcome are involved if one moves from this minimal imputation of a
collective interest in mobilization to asserting such an interest in a
general strike, revolution or in the establishment of socialism conceived
of as a radically different new form of society. When invoked to
legitimate such projects, the notion of objective interests essentially
connotes an ideal, masked however as something more concrete,
empirically demonstrable, and linked to the utilitarian rather than the
normative concerns of actors, in Etzioni's terms. To move from the
imputation to collectivities of a potential for conflict consciousness to

the imputation of a potential for revolutionary consciousness is to make a leap into faith.

Whether the ideal of a new order in which all interests are fulfilled and harmonized is realizable may be subject to doubt and also whether the struggle to realize it, even if it is seen as attainable, is worth the cost in light of Arendt's 'near is my shirt, but nearer is my skin' dictum, not to speak of the Olson problem.[120] The elimination of the present order is obviously possible and with a minimum of violence if only the masses, or the relevant classes, would become aware of it and achieve the necessary unity and determination. The radical's 'if only', however, is simply another version of the 'they could if they wanted to' argument of the pluralist defender of contemporary democracy who contends that the formal freedom to mobilize politically means that all the discontented and victimized are 'potential groups' able to organize and exert power to rectify their complaints. In both cases 'they could if they wanted to' begs the fact that they usually don't want to and confront formidable obstacles to mobilization that set limits to their capacity to exercise the freedom they possess in law or in principle.

Social movements, of course, are founded on the convergence of ideals and short-run, tangible, usually material, collective interests. Ideals may be necessary to inspire unorganized individuals to make the effort to mobilize and achieve the real if limited gains that result. 'Certainly all historical experience confirms the truth that man would not have attained the possible had he not first reached out for the impossible.'[121] Sorel wrote of the 'myth of the general strike', there is also the myth of the revolution that will make all things new, the myth of a 'classless society' or of a socialism that will by definition solve all existing social problems without sacrificing the positive achievements of capitalism. The potency of these myths is not to be doubted. It is the task of the sociologist to discern the developmental potentialities inherent in power relations, including tendencies to conflict and dissolution. He also has the broader responsibility of exploring the outer limits of the possible by considering alternative social arrangements that reduce inequalities of power; for example, by dispensing with widespread reliance on coercion and restricting power relations as much as possible to a minimum of scope-specific competent authority. To the extent that the sociologist assumes these intellectual responsibilities, he is not confined to what Lukes calls a 'one-dimensional' view of power limited to the observation of what actually happens in conflicts over publicly articulated issues and decisions while taking for granted the existing power structure and the consciousness of its actors as irreducibly given.

The concept of objective interests, however, obfuscates the tension between interests and ideals by covertly collapsing the latter into the former. It reflects a pseudo-scientific or 'objectivistic' manœuvre that imputes a spurious air of rationality and realizability to ideals. The notion of 'latent interests', referring to the suppressed or repressed needs and aspirations of an aggregate of persons sharing a common fate, is, on the other hand, entirely acceptable and even indispensable. The existence of such latent interests indicates a potential for mobilization and identifies a target group for mobilizing efforts. It also frequently leads to the exercise of some degree of anticipatory power by the group in question.

CHAPTER EIGHT

The Bases of Power: Numbers and Political Democracy

Numbers are a formidable collective resource. The volume of aggregated individual resources depends crucially on the size of the group contributing to a common pool whether the resources in question are money, goods, labour time, votes, small weapons, muscular strength or sheer occupation of space. For this reason, I chose in Chapter 6 to classify numbers as a non-reducible or global collective resource notwithstanding the fact that the size of a group or population is no more than the sum of its individual members. Yet, in contrast to a small group, it is notoriously difficult to mobilize large numbers of people, to keep them mobilized and contributing their individual resources to the common stock, and to co-ordinate their activities to wield the collective power they bring into being – so much so that some writers have even referred to a 'law of the superiority of small numbers'.

Political democracy comprising regularly scheduled elections based on universal adult suffrage can be regarded as the institutionalization of the power of numbers in accordance with the normative principles of majority rule and one person-one vote. Democracy grants to every individual person regardless of what other resources he or she may possess a specifically political resource, the right to vote.[1] Democracy also gives exclusive precedence to this resource when aggregated as a collective electoral choice in the selection of a government. The one individual resource that is equally distributed in a population is, in short, accorded decisive weight. The collective resource of numbers, therefore, gives potential political ascendancy by majority vote to those segments of the population most lacking in all of the other individual and collective resources which remain unequally distributed and concentrated in the possession of a minority. Introduced into a class-divided society, democracy represents a formal, that is, legal and constitutional, equalizing tendency. The possibility that the lower classes may use the power of the ballot to win control of the state and carry

out a redistribution of those resources that remain unequally distributed
is inherent in mass democracy. Its introduction was therefore feared
and opposed by many spokesmen for the privileged classes in the
nineteenth century and even earlier whereas extension of the franchise
became a major demand of populist and socialist egalitarian
movements. The battle was chiefly waged over property restrictions on
the right to vote. In their later years both Marx and Engels thought that
the achievement of universal suffrage eliminated the necessity of violent
revolution by making the victory of the proletariat possible by legal and
peaceful means.[2]

But, of course, it hasn't worked out that way in practice. In the long-
established constitutional democracies there has been some movement
towards greater equality in the distribution of resources other than
citizenship (which includes the right to vote), but the movement has on
the whole been a modest one.[3] One must ask the deliberately naïve yet
significant question: why don't the parties of the numerically
preponderant lower classes win most of the elections and create a
classless society in which the three p's of power, privilege and prestige
are more or less equally distributed? Or – to achieve the feat of quoting
two American presidents in a question – why, if 'God must love the
poor people because he made so many of them' (Lincoln), is
'conservative government in the saddle most of the time' (Wilson)?

There are two main answers. First, it is, as already noted, hard to
mobilize large numbers of people even for so limited a purpose as
casting their votes for the same candidate. And the process of
mobilization takes time – decades rather than years. Second, resources
other than the vote remain in the predominant possession of minorities:
wealth; status; political skills based on superior information; education;
range and variety of social contacts; access to means of persuasion; free
time; traditional legitimacy. The upper and middle classes are at an
advantage with respect to all of these resources which enable them to
exercise greater influence not only on government policy between
elections but also on electoral mobilization up to the very moment of the
actual voting when formal equality prevails. As Lehman summarizes
the situation:

> Elections . . . benefit the less privileged since the act of voting itself is not
> terribly costly. Elections occur only periodically and casting a ballot
> takes little time. On the other hand, costs jump the further away from
> election day we are. As we move back from casting the ballot – to being

active in the campaign, to raising funds, to shaping platforms and issues, to putting forward and selecting candidates, and to keeping party structures alive between election – the cost for weaker groups skyrockets. Only at the very end of the electoral process does the leveling effect of one person-one vote prevail. The more remote the event, the greater differentials in influence.[4]

It is possible even to argue that the introduction of formal political equlity into a society that remains highly inegalitarian in most other respects actually favours those with the greatest advantages. As Frank Parkin puts such a case:

> A political system which guarantees constitutional rights for groups to organize in defence of their interests is almost bound to favour the privileged at the expense of the disprivileged. The former will always have greater organizing capacities and facilities than the latter, such that the competition for rewards between different classes is never an equal contest. This is not merely because the dominant class can more easily be mobilized in defence of its interests, but also because it has access to the all-important means of social control, both coercive and normative. Given this fundamental inequality in the social and economic order, a pluralist or democratic political structure works to the advantage of the dominant class.[5]

Though it is clear that Parkin is describing rather than advocating a political conclusion sometimes drawn from these circumstances,[6] he presents the rationale of left-wing authoritarians for favouring the sacrifice of liberty to equality, whether in the form of a Marxist-Leninist 'dictatorship of the proletariat' or of a Marcusean 'temporary' educational dictatorship as a means of overcoming the stasis of 'repressive tolerance'.[7] However, comparing the command economies of the Communist world with the capitalist democracies, Parkin recognizes that in the former

> the party's monopoly of power has often resulted in gross abuses of constitutional rights and the use of terroristic methods of social control. Similarly, power has been used to exercise tight control over areas of social life which have little direct bearing on the maintenance of social equality.[8]

The same considerations that give rise to justified suspicion of the fundamental and enduring egalitarianism of even a hypothetical dictatorship claiming to represent the masses also apply to such mass organizations as unions and socialist parties within the context of democracy itself. The Italian neo-Machiavellians at a level of sweeping transhistorical generality and Weber and Michels with specific reference to existing mass organizations asserted the inevitability of differentiation between leaders and the rank-and file within the most formally democratic unions and political parties. The history of labour and left-wing movements is punctuated with cries of 'betrayal', 'class renegadism', 'mis-leaders of labour', 'sell-out', 'co-optation' and the like directed against leaders, especially those who have achieved some electoral success under 'bourgeois' democracy. The assumption expressed in these accusations – shared also by Michels – that leaders are always likely to be less radical and militant than the working-class constituencies that they represent is often very far from being true, as Guenther Roth has shown with respect to Michels' own classic case, the Social Democratic Party in Imperial Germany.[9] But there can be no question that the very size of the constituency served and represented by mass organizations requires their bureaucratization and the emergence of an internal hierarchy separating the leaders from the led. Nor can it be doubted that the electoral successes of left-wing parties since Michels' time have in the long-run had a moderating effect on their commitment to radical egalitarianism, even if members and voters are affected as well as politicians and officials. There is truth in the poignant complaint that 'socialists will triumph, socialism never!'[10]

But whatever its frequent pathos, the charge that leaders are corruptible and prone to *embourgeoisement* has an ominous, self-serving ring, especially when the followers are not in fact more radical, and when it is combined with the doctrine of 'objective interests' and 'false consciousness'. I think it is preferable, therefore, to see the 'Michels thesis' and its variants as a subordinate part of the broader explanation already suggested for the failure of mass democracy to produce a general equalization of resources: namely, the difficulty of mobilizing large numbers of people who are, by comparison with their opponents, relatively lacking in resources other than their enfranchisement. Mobilizing the resource of numbers to prevail in elections requires, as Michels insisted, the creation of bureaucratic party machines. Electoral success becomes their overriding goal and acquires ritualistic and symbolic overtones independently of any substantive reductions in social and economic equality. These developments are a consequence of introducing democracy into old hierarchical class societies in which new inequalities created by the market economy and the general process of bureaucratization are added to surviving class divisions with their roots in the past. Yet none of the attempts to impose a centralized dictatorship in the name of oppressed classes has succeeded even in eradicating all the old inequalities, let alone in avoiding the creation of new and more oppressive ones.

The greatly improved living standards in the advanced industrial countries owe vastly more to general economic growth than to any politically directed changes. But the relatively modest gains towards greater equality that have been made under democracy should not be discounted. Parkin minimizes them, Lenski stresses them, although there is no significant disagreement between the two concerning their nature and extent. It is essentially a matter of whether the glass is described as half-full or half-empty. Also, the ritualistic and symbolic trappings of democracy, for instance the 'democracy of manners' that so impressed Tocqueville in the America of the 1830s, reflect a deeper ethos that provides a climate in which the egalitarian demands of parties of the left attain a certain legitimacy and this can facilitate the conversion of power into full-fledged legitimate authority when events produce a shift of opinion to the left.

The Democratic Class Struggle

Voting studies have documented the fact that the vote for conservative parties by the upper and middle classes is proportionately higher than the vote of the lower classes for parties of the left; the upper and middle classes also show higher rates of turnout.[11] Lipset, from whom I have borrowed the heading for this section of the chapter, has addressed himself in a valuable essay to the question of how conservative parties manage to compete successfully with parties of the left despite the fact that the latter's potential constituency amounts to a majority of the electorate.[12] He argues that 'there are two important sources of deviation from a purely class model of party choice': first, effects inherent in class inequality itself; and second, the existence of political issues arising out of religious and ethnic differences that are not directly class-related.[13]

The problem of mobilizing numbers as a collective resource is of primary importance with regard to the first of these two sources of deviation from a class model. Ethnic and religious communities, as I noted in Chapter 7, present a more salient base for mobilization than classes because they possess at least a diffuse solidarity rooted in shared values. Moreover, these values, politically relevant and divisive though they may on occasion become, are usually not intrinsically political or conflict-oriented. Class solidarity differs, since a disposition to political action and conflict tends to be central to it; even purely economically oriented trade unions are power-seeking groups engaged in conflict with management. Classes are essentially relational groups characterized by a dichotomous 'we-them' outlook.[14] This is not necessarily true of religious and ethnic groups, which may or may not acquire conflict consciousness and become politically mobilized.

Lipset lists seven separate consequences of class inequality that reduce the disposition and opportunity of the lower classes to muster their full strength at the polls in support of egalitarian parties, candidates or policies. They are, with some comments and amendments of my own, as follows:

(1) The lower classes are more likely to share the values of the upper classes than the reverse. Lipset confines himself to stating this as a fact, but it results, of course, from the greater institutional power of the upper classes. As Parkin notes, 'Normative consensus is better understood in terms of the socialization of one class by another than as independent class agreement or convergence on values.'[15]

(2) The lower classes are more exposed to conflicting normative pressures as a result of their socialization in both the culturally dominant values of the upper classses and their own more egalitarian and politically left-wing class subculture.

(3) The lower classes are more exposed to conservative values because the upper classes have greater control over the means of persuasion, including the educational system and the mass media of communications. This statement seems to be no more than a spelling out in greater detail of what has already been asserted in (1). Lipset appears to be referring here to specifically political sentiments and attitudes whereas (1) refers to more general values which play a role in shaping political outlooks. In any case, propositions (1) and (3) help to account for the greater deviation from modal lower-class attitudes and voting patterns by lower-class members than that of middle- and upper-class members from the modal attitudes and voting behaviour of their class. Proposition (2), on the other hand, suggests that because lower-class voters are more exposed to normative conflicts, more of them are likely not to vote at all, for voting studies have shown that apathy and withdrawal are common responses of citizens who

experience 'cognitive dissonance' as a result of exposure to political cross-pressures.

(4) Parties of the left appealing to lower-class voters are advocates of change in the direction of a redistribution of rewards. It is harder to persuade people to believe in the possibility of beneficial change than to strengthen their adherence to the present order, especially in the case of relatively socially isolated and tradition-minded lower-class groups. No one has stated this better than Machiavelli, who remarked on 'the incredulity of mankind, who do not truly believe in anything new until they have actual experience of it'.[16]

(5) The social environment of the upper classes tends to be more homogeneous and more actively involved with politics than the environment of the lower classes. Hence upper-class persons are more continuously exposed to political information and advocacy in line with their predisposition.

(6) Inter-class communication is more likely to influence the attitudes of the lower-class person to conform more closely to those of the upper-class person because of the latter's higher status. This is largely a corollary of propositions (1), (2) and (3).

(7) Higher-status individuals are more aware of the relevance of political action to their group interests as a result of their greater education and wider social and political contacts. I listed this as a prerequisite for political mobilization in Chapter 7.

Lipset regards these seven conditions favouring higher electoral turnout and greater support for conservative parties by the middle and upper classes as inherent in the existence of a class-divided society itself. He then mentions four strategies available to conservative parties to 'reduce the saliency of class as the principal basis of party controversy in order to win lower-class votes': (1) An emphasis on national patriotic issues and the nomination of military heroes as candidates; (2) Stressing non-economic bases of cleavage, such as ethnic or religious differences or moral issues; (3) 'Tory socialism': the adoption by conservative parties of some egalitarian proposals of the sort usually associated with the parties of the left; and (4) the employment of a populist rhetoric to scapegoat unpopular minorities as a way of both exploiting and deflecting the anti-elitism of the lower classes.[17]

Lipset's generalizations are drawn from survey research, voting studies and some historical evidence. Despite their comparative and historical range, however, they are presented as static, ahistorical propositions summarizing constants in the experience of class-divided democratic societies. But if electoral mobilization is a temporal process and the lower classes start out at a disadvantage when universal suffrage is introduced into societies in which most resources remain unequally distributed, this does not mean that no progress is made in overcoming the disadvantage. The fifty to a hundred years that have witnessed the democratization of politics in most Western nations are not very long,[18] but the pattern of politics has scarcely remained the same in these nations over that period. There is in fact a discernible pattern of short-run and long-run development over time in democratic politics as the tempo of lower-class mobilization accelerates and as the upper-class parties seek new ways of trying to contain their opponents' potential majority that is inherent in democracy based on universal suffrage – in what I have called the institutionalization of the power of numbers as a decisive collective political resource. Movement can be introduced into Lipset's static generalizations and in doing so the characteristic ways in which democracy itself breeds frustration and disappointment as well as its routine achievements can be noted.

The Rhythm of Democratic Politics and the Spiral Pattern it Traces[19]

Democratic political orders with universal suffrage and competing political parties experience a cyclical alternation of periods dominated by protest from the left and retrenchment by the right. The notion that politics conforms to such a cycle is hardly a new one: it is implicit in the most commonplace language of political journalism which regularly uses such metaphors as 'swing of the pendulum', 'rising and ebbing tides', or 'waxing and waning' forces.

The conception of a one-dimensional left-right continuum along which parties, movements, regimes and ideologies can be located has often been justly criticized, yet some such conception seems indispensable and creeps back in different guises if the familiar tainted terminology is renounced.[20] The dictum that 'if men define situations as real, they are real in their consequences' is especially applicable to political conflict and the alignments it produces. The idea of a left-right spectrum or of a liberal-conservative polarity is constitutive and not merely descriptive of political reality itself. To be sure, it is nearly always in the interests of democratic parties and politicians to gravitate toward the centre by blurring the rigid distinctions made by ideologists and intellectuals, but even the blurring takes place with reference to recognized polar points.[21]

I shall use 'left' to refer to programmatic political demands for planned or enacted social change towards a more equal distribution of economic rewards, social status and power; or, in unpropitious times, to the defence of an existing, achieved degree of equality against advocates of increased inequality. The classic left demand is to realize for all mèn '*liberté, égalité, fraternité*'. But the emphasis of the left in the past century has been, as noted in my definition, to an increasing degree on equality, apart from the existence and influence of Communist states that have laid claim to the heritage of the left while renouncing 'bourgeois' democracy and civil liberties. Liberty and equality partially entail one another, as is recognized in Anatole France's well-known jibe that the law with majestic impartiality grants freedom to both the rich and the poor to sleep under the bridges over the Seine.[22] But they may also be at odds when the demands for certain kinds of equality require the suppression of the liberty of some individuals and groups, a fact repeatedly stressed by conservative thinkers and ideologues anxious to lay claim to at least a part of the liberal heritage or to identify freedom with 'free enterprise'. Since the left as a permanent political tendency came into being at the time of the French Revolution, 'right' is best defined residually as resistance on any grounds whatever to further movement towards equality in the distribution of material rewards, status and power, or as the demand for restoration of a (usually idealized) *status quo ante* in which greater inequality prevailed. Because the left, in the modern sense of support for a more egalitarian society to be created by organized political effort, did not exist before the Enlightenment, an identifiable right emerged only in response to the challenge of the left. As Mannheim wrote: 'Goaded on by opposing theories, conservative mentality discovers its *ideas* only *ex post facto*'.[23]

Obviously, these sparse definitions raise problems if they are applied to the rich diversity of past and present political parties and movements. Yet in emphasizing, however broadly, the *content* of political demands, they avoid the relativism of defining left and right solely in relation to attitudes towards the existing order. Thus a party of the left that is in office does not cease to be left because it conducts an election campaign with such literally conservative slogans as 'Don't let them take it away' or 'You never had it so good'; it remains committed to an achieved degree of equality perceived as threatened by the right. Similarly, a party or candidate of the right may often appear as innovative and 'radical' when challenging an entrenched administration of the left, but the challenge still comes from the right if it defends the relatively well-off social groups and attacks enacted or proposed egalitarian reforms.

Defining left and right by the broad content of political demands also avoids the difficulties raised by classifying power-seeking groups as left or right solely according to their social bases – whether they are supported by or direct their appeals to the victims or the beneficiaries of the existing distribution of rewards and privileges. Thus Peronism in the 1940s and 1950s was not necessarily a movement of the left because its main following was among industrial workers; nor must New Left student movements of the 1960s be considered 'really' right-wing because their members were disproportionately drawn from upper middle-class backgrounds.[24] Nor need the structure of a party or regime affect its classification as left or right: parties of the left may be led and controlled by tiny, self-perpetuating elites, while parties of the right may be organized in a loose, decentralized, 'populistic' manner. The subordination of internal democracy and liberties to the demand for greater equality is, of course, characteristic of Communist movements.

The periodicity of left and right in democratic politics is not necessarily equivalent to the alternation of parties in power. Sometimes a conservative party may be able to take advantage of a turn to the left of popular opinion in response to an economic crisis and win over part of the left's normal constituency by advocating 'Tory socialist' reforms. This is particularly likely to happen when a party of the left is in office and incurs blame for the crisis.[25] More commonly, the left-right cycle or dialectic may take place within a single party that has remained in office for long periods of time and which electorally overshadows its opponents. For parties of both the left and the right are usually factionalized into moderate and militant wings, dividing reformers from radicals and conservatives from reactionaries. Intra-party success usually goes to those politicians capable of skilful manœuvring in the capacious centre, as in the case of inter-party competition. But the ideological dynamic that shapes the party's posture comes from the wings.

Nor, as the previous paragraph may seem to suggest, is it always a matter of a changed public mood turning to protest or expressing a sense of crisis that wells up from the substratum of politics and sets the rhythm in motion. A change of parties in power can initiate rather than merely reflect the workings of the rhythm. For example, John F. Kennedy's narrow presidential victory in 1960 – if indeed it was a real victory untainted by fraudulent vote-counts in Texas and Chicago – began the turn to the left in the 1960s, although it is highly probable that

President Eisenhower could have been re-elected if it had been legally possible for him to run again. Also Nixon's close victory over a divided Democratic party and administration in 1968 intensified the backlash against the protest movements of the sixties which might otherwise have remained inchoate and politically unfocused. In multi-party systems where coalition governments of the same several parties remain in office for long periods, shifts in the proportions of the vote won by different coalition partners may play a similar role.

The left-right rhythm, then, is neither to be identified simply with an alternation of parties in power nor with an eruption of 'deeper' social forces that penetrate and transform party politics, although both, of course, combine to play a part in it. The rhythm or cycle is essentially one of a pronounced shift in the mood and the *kinds of issues* that dominate political debate, electoral competition, and often intellectual and cultural life as well. It is not the effect of a mysterious cosmic law: a description of the rhythm, however accurate, *explains* nothing whatsoever, for the rhythm is an *explanandum* rather than an *explanans* – an effect of underlying causes rather than a causal agency itself.[26] An explanation of it must be historically bounded because party politics under conditions of mass suffrage are less than a century old in most of the stable, economically advanced, constitutional democracies of the West. Yet it is at least worth observing in passing that there is some evidence of a similar periodicity in non-democratic states. Despotic rulers of absolutist monarchies have often been followed by rulers more responsive to pressures from below. Totalitarian dictatorships undertake 'great leaps forward' that are followed by periods of relaxed discipline in which 'a hundred flowers' are encouraged to bloom. An analyst of Stalin's rule has written of the 'artificial dialectic' imposed by him on Soviet society, where rigorous demands for total ideological conformity and the use of terror to deter even the mildest dissent alternated with periods of greater permissiveness or 'thaw'.[27]

The fullest periodization of American politics into successive left and right eras – from 1765 to 1947 – was presented by Arthur Schlesinger, Sr. in an article first published in 1939 and later revised and expanded.[28] Schlesinger divided American history into eleven periods of alternating 'conservative' and 'liberal' ascendancy, each one averaging 16.5 years with very slight deviations around the mean except in the period from the Civil War to the end of the nineteenth century. Schlesinger's attempts to explain the cycle were not very adequate, scarcely going beyond the assertion of inevitable 'changes in mass psychology' resulting from boredom or disappointment with the prevailing phrase of the cycle. Also, although he acknowledged the existence of a similar cycle in the Western European democracies, his explanatory remarks refer largely to alleged peculiarities of the American people, such as their preference for 'empiricism' rather than 'preconceived theory' and their belief in the virtues of competition. The very influence of Schlesinger's article on politicians may have helped to make his cyclical 'theory' self-fulfilling in recent decades: in his autobiography published just two years before his death in 1963, Schlesinger reports that Franklin D. Roosevelt's adviser, David Niles, once told him that FDR was influenced in his decision to run for re-election in 1944 by Schlesinger's calculation that liberalism would remain dominant until 1948 (not a bad forecast).[29] Schlesinger also mentions a pre-election column by James Reston in 1960 maintaining that John F. Kennedy 'based his campaign on the assumption' derived from Schlesinger's theory that a turn to the left was in the offing within a year or two.[30] Also, Arthur Schlesinger, Jr., who was active in the liberal wing of the Democratic Party in the late 1950s, revived and updated his father's thesis to argue that the 1960s were destined to be a period of reform and innovation (not a bad prediction either!). But if presidents, presidential candidates and their advisers acted on a belief in Schlesinger's theory, then they helped make it partially self-confirming. For the decisions and actions of powerful politicians are to a considerable extent what activates the cyclical pattern rather than mere epiphenomenal effects of an underlying causal law.

The cyclical rhythm is explained neither by such a law nor by Schlesinger's observations on 'mass psychology'. It represents, rather, a pattern of change that is inherent in the workings of a democratic political system in a class-divided society. Political democracy based on universal adult suffrage was itself originally a demand of the left introduced into previously authoritarian and hierarchical social orders. In Europeans nations, though not in the United States, it was the central issue around which new working-class and socialist parties organized in the last decades of the nineteenth century. For the formal, i.e. the legal and constitutional, redistribution of power achieved by universal suffrage to lead to reforms reducing social and economic inequalities, a long period of political mobilization of the lower classes had to take place, a process that is hardly complete even today in many countries, including the United States. The higher turnout and more unified support for parties of the right by the upper and middle classes compared with working- and lower-class support for parties of the left indicates that the political mobilization of the lower classes is still by no means fully accomplished.

But left parties and movements succeed in mobilizing a large enough proportion of their potential constituency to become leading opposition parties. Sometimes they displace older parties, as in the rise of Labour at the expense of the Liberals in Britain. Sometimes they emerge as the first and largest organized mass parties confronting electoral or government coalitions of smaller parties of the right, as on the European continent. Sometimes they partially transform an older, heterogeneous and factionalized party into a vehicle for the demands of newly mobilized lower-class groups, as in the United States. Once parties of the left have been organized, or the working class has been at least partially mobilized by older parties, some crisis such as economic depression or defeat in war, or a split in the ranks of the right, is bound to give the party that is supported by the working and lower classes the opportunity to win office, whether on their own or as part of a coalition. They are then able to carry out reforms that constitute at least their minimum programme. It has often been the fate of left parties to come to power at a time of such acute crisis for the entire society that they are forced to concentrate on improvised short-run policies to restore or maintain internal peace with the result that their long-range goals of social reconstruction have to be shelved or severely modified, inspiring accusations of 'class betrayal' from their more militant followers. The German Social Democrats in the first and last years of the Weimar Republic are the classic case.[31] Nevertheless, by coming to office the left party wins a kind of legitimacy in the eyes of the electorate that it previously lacked. Not only is it able to enact at least its minimum programme, but it gains plausibility as an alternative to the previously dominant conservative party, which increases the probability that it will be again returned to office. Power, in effect, becomes partially self-legitimating.

But failure to resolve the crisis that brought the party to office; the passing of the crisis whether or not the government's policies are given credit for it; splits between the party's or government's radical and moderate wings once the minimum programme has been passed; the temporary appeasement of the left's constituency by the limited gains − actual or symbolic − that have been won; and the retrenchment of the right all result in electoral defeat or the 'co-optation' of prominent leaders before the left party has done more than institute 'incremental' or 'token' reforms. The party of the right then returns to office after successfully persuading a sufficient segment of the left's following that a conservative government will not wipe out the gains that have been made, that it will not 'turn the clock back' on the reforms achieved by the left. Old issues bitterly contested by the parties in the past suddenly become obsolescent and periods of 'Butskellism' (as in Britain in the 1950s) or even Grand Coalitions between the rivals (as in West Germany in the late sixties) become the order of the day, isolating and infuriating the more militant partisans on each side who may break away and create splinter or 'ginger' groups within legislatures or 'extraparliamentary opposition' movements outside. The right party, in an effort to enhance or consolidate its appeal to the constituency of the left, may adopt hybrid, apparently oxymoronic names or slogans designed to suggest that it has outgrown past hostility to left policies, such as 'Tory socialism', 'Progressive Conservatism',[32] 'Christian Democracy' or 'Moderate Republicanism'.[33] The most flagrant example of such an attempt to insert an appeal to all political tendencies into the very name of the party was the National Socialist German Workers' Party, in which the first and third words were designed to attract the nationalist right and the second and fourth the proletarian left. But the Nazis can hardly be regarded either as a democratic party or as a product of the 'normal' workings of electoral politics.

This recurrent sequence of events is the rhythm or dialectic of democratic politics. It falls far short of realizing either the far-reaching hopes of the advocates or the apocalyptic fears of the opponents of universal suffrage in the nineteenth century. Yet if it ensures that sooner or later reformist parties of the left will come to office, and if the return to office of conservative parties is contingent on their leaving untouched the popular reforms carried out by left administrations, then *there is an unmistakable leftward drift inherent in the functioning over time of democratic politics*. The metaphors of pendular or tidal movements are misleading, for the overall pattern is not one of a mere repetitive oscillation between fixed points. In Schlesinger's words, 'A more appropriate figure than the pendulum is the spiral, in which the alternation proceeds at successively higher levels.'[34] The classical Marxist conception of the movement of history has also been described as a spiral, combining a cyclical with a secular or unilinear motion. Another apposite image would be that of a ratchet mechanism, as in an automobile jack.[35]

Support for the idea of a leftward drift – at least in recent decades – can be found in Lipset and Ladd's study of the political attitudes of college generations from the 1930s to the 1960s. They see the 1930s as a left era marked by student radicalism, the 1940s as rather less so, the 1950s as conservative on the campuses and elsewhere, and the 1960s, at least after 1964, as a time of intense radical activism among students. Though confined to college students, these periods reflect the alternating left-right rhythm. Drawing on opinion survey data from a number of sources, Lipset and Ladd compare the youthful with the mature attitudes of student cohorts from the thirties through the sixties. They find confirmation of Aristotle's assumption that people become more conservative with age. However, for each successive cohort the shift to the right takes place from a starting position further to the left:

> To say that as they grow older alumni become more moderate, less committed to the support of current proposals for major change, than they were in their college years does not mean that they necessarily become more conservative in any rigid policy sense. The crucial point is that the shift is *relative*: They become more moderate, *as against* an earlier position closer to the extreme. But though relatively more conservative, they may remain as liberal in terms of the issues dominant in their college years. This results from a second, perhaps more important fact: While *each* college generation seems to go through the same process, any given later generation will have started at a more liberal or left position than the preceding one. In short, the *historical slope* of political attitudes among American college generations (as among Republican presidents) has been toward a more liberal position over time.[36]

To counter the leftward drift rooted in the incompletely realized demographic superiority of the left, the most reliable strategy of the right is, as Lipset noted, an appeal to nationalist sentiment. Modern nationalism is itself a product of democratic ideology, born in the wake of the American and French revolutions. But this very fact has served to enhance its appeal in opposition to the class and anti-élitist appeals of the left, which has so tragically underestimated the strength of national loyalties on so many occasions in the present century. The right lays claim to the symbols of legitimacy identified with the past of the nation, indeed with its very existence in a world of competing nation-states, an existence usually achieved by wars of conquest or revolts against foreign domination that usually, though not in the case of the United

States, antedated the creation of democratic institutions and the extension of the franchise. Thus parties of the right tend to wave the flag, to nominate generals who stand 'above politics' as candidates for office, and to invoke the need for national unity against enemies abroad to counter the divisive appeals of the left. National leaders of the right have sometimes engaged in foreign adventurism and even embarked upon limited expansionist wars in order to overcome internal tensions generated by the domestic class struggle. War has often in this sense been 'the health of the state', in Randolph Bourne's dictum. Parties of the left, on the other hand, have traditionally been isolationist in the United States, internationalist and anti-imperialist on the European continent, and Little Englanders in Britain.

One might conclude that outbreaks of war and international crises often initiate the rightist phase of the cycle. Schlesinger, however, denied this with respect to American politics, arguing that there was no 'correlation between foreign wars and the mass drifts of sentiments' and that 'conflicts have taken place about equally in conservative and liberal periods, sometimes coming at the start, sometimes at the end and sometimes midway'.[37] The Civil War would seem to have been another matter: the longest period of conservative rule, twice as long as Schlesinger's mean figure of 16·5 years, witnessed the emergence of the Republican Party as the undisputed champion of big business and coincided with their persistent 'waving the bloody shirt' at the Democrats. Moreover, the association of patriotism and militarism with the right was much more pronounced in Britain and on the European continent, both because democracy did not coincide there with the birth of the nation and because of inescapable involvement in wars and power politics in contrast to traditional American isolationism.

It can also be argued that the ideological significance of wars and international alignments for domestic division of opinion has become much greater in the present century. World War I divided the left; the Russian Revolution further divided it and enabled the right to make use of the 'red scare' as a political tactic. World War II, on the other hand, was fought against nations seen as the incarnation of the values most bitterly opposed by the left and therefore did not displace its ideological ascendancy. In America at least, the cold war and Korea, fought against an enemy laying total claim to the ideological heritage of the left, delegitimated the American left, almost completely obliterating its radical wing. The unpopularity and failure of the war in Vietnam played a large, even a major, part in the revival of radical protest movements in the 1960s and greatly reduced the identification of the left with international involvements that dated back to the anti-fascist ambience of the 1930s. This had been particularly pronounced in America because of Roosevelt's internationalism which was most vigorously opposed by anti-New Deal Republicans. Even the war in Vietnam was not unjustly described as a 'liberals' war'. More recently, both in America and elsewhere, the left has tended to resume its instinctive resistance to the salience of foreign policy and the government agencies, civil and military, that conduct it – the 'natural' posture, as it were, of the left, which defines itself by the priority it gives to domestic reforms implementing greater equality. Foreign policy choices – war and peace, military spending, international alignments (what George Washington called 'entangling alliances') – have more than any other issues been responsible for the factionalism to which the left is so notoriously prone.

One cannot, therefore, simply treat wars, international crises and issues of foreign policy as irrelevant to the rhythm of democratic politics or as *dei ex machina* that occasionally impinge upon and alter it. Nationalism and foreign policy have been, if not always in the United States, the stock-in-trade of the right in electoral politics, but in the increasingly interdependent and pervasive world of nations of the later twentieth century differences over foreign policy have frequently become associated with left-right differences on domestic issues.

The identification of the right with nationalism, however, is largely confined to the older Western democracies. Nationalism of the left has been a common phenomenon of independence movements in the Third World. The élites of new, formerly colonial nations have tended to be ideologically leftist, often having acquired their outlook as students in the former metropolitan countries or in the Communist world. As Lipset observes:

> In a context in which a large section of the élite supports leftist ideological goals, and in which the large majority live in poverty, the chances for conservative parties representing the traditional élite to remain viable electoral alternatives to the predominant leftists are quite rare.[38]

My concern has been with the politics of relatively stable democracies and the new nations of the underdeveloped world have not, alas, produced many of these. But the legitimacy acquired by the left in these nations through identification with their foundation emphasizes the historical limitations of the association of nationalism in the West with the right, and of the greater availability of patriotic symbols to parties of the right, striving to overcome the left's potential advantage in the collective resource of numbers by appealing to the wider community of the nation.

Recognition of the leftward drift inherent in democracy is likely to disturb and alarm partisans of the right who may see themselves as winning most of the battles but losing the war. But right-wing dis-illusionment with democracy need not stem solely from the increasing conviction that in the long-run the right is playing a losing game. The genuine commitment of some conservatives to the national community as a historical entity preserving a deep continuity with the past may give rise to distaste and contempt for the endless higgling and bickering of the politicians and their cynical pandering to the shallow and ephemeral emotions of the crowd in the constant quest for votes. The unity of the nation as 'a pact between the living and the dead and those who are yet to be born', in Burke's famous words, counts for more with such conservatives than party or class victories in electoral competition. Democracy thus produces what Aron calls a Right Opposition appalled by the pettiness and baseness of its political struggles. But it also produces a Left Opposition which, outraged by the persistence of class division and social injustice, views the parliamentary 'game' as a fraud perpetrated by a capitalist ruling class engaged in manipulating a shadow contest between venal political parties that never produces more than token changes in the direction of a fully classless or egalitarian society.[39] Militants of the left become disillusioned and radicalized by the glacial slowness of the leftward drift and the many counter-pressures and setbacks to which it is subject. They proceed to dismiss parliaments as 'talking-shops', the major parties as 'Tweedledum and Tweedledee', and the 'system' itself as a fraud in professing to offer opportunities for fundamental – nowadays often called 'structural' – change.

When a democratic political system and the leftward drift inherent in it have been in operation for some time, the *status quo* does not fully correspond to the interests, values or aspirations of either left or right: It reflects what John Rex describes as a 'truce situation' resulting from a balance of power rather than the complete ascendancy of either side.[40] If there are enough conservatives who regard themselves, like one cited by Collingwood, as 'a "brake" on the vehicle of progress', then the rhythm of democratic politics continues and the spiral pattern it traces moves to a higher level. ('He meant,' Collingwood explains, 'that the Conservative policy was not to stop the vehicle but to slow it down when it seemed likely to go too fast.'[41]) The pattern of movement is also maintained if there are enough men of the left who persist in seeing democracy itself as a partial but crucially important fulfilment of their values and who do not therefore countenance abandoning it in order to maximize other kinds of equality.

But there is no guarantee that these conditions will last. If Aron's Right and Left Opposition are products of the 'normal' workings of democracy, segments of them are attracted by violent revolutionary or counter-revolutionary short-cuts: in the case of the right, to arrest and even reverse the leftward drift; in the case of the left, to accelerate and complete it. In periods of acute national crisis and distress, a 'dialectic of the extremes', to use Aron's phrase, in which each side violently confronts the other, often enough in the streets, may take centre stage and threaten the very survival of democratic institutions. The last years of the Weimar Republic are, of course, the classic example. At such times, *les extrèmes se touchent* and the left-right spectrum itself resembles a horseshoe rather than a semi-circle or a straightline continuum. The dialectic of the extremes represents an effort to short-circuit the 'normal' pattern of alternating periods of protest and stabilization with its built-in tendency toward a glacially slow leftward drift. Democrats suspect those on both the left and the right who, out of impatience with the stately rhythm of democratic politics, wish to fracture it by making a forward 'leap to socialism' or the restoration of an idealized *status quo ante*, and this suspicion is surely well-founded. But, in a spirit of irony, democrats might well adopt as a motto for the institutions of political democracy Galileo's famous aside when forced to recant his belief in the Copernican theory: *eppur si muove* – 'yet it still moves'.

The 'democratic class struggle' and the left-right alignment it produces are not the sole content of democratic politics although they are probably the most universal and enduring basis of conflict. Ethnic, religious and racial divisions are central issues in the politics of a large number of democratic states and such subcultural cleavages clearly pose a much greater threat than class politics, not only to democracy but to the survival of the existing nation-state itself.[42] The interaction between ethno-religious differences and class divisions, how they intergrade in overlapping or cross-cutting ways, is a subject that requires greater attention than it has yet received. Critics of the Marxist insistence on the primacy of class have been too much inclined to present ethnicity as an alternative to class in providing a basis for group identity and conflict rather than as a difference which sometimes itself depends on and sometimes contributes to class division.[43] Obviously, in democratic politics the collective resource of numbers plays as crucial a role in the strategies of rival ethnic groups and in the outcome of their struggle as in the case of classes. The size and territorial concentration of an ethnic group may determine whether it adopts secessionist aims, seeks constitutionally guaranteed national rights within a multi-national state, or strives only for limited representation. The long-term process of political mobilization that so centrally shapes the rhythm of the democratic class struggle is less relevant to ethnic politics, but there may also be a rhythmic and a long-term pattern in the electoral competition of ethnic and religious groups, a movement that intersects, is superimposed upon, or varies inversely with the left-right rhythm. But my concern here has been solely to abstract out of the welter of democratic political experience a discernible rhythm or dialectic of the latter.

If the left should ever succeed in fully and permanently mobilizing its constituency the rhythm would come to an end. The left party would win all the elections and would presumably carry out egalitarian reforms eventuating in a socialist utopia. Even in Scandinavia, however, this millennium has not yet arrived. There is also the possibilty that the left's constituency of the lower classes may become more conservative with regard to future egalitarian reforms than important segments of the right's constituency.[44] There were at least intimations of this in the 1960s when such phrases as 'radical chic' and 'limousine liberal' entered political discourse. This possibility provides an additional cogent reason for separating the definition of 'left' and 'right' from the social basis of parties advocating egalitarian or anti-egalitarian programmes. But, at least in the United States, this dispensation remains a long way off, as revealed in particular by the detailed work of Richard Hamilton which shows that there is considerable latent support by the lower-middle, working and lower classes for egalitarian tax and welfare policies going far beyond those publicly advocated by spokesmen for the two major political parties.[45]

Epilogue

The theory of democratic politics here presented has, of course, implications going far beyond the particular connection in which I have introduced it. My purpose has been mainly to use it as an illustration of how mobilization of the collective resource of numbers, which is given legal priority in the selection of a government under political democracy with universal suffrage, produces over time a shifting balance of power between classes and parties regarded as vehicles of class interests. The significance of numbers as a collective resource might have been illustrated quite differently. Numbers are central, for example, to Mancur Olson's economic model of collective action[46] and to élitist theories of the greater cohesiveness of minorities as opposed to majorities[47]; both are approaches that emphasize the advantages of small rather than large numbers from the standpoint of creating the collective resources of solidarity and organization on which all other collective resources, including numbers, depend. Size has also been recognized increasingly as a key variable in organization theory.[48] The conception of democratic politics and the concepts of mobilization and collective resources can and should be evaluated independently of one another. I freely confess that my idea of the rhythm of democratic politics was formed long before I became interested in the conceptualization of power and of the individual and collective resources that are bases for exercising it. The reader will have to judge whether or not it serves as a useful illustration of the importance of numbers as a collective resource.

CHAPTER NINE

The Uses of Power

Why do people want power? Is it a nearly universal object of human striving? What good is it? What are its uses? Is its possession and exercise intrinsically gratifying or is it primarily sought as a means to a multitude of different ends? To what extent is the striving for power rooted in the most fundamental drives and motivations of human nature? How is power related to universal desires for material comforts and the approval of others – to Hobbes's gain and glory? Whatever the status of power as a generic psychological desideratum, are differences in power unavoidable prerequisites for effective social organization to pursue collective goals? Is power itself a necessary resource for the attainment of collective goals as well as being, as we have seen in the preceding chapters, the result of the mobilization of other resources? I shall try to answer these questions in this final chapter.

Power and Human Nature

The idea that a 'power drive', a 'will to power' or even a 'lust for power' is a major constituent of human nature is widely entertained and has deep roots in Western political thought. It is central to the Machiavellian tradition, although the insistence that in all societies the many are ruled by the few requires the assumption that either the ruling élite possesses exceptionally strong power drives or that, for the vast majority of men, a complementary desire to submit to the power of others outweighs the desire to wield it. If everyone had an equally strong power drive the result would more probably be a Hobbesian state of nature than a stable oligarchical political order. And Hobbes indeed in one of his most quoted statements maintained 'in the first place, I put for a general inclination of all mankind, a perpetual and restless desire of power after power, that ceaseth only in death'.[1] Probably no assertion is more often cited to illustrate the view that striving for power is a universal and elemental human motive, although Hobbes's very next sentence explicitly repudiates such a view:

> And the cause of this, is not always that a man hopes for a more intensive delight, than he has already attained to; or that he cannot be content with a moderate power: but because he cannot assure the power and means to live well, which he hath present, without the acquisition of more.[2]

In sum, even though men may be of peaceable disposition and 'content with a moderate power', they have to seek continually more power in order to secure the advantages they have already attained or else they will be deprived of what they have by the less successful who in a world of scarcity are prepared to 'kill, subdue, supplant or repel' them. Men seek power, according to Hobbes, not as an end-in-itself, a source of 'intensive delight', but as a means of acquiring scarce possessions and reputation in the eyes of others and, having acquired these, they must continue to augment their power for strictly defensive reasons in order to retain what they have won.

Machiavelli and Hobbes are undoubtedly the writers chiefly responsible for the claim that lust for power is a fundamental human endowment. Yet for the Machiavellians it is dominant only in the ruling minority and for Hobbes it is essentially a means to an end in a situation of scarcity in which

> if any two men desire the same thing, which nevertheless they cannot both enjoy, they become enemies; and in the way to their end, which is principally their own conservation, and sometimes their delectation only, endeavour to destroy, or subdue one another.[3]

The plausibility of the view that power is a basic drive rests in part on the ambiguity of the term 'power' itself. If power is broadly understood as 'man's present means to any future apparent good' (Hobbes) or as the capacity to 'produce intended effects' (Russell), then obviously all men seek power in the sense of striving to acquire the means and capacities to satisfy their needs and wants. So defined, power is equivalent to capability, potency or mastery, as we saw in Chapter 1. Needs and wants are conditions of deficit requiring action to alter the actor's relation to objects in his environment if the deficit is to be eliminated. To say therefore that men seek power is tautological if no more is meant than that men strive to satiate their needs and wants in a world in which instant, effortless gratification is unavailable. Clearly, everyone seeks to acquire the power to satisfy their wants and achieve their goals, but this is implied by the very concepts of 'want' and 'goal' themselves.

It does not, however, follow from this truism that everyone seeks power *over* other people, that is, strives to acquire the capacity to produce intended effects on the actions and attitudes of others. To compel or induce others to undertake the efforts necessary to satisfy one's own needs and wants is certainly a most effective way of ensuring satisfaction, one that even approximates to instant gratification. The infantile illusion of omnipotence reported by psychoanalysts involves just such an experience of effortless gratification resulting from constant parental ministration to the infant's needs. But it is, of course, short-lived: the infant's eventual awareness of his utter helplessness and total dependence on the parent is a traumatic experience producing 'separation anxiety' and the intrusion of the 'reality principle' into a psychic life previously governed by the 'pleasure principle'. Fantasies of total gratification easily merge into fantasies of God-like omnipotence over the lives of others, and *vice-versa*. A Jules Feiffer cartoon pictured Bernard, Feiffer's Woody Allen-like anti-hero, imagining himself the absolute ruler of the world using his power to achieve such noble objectives as peace for mankind, the liberation of the oppressed, restoration of the environment and the like. Then Bernard reflects with an apologetic leer, 'And I'll have lots and lots of girls!' The mad scientist holding the entire world up to ransom by means of a lethal instrument of destruction has long been a theme of popular culture, one that has moved uncomfortably closer to reality in recent years as a result of the rise of political terrorism combined with developments in nuclear technology.

Power over others, then, is readily seen as an instrument for the achievement of a wide range of goals. Power is the most universal means, indeed even more so than money because it can command that as well. Many recent writers have therefore described it as a 'medium' and classified it with such other general media as money, love, truth and linguistic competence.[4] To Hobbes, security, especially the avoidance of violent death at the hands of another person, is the overriding human motive, so the attainment of power is the surest way of deterring the depredations of others. Since the war of all against all is not always waged overtly but is rather a constant tendency or latent potentiality in the relations among men, reputation for power is the individual's most effective insurance policy. Therefore personal vanity and the desire for glory on which Hobbes lays considerable stress are ultimately reducible to reputation for power. Touchiness about personal honour, sensitivity to such

> trifles, as a word, a smile, a different opinion, and any other sign of undervalue, either direct in their persons, or by reflection in their kindred, their friends, their nation, their profession, or their name,[5]

ultimately reflect a defensive concern about one's reputation for power rather than a self-sufficient wish to enhance one's self-esteem by receiving deference from others.[6]

Yet the difference between 'power to' and 'power over' remains an important one. It has recently been much discussed at the level of collective power, a debate I shall review at a later point, but the distinction is clear at the level of individual motivation as Hobbes's progression from the neutral definition of power as capacity to attain ends to power over other men makes clear.[7] But even for Hobbes power over other men remains instrumental, a means to safe-guarding oneself against the possibility of coercion by others. He cannot therefore be credited with the belief that power over others is desired for its own sake and is innately grounded in human nature.[8]

If there is such an elemental lust for power, the primitive impulse from which it develops must surely be the propensity to aggression. In regarding aggression as one of the two basic human instinctual drives, Freud was more 'Hobbesian' than Hobbes, as is clear in the following well-known passage in which he actually cites a Latin phrase from Hobbes about man's wolfish treatment of his fellows:

> ... men are not gentle, friendly creatures wishing for love, who simply defend themselves if they are attacked, but ... a powerful measure of desire for aggression has to be reckoned as part of their instinctual endowment. The result is that their neighbor is to them not only a possible helper or sexual object, but also a temptation to them to gratify their aggressiveness on him, to exploit his capacity for work without recompense, to use him sexually without his consent, to seize his possessions, to humiliate him, to cause him pain, to torture and to kill him. *Homo homini lupus*; who has the courage to dispute it in the face of all the evidence in his own life and in history? This aggressive cruelty usually lies in wait for some provocation, or else it steps into the service of some other purpose, the aim of which might as well have been achieved by milder measures. In circumstances that favour it, when those forces in

the mind which ordinarily inhibit it cease to operate, it also manifests itself spontaneously and reveals men as savage beasts to whom the thought of sparing their own kind is alien.[9]

To Freud, aggression is the externalization of a primary suicidal or death instinct, but he frequently refers, as in the passage quoted, to aggression itself as innate. The passage makes clear that he regards aggression as intrinsically satisfying apart from the uses to which it may be put in serving other drives; this goes beyond Hobbes's instrumental view in making aggression inherent in human nature itself. Freud, of course, also postulated Eros as a rival basic drive impelling men to form positive emotional bonds with each other and there is no equivalent of this in Hobbes for whom 'men have no pleasure, but on the contrary a great deal of grief, in keeping company'.[10] The combinations and vicissitudes of the two instincts lead to the formation of the superego which internalizes the formerly external constraints imposed by the parents whereas to Hobbes only the external authority of the state restrains men from endeavouring to subdue and destroy one another.

Even most orthodox Freudian psychoanalysts have rejected the death instinct, although they have continued to regard hostile and aggressive impulses as universally human. The neo-Freudian revisionists reacted against Freud's 'pessimism' by interpreting aggression as a response to frustrations that are potentially removable by more permissive methods of socializing children or by creating a more egalitarian, less competitive society. Most of them abandoned Freud's dualistic instinct theory altogether and returned to more traditional pre-Freudian, conflict-free conceptions of human nature. Thinkers in the left Freudian tradition, such as Norman Brown and Herbert Marcuse, fully accepted the instinct theory but sought 'a way out' of its pessimistic implications by envisaging the dialectical overcoming of conflict between the instincts through the abolition of repression (Brown) or by the achievement of material abundance through technological progress which will transform human nature itself by eliminating the Hobbesian condition of scarcity and 'pacifying' the struggle for existence (Marcuse).[11]

But whether aggression is inherent in human nature or a response to remediable social conditions, its relevance to institutionalized power vested in social roles is limited. This applies even to violence, especially where the most technically advanced instruments of modern warfare are employed. Both contemporary ethologists and sociobiologists who have insisted that human aggressiveness is genetically based and their liberal-radical environmentalist critics have concentrated on the alleged implications of the hereditarian argument for the inevitability of war and violent conflict between organized groups in general. Yet the satisfactions of the aggressive impulse derived from dropping bombs from above the clouds on invisible human targets below would seem to be highly indirect and 'sublimated' at best – feeble indeed by comparison with a solid punch on the nose or a sword-thrust. Even the opportunity for the delight expressed by Bruno Mussolini on witnessing his aerial bombs set fire to African straw huts is lacking in modern air warfare.[12] Even without complex instruments of violence, the best soldiers are not necessarily those most strongly driven by motives of aggression.

Believers in innate aggression would be better advised to argue that human society cannot hope to eliminate bar-room brawls or violent domestic quarrels than to insist on the genetic inevitability of warfare. Apart from the impersonal, technologically routinized nature of much contemporary military violence, the motivational basis of violent behaviour which is normatively prescribed obviously differs from that of spontaneous violence, whether the latter expresses an autonomous instinct of aggression or is a response to a perceived threat. Freud himself was guilty of the psychologistic fallacy in regarding wars as no more than outlets for repressed aggression, thus treating a complex collective enterprise as human nature in the raw writ large.[13] As Philip Rieff has observed:

> By presuming that the super-ego counts for little in war, he misses the more terrifying fact that mass murder often presupposes a strong super-ego and positive identification with national ideals.[14]

If even violence, which (though often rule-governed[15]) is non-social behaviour below the level of symbolic communication, frequently does not express an innate aggressive drive, this is bound to be more true of power as a form of social relation or social interaction. At the very least a power drive acted out in a power relation must represent a refined, sublimated and socially modified manifestation of aggressiveness rather than a primitive urge emanating from original human nature. Even threatened violence, as distinct from its actual use, must amount to a partial inhibition and frustration of an innate aggressive drive – comparable perhaps to talking and fantasizing about sex as a

substitute satisfaction of the sexual drive.[16] In contrast to their concern
with the myriad forms of eroticism, psychoanalytic thinkers have given
less systematic attention to the sublimations, displacements and
symbolic substitutions to which aggressive impulses are subject.
Perhaps this is because, as Freud recognized in *Civilization and Its
Discontents*, the control of aggression is a *sine qua non* for the very
existence of human society whereas the necessity of sexual repression –
which, of course, he also upheld – is less obvious and has been precisely
the ground on which left Freudians like Reich, Marcuse and Brown
have challenged him.

People who have strong aggressive drives are more likely to end up in
jails or hospitals for the criminally insane than in positions of power.
Robert Lane notes with a caution that is perhaps excessive:

> A person with a raging desire for power who 'attaches great importance
> to imposing himself on others' will constantly alienate his supporters,
> thereby making the achievement of power impossible for him. On the
> whole persons with this value-orientation are relegated to minor roles in a
> democracy and the top positions go to people who value power as an
> implement to other life goals.[17]

Psychopaths who cannot control their aggressive drives are the least
likely candidates for positions of institutionalized power, although they
may be utilized by major power holders to do the dirty work of criminal
investigation, running prisons and concentration camps, and terrorizing
political opponents. Even in authoritarian or totalitarian societies, those
who give the orders to carry out brutal and violent actions do not
achieve full, direct satisfaction of their aggressive drives because they
rarely see what takes place 'at the end of the telegraph line'.[18]
When such bureaucrats of murder do happen to witness the carrying
out of their commands, they may recoil in horror: Heinrich Himmler
was present at one mass killing in occupied Russia and screamed
hysterically and came close to fainting.[19] This is partly what
Hannah Arendt meant by the phrase 'the banality of evil' with
reference to the Nazi mass murderers. Whatever the facts of Adolf
Eichmann's personal psychology, the calculated and unemotional use
of violence was characteristic of the Nazis, from those at the top who
initiated 'the final solution' for abstract ideological reasons to many of
its executors at the bottom of the chain of command who felt obliged

to comply with the orders of their superiors without questioning or resisting them.

If this is true of a collective policy of destructive violence, the connection between the non-violent commands and directives of most power holders and the satisfaction of aggressive impulses must be even more attenuated. Yet the historical record provides plentiful examples of psychopathic and paranoid personalities achieving or inheriting positions of political power. Hitler, Stalin, Idi Amin and Pol Pot are among the recent cases of national leaders who come to mind and the politics of stable constitutional democracies are not lacking in examples of power-seeking demagogues even if few of them have had long careers or have succeeded in reaching the summits of power in their nations. On a smaller scale, such personality types often seek out and achieve organizational positions in which they have the opportunity to exercise a modicum of authority and to make life miserable within limits for their subordinates. A rarer type of personality is the ego-dominated individual capable of a cold, intelligent, manipulative ruthlessness that makes him a far more promising candidate for leadership than the greedy, undisciplined psychopath whose aggressiveness and hunger for power rather quickly antagonize prospective supporters and patrons. Elaborating on some observations of Freud's, Philip Slater has suggested that the combination of rationality, boldness, and lack of superego inhibitions displayed by such narcissistic characters exerts a potent force of charismatic attraction on others which provides especially favourable opportunities for seeking and winning power.[20] Slater's illustrations are largely literary and such character types, often suggested by historical figures, have indeed fascinated writers and film-makers. Psychohistorical studies of powerful individuals can be expected to increase our understanding of such leaders and the quality of the allegiance given them by their followers.

Yet these examples of psychopathic and power-driven leaders attract notice and interest primarily because of their rarity or the enormity of the deeds they commit or set in motion. For most men of power, power-seeking is, if present at all, a motive shaped and moderated by socialization rather than an elemental impulse. The exercise of institutionalized power in modern societies involves little in the way of direct body-linked satisfactions but consists rather of handling abstract symbols and communicating decisions through relatively impersonal channels. The executive sitting at his desk behind a telephone 'dictating' memos to his secretary is an appropriate image. Positions of power are usually highly rewarded financially and carry great prestige; if, however, they are sought for gain or prestige, power is not valued as an intrinsic reward but as a means to other satisfactions at the level of egoistic motivation.

The desire for power seems to be both less psychologically primitive and less universal in humans than the desire for material rewards and for prestige. Material comforts and indulgences (including sexual gratification) are rooted in the body, and the wish to be thought well of as a prerequisite for thinking well of oneself is inherent in the self, for, as George Herbert Mead showed, the self is constituted by the reflexive nature of language and self-regarding attitudes are originally dependent on the 'reflected appraisals of others', in Harry Stack Sullivan's phrase. The greater prestige of roles invested with power makes it especially difficult to separate the enjoyment of power from the enjoyment of the prestige it brings; also, power is an asymmetrical relation in which the power subject submits to the power holder who may demand flattery and ceremonial gestures of respect. What looks like avid power-seeking may really be avid status-seeking when the powerful are assured of high status. Some writers have considered there is no difference between them; such a one is Bertrand Russell, who contended that

> the desire for glory ... prompts in the main the same actions as are prompted by the desire for power, and the two motives may, for most practical purposes, be regarded as one.[21]

Harold Lasswell sees power both as a value in itself and as a base for the attainment of other values, including wealth and prestige (or respect).[22] He characterizes the political man as one who

> pursues power as a means of compensation against deprivation. *Power is expected to overcome low estimates of the self*, by changing either the traits of the self or the environment in which it functions[23] (italics in text).

One can readily distinguish between the ego-enhancement that comes from the ability to control other people's lives and even to induce fear in them and the sense of self-importance resulting from the praise and deference bestowed by others — between the blood-thirsty tyrant and the celebrity adored by millions, to take extreme examples of each. But

Lasswell's definition is too broad to encompass this distinction; neither his character types linked to particular political roles (agitator, bureaucrat, etc.) nor his case studies of individuals establish a very close fit between personality needs and role performances.[24]

If we overlook the sadistic tyrant who finds gratification in inflicting pain and death on others, one might expect to find people strongly attracted to power as such to be drawn to positions permitting the manipulation of others in which the very existence of the manipulator remains unknown to all but a few. One thinks of 'grey eminence' roles: behind-the-scenes intriguers and wire-pullers, advisers to princes, political bosses controlling from smoke-filled rooms the politicians who receive the plaudits of crowds, and members of presidential 'kitchen cabinets', although the latter have in recent decades received a good deal of attention from the media – Haldeman and Ehrlichman, and even Rebozo and Albanalp, were hardly unknown figures even before the Watergate scandal became public. But the satisfaction of knowing that one is secretly controlling careers and important historical events, even though others are given the credit (or the blame) for doing so, would seem to be a highly refined, sophisticated and cerebral kind of pleasure quite remote from the crude lust for power postulated by so many psychologists of politics.

Types of Orientation towards Power

The motives of most power seekers and power holders, like those of most power subjects and indeed of most people most of the time, are compounds of fundamental human impulses, shaped, channelled and sublimated – 'cribbed, cabined and confined', if you like – by the social and socializing experiences they have undergone. It is nevertheless possible to distinguish the predominance of one or another basic motive in individuals even if there is no neat correspondence between forms of conduct, such as seeking and exercising power over others, and the motives that actuate it, such as a specific power drive reflecting an underlying aggressive impulse. As one author has put it,

> The difference between a rich man, a celebrity and a ruler is something like this: A rich man collects cattle and hoards of grain, or the money which stands for them. . . . A ruler collects men. Grain and cattle, or money, mean nothing to him except insofar as he needs them to get hold of men. . . . A celebrity collects a chorus of voices. All he wants is to hear them repeat his name.[25]

Or, as W. G. Runciman concludes more prosaically:

> To want wealth is not necessarily to want prestige or power; to want
> prestige is not necessarily to want power or wealth; to want power is not
> necessarily to want wealth or prestige.[26]

The differences can be significant. In his biography of Senator Joseph
McCarthy, Richard Rovere attributes McCarthy's meteoric career and
his quick decline and death after the Senate censured him to the fact that
he was essentially a 'man of glory' rather than a 'man of power'. Rovere
concludes:

> It was the lack of conviction that made McCarthy at once a more
> vulnerable and a more interesting human being than any of his followers
> or imitators. The conviction he lacked was an absurd thing. He was
> somewhat the better for lacking it – as we were the better for the fact that
> he sought glory more than power. The glory drive is always less
> dangerous because it is more easily frustrated. It is selfish, or self-seeking,
> in the narrowest sense, and it makes defeat and humiliation a personal
> affair. A discouraged politician with no deep sense of mission can go off
> with his reveries of peace into the Arizona desert, but a man possessed
> could never do so, for he knows that his dreams and his demons could not
> follow him.[27]

When Rovere contrasts McCarthy's craving for glory, for making a
splurge in the media and acquiring the reputation of the Great Accuser,
with his lack of 'belief in the sacredness of his mission', he is not
contrasting the desire for glory with the desire for personal power but
rather the glory drive with the determination to wield power in the
service of a collective ideal or cause. There is no reason to regard a
craving to enjoy the intrinsic satisfactions of exercising power as any
less selfish or narrow than a craving for fame or notoriety and it is
usually far more dangerous. Compare McCarthy with Stalin, originally
a shadowy bureaucrat in the background with no oratorical ability. Of
course, McCarthy's medium was words in the form of accusations,
words as deeds or 'performative utterances',[28] and, in addition to
attracting attention, this gave him the power to damage the reputations
of others. Yet Rovere is surely right in contending that McCarthy's
'selfishness' accounts for his apparent acceptance of total defeat after
the Senate had censured him. The archetypal charlatan or con-man in
politics, McCarthy was incapable of enduring a period in the wilderness

from which he might well have emerged after a few years to become a powerful figure in the Republican Party when the Party turned to the right in the early 1960s and awarded its presidential nomination to a man of very different personality who came, it so happened, from the Arizona desert.

It can be argued that great prestige and great wealth imply power because each is acquired as a result of the capacity to produce intended effects on others. High prestige accrues to those who succeed in 'cashing in their status claims', as C. Wright Mills put it,[29] by successfully eliciting respectful and approving responses from others. Wealth in the form of money is commonly referred to as 'purchasing power'. More important, those who control men's labour and its products exercise power over them that C. B. Macpherson calls 'extractive power'.[30] Inequalities of wealth resulting from inequalities in extractive power are lacking only in unstratified tribal societies and communities of independent agriculturalists, as was recognized, of course, by both Rousseau and Marx. In Max Weber's well-known discussion of social stratification he stated at the outset that 'the distribution of power in a community is reflected in the existence of "classes", "status groups" and "parties"',[31] after first noting that wealth, status and power may either be valued for their own sakes or employed as means to obtaining one another. Parties, as distinct from classes or status groups, 'are primarily at home in the sphere of power' in that they are organized groups mobilized to pursue a definite goal in competition or conflict with other groups. Weber has been the major influence on contemporary sociologists who make use of the triad of wealth, status and power (or the three p's: privilege, prestige and power) to refer to three kinds of unequally distributed rewards on which the stratification of modern societies is held to be founded. But he regarded the distribution of wealth and status as themselves the consequence of differences in power and he was primarily concerned with the groups or potential groups formed on the basis of common economic, status and political interests rather than with the rewards of individuals. He recognized, of course, that some people sought power for its own sake, but his major emphasis was on power as the most effective means for securing other rewards and on parties as mobilized conflict groups seeking a variety of objectives which might or might not include gaining for their members the pleasures of exercising power as well as other 'sinecures'.

In 'Politics as a Vocation' Weber distinguished those who live 'off' politics from those who live 'for' it. Although his first and most obvious example of the former is the man who makes his living from politics just as other men do from other occupations, Weber also includes under the same rubric the man who engages in politics primarily for *any* self-centred motive, including the desire to enjoy power for its own sake:

> Either he enjoys the naked possession of the power he exerts, or he nourishes his inner balance and self-feeling by the consciousness that his life has *meaning* in the service of a 'cause'.[32]

Only the latter lives *for* politics. Later in the essay, Weber asks directly, 'What can politics as a vocation offer in the way of satisfaction?' and answers, 'Well, it offers first of all the sense of power.'[33] He distinguishes this from 'vanity – the need to occupy the limelight as much as possible' and observes that, although vanity is 'a kind of occupational disease' of academic men, it usually does not interfere with their scholarly activity whereas for the politician it is a 'mortal sin' to which the 'demagogue' in particular is tempted because he

> is forced to take into account the 'effect' which he produces: indeed just because of this he runs a constant risk of becoming a play-actor, making light of the responsibility for the consequences of his actions and asking only what 'impression' he is making.

One recalls Rovere's discussion of Joseph McCarthy.

Weber clearly distinguishes between vanity – the desire for prestige or glory – and the urge for power. Of the latter he observes:

> Even in positions which are, formally speaking, modest, the professional politician can feel himself elevated above the everyday level by the sense of exercising influence over men, of having a share in power over their lives, but above all by the sense of having his finger on the pulse of historically important events.

But the urge to power as much as vanity can become a mortal sin if it is the politician's primary motivation or if he allows himself to be intoxicated by it:

> ... there is no more pernicious way to distort the political drive than for a politician to boast of his power like a parvenu and luxuriate conceitedly in the sensation of power – in short, to worship power for its own sake.

Weber's argument is that only men with a goal that transcends narrow self-interest can achieve an unwavering sense of responsibility for the consequences of political action and what David Riesman once called 'the nerve of failure'[34] – for frustrations and defeats are inevitable in politics which is always 'a strong and slow boring of hard boards'.[35]

A fourfold classification of individual orientations towards power, combining positions on the two variables of whether power is sought as a means or as an end and whether it serves an individual ('selfish') or collective aim, suggests itself and is presented below. All four

Goals for which power is sought:

Power sought as:	Individual	Collective
Means	A	C
End-in-itself	B	D

orientations may, of course, be present to some degree in any particular political man: human motivation is usually, as we have had occasion to remark before, a complex mixture of often contradictory and conflicting impulses, affects and internalized values. A scatter diagram would perhaps capture this intergrading of the four orientations better than a fourfold table. Nevertheless, considering its boxes as ideal types, the table serves to highlight and summarize the varying attitudes individuals may have to political power.

Box A contains those who seek power as a means to secure other, purely personal satisfactions, such as the ordinary professional politician, the *apparatchik* who simply makes his living from politics. The boodling politician and the corrupt official are obvious extreme cases. The glory-seeker for whom fame is the spur also clearly belongs in this cell.

Box B includes the psychopath, the paranoid and the narcissistic leader type described by Freud and Slater who is equipped with a strong ego to control his insistent id impulses and a weak superego that imposes few restraints on him. The classical stereotype of the 'Machiavellian' or 'Hobbesian' power seeker, driven by an insatiable hunger to impose his will on others, belongs in this cell. Individual examples are the notoriously cruel tyrants and conspirators of history from Richard of Gloucester and Cesare Borgia to Stalin and Hitler in our own day.

The two cells on the right-hand side of the table include individuals who may have little disposition to seek power either for instrumental reasons or as a consummation in itself. They may nonetheless exercise power out of a sense of duty in the service of an ideal or as an obligation to their group or community. An extreme case would be Cincinnattus who, after heeding a summons to lead the Roman armies to victory in the field, declined the Consulship and chose to return to his plough. If the well-known anthropological accounts of the Mountain Arapesh of New Guinea and the Zuni Indians of New Mexico are to be believed, whole cultures – at least primitive ones – may induce in their members a profound distaste for assuming the tasks of leadership. If power is sought as a satisfaction or an opportunity by some men, there are others who experience it as a burden and take pains to avoid exercising it. There are, of course, also ascetics who starve themselves and mortify their flesh and psychological masochists who seek humiliation and continually denigrate themselves. (Although, as Nietzsche said: 'A man condemns himself yet praises himself as a self-condemner'.) But there seem to be far fewer ascetics and masochists than people who have a positive disinclination to wield power over others. This is a further indication that material acquisitiveness and the wish to be personally valued by others are universally human motives, but that the striving for power as an intrinsic source of pleasure is not. Although the power drive may be an expression of impulses to aggression that *are* universally human, the actual exercise of power in social roles that enjoin or permit it is, as we have seen, far removed from any direct, emotionally satisfying release of hostile or aggressive feelings. Power is, of course, widely sought as a means to obtain all kinds of other direct satisfactions (as in cell A of the table), but it is scarcely unique in this respect. We regard the man who accumulates money for itself rather than for the things it can buy as an abnormal deviant called a miser; the sadist or despot who values power for its own sake might be regarded as similarly abnormal and indeed often is so regarded. I do not mean to suggest that people who belong in cells C and D of the table are necessarily free of any craving for power as such and wield it only out of duty or as a burden 'thrust upon them'. All that is assumed is that a taste for power, whether as an instrument for obtaining other purely egoistic rewards or for its own sake, is not an essential nor even a primary element in their motivation.

Cell C contains persons who seek or wield power in the service of ideals, values or the collective interests of a group to which they have made a commitment. The group may be a nation, an institutional structure, a church, an ethnic group, a class, a party or social movement, or a limited special-interest group. It may see itself as the incarnation or embodiment of comprehensive ultimate religious or secular values, or as a crusading army striving to realize an ideal by transforming the world; it may seek to defend and represent the diffuse sentiments and interests of a larger constituency; it may endeavour to promote a single cause, ideal or reform such as conservation, civil liberties or minority rights; or it may be concerned only with limited economic and utilitarian interests of its members, as in the case of the political activities of many professional associations, business lobbies and trade unions. In all of these examples, binding norms or commitments to a collective goal lead to a concern with objective consequences that serves to discipline the pursuit of power and avoid a surrender merely to savouring it as a subjective sensation.

Cell D is probably less thickly populated, at least in most historical epochs, than the other three cells, but it has been of considerable significance in the twentieth century. The supporters of movements with the primary objective of winning collective power unrestrained by substantive norms or ideal goals belong in this cell, although the Actonian corruption of power may produce such a tendency in the leaders of any power-seeking group. A fictional member of the cell would be Orwell's O'Brien who proclaimed that 'power is not a means; it is an end' and 'the object of power is power', referring to the potentially eternal collective power of the Party rather than to power for himself alone as we saw in Chapter 5. Granting that her description of totalitarianism is visionary and suffers from an excess of ideal-typical exaggeration, Hannah Arendt's discussion of the totalitarian's central belief in 'organizational omnipotence' remains outstanding:

Power, as conceived by totalitarianism, lies exclusively in the force produced through organization . . . Whatever connection power had in the minds of Western man with earthly possessions, with wealth, treasures, and riches, has been dissolved into a kind of dematerialized mechanism whose every move generates power as friction or galvanic currents generate electricity. The totalitarian division of states into Have and Have-not countries is more than a demagogic device; those who make it are actually convinced that the power of material possessions is

negligible and only stands in the way of the development of
organizational power.[36]

To Max Weber, the members of the two left-hand cells are sub-
ethical, below the level of 'the *ethos* of politics as a cause' and lacking
any true 'sense of vocation' for politics. What about the members of cell
D? Belief that 'the end justifies the means' is hardly peculiar to a
totalitarian outlook for it characterizes anyone who engages in politics,
who is necessarily committed, as Weber insisted, to the use of violence
as a means. The totalitarian is, perhaps, he who acts as if the end
justifies *any* means, Brecht's Communist in that prophetic play of
1930, *Die Massnahme*, who is prepared to 'lie down in the dirt, embrace
the butcher' and 'of all the virtues has but one, that he fights for
Communism'.[37] But this is still insufficient because, for Brecht at least,
the eventual triumph of the Communist Party remains a means: 'Alas,
we who wished to lay the foundations of kindness could not ourselves be
kind'. For the full-fledged totalitarian, the collective power of the
movement or organization is itself his end. The organizational weapon
has ceased to be a mere instrument but has become the final measure of
value. The slogan 'my country right or wrong' expresses the same
morality and, needless to say, extreme nationalism has been a fertile
seedbed of totalitarian politics.

Since cell C clearly contains those who are committed to Weber's
'ethic of responsibility' (*Verantwortungsethik*), there is a temptation to
assign to cell D the followers of the rival 'ethic of intentions'
(*Gesinnungsethik*). Many writers have grouped together as followers of
Gesinnungsethik the totalitarian man of violence ready to countenance
any measures that will advance his end and the saint or exemplary
prophet who believes in living according to his vision and his values no
matter what the consequences. They have doubtless been encouraged to
make this equation by the frequent translation of *Gesinnungsethik* as
'ethic of absolute ends'. The saint and the totalitarian – 'the yogi and the
commissar' – are indeed alike in believing in an absolute end, but only
the former is indifferent to the consequences of his actions and primarily
concerned with the ethical intentions motivating them. The totalitarian,
by contrast, is interested *only* in the consequences according to whether
they promote or hinder his end, the acquisition of power. ('How many
divisions has the Pope?' as Stalin asked rhetorically.) The saintly
adherent to the Sermon on the Mount is not a political man at all if he
truly practises what he preaches; nor does he belong in any of the cells

of our fourfold table, which presuppose a readiness to make use of all forms of power including force. Weber recognized anarcho-syndicalists as secular practitioners of an ethic of intentions because their advocacy of violence stemmed not from a calculation of its probable consequences but from a determination to ensure that 'the flame of pure intention, the flame of protest against the injustice of the social order, is not extinguished'. This is hardly the attitude of the totalitarian activist, nor even of contemporary Italian and German terrorists who contend that their acts of violence will provoke the state to 'fascist' counter-measures which will then arouse the apathetic masses to revolt; such a policy of 'the worse, the better' continues to justify itself by an appeal to consequences.

By the criterion of giving priority to the consequences over the intentions of an act, the totalitarian is an extreme practitioner of the ethic of responsibility, extreme in that he does not like the moderate practitioner combine at some point the two ethics by ruling out the use of some morally questionable means however effective they might be or by avoiding some actions because they will have undesirable consequences in addition to those intended.[38] The problem of where to classify the totalitarian perhaps emphasizes the failure of Weber's categorization of the two ethics to cover all possible resolutions of the means-ends dilemmas posed by politics.[39] The difference between cells C and D in the table, however, is not equivalent to that between Weber's two types of ethic.

The preceding discussion has for the most part dealt with political power, which, virtually by definition, is the most extensive, comprehensive and intensive kind of power, at least for those in top leadership roles. The institutionalized power vested in lower and non-political positions is less extensive, more scope-specific and more restricted in intensity. Those who occupy positions of authority in total institutions – prison guards, hospital and nursing home attendants, junior officers and NCOs in the armed forces, boarding school teachers – are at least partial exceptions where comprehensiveness and intensity are concerned and, of course, families notoriously provide a limited arena for domestic despots. But middle-level bureaucrats, professionals, and most teachers have rather narrow outlets for their putative power drives; even their opportunities to 'abuse' power tend to be confined to making sexual advances to secretaries and female clerical workers or taking advantage of students to obtain their services as baby-sitters or house-cleaners. Except for bank employees, even the

chances for financial peculations are fairly restricted in most bureaucratic and service occupations. Moreover, as critics of Mills's *The Power
Elite* pointed out, there are many things that the high and mighty who
control the executive branch of the American government cannot do,
especially in domestic policy: defy Supreme Court verdicts, nationalize
the steel industry, give preferential treatment to Catholics, or, as we
learned from Watergate, break into the opposition party's campaign
headquarters, burgle the offices of psychiatrists, or keep records of
conversations among themselves out of the hand of congressional
committees and the courts.

Power, in short, may be a medium, but it is not a very generalized
medium, at least as it is exercised in most established social roles.
Considerably less so than money, in fact: as Roderick Martin remarks,
'Power relations are more comparable to barter than to open-market
relations'.[40] Nor is it possible to compare the 'amounts' of power
possessed by different roles even to the extent that this is possible in
constructing occupational status scales.[41] Does the policeman who can
compel me to appear in court and pay a fine for a traffic offence have
more power than the professor who can give a student a failing grade
that may affect his or her future career opportunities? The policeman's
power is considerably more extensive (there are more citizens than
students even in university towns), but the professor's power may have
wider effects that last for a much longer time.

In conclusion, the concept of a quasi-biological or universally human
psychological power drive is neither a tenable nor a useful one. People
are undoubtedly often able to express hostile and aggressive impulses
by wielding power over others, but it is usually a highly indirect,
canalized and symbolic form of expression. Power is more often sought
as a means to other satisfactions such as wealth, sexual gratification,
prestige, and a wide range of valued experiences in general. Absolute
power over others, as we have seen, is indeed a universally effective
means capable of obtaining almost any object of desire (though not
respect and love, or at least the assurance that a declaration of respect
or love is genuine and freely given rather than expediential or coerced).
But for all but a tiny few absolute power is a fantasy rather than a
realistic goal and bears slight resemblance to the hedged-in power
exercised in social roles. The power vested in social roles other than the
'command posts' at the top of institutional hierarchies is too scope-
specific and limited in extent to be transferable to other situations.
Political power is most persistently and successfully sought by persons

committed to a cause or collective goal; politics as a vocation reflects therefore a socialized purpose rather than a primitive craving.

Whatever the motives of individuals for seeking and using power to attain their own ends, collective goals are attributes of groups rather than individuals. Personal enjoyment of power and its use to achieve other satisfactions are essentially by-products or side-effects of the contribution the exercise of power makes towards the realization of collective goals. Does the collective power created by pooling and mobilizing the resources of individuals represent a gain for some groups at the expense of others, or can the generation of collective power result in a net gain for the entire community who are influenced by its exercise? Let us turn to this much-debated question.

Collective Power and the 'Zero-Sum' Debate

The debate revolves around the distinction between 'power to' and 'power over' and to *whom*, that is, to what groups or collectivities, each or both kinds of power should be imputed.[42] The distinction itself is scarcely a new one. It is recognized at least implicitly by many writers of the past. Machiavelli, for example, dwelt at length on the cruelties and deceits – the techniques of 'force and fraud' – practised by successful princes in their dealings with rivals and subordinates, but he argued that such practices were necessary in order to ensure and enhance the security and strength of the state. *Raison d'état* clearly implies a collective goal.

Hobbes, as we have seen, initially defined power very broadly as generalized capacity and then argued that power, or reputation for power, to subdue or destroy others was essential for the security of any man's person and possessions. Power *against* can be considered a particular form of power *to*, namely, the power to defend oneself against the attacks of others. Power *over* others is never securely won in Hobbes's state of nature in which, as he repeatedly insisted, all men are ultimately equal, their equality consisting in their equal ability to kill and despoil one another. True, a man may sometimes succeed 'by force, or wiles, to master the persons of all men he can',[43] but such power relations are unstable 'for there are very few so foolish, that had not rather govern themselves, than be governed by others'.[44] Stable power over others only comes into being when men have made a covenant to end 'that dissolute condition of masterless men, without subjection to laws, and a coercive power to tie their hands from rapine and revenge'[45] by agreeing to create and submit to just such a 'coercive power' in the form of civil government, 'that great Leviathan, called a Commonwealth, or State . . . which is but an artificial man'. Only when such a 'common power' *over* them 'able to keep them all in awe' exists can individual men realize their power *to* achieve their diverse ends.

The contrast between the views of C. Wright Mills and Talcott Parsons has been the main focus of the recent debate over the uses of power. Both men were primarily concerned with collective power, but for Mills the power of a group in a stratified society is necessarily exercised over and at the expense of a subordinate group whereas for Parsons power is a collective resource utilized to advance the goals of the entire community or the social system at large.[46] Parsons first put forward his alternative conception in a critical review of Mills's *The Power Elite*; Mills never replied directly, although in a later book he scathingly attacked Parsons's sociological theory in general and dismissed in particular Parsons's emphasis on 'common values' by redefining them as 'master symbols of legitimation' serving to 'justify or oppose the arrangement of power and the position within this arrangement of the powerful'.[47] Parsons later elaborated his concept of power in a series of articles published after Mills's death.[48]

Some of the difficulties with Mills's formulation followed from the fact that he wished to abandon many traditional Marxist assumptions, especially those pertaining to political and military power, while retaining others. He therefore sought to combine a Marxist view of deep-rooted conflict of interests between classes with an élitist conception of political power similar to that of the neo-Machiavellians. Insisting that a small group of men were able to make decisions of enormous consequence for the rest of the population, his vehement expressions of moral indignation over this fact often appeared gratuitous in light of his failure to specify the precise nature of the conflicting interests at issue between the élite and their subjects, the existence of which he nevertheless assumed. The decisions he mentioned were exclusively major foreign policy decisions and he remained vague as to how group rather than national interests dictated them. For example, two critics with quite opposite views of the nature of the Cold War, one an anti-Communist social democrat and the other at that time a fellow-traveller, charged him with failure to make clear whether he considered American foreign policy after 1945 to be primarily a response to the threat of Soviet expansion or whether he regarded the alleged threat as a non-existent bogey invented by the power élite in order to justify its tight control over American society and to discredit any protest from the left.[49] Presumably, the élite was regarded as having a primary interest in retaining its power and excluding the rest of the population from sharing in it, but, since Mills did not appear to accept the neo-Machiavellian belief that this inevitably followed from unalterable psychological constants in human nature, the absence of even a conventional Marxist notion of the conflicting interests of owning and labouring classes left large ambiguities in his position. On the one hand, he seemed to view politics as a simple and ceaseless 'struggle for power' – as indeed he described it. On the other hand, his tone of moral condemnation lent justice to Parsons's complaint that Mills appeared to cherish 'a utopian conception of an ideal society in which power does not play a part at all'.[50]

In his earliest theoretical statement on power, the review of Mills, Parsons made plain at the outset that his view of power in contrast to Mills's was centred on 'power to', noting that 'Mills . . . adopts one main version of the concept without attempting to justify it. This is what may be called the "zero-sum" concept; power, that is to say, is power *over* others'[51] (italics in text). He then states: 'What this conception does is to elevate a secondary and derived aspect of a total phenomenon into the central place.' The idea of power as a zero-sum concept seems to have fascinated later commentators, perhaps because it is borrowed from game theory and sounds impressively precise. The characterization of 'power over' as a zero-sum concept has become sufficiently widespread to justify my using the term to label the whole debate. In general, Parsons's theorizing about power has set the terms of the debate to such a degree that his formulations deserve a brief review.

Parsons cross-classifies the forms of power according to two binary variables which yield, as so often in his work, a four-fold typology.[52] His variables are whether the sanctions employed to achieve compliance are positive or negative (rewards or penalties), and whether the power holder alters the power subject's situation or his intention. Parsons calls positive situational sanctions *inducement*, and negative situational sanctions *coercion*. Positive intentional sanctions constitute *persuasion*, negative intentional sanctions *activation of commitments*, that is, appeals to duty. Parsons's 'inducement' and 'coercion' do not differ from what I classified, using the same terms, as forms of authority. His 'persuasion' is broader than mine, including also what I called 'competent authority', and his 'activation of commitments' is equivalent to my 'legitimate authority'. However, only the latter constitutes 'power' in Parsons's sense; he explicitly denies that the other three types are to be regarded as 'forms of power.'

To Parsons, power must be a 'symbolic' or 'generalized medium' for obtaining compliance with collectively acknowledged obligations. For this reason, he regards neither 'personal authority', 'manipulation' nor 'coercion' as forms of power for none of them need be institutionalized. He argues that

> by my definition, securing compliance with a wish, whether it be defined as an obligation of the object or not, simply by threat of superior force, is not an exercise of power. . . . The capacity to secure compliance must, if it is to be called power in my sense, be generalized and not solely a function of one particular sanctioning act which the user is in a position to impose, and the medium used must be 'symbolic'.[53]

This definition excludes both force and many instances of the threat of force. Of course one would not want to call a single exercise of coercion, say an armed robbery, an instance of a power relation, which implies recurrent interaction.[54] But force and the threat of force are not always 'a function of one particular sanctioning act'. Parsons, nevertheless, does not deny force any role in institutionalized power relations. His writings on power were partly an attempt to remedy the criticisms levelled at his theorizing by conflict and coercion theorists, including Mills, for its alleged overemphasis on value-consensus and he assigns an apparently central role to force in his formulations. He sees force as 'backing up' commands and obligations analogously to the way gold or the gold standard backs up money as a medium of economic exchange. The ultimate threat of force to deter noncompliance is what gives power its symbolic status as a medium for obtaining compliance.

If Parsons's definition of power excludes both the use of force and the threat of force as 'a function of one particular sanctioning act', one might interpret him as accepting the threat of force provided it is 'generalized' — that is, serves to maintain a stable recurrent power relation of some comprehensiveness and intensity. From such a standpoint, his position would not differ from that of David Easton and myself who have insisted that it is meaningful to speak of 'coercive authority' or from several recent theorists who have sharply distinguished between force and the threat of force.[55] But this interpretation is not justified: it is only 'the legitimate use of force', as Weber put it in his famous definition of the state, with which Parsons is concerned – force, that is, which is threatened or applied against recalcitrant actors *with the approval or consent of those other members of the community who are not themselves recalcitrant.*[56] 'Illegitimate' uses or threats of force, however effectively 'generalized' in maintaining a comprehensive and intensive power relation over time, are not considered. Thus Parsons ends up, despite his explicit claim that force undergirds power as gold does currency, 'by treating', in the words of Giddens, 'power as necessarily (by definition) legitimate, and thus *starting* from the assumption of consensus of some kind between power holders and those subordinate to them'.[57]

Parsons's formulation leads back to a prior assumption of consensus by yet another route. Power, he insists, is primarily a facility that makes possible the attainment of collective goals to which a normative commitment has been made. Power is not therefore a zero-sum phenomenon in which the power holder's gain necessarily entails a loss on the part of the power subject. This emphasis is a justified corrective to extreme Thrasymachean or anarchistic views of power, but it presupposes the existence of collective goals grounded in the shared values of a public that benefits from their attainment by means of an organized and established system of power.[58] Neither the reality of the underlying consensus nor the process by which the system of collective power becomes organized and established are problematical to Parsons. He takes them for granted.

Parsons defends his conceptual approach to power as opposed to 'diffuse' classifications of 'the "forms" of power' (such as, presumably, my own in Chapters 2 and 3) on the grounds that such classifications

> make it logically impossible to treat power as a *specific* mechanism operating to bring about changes in the action of other units, individual or collective, in the processes of social interaction[59] (italics in text).

I fail to see how a close description of the processes of social interaction involved in persuasion, coercion or the exercise of legitimate authority can be characterized as insufficiently specific to account for the intended effects they produce on the actions of individuals or groups. Parsons's real complaint seems to be that classifications of the forms of power are insufficiently generalizable to account for the way power operates as a symbolic medium. As Lehman, whose own approach is explicitly at the 'macro' level, notes, Parsons is primarily concerned with *political power* in large-scale societies 'with structurally differentiated and powerful *states*.[60] Indeed, Parsons's focus on legitimate political power in conjunction with his idea that power is the servant of collective goals rooted in a majority consensus sounds, as several critics have noted, like a somewhat idealized conception of American democracy. The range of power relations which the sociologist, even – or perhaps especially – the political sociologist, may wish to analyse is likely to be a good deal broader than that of total 'system effects' at the so-called 'macro' level in stable advanced industrial societies.

Parsons regards power as one of a class of media that also includes money, influence and value-commitments. His treatment of power is considerably shaped by his effort to show that its role in the polity as a medium for implementing collective goals is analogous to the role of money as a medium of exchange in the economy. Clearly, he is referring to the power of the state to adopt policies affecting the entire society, for power as an attribute of social roles below the apex of political power is, as we saw above, too scope-specific to be transferable to a very wide range of scopes and can hardly therefore be regarded as a medium comparable to money. The analogy between power and money has been examined in exhaustive detail and rejected by Cartwright and Warner.[61]

Giddens argues that in making 'legitimacy part of his very definition of power' Parsons avoids the confusion made by other writers between the bases and forms of power:

> Parsons thus rejects the frequently held conception that authority is a 'form' of power or is 'legitimate power'. . . . Authority refers to the legitimate position of an individual or group, and is therefore properly regarded as a *basis* of power (for Parsons, the only basis of power), rather than as a kind of power. It is precisely the confusion of the forms with the bases of power which causes Parsons to specify a very restricted definition of power. Authority is no more a form of power than force is a form of power.[62]

Giddens' use of the notions of bases and forms of power clearly differs from my own. Legitimate authority (which, like so many other writers, he calls simply 'authority') is indeed based on the *right* of the power holder to command by virtue of incumbency in a role which grants the right (or imposes the responsibility as an obligation) in accordance with the norms of a 'collectivity of subordinates' in Blau's terms.[63] In this sense, legitimate authority can be considered a base or resource enabling someone to exercise power, just as the possession of a large bank account or of a gun constitutes such a base or resource. In Etzioni's terms, the latter two are utilitarian and coercive resources respectively whereas legitimacy is a normative resource. My own approach has explicitly treated both force and legitimate authority as 'forms' rather than 'bases' of power. Force is a form of power; guns and other instruments of force are a basis for its application (and, more importantly, as argued in Chapter 3, for its threatened application). The issuance of an order by the incumbent of a role empowered with the right (or obligation) to command is a form of power if the order is obeyed; incumbency in the role is a basis for the exercise of power in the form of legitimate authority. Parsons equates the latter with power itself because he sees only legitimate authority as generalized enough to cover an indeterminate range of possible decisions favourable to the attainment of collective goals. But all forms of power possess some comprehensiveness and intensity, which is essentially what he means by 'generalizability'. Nor is legitimate authority always the most extensive form of power.

The collective power of organized and solidary groups controlling the aggregated resources of individuals is capable of achieving goals far beyond the capacities of individuals; it is also more enduring and superior to the power of unorganized aggregates of people as well as to that of the most powerful individual. I referred to these as virtually sociological platitudes in Chapter 6. If this is all that Parsons means in insisting that power is a facility or resource for the attainment of collective goals, it is acknowledged in such hoary maxims as 'in unity there is strength', 'united we stand, divided we fall' and 'divide and conquer'. These maxims implicitly refer to conflict situations in which 'power to' takes the form of 'power against' other groups or oppressive power holders and they therefore ignore 'power over' as a relation between individuals and groups.

Several commentators have pointed out that, although Parsons describes himself as a liberal, his conception of power as a collective resource is similar to that of Robert S. Lynd, who was a socialist.[64] In criticizing the view that political power is invariably used by the powerful to promote their selfish interests, Lynd was attacking the traditional checks-and-balances outlook of eighteenth-century liberalism in the name of national economic planning whereas Parsons's arguments were originally directed against the anarchistic and utopian overtones of Mills's radicalism. That collective power can be used to further the aims of a majority has long been recognized. As Giddens points out, 'This possibility is, of course, envisaged in classic Marxist theory, and in most varieties of socialist theory, in the form of 'collective' direction of the instruments of government.'[65] In recent decades, many socialists have become, in recoil from the example of the state socialist societies, sensitive to the problem of bureaucracy and more inclined to identify socialism itself with decentralized forms of workers' control, autogestion and participatory democracy rather than with state planning as such. There is, in fact, a curious underlying resemblance between the orthodox Marxist-Leninist view of power in a society that has abolished private ownership of the means of production and Parsons's conception of the fundamental benignity of power in the service of collective goals. To the early Soviet Marxists, the party bureaucracy could not represent a new form of exploitative power exercised by the few over the many because its power was not based on private ownership of property; even the Trotskyist critics of Stalin's party machine treated 'bureaucratism' as a 'deformation' of what remained fundamentally a 'workers' state', still a position widely held on the Left. Similarly, to Parsons the actual and potential use or abuse of power for minority ends remains no more than 'a secondary and derived aspect of a total phenomenon' when power has been legitimated by 'public' commitment to collective goals and its exercise vested in official roles.

Apart from the ultimately unconvincing analogy between power and money, the statement that power can be a resource for the attainment of collective goals hardly seems very novel or revelatory. If Parsons were simply affirming in elaborate sociological language that 'in unity there is strength', as some of his critics have come close to suggesting, his views would scarcely deserve close attention. But his claim that the *production* of power is a separate and prior issue from that of its *distribution* goes much further than this. That collective power must be produced or generated by a process of mobilization in which individual resources are aggregated to become collective resources and new *sui generis* collective resources are created was my own major argument in Chapters 6, 7 and 8. My emphasis, however, especially in Chapters 7 and 8, was on *which* groups within a society achieve mobilization; from Parsons's standpoint, this too focuses on the distributive aspects of power even though it deals with collective power and goal attainment rather than remaining at the level of individuals.

Parsons, by contrast, is concerned with power as an agency or resource of a total society: power to him is a 'system property' rather than a relation between individuals or groups.[66] The focus on goals at the systemic level results in his apparent neglect of the asymmetry of power relations by eliminating any possible non-participants in the system over whom power might be exercised, that is, anyone who is not a party to the consensus that legitimates the use of power to attain collective goals. Presumably, those who are defeated in conflicts between systems are absorbed into the winning system or remain outside of it. This is the source of Parsons's relative neglect of 'power over'.

But this neglect has been overstated by many of his critics, for he actually discusses at some length what he calls 'the hierarchical aspects of power systems' and even in his early critique of Mills accused him of utopianism for implying that inequalities of power might be eliminated altogether. Parsons recognizes that the power to attain collective goals requires that some men exercise power over others in an established chain of command. This specific requirement makes power over others itself a collective resource distinguishable from the overall power of the system or society to attain collective goals as a result of mobilization. In addition to the aggregated resources of individuals and the non-reducible or global resource of solidarity based on awareness of common interests or values, the non-reducible resource of organization implies the emergence of a differentiated power structure – at least when the permanent mobilization of large numbers of people is involved. Thus power becomes itself a collective resource or a partial but crucial aspect of organization as a collective resource. A stable system of 'power over' is a prerequisite for 'power to' in the broadest sense. Parsons affirms, in effect, that 'who says organization, says oligarchy',[67] although he says it in a very different tone of voice from Michels. Nor, in contrast to Michels, does he regard the emergent oligarchy as necessarily leading to a conflict of interests between the oligarchs and their subjects that subverts or displaces the goals to which a collective commitment had been made and in the name of which organization was originally undertaken. Parsons, indeed, minimizes the dominance-submission aspect of power relations in suggesting that their asymmetry lies essentially in unequal rights to make decisions on behalf of collective goals.[68]

Does not Parsons's stress on the production of power contradict my earlier statement that he presupposes consensus between rulers and ruled and thus treats the genesis of legitimate authority and of collective goals themselves as non-problematical? I do not think so, for, although Parsons correctly regards power as a collective resource, he does not specifically discuss the *process* as distinct from the fact of its production and he implicitly assumes that the process is one of building consensus. He writes as if society as a whole, or the social system, were a social movement in its early stages when collective enthusiasm and the emotional bonds uniting leaders and followers are at their maximum strength. He ignores the fact that organizations can be formed by coercion and material or non-material inducements and that the compliant actions of subordinate members may contribute to the attainment of collective goals in the absence of any consensus between superiors and subordinates – that, in short, organization and solidarity are not always associated but are sometimes negatively correlated.[69] If this is true of many economic and political organizations, it applies even more to the large-scale institutional structures that give an entire society its coherence and identity – the macro-system with which Parsons is chiefly concerned. The economy and the polity are not the results of a social contract once agreed upon but the unintended and unforeseen precipitates of history that confront individual actors in all their massive, reified bulk.

As I noted in Chapter 4, there is an affinity between Parsons's consensual view of power and those of Hannah Arendt and Jürgen Habermas. In one sense Parsons is more 'realistic' than either of them in explicitly recognizing the necessity of inequalities in power for the realization of collective goals in a large-scale society. Arendt regards authority as grounded in a past consensus when the historical act of foundation establishing a new political order took place. She tends, at least in *On Violence*, to stress consensus to such a degree that command-obedience relations as such are seen as not differing in kind from force and violence.[70] Habermas envisages the possibility of a world in which men are completely emancipated from domination and all collective decisions are arrived at after public debate in which rival 'truth claims' are assessed and 'discursively redeemed' or rejected. He fails to mention the possibility that power relations based at best on the generalized trust of superiors by subordinates so emphasized by Parsons, at worst on irreducible elements of coercion, may be 'functionally necessary' in any complex large-scale society. Arendt's consensual polity is located in the Greek and Roman past and she regards contemporary political power as a degenerate form in which force, violence and manipulation predominate. Habermas's polity based on his 'ideal speech situation', on the other hand, is explicitly utopian and he sees existing political and social orders, whether capitalist or state socialist, as founded on domination. Parsons, by contrast, often appears to be describing contemporary America, or democratic capitalist society, as if it were a utopia in which group conflict, abuses of official power and latent tensions between power holders and power subjects were at most minor blemishes or secondary byproducts.[71] In this respect, his views seem more abstract and remote from reality than those of Arendt and Habermas.

In conclusion, whether power should be regarded as a zero-sum phenomenon or as a collective resource does not appear to be a genuine theoretical issue in which two incompatible views confront one another. Only the most doctrinaire anarchist or proponent of direct democracy would maintain that authorizing some men to direct the activities of others is so corrupting and conflict-producing for all concerned that it should never be considered as a means of achieving collective goals. And only the most naïve believer in the malleability of men, in their almost infinite capacity to be socialized to serve larger collective ends in a heterogeneous society in which many resources are unequally distributed, would deny that power is peculiarly susceptible to being diverted into use for self-interested purposes by individuals and groups. Vulgar anti-Parsonians have long accused Parsons of just such naïveté, but the one-sidedness of his conception of power as a collective resource is primarily the consequence of his determination to treat societies as total systems and the level of abstraction to which this commits him. Whether systems or total societies have – or can have – collective goals may be arguable, but few would deny that groups within societies have collective goals for which power serves as a resource. As Lehman observes:

> Once we dismiss the theoretical possibility of societal goals, the prospect of collective goals for other groups disappears too. If, on a priori grounds, American society does not have goals, how can the corporate establishment, workers, blacks or the poor have them?[72]

It is worth noting that in recent years a number of writers who do not share Parsons's pervasive consensual bias have nevertheless found his system-level approach useful for their own purposes and their number even includes some Marxists.[73]

Power and Structure

That power relations are indispensable wherever men pursue collective
goals is asserted with superb economy by R. G. Collingwood:

> Command and obedience are found, not in all societies, but in all where
> the nature of the common task is such as to require them. Watch two men
> moving a piano; at a certain moment one says 'lift', and the other lifts.[74]

Such simple tasks as lifting a piano are surely found in all societies –
even Neanderthal men must have confronted the necessity of moving
fallen tree-trunks blocking their path through the forest. When
Collingwood suggests that command and obedience are not present in
all societies, he presumably means *recurrent* command-obedience
relations required for the regular performance of collective tasks which
result in permanent institutionalized role differences between those who
command and those who obey.

Collingwood's claim for the ubiquity of power relations is based on
the need for co-ordination of the activities of plural actors striving to
achieve a common goal. Consensus on the goal itself is presupposed.
Marx and Engels acknowledged the universal necessity for co-
ordination as a source of authority in any society with complex means
of production, even a future communist society. Engels specifically
repudiated what he regarded as the retrograde position of the anarchists
in denying this, maintaining that organization by its very nature
required authority and never more so than where the techniques of
large-scale industrial production are employed.[75] Marx and Engels
unmistakably shared Parsons's doubts about the possibility of an 'ideal
society in which power does not play a part at all'. All three tend to
assimilate the co-ordinating role of power to a form of what I have
called competent authority: the exercise of authority, though not
necessarily based on certified scope-specific expertise, is an intrinsic
part of goal-directed collective action. Marx used the analogy of the
orchestra conductor to describe it, a frequently employed latter-day
version of the ancient Platonic metaphor of the helmsman.[76] Engels
argued that 'the social organization of the future would restrict
authority solely to the limits within which the conditions of production
render it inevitable'.[77]

But the need for *co-ordination* in the performance of complex
collective tasks is only one aspect of the necessity for power relations
and not the most significant. There is also the need for *discretionary*

judgement in deciding which tasks should be carried out, which immediate goals pursued, in concrete situations. Discretion differs from co-ordination in that it involves what is done rather than how it is done, the choice of goals rather than their implementation, strategical rather than tactical decision-making. Thus leaders whose judgement is trusted on grounds of character or expert knowledge emerge and are able to obtain the compliance of others to their directives. Leadership becomes institutionalized in 'head roles' or 'command posts'[78] and elaborate pyramidal structures of power develop. Conflict situations in which flexible tactics and rapid decision-making are at a premium are especially likely to give rise to hierarchies of power conferring the right on some to command and imposing the duty on others to obey while concentrating control over coercive and utilitarian resources for use as sanctions to ensure compliance. Armies are the most obvious case in point. But the greater the size and complexity of the society, the greater the reliance of the many on the discretionary judgment of the few in a wide range of scopes, even as the power-holding few themselves become more dependent on subordinate power holders and expert advisers.

To argue that permanent hierarchies of power relations are indispensable in any moderately complex society is not, of course, to stamp the seal of necessity on the power structures of particular existing societies. Functionalist arguments have too often been vulnerable to the charge that they imply just this and have accordingly lent themselves to conservative ideological uses even when, as in the case of Parsons, theoretical statements are pitched at so high a level of abstraction that their authors are able to claim that such uses represent 'false concretization'. Parsons, as we have seen, is open to the accusation that he idealizes the *status quo* because he minimizes to the point of neglect the use of power on behalf of some group interests at the expense of others. Yet one of his harshest critics has conceded that his theorizing will acquire new and greater relevance 'after the revolution' when class conflict has presumably ended and democratic consensus becomes a reality.[79] One can, however, also charge Marx and Engels with ignoring the conflict-producing potential inherent in power differences as such: commenting on Marx's analogy with the conductor of an orchestra, a recent interpreter remarks:

Assuming agreement on what to play, there are often considerable disagreements between the conductor and the members of the orchestra about the interpretation of the music. And in no society of any complexity has it ever been the case that everyone has wanted to play the same tune.[80]

If power relations are necessary, they might perhaps be described as a necessary evil. The evil lies in the proneness of power to abuse, in its tendency to spread from the scopes in which it has been legitimated to other scopes, which is essentially the result of its status as a potential universal means capable of serving any group or individual purpose. The greater prestige attached to positions of authority and the higher material rewards they usually receive enhance the tendency of power to overflow scope-specific boundaries. This is even true of the authority of experts that is primarily exercised in decentralized dyadic professional-client relationships, as Freidson's study of the medical profession illustrates.[81] Their dependence on the powerful reduces the opportunities of the powerless to resist or evade the expansiveness of power. Critics of Marxism who have argued that the economic dependence of the propertyless on those who own the means of production is only a special case of a wider dependence that is inherent in all power relations are certainly correct. In addition, the inherent inequality of power relations creates a sense of inferiority and resentment on the part of subordinates in all but the most obviously unavoidable and scope-specific relations of competent authority. Because power is relational, creating and maintaining complex structures of interdependent social bonds, power differences are more consequential than inequalities in wealth and prestige. To be sure, wealth and prestige may be used as bases for obtaining power as well as the reverse, but they, unlike power, represent terminal want satisfactions and thus have an inherently distributive aspect whereas power always involves an ordering of the lives of others that sets limits to their autonomy of action. In contrast to making money, to recall Dr. Johnson's famous aphorism, no one is ever 'innocently employed' when exercising or seeking to exercise power.

There is, however, another way in which power relations in actual societies fail to conform to the minima required for the co-ordination of collective action and for discretionary judgement in some situations. This way stands in marked contrast to the dangerous, not to say demonic, potential of power that I have been stressing up to now. Social institutions, including the structured power relations partly constitutive of them, consist of rules and practices handed down from the past which possess a massive resistance to change grounded in the petty and fragmented interests of the individuals who operate them and on whom they impinge. Far from being a conscious instrumentality of individual or collective aims, power is often exercised in a perfunctory manner subject to no more than pragmatic matter-of-fact legitimations: 'I don't make the rules, Madam, it's just my job to apply them.' Even if the rules were created in the past to secure or promote the interests of a particular group and although they may continue to restrict the alternatives open to non-favoured groups, this is less a matter of design – let alone conspiracy – or even of anyone's complete understanding than a result of the sheer weight of routinized ways of acting that go unchallenged *faute de mieux*.

This is the aspect of power that Schattschneider referred to as 'mobilization of bias' and that Bachrach and Baratz discerned in noting the 'agenda-setting' function of established institutions that relegates possible alternative policies to the limbo of 'non-issues' or 'non-decisions'.[82] Hannah Arendt has the same aspect in mind when, availing herself of a certain amount of poetic licence, she describes bureaucracy as 'rule by Nobody' on the grounds that 'in a fully developed bureaucracy there is nobody left with whom one can argue, to whom one can present grievances, on whom the pressures of power can be exerted'.[83] At a more abstract level, a 'structuralist' conception of power is opposed to an 'actionist' one. Structural determinants of action are sometimes considered to be the antithesis of power, a view which identifies power essentially with capacity or 'power to' and, in effect, equates power with freedom or autonomy – a paradoxical consequence if one thinks of power from the standpoint of the power subject whose choices are constrained by the power exercised over him by others. On the other hand, structure may be regarded as the most formidable and comprehensive kind of power constraining individual actions, reducing men to mere players of roles or bearers of positions in a larger predetermined system of relations.[84]

Many of these issues have been raised in colloquia at various universities where I have presented sections of the present book. I have been charged with taking an excessively social psychological and methodologically individualist view of power, one that ties it too closely to individual and group aims instead of seeing it as the product of structural determination to which the feelings, legitimations, and consciousness of individuals are largely irrelevant. Such criticisms have usually focused on my ascription of intentionality to power, so, at the risk of some repetition, it is worth reexamining the argument presented in Chapter 1 for regarding power as necessarily intentional.

To insist that power can be validly imputed to an actor only when he produces *intended* and *foreseen* effects on others in no way precludes the possibility that he may in doing so also produce a wide range of far more significant unintended and unforeseen effects. Effects that are foreseen but not intended count as exercises of power notwithstanding the fact that the power wielder may regard them as incidental byproducts or as painfully heavy but unavoidable costs of his effort to achieve his ends. Those effects that were both unintended and unforeseen do not by my definition constitute an exercise of power, but when conjoined with intended and foreseen effects they are certainly the results of such an exercise. In short, to be in a position to produce intended and foreseen effects on others is also to be in the most favourable position to produce unintended and unforeseen effects. The latter are in no way excluded or minimized by identifying power with intentionality, a definition that has the additional advantage of conforming to the canons of interpretation of human action stressed by contemporary *verstehende* philosophies of social science.[85]

But if the unintended and unforeseen effects of the exercise of power are often more enduring and consequential than the intended effects, why not, it might be argued, include them in the very definition of power? The answer is that to do so would make *any* social effect equivalent to an exercise of power. Power relations would then become identical with the entire subject-matter of sociology as the study of how human action (including beliefs and emotions) is generated, shaped and constrained by the structures and networks of social relations in which we are all of us enmeshed from birth. Power would be collapsed into social control and would include the diffuse control of the One by the Many as well as the relatively permanent past effects of power embodied in internalized norms (the superego), taken-for-granted beliefs and even language itself which, as contemporary linguistic philosophers have shown, contains built-in preconceptions, prejudgements and evaluations. Solipsists, complete libertarian individualists, and believers in the possibility and desirability of a 'natural man' uncontaminated by social influence might be prepared to accept such an equation of power and social control, but it is unlikely to appeal to many others. Even if the power of the parent over the child is the very matrix of human character formation, it hardly seems useful to treat socialized human nature itself as entirely the product of the exercise of power, which would rob the concept of power of all specificity. Power would cease to be *a* 'key concept in the social sciences' but become *the* key concept, identical with society and the very realm of the social itself. Nevertheless, one can and should recognize that power is inherent in all social interaction, which consists of actors reciprocally producing effects on one another. Moreover, no two actors bring to their inter-action exactly the same combination of resources to exercise influence and power even when the general conditions fulfilling Habermas's ideal speech community are met.[86] But definition of a power relation as a distinctive form of social relation requires the exclusion of these two senses in which power is implicit in all social relations and the criteria of intentionality and patterned asymmetry (see Chapter 1) achieve this exclusion.

No doubt I am in some sense a 'methodological individualist', although ultimately, I am prepared to argue, so are those who purport to deny that they are. That, of course, is what a methodological individualist might be expected to claim, but this is not the place to enter into debate over that embattled epistemological issue.[87] With reference to power, it will have to suffice to contend that structural determination is at least mediated by the intentional acts of individual persons; this entails, however, no assumption that the actors' intentions are unmoved movers, voluntaristic choices, or even dispositions external to and antedating the situation in which action takes place. Or, if a more positivistic and behaviouristic language is preferred, intentions and motives are 'intervening variables' between the stimulus of the structural context and the response in the form of acts of power. Intentional acts designed to produce effects on others are, in Aristotelian terms, the efficient causes of the workings of social structures – and social structures *are* nothing but their recurrent workings. The bored, distracted official perfunctorily applying a regulation, or the businessman obsessed with the figures shown on his balance sheet, still act intentionally in giving orders or making decisions however limited their consciousness of the impact of their orders and decisions. Actors may make decisions only as agents serving a collective goal or in their capacity as representatives of a group or collectivity, but collective goals must be pursued through the intentional acts of individuals although they need not be identical with the self-chosen goals of any individual in particular. If this amounts to methodological individualism, so be it.

The preceding discussion has centred on the intentionality of the wielder of power because I made this part of the very definition of power. But – except in the cases of force and manipulation – intentionality also applies to the compliance of the power subject.[88] Undoubtedly, the awareness of power subjects complying with a command may shade off into sheer 'unthinking habit' to an even greater extent than the awareness of the power holder who issues a command expecting the subject's compliance. Also, as was noted in Chapter 4, the power subject's motives for compliance may be mixed and he may be unable to articulate his grounds for compliance or even deceive himself about them. This, of course, may also be true of the underlying motives of the power holder, but because he initiates the asymmetrical interaction of a power relation he must at least be able to articulate what he demands or expects of the power subject. But short of the automatic response given by a trained soldier ordered to stand at attention, the power subject 'knows' that he complies with another's directives even if his consciousness is too impoverished for him to imagine doing otherwise.

To Marxists, structure is equated with the system of classes determined by the forces and relations of production. Marxists might argue that my conceptualizations of power relations are too psycho-logical to allow for such assertions as that capitalist societies are based on 'class domination'. Examination of what precisely is meant by class domination reveals that it usually connotes no more than that power, prestige and privilege are unequally distributed among individuals, that the unequal distribution is perpetuated inter-generationally, and that owners of productive property are greater beneficiaries of inequality than non-owners. But we knew all this at the outset, so it verges on the tautological to adduce class domination as a presumptive explanation rather than simply as an alternative and largely metaphorical way of summing up the facts of class inequality.[89] Max Weber, to be sure, saw differences in prestige and wealth as reflecting 'the distribution of power in a community' and in this sense one may regard the class system itself as a phenomenon of power. Yet to speak of class domination is at best elliptical: the greater income and prestige received by the upper classes, as well their superior access to roles involving the exercise of authority in organizational positions, remain essentially distributive phenomena. Class domination implies collective power and thus raises the question of the relation between economic location, the defining criterion of class, and political power. This is the arena of debate between Marxist and élitist theorists over the identity and basic interests of those who actually wield political power. Weber's definition of 'party' as both a phenomenon of the general distribution of power in a community *and* as a group primarily oriented to the pursuit of political power implies the distinction between the distributive and collective aspects of power.[90] If the state were in fact no more than the 'executive committee of the bourgeoisie', one could speak unambiguously of class domination, but contemporary Marxists profess to reject so crudely 'instrumentalist' a view of the state.[91] Collective power is located in institutions and organizational structures rather than in diffusely solidary quasi-groups such as classes. Poulantzas with a great display of italics appears both to affirm and to deny this:

> The various social institutions, in particular the institutions of the state, do not, strictly speaking, have power. Institutions, considered from the point of view of power, can be related only to *social classes which hold power*. As it is exercised this power of the social classes is organized in specific institutions which are *power centres*: in this context the state is *the centre of the exercise of political power*. But this does not mean that power centres, the various institutions of an economic, political, military, cultural, etc., character are mere instruments, organs or appendices of the power of social classes. They possess their autonomy and *structural* specificity which is not as such immediately reducible to an analysis in terms of power.[92]

I would reverse Poulantzas' statement and maintain that 'strictly speaking' only social institutions embodied in concrete organizations can be said to have and to exercise power. To speak of classes as collective actors possessing power is misleading.[93] In contending that organizations are the real locus of collective power, I am committed to what Westhues calls the 'organization paradigm' as opposed to the 'class paradigm' in sociology – the only useful employment by a sociologist that I have seen, incidentally, of the much-abused Kuhnian term.[94] Such a view, of course, in no way rules out investigation of the links between organizations as hierarchical power structures and the more inclusive society-wide 'horizontal' divisions that social classes represent. Organizations may or may not promote the diffuse interests and values of classes or other 'macrosolidary groups' in Lehman's sense. But organizations, not classes, are the collective historical actors in contemporary advanced industrial societies. As Weber correctly foresaw less than a year after the Russian Revolution, socialism even more than mature capitalism results in 'the dictatorship of the official, not that of the worker'.[95]

Such a view disposes of the numerous 'new class' theories put forward in the last century and a half, as well as of the critical importance of the long and continuing debate over whether modern corporations are controlled by their managements or by owning groups.[96] Although the earliest version of a 'new class' theory, that of Saint-Simon, actually antedated Marx's baptism of the proletariat as the revolutionary class destined to ascendancy in the future, most new class theories have been presented as alternatives to the forecast of proletarian revolution.[97] Some new class theorists have favoured the 'managers', 'scientific and technical intelligentsia' or 'experts' whose advent they predict. Others have opposed them, treating bureaucratic or technocratic visions of the future as ideologies making universal claims while actually, like all ideologies, promoting the particular interests of a limited group. If technicians and experts – though rarely bureaucratic officials – have sometimes been welcomed as heirs to the failed mission of the proletariat, they have also been assailed as an actual or prospective new ruling class frustrating the dream of a classless society. Some writers have assigned to the new class the parts of *both* the bourgeoisie and the proletariat in the Marxist drama, seeing it as an outgrowth of the 'old middle class' that is nevertheless destined to be the carrier of an anti-capitalist ethos rooted in antagonism to the planlessness and waste of the market and the vulgarities of a commercial culture.

Apart from the vagueness with which the new class and its boundaries are usually defined – epitomized by the very multiplicity of new class theories – the major problem confronting such theories has been their manifest failure to show that the proposed class actually possesses a degree of social cohesion, a common ethos or world-view, and at least nascent political aims, all necessary attributes if it is to constitute an identifiable collective actor. New class theorists rarely avoid some version of the fallacious argument that the functional indispensability of a group is a sufficient as well as a necessary condition for its exercise of collective power, or, in Robert Dahl's terms, that a group's 'potential for control' is inseparable from its 'potential for unity'.[98]

The limited potential for unity of new classes is a consequence of the fact that all of the candidates proposed are groups within large organizations, whether administrators holding positions of 'line' authority or technical and scientific experts in 'staff' positions. Identification with the organization as a vertical structure or with autonomous professional associations tends to fragment the group and take precedence over horizontal class loyalties.[99] Thus a new class resembling the old bourgeoisie and proletariat fails to emerge despite the great increase in the numbers of persons whose social position depends on bureaucratic office or educationally certified skill and knowledge rather than on ownership of property or nothing but manual labour power.

Large-scale organizations are the prototype of structural determination, encasing men in Weber's 'iron cage', suggesting Arendt's 'rule by Nobody' as an addition to the venerable Aristotelian classification of forms of government, and subject even when originating in popular ferment and solidarity to Michels's 'iron law of oligarchy' and Lowi's 'iron law of decadence'. The depersonalized, 'structural' face of power is nowhere more evident than in the routine workings of large-scale bureaucracy. Yet bureaucratic organizations are manifestly man-made instruments, entirely secular concentrations of collective resources subject to evaluation solely by standards of efficiency in achieving tangible goals. To primitive man, culture is as fixed and unalterable as nature; the idea of reforming his institutions to improve their efficiency or to make them more responsive to human desires and yearnings does not occur to him.[100] Yet neither he nor men of earlier civilizations dominated by coercive and arbitrary traditional authorities experience the 'alienation' of modern man. Like all men, modern men are thrust into a world they never made, but they know that it was made by other men rather than by God or nature and it appears to them therefore as a world of makeshift social arrangements which they can readily imagine otherwise. It is not so much that they 'reify' the institutions and power structures controlling their lives, attributing to them an existence and weight independent of human activity and choice, as that they are *unable* to see them in such a manner and thus view them as arbitrary creations to which they are forced to accommodate. Hence the emptiness of their freedom, the combination of nostalgia towards the past when power was clothed in 'miracle, mystery and authority' with utopian greed towards the future, the frenzied efforts to re-enchant the world in new cults based on esoteric borrowings, and the disposition to magnify the irksomeness of organizational power that lacks a human face.

Notes
Chapter One

1. Geoffrey Gorer quoted by Erich Fromm, *Escape from Freedom* (New York: Farrar and Rinehart, 1941), n. 6, p. 157.
2. Gilbert Ryle, *The Concept of Mind* (New York: Barnes and Noble, 1949), pp. 116–125.
3. Thomas Hobbes, *Leviathan*, Parts I and II (Indianapolis: Bobbs-Merrill, 1958), p. 78.
4. Bertrand Russell, *Power: A New Social Analysis* (London: George Allen and Unwin, 1938), p. 25.
5. Ryle, *op. cit.*, p. 117.
6. See especially the passages in *Power: A New Social Analysis*, pp. 21–22, referring to and generalizing from Bruno Mussolini's account of his air-bombing of villages in the Abyssinian war.
7. For example, John McDermott, 'Technology: The Opiate of the Intellectuals', *New York Review of Books*, 31 July, 1969, pp. 25–35.
8. Lasswell and Kaplan also accept with modification Russell's definition; see Harold Lasswell and Abraham Kaplan, *Power and Society* (New Haven: Yale University Press, 1950), pp. 75–76.
9. See Dennis H. Wrong, *Skeptical Sociology*, (New York: Columbia University Press, 1976), Chapter Two, pp. 31–46.
10. R. G. Collingwood, *The New Leviathan* (Oxford: The Clarendon Press, 1942), p. 176.
11. Robert A. Dahl and Charles E. Lindblom, *Politics, Economics and Welfare* (New York: Harper and Brothers, 1953), pp. 99–104.
12. Robert K. Merton, *Social Theory and Social Structure* (rev. ed.; New York: The Free Press, 1957), p. 68. Several writers have defined power in such a way as to include explicitly *unintended* effects on others, such as Felix E. Oppenheim, *Dimensions of Freedom: An Analysis* (New York: St Martin's Press, 1961), pp. 92–95 and J. A. A. Van Doorn, 'Sociology and the Problem of Power', *Sociologia Neerlandica* 1 (Winter 1962–63), 12. The majority of the authors cited in this chapter, however, as well as many others, have implicitly or explicitly restricted the term power to *intentional* influence on others. See the discussion by P. H. Partridge, 'Some Notes on the Concept of Power', *Political Studies* 11 (June 1963),

113–115; also Jack H. Nagel, *The Descriptive Analysis of Power* (New Haven: Yale University Press, 1975), pp. 20–22.

13. The importance of making this distinction for basic epistemological and 'meta-theoretical' reasons as well as on empirical grounds is stressed by Peter Winch in *The Idea of a Social Science* (London: Routledge and Kegan Paul, 1958), p. 110. Winch mentions Durkheim's well-known definition of suicide as an example of a failure to distinguish between intended and foreseen outcomes, an example that is discussed at greater length by Alasdair MacIntyre in his critique of Winch; see MacIntyre, 'The Idea of a Social Science' in Bryan R. Wilson, editor, *Rationality* (Oxford: Basil Blackwell, 1970), pp. 124–127. In the context of developing a more adequate theory of suicide, Anthony Giddens shows that Durkheim's suppression of the distinction accounts for the shortcomings of his own famous study, in *Studies in Social and Political Theory* (London): Hutchinson, 1977), pp. 303–304; see also, Giddens, *Durkheim* (Glasgow: Fontana/Collins, 1978), pp. 118–120. Giddens also criticizes Merton for failure to distinguish between unintended and unanticipated consequences in his concept of 'latent function'; see *Studies in Social and Political Theory*, pp. 106–109. The implications of the distinction for the assessment of responsibility, including legal responsibility, are discussed by William E. Connolly, *The Terms of Political Discourse* (Lexington, Mass.: D. C. Heath, 1974), pp. 105–106; see also, Steven Lukes, *Power: A Radical View* (London: Macmillan, 1974), pp. 51–52.

14. Ryle, *op. cit.*, p. 116.

15. See the full discussion of this distinction by Oppenheim, *op. cit.,* pp. 100-102. See also Richard M. Emerson, 'Power-Dependence Relations', *American Sociological Review,* (27 February 1962), pp. 31-32.

16. See the discussion of this distinction by Van Doorn, *op. cit.*, pp. 8–10.

17. Carl J. Friedrich, *Constitutional Government and Politics* (New York: Harper and Brothers, 1937), pp. 16–18; for a later and fuller discussion, see Friedrich's *Man and Government* (New York: McGraw-Hill, 1963), pp. 199–215. Friedrich treats 'the rule of anticipated reactions' as a form of *influence* rather than of *power*, which he regards as a broader category – just the reverse of the position adopted here. The best recent account of anticipated reactions is that of Nagel, *op. cit.*, pp. 15–19, 30–32.

18. Robert Bierstedt, *Power and Progress: Essays on Sociological Theory* (New York: McGraw-Hill, 1974), p. 236.

19. Max Weber, *Economy and Society*, Guenther Roth and Claus Wittich, eds, 3 vols. (New York: Bedminister Press, 1968), vol. 1, p. 53.

20. Arnold M. Rose notes that many social scientists have in effect taken this position without consistently committing themselves to its implications. Rose, *The Power Structure: Political Process in American Society* (New

York: Oxford University Press, 1967), pp. 44–50. See also Partridge, *op. cit.*, pp. 115–117.

21. Van Doorn, *op. cit.*, p. 9.

22. An at least partial instance of this is the case of a small-town leader mentioned by Arthur Vidich and Joseph Bensman in *Small Town in Mass Society* (Princeton: Princeton University Press, 1958), pp. 276–277.

23. See Nelson W. Polsby, *Community Power and Political Theory* (New Haven: Yale University Press, 1963), pp. 47–53, and 'Community Power Meets Air Pollution', *Contemporary Sociology* 1 (March 1972), 99–101; Robert A. Dahl in William V. D'Antonio and Howard I. Ehrlich, eds, *Power and Democracy in America* (Notre Dame, Ind.: University of Notre Dame Press, 1961), pp. 101–104; Raymond Wolfinger, 'Reputation and Reality in the Study of Community Power', *American Sociological Review* 25 (October 1960), 636–644.

24. Raymond Aron, '*Macht, Power*, Puissance: prose démocratique ou poésie démoniaque?' *European Journal of Sociology* 5 (1964) 27–33.

25. See Georg Simmel, *The Sociology of Georg Simmel*, Kurt H. Wolff, ed. and trans. (Glencoe, Ill.: The Free Press, 1950), pp. 181–182.

26. Hans Gerth and C. Wright Mills, *Character and Social Structure* (New York: Harcourt, Brace, 1953), p. 193.

27. Peter M. Blau, *Exchange and Power in Social Life* (New York: John Wiley and Sons, 1964), p. 118.

28. This distinction was formulated by Theodor Geiger. See the discussion, to which I am much indebted, by Van Doorn, *op. cit.*, pp. 16–18. Geiger's distinction resembles that of Edward W. Lehman between what he calls *systemic* and *inter-member* power in 'Towards a Macrosociology of Power', *American Sociological Review* 34 (August 1969), 453–463. See also William Gamson, *Power and Discontent* (Homewood, Ill.: Dorsey Press, 1968), chapter 1.

29. David Riesman *et. al.*, *The Lonely Crowd* (New Haven: Yale University Press, 1950), pp. 244–255.

30. Franz Neumann, *The Democratic and the Authoritarian State* (Glencoe, Ill.: The Free Press, 1957), p. 7.

31. *Ibid.*, p. 17.

32. *Ibid.*, pp. 257–269. Neumann points out that in foreign policy, integral power ('the political element') 'prevails absolutely and without regard for Law'; p. 259.

33. See the discussion of this issue by Jack H. Nagel, 'Some Questions about the Concept of Power', *Behavioural Science* 13 (March 1969), 133–134; also, Nagel, *The Descriptive Analysis of Power*, pp. 12–14.

34. Peter Bachrach and Morton S. Baratz, 'Decisions and Non-decisions: An Analytical Framework', *American Political Science Review* 57 (September 1963), 632–642.

35. Bertrand de Jouvenel, 'Authority: The Efficient Imperative', in Carl J. Friedrich, ed., *Authority*, Nomos I (Cambridge, Mass.: Harvard University Press, 1958), p. 160. P. H. Partridge identifies independently the same three 'dimensions' of power, calling the first *range*, the second *zone of acceptance*, and the third *intensity*; *op. cit.*, p. 118. So does William E. Connolly, using a still different set of terms, *op. cit.*, p. 86.

36. Aristotle, *Politics and Poetics*, Benjamin Jowett and Thomas Twining, trans. (Cleveland: Fine Editions Press, 1952), 'Politics', book 3, Chapter 7, pp. 69–70.

37. This statement is, as T. B. Bottomore notes, less applicable to Mosca than to Pareto; Bottomore, *Elites and Society* (London: C. A. Watts, 1964), pp. 4–5.

38. Robert A. Dahl, *Modern Political Analysis* (Englewood Cliffs, N.J.: Prentice-Hall, 1963), pp. 45–46.

39. Erving Goffman, *Encounters* (Indianapolis: Bobbs-Merrill, 1961), p. 96.

40. Mark DeWolfe Howe, ed., *Holmes-Laski Letters* (Cambridge, Mass.: Harvard University Press, 1953), vol. I, p. 8. See also p. 762.

41. Herbert A. Simon, 'Notes on the Observation and Measurement of Power', in Roderick Bell, David V. Edwards, and R. Harrison Wagner, editors, *Political Power: A Reader in Theory and Research* (New York: The Free Press, 1969), p. 76.

42. Partridge, *op. cit.*, p. 118.

43. *Ibid.*

44. Philip E. Slater, 'On Social Regression', *American Sociological Review* 28 (June 1963), 348–361.

45. Hannah Arendt, *The Origins of Totalitarianism* (New York: Harcourt, Brace, 1951), pp. 303–305; Michael Polanyi, *Personal Knowledge* (London: Routledge and Kegan Paul, 1958), pp. 224–225.

46. Arendt, *op. cit.*, pp. 414–428.

Chapter Two

1. Max Weber, *Economy and Society*, three volumes, edited by Guenther Roth and Claus Wittich (New York: Bedminster Press, 1968), Volume Two, p. 926. Anthony Giddens has recently made the point that many versions of Weber's definition of power as 'the capacity of an individual to realize his will, even against the opposition of others' omit the 'even' and thus make coercion and conflict of goals and interests inherent in the very nature of power. He is certainly correct on this conceptual point and I agree with the implication that coercion in other than an attenuated psychic sense which *may* be inherent in all power (see Chapter 5, pp. 114–121 above) should be regarded as only one form of power rather than the essence of the phenomenon itself. However, the page reference to the

Roth-Wittich English translation of *Economy and Society* that Giddens
gives for Weber's definition is wrong; see Giddens, *New Rules of Sociological Method* (New York: Basic Books, 1976), p. 173, n. 26. Although
the wording is not exactly the same, he appears to be referring to the
definition on p. 926 in the citation at the beginning of this note. This
definition occurs at the beginning of the famous section on 'Class, Status
and Party' which first appeared in English in the 1946 translation by
Gerth and Mills; H. H. Gerth and C. Wright Mills, editors and
translators, *From Max Weber: Essays in Sociology* (New York: Oxford
University Press, 1946), p. 180. In volume 1 of *Economy and Society*,
however, another definition of power appears which omits the 'even':
"'Power" (*Macht*) is the probability that one actor within a social
relationship will be in a position to carry out his own will despite
resistance. . . .' *This* definition has been available to English-speaking
sociologists since 1947 in Talcott Parsons's translation of sections of
Economy and Society: Max Weber, *The Theory of Social and Economic
Organization* (New York: Oxford University Press, 1947), p. 152. The
omission of the 'even', therefore, is the fault of Weber himself (or his
translators) rather than of commentators on his work who have relied
upon the definition from the first (but later written) part of *Economy and
Society*. In raising this point Giddens has cleared up a question that has
puzzled and even confused interpreters of Weber's political sociology,
including myself; Wrong, editor, *Max Weber* (Englewood Cliffs, N.J.:
Prentice-Hall, 1970), pp. 54–58.

2. Robert Bierstedt, *Power and Progress: Essays on Sociological Theory*
   (New York: McGraw-Hill, 1974), p. 231.
3. Harold Lasswell and Abraham Kaplan, *Power and Society* (New Haven:
   Yale University Press, 1950), p. 75.
4. J. A. A. Van Doorn, 'Sociology and the Problem of Power', *Sociologia
   Neerlandica*. 1 (Winter, 1962–1963), p. 7.
5. Bierstedt, *op. cit.*, pp. 247–249.
6. Peter Bachrach and Morton S. Baratz, 'Decisions and Nondecisions: An
   Analytical Framework', *American Political Science Review*, 57
   (September 1963), pp. 633–634.
7. Herbert Goldhamer and Edward A. Shils, 'Types of Power and Status',
   American Journal of Sociology, 45 (September 1939), p. 171.
8. H. H. Gerth and C. Wright Mills, *Character and Social Structure* (New
   York: Harcourt, Brace, 1953, p. 193.
9. *Ibid.*, p. 195.
10. Weber, *Economy and Society*, Volume One, p. 53.
11. Gerth and Mills, *op. cit.*, p. 195.
12. Georg Simmel, *The Sociology of Georg Simmel*, edited and translated by
    Kurt H. Wolff (Glencoe, Ill.: The Free Press, 1950), pp. 182–183.

13. Hannah Arendt, *On Violence* (New York: Harcourt, Brace and World, 1970), p. 56.

14. David Easton, 'The Perception of Authority and Political Change', in Carl J. Friedrich, editor, *Authority*, Nomos I (Cambridge, Mass.: Harvard University Press, 1958), p. 183.

15. E. V. Walter, 'Power and Violence', *American Political Science Review*, 58 (June 1964), p. 354; Harold Garfinkel, 'Conditions of Successful Degradation Ceremonies', *American Journal of Sociology*, 61 (March 1956), pp. 420–424.

16. Easton, *op. cit.*, p. 179.

17. Robert A. Dahl and Charles E. Lindblom, *Politics, Economics and Welfare* (New York: Harper and Brothers, 1953), p. 105.

18. *Ibid.*

19. Robert K. Merton, *Mass Persuasion: The Social Psychology of a War Bond Drive* (New York: Harper and Brothers, 1946), p. 142.

20. Harold Garfinkel, 'Aspects of the Problem of Common-Sense Knowledge of Social Structures', in *Transactions of the Fourth World Congress of Sociology*, Volume 4 (International Sociological Association, 1959), pp. 51–65.

21. Dahl and Lindblom, *op. cit.*, pp. 175–177.

22. Merton, *op. cit.*, pp. 142–143.

23. Robert Jay Lifton, *Thought Reform and the Psychology of Totalism* (New York: W. W. Norton, 1963), Chapter 1.

24. An acknowledged masochist would be an idiosyncratic exception.

25. See pp. 99–103 above.

26. Hannah Arendt, *Between Past and Future* (New York: The Viking Press, 1961), p. 93.

27. William A. Gamson, 'Reputation and Resources in Community Politics', *American Journal of Sociology*, 72 (September 1966), p. 130; see also Gamson, *Power and Discontent* (Homewood, Ill.: The Dorsey Press, 1968), pp. 102–105. Gamson, however, defines persuasion much more broadly than I do, including under it the two forms of authority that I discuss in the next chapter under the labels of *competent* and *personal* authority; see *Power and Discontent*, pp. 79–81.

28. Daniel Bell, 'Marxian Socialism in the United States', in Donald Drew Egbert and Stow Persons, editors, *Socialism and American Life*, two volumes (Princeton: Princeton University Press, 1952), Volume One, pp, 365–369. Roger O'Toole, in a study of small radical groups in Toronto in the late 1960s, stresses the ritualistic nature of the proselytizing activities followed by such groups in handing out leaflets, advertising meetings, and the like; O'Toole, *The Precipitous Path: Studies in Political Sects* (Toronto: Peter Martin Associates, 1977), pp. 54–56, 68–72.

Chapter Three

1. Quoted by David Easton, 'The Perception of Authority and Political Change', in Carl J. Friedrich, editor, *Authority*, Nomos 1 (Cambridge: Harvard University Press, 1958), p. 179.
2. Thomas Hobbes, *Leviathan*, Parts I and II (Indianapolis: Bobbs-Merrill, 1958), p. 203. However, it does not necessarily follow, as Hobbes contends, that 'he that commands pretends thereby his own benefit, for the reason of his command is his own will only, and the proper object of every man's will is some good to himself', although one can agree that 'it is evident that he that gives counsel pretends only, whatsoever he intends, the good of him to whom he gives it' (*ibid.*). For the complex relations between persuasion and legitimate and competent authority, see pp. 76–79 above.
3. Easton, *op. cit.*, p. 182.
4. Bertrand de Jouvenel, 'Authority: The Efficient Imperative', in Friedrich, editor, *op. cit.*, p. 161.
5. Max Weber, *Economy and Society*, three volumes, edited by Guenther Roth and Claus Wittich (New York: Bedminster Press, 1968), Volume One, p. 53. I have drawn for this discussion of Weber from my 'Introduction' to Dennis H. Wrong, editor, *Max Weber* (Englewood Cliffs, N.J.: Prentice-Hall, 1970), pp. 55–57.
6. Weber, *op. cit.*, Volume Three, p. 946 (italics in text).
7. Talcott Parsons, 'Max Weber', *American Sociological Review*, 25 (October 1960), p. 752.
8. Reinhard Bendix, *Max Weber: An Intellectual Portrait* (Garden City, N.Y.: Doubleday Anchor Books, 1962), p. 482.
9. Weber, *op. cit.*, p. 946.
10. The quotations and references in this paragraph are from *ibid.*, Volume One, pp. 212–213.
11. *Ibid.*, p. 334.
12. Talcott Parsons, *Politics and Social Structure* (New York: The Free Press, 1969), pp. 361–362.
13. Robert Bierstedt, *Power and Progress: Essays on Sociological Theory* (New York: McGraw-Hill, 1974), pp. 249–259; Peter M. Blau, *Exchange and Power in Social Life* (New York: John Wiley and Sons, 1964), pp. 205–213.
14. Hannah Arendt, *On Violence* (New York: Harcourt, Brace and World, 1970), p. 43.
15. *Ibid.*, p. 37.
16. *Ibid.*, p. 44.
17. *Ibid.*, p. 44.
18. *Ibid.*, p. 47.

19. *Ibid.*, p. 45.

20. Hannah Arendt, *Between Past and Future* (New York: The Viking Press, 1961), p. 93.

21. Arendt, *On Violence*, p. 53.

22. E. V. Walter, 'Power and Violence', *American Political Science Review*, 58 (June 1964), pp. 355–360; Ralf Dahrendorf, *Essays in the Theory of Society* (Stanford, Calif.: Stanford University Press, 1968), pp. 129–150; P. H. Partridge, *Consent and Consensus* (New York: Praeger, 1971), pp. 80–95.

23. Kenneth Boulding, 'Toward a Pure Theory of Threat Systems', in Roderick Bell, David V. Edwards, and R. Harrison Wagner, editors, *Political Power: A Reader in Theory and Research* (New York: The Free Press; 1969), p. 288.

24. *Ibid.*, p. 288.

25. Blau, *op. cit.*, p. 117.

26. Barrington Moore, Jr., *Political Power and Social Theory* (Cambridge: Harvard University Press, 1958), pp. 30–88.

27. William J. Goode, 'The Place of Force in Human Society', *American Sociological Review*, 37 (October 1972), p. 516.

28. Amitai Etzioni, *The Active Society* (New York: The Free Press, 1968), pp. 361–364.

29. Blau, *op. cit.*, pp. 115–125; George Homans, *Social Behavior: Its Elementary Forms* (New York: Harcourt Brace Jovanovich, Revised Edition, 1974), pp. 89–93; Alvin W. Gouldner, *For Sociology* (New York: Basic Books, 1974), pp. 233–236.

30. Blau, *op. cit.*, pp. 76–85.

31. *Ibid.*, p. 92.

32. *Ibid.*, p. 32; Homans, *op. cit.*, p. 89. See also Richard M. Emerson, 'Power-Dependence Relations', *American Sociological Review*, 27 (February 1962), pp. 37–39.

33. Bierstedt, *op. cit.*, p. 257.

34. Blau, *op. cit.*, p. 209.

35. Bierstedt, *op. cit.*, pp. 257–258.

36. *Ibid.*, pp. 257–258.

37. Lewis A. Coser, *Greedy Institutions* (New York: The Free Press, 1974), p. 4.

38. Franz Neumann, *The Democratic and the Authoritarian State* (Glencoe, Ill.: The Free Press, 1957), p. 4.

39. Talcott Parsons, 'Introduction' to Max Weber, *The Theory of Social and Economic Organization* (New York: Oxford University Press, 1947), p. 59. See also Bierstedt, *op. cit.*, p. 246.

40. Carl J. Friedrich, 'Authority, Reason, and Discretion', in Friedrich, editor, *op. cit.*, p. 35.

41. Eliot Freidson, 'The Impurity of Professional Authority', in Howard S.

Becker, Blanche Geer, David Riesman, and Robert S. Weiss, editors, *Institutions and the Person* (Chicago: Aldine, 1968), pp. 30–31.

42. Aristotle, *Politics and Poetics* (Cleveland: Fine Editions Press, 1952), p. 68.

43. Etzioni, *op. cit.*, pp. 356–357.

44. Freidson, *op. cit.*, p. 34.

45. Eliot Freidson, *Profession of Medicine* (New York: Dodd, Mead, 1972), p. 337.

46. Renford Bambrough, 'Plato's Political Analogies', in Peter Laslett, editor, *Philosophy, Politics and Society* (New York: Macmillan, 1956), pp. 105–106.

47. The common interest in safely completing a voyage, or surviving an experience fraught with danger, may partially account for the fact, recently noted by Dorothy Rabinowitz, that American hostages of aeroplane hi-jackers and other terrorists have shown a pronounced tendency to sympathize with their captors even after they have been rescued by official authorities such as the police or the military. Hi-jackers, unlike ordinary navigators, usurp the right to decide the route and destination of a journey rather than merely direct the vehicle over a preselected route to a preselected destination; in fact, they rarely take over the controls of a plane themselves but coerce the pilot and crew to direct it where they want to go. Yet they are nevertheless 'in the same boat' with the crew and the passengers in wanting a safe journey. Miss Rabinowitz attributes the expressions of compassion by the victims after their ordeal has ended to the ideological influence of 'liberal-progressive orthodoxy' – all of the examples she cites involved hi-jackers or terrorists who acted ostensibly in the service of a political or religious cause. Perhaps ideology plays a part, but she ignores entirely the temporary bonds created by the shared ordeal, granting that the actions of the terrorists themselves are responsible for the ordeal. This is most obviously the case in plane hi-jackings, but it is not absent from Miss Rabinowitz's other major example of the seizure of a building and the holding of its occupants as hostages: the victims as much as the victimizers had reason to fear death or injury if the police stormed the building and shot it out with the terrorists. Miss Rabinowitz's own interpretation strikes me as being excessively ideological; Dorothy Rabinowitz, 'The Hostage Mentality', *Commentary*, 63 (June 1977), pp. 70–72.

48. This example is based on observations made during several trips I took as a merchant seaman in the 1940s.

49. I have actually combined *two* separate statements in the quotation. The first sentence is from Weber, *The Theory of Social and Economic Organization*, p. 339; the second is from H. H. Gerth and C. Wright Mills, editors, *From Max Weber: Essays in Sociology* (New York: Oxford University Press, 1946), p. 214.

50. Charles Perrow, *Complex Organizations: A Critical Essay* (Glenview, Ill.: Scott, Foresman, 1972), pp. 56–58.

51. Etzioni, *op. cit.*, pp. 357–359.

52. Freidson, *Profession of Medicine*, p. 337.

53. Bambrough, *op. cit.*, 98–115 provides a thorough critique of these analogies; see also T. D. Weldon, *The Vocabulary of Politics* (Harmondsworth, Middlesex: Penguin Books, 1953), pp. 138–143. I have drawn here, and elsewhere in this section, on an essay of mine which examines more fully the use of competent authority as a legitimating ideal; Dennis H. Wrong, *Skeptical Sociology* (New York: Columbia University Press, 1976), pp. 196–208.

   Mao was regularly described as 'The Great Helmsman' in Communist China. I do not know whether the metaphor was borrowed from Western Marxism and thus may ultimately derive from Plato, or whether it is also indigenous to traditional Chinese culture. Stalin, from whom Mao imitated what Stalin's heirs later anathematized as 'the cult of personality', used to prefer more modern, industrial metaphors such as 'the Great Driver of the Locomotive of History'. After his famous visit to China in early 1972, Richard Nixon was frequently described in the campaign literature of the ill-fated Committee to Reelect the President (known as CREEP) as 'the helmsman of the American ship of state', so there may have been a three-step West to East and back again diffusion of this ancient metaphor.

54. R. G. Collingwood, *The New Leviathan*, Oxford, The Clarendon Press, 1942, p. 183.

55. Friedrich, 'Authority, Reason, and Discretion', p. 34.

56. Collingwood, *op. cit.*, p. 205.

57. Blau, *op. cit.*, pp. 76–85.

58. Bierstedt, *op. cit.*, p. 248.

59. Talcott Parsons, *The Structure of Social Action* (New York: McGraw-Hill, 1937), pp. 658–672; Edward A. Shils, 'Charisma, Order and Status, *American Sociological Review*, 30 (April 1965), pp. 199–213; Robert A. Nisbet, *The Sociological Tradition* (New York: Basic Books, 1966), pp. 251–257.

60. Weber, *Economy and Society*, Volume 1, pp. 37, 226.

61. For a perceptive discussion of the special vulnerabilities of charismatic leadership, see Reinhard Bendix, 'Reflections on Charismatic Leadership', in Wrong, editor, *Max Weber*, pp. 166–181.

Chapter Four

1. Each of the different conceptions and definitions summarized in this paragraph has been advanced by one or more of the writers cited in the

first three chapters. It is superfluous to cite all of them again, but they include Arendt, Bachrach and Baratz, Bierstedt, Blau, Boulding, Connolly, Dahl and Lindblom, Easton, Emerson, Etzioni, Friedrich, Gamson, Gerth and Mills, Goldhamer and Shils, Goode, Homans, de Jouvenel, Lasswell and Kaplan, Lehman, Lukes, Nagel, Neumann, Oppenheim, Parsons, Partridge, Rose, Russell, Simmel, Simon, Van Doorn, Walter, Weber and Weldon.

2. William J. Goode has suggested eliminating the term 'power' altogether, at least 'for the next decade', in 'The Place of Force in Human Society', *American Sociological Review*, 37 (October 1972), p. 510.

3. Robert Bierstedt has discussed at length the distinction between nominal and what he calls 'real' definitions in sociology in *Power and Progress: Essays on Sociological Theory* (New York: McGraw-Hill, 1974), pp. 150–187.

4. Max Weber, *Economy and Society*, 3 vols., edited by Guenther Roth and Claus Wittich, vol. 1, pp. 37–38, 262–266; vol. 3, p. 954. In the last citation, Weber observes after identifying 'the "pure" types of domination' that 'the forms of domination occurring in historical reality constitute combinations, mixtures, adaptations or mixtures, adaptations or modification of these "pure" types'.

5. This was a central issue in the trial for armed robbery of Patricia Hearst in San Francisco in early 1976. The defence argued that she had been subjected to 'coercive persuasion' by her kidnappers and therefore should not be held legally responsible for her later participation in crimes planned and carried out by the group. 'Coercive persuasion' is a good example of an oxymoron. The case for it as a psychological possibility, both in general and in the particular case of Miss Hearst, was made by three psychiatrists who testified as defence witnesses. One of them, Robert Jay Lifton, briefly stated his views in 'On the Hearst Trial', *New York Times*, 16 April 1976, p. 27. Actually, Miss Hearst was a victim of *both* physical and psychic force, so 'coercive persuasion' cannot, at least in her case, be identified solely with the latter.

6. Examples of mixed motives underlying compliance with authority are given by Weber, *op. cit.*, vol. 1, pp. 31–32; Peter Bachrach and Morton S. Baratz, 'Decisions and non-Decisions: An Analytical Framework', *American Political Science Review*, 57 (September 1963), p. 637; Alvin W. Gouldner, *The Coming Crisis of Western Sociology* (New York: Basic Books, 1970), pp. 293–294; Goode, *op. cit.*, p. 512. Many other writers might also be cited.

7. For the distinction between *intention* and *motive*, see G. E. M. Anscombe, *Intention* (Ithaca, N.Y.: Cornell University Press, Second Edition, 1966), pp. 18–20.

8. Talcott Parsons, *The Structure of Social Action* (New York: McGraw-Hill, 1937), pp. 43–51.

9. Talcott Parsons, *The Social System* (Glencoe, Ill.: The Free Press, 1951), pp. 37–51.

10. See John Rex's criticism of Parsons's model in *Key Problems of Sociological Theory* (London: Routledge and Kegan Paul, 1961), pp. 103–112; for a much fuller recent statement by Rex of the different possible relations between ego and alter, see his *Sociology and the Demystification of the Modern World* (London and Boston: Routledge and Kegan Paul, 1974), pp. 69–77.

11. Amitai Etzioni, *The Active Society* (New York: The Free Press, 1968), pp. 357–359. The classification of power as either coercive, utilitarian or normative was first developed in Etzioni's earlier book *A Comparative Analysis of Complex Organizations* (New York: The Free Press of Glencoe, 1961), pp. 5–6. See also William Gamson, *Power and Discontent* (Homewood, Ill.: The Dorsey Press, 1968), pp. 163–183.

12. Etzioni, *The Active Society*, pp. 364–366.

13. Robert K. Merton, *Mass Persuasion: The Social Psychology of a War Bond Drive* (New York: Harper and Brothers, 1946), pp. 45–47; Etzioni, *The Active Society*, pp. 366–367.

14. Etzioni, *The Active Society*, p. 366 (italics in text).

15. Edward W. Lehman, 'Towards a Macrosociology of Power', *American Sociological Review*, 34 (August 1969), p. 457.

16. Lehman makes the point that 'macro-power' is more likely than 'micro-power' to be based on the control of multiple resources; *ibid.*, pp. 456–457.

17. Niccolo Machiavelli, *The Prince and the Discourses* (New York: Random House, The Modern Library, 1940), p. 61.

18. Hannah Arendt, *The Origins of Totalitarianism* (New York: Harcourt, Brace, 1951), pp. 333–353.

19. The possibility that change rather than maintenance of equilibrium may be inherent in recurrent patterns of interaction even when conflict is absent was suggested as long ago as 1955 by Alvin W. Gouldner in an article reprinted in *For Sociology* (New York: Basic Books, 1974), pp. 181–182.

20. Carl J. Friedrich, 'Authority, Reason, and Discretion', in Friedrich, editor, *Authority*, Nomos 1 (Cambridge: Harvard University Press, 1958), pp. 29, 35–36.

21. Karl Mannheim, *Essays on Sociology and Social Psychology* (New York: Oxford University Press, 1953), pp. 98–101; also *Ideology and Utopia* (Harcourt, Brace, 1946), pp. 207–208.

22. Hannah Arendt, *On Violence* (New York: Harcourt, Brace and World, 1970), p. 38.

23. *Ibid.*, pp. 40–41. This view is expressed much more fully in a number of other works by Hannah Arendt; see especially *Between Past and Future* (New York: The Viking Press, 1961), pp. 91–141 where it is explicitly

presented as a concept of authority in an essay that first appeared in Friedrich, editor, *op. cit.*, pp. 81–112; it is adumbrated in *The Human Condition* (Chicago: University of Chicago Press, 1958), pp. 200–204; and is central to the thesis of *On Revolution* (New York: The Viking Press, 1963), especially Chapters 4 and 5, pp. 139–215.

24. One of the few writers who has commented on the similarity of Arendt's and Parsons's concepts of power is Steven Lukes, *Power: A Radical View* (London: Macmillan, 1974), pp. 27–31; see also Jürgen Habermas, who emphasizes, however, the differences between them more than the similarities, in 'Hannah Arendt's Communications Concept of Power', *Social Research* 44 (Spring, 1977), pp. 5–7, 19–20.

25. Jürgen Habermas, *Legitimation Crisis* (Boston: Beacon Press, 1973), especially pp. 95–117.

26. Erich Fromm developed such a distinction between 'rational' and 'irrational' authority in *Escape from Freedom* (New York: Farrar and Rinehart, 1941), pp. 164–166. This was, however, long before concern arose among Western intellectuals over the rise of new forms of 'technocratic domination' which appeal to the model of rational or competent authority to legitimate themselves. This theme is particularly associated with Habermas's writings, especially *Toward A Rational Society* (Boston: Beacon Press, 1970), Chapter 6, pp. 81–122, and has become linked to a general critique of 'positivistic' social science seen as originating with Comte and Saint-Simon. For a more detailed discussion of its relationship to the model of competent authority, see Dennis H. Wrong, *Skeptical Sociology* (New York: Columbia University Press, 1976), Chapter 12, pp. 196–208.

27. See the rueful account of his encounter with this attitude by Paul Goodman, *New Reformation: Notes of a Neolithic Conservative* (New York: Random House, Vintage Books, 1971), pp. 47–9.

28. 'World history is not a seminar', observes Richard Lowenthal in a critique of Habermas's *Legitimation Crisis* in 'Social Transformation and Democratic Legitimacy', *Social Research*, 43 (Summer, 1976), p. 264. See also Richard J. Bernstein, *The Restructuring of Social and Political Theory* (New York: Harcourt Brace Jovanovitch, 1976), pp. 223–225; also, Anthony Giddens, *New Rules of Sociological Method* (New York: Basic Books, 1976), pp. 68–69.

29. Anthony Giddens, '"Power" in the Recent Writings of Talcott Parsons', *Sociology*, 2 (September 1968), p. 266.

30. See also Wrong, *op. cit.*

31. Machiavelli, *op. cit.*, p. 61.

32. I believe that the origin of this phrase is a story once told by Senator, later Vice-President, Alben Barkley, who received this response from a Kentucky constituent whose vote he had solicited after enumerating the many favours he had done for the constituent while in office.

33. Denis de Rougement, 'The Crisis of the Modern Couple', in Ruth Nanda Anshen, editor, *The Family: Its Function and Destiny* (New York: Harper and Brothers. Revised edition, 1959), pp. 449–462.

34. This was one of George Homans's propositions about leadership in *The Human Group* (New York: Harcourt, Brace, 1950), pp. 431–433.

35. W. G. Runciman, *A Critique of Max Weber's Philosophy of Social Science* (Cambridge: Cambridge University Press, 1972), pp. 33–48.

Chapter Five

1. George Orwell, *Collected Essays, Journalism and Letters*, 4 vols. (Harmondsworth, Middlesex: Penguin Books, 1970), vol. 4, pp. 210–211.

2. Jean-Jacques Rousseau, *The Social Contract* (Harmondsworth, Middlesex: Penguin Books, 1968), p. 53.

3. *Ibid.*, p. 52.

4. Franz Neumann, *The Democratic and the Authoritarian State* (Glencoe, Ill.: The Free Press, 1957), p. 18.

5. H. H. Gerth and C. Wright Mills, editors and translators, *From Max Weber: Essays in Sociology* (New York: Oxford University Press, 1947), p. 78.

6. I have analysed Weber's definition at greater length in Dennis H. Wrong, editor, *Max Weber* (Englewood Cliffs, N.J.: Prentice-Hall, 1970), pp. 36–41.

7. Gerth and Mills, *op. cit.*

8. L. J. Macfarlane ably analyses the concept of legitimacy in relation to the state's use of force in *Violence and the State* (London: Thomas Nelson and Sons, 1974), Chapter 4. I have not adopted, however, his distinction (derived from Sorel) of *force* as the legitimate use of coercive power and *violence* as its illegitimate use.

9. Gerth and Mills, *op. cit.*, pp. 123, 126.

10. Although he does not mention Weber, Isaiah Berlin's view of Machiavelli closely resembles Weber's. Machiavelli's distinctive achievement, Berlin argues, was to insist that the equally cherished values of private virtue and the political independence of the community inescapably conflict and cannot be reconciled; his stark insistence on this painful fact is the reason why 'Machiavelli's writings, more particularly *The Prince*, have scandalized mankind more deeply and continuously than any other political treatise' (p. 30). 'The Question of Machiavelli', *New York Review of Books* (4 November 1971), pp. 20–32.

11. C. Wright Mills, *The Power Elite* (New York: Oxford University Press, 1956), p. 171.

12. Hannah Arendt has noted the similarity between this attitude and that of

Communists in the 1930s towards Hitler's coming to power, although she notes that the latter policy was not spontaneous but was dictated far from the scene by Stalin; *On Violence* (New York: Harcourt, Brace and World, 1970), pp. 99–100. The attitude in question, however, is clearly an application of 'the worse, the better' assumption sometimes adopted by radicals and revolutionaries.

13. *Ibid.*, pp. 53, 56; Neumann, *op. cit.*, p. 4; earlier writers who have described force or violence as the 'failure' or 'breakdown' of power are Robert M. MacIver, *The Modern State* (Oxford: Oxford University Press, 1926), pp. 222, 230–231; also, *The Web of Government* (New York: Macmillan, 1947), p. 16; and Charles E. Merriam, *Political Power* (New York: McGraw-Hill, 1934), pp. 21, 226.

14. E. V. Walter, 'Power and Violence', *American Political Science Review*, 58 (June 1964), p. 358. I have learned much from this valuable statement which has been partly incorporated into the author's *Terror and Resistance* (New York: Oxford University Press, 1969), Chapter 3.

15. Walter, 'Power and Violence', p. 360.

16. Dahrendorf's argument first appeared in 'Out of Utopia: Towards a Re-Orientation of Sociological Analysis', *American Journal of Sociology*, 64 (September 1958), pp. 115–127; it was restated at much greater length in *Class and Class Conflict in Industrial Society* (Stanford, Calif., Stanford University Press, 1959), pp. 157–173. The earlier essay and several later ones on the same general theme appear in *Essays in the Theory of Society* (Stanford, Calif.: Stanford University Press, 1968).

17. I am borrowing a comment of Alvin W. Gouldner's in *For Sociology* (New York: Basic Books, 1974), p. 183. (The comment is from an article first published in 1955).

18. Peter Weingart, 'Beyond Parsons? A Critique of Ralf Dahrendorf's Conflict Theory', *Social Forces*, 48 (December 1969), pp. 151–165; Dick Atkinson, *Orthodox Consensus and Radical Alternative* (London: Heinemann Educational Books, 1971), pp. 89–95, 101–104; Jonathan H. Turner, *The Structure of Sociological Theory* (Homewood, Ill.: The Dorsey Press, 1974), Chapter 6.

19. This point is particularly stressed by Desmond P. Ellis, 'The Hobbesian Problem of Order', *American Sociological Review*, 36 (August 1971), pp. 692–703.

20. Thomas Hobbes, *Leviathan* (Indianapolis, Ind.: Bobbs-Merrill, 1958), pp. 106–107. For an appreciation of Hobbes as a dialectical thinker, see R. G. Collingwood, *The New Leviathan* (Oxford: The Clarendon Press, 1942), p. 183.

21. These constitute what Turner calls 'intervening empirical conditions' and are, he argues, omitted by Dahrendorf in contrast to Marx; Turner, *op. cit.*, pp. 97–101. I do not agree with Turner, however, that the initial existence of institutionalized power relations is 'considered

nonproblematic' by Marx as well as by Dahrendorf. A fuller comparison which criticizes Dahrendorf but argues that Marx's theory, whatever its empirical truth, is logically and conceptually superior, may be found in Hugh Stretton, *The Political Sciences* (New York: Basic Books, 1969), pp. 318–319, 327–339.

22. Dahrendorf, *Essays* . . . , p. 150.

23. *Ibid.*, pp. 151–178. I have made no effort here to assess this essay as an argument 'on the origin of inequality among men', which is its title.

24. *Ibid.*, p. 173.

25. *Ibid.*, p. 174.

26. *Ibid.*, n. 21.

27. *Ibid.*, p. 173.

28. For a useful discussion of these in the context of a criticism of 'coercion theory', see Robert E. Dowse and John A. Hughes, *Political Sociology* (New York: John Wiley and Sons, 1972), pp. 25–26 (also pp. 90–95).

29. Dahrendorf, *Essays* . . . , p. 173, n. 20.

30. One of the best systematic comparisons of the different principles underlying a system-integration (or 'structural-functional') and a conflict-power (or 'historical-comparative') approach, which, unlike that of Dahrendorf, focuses on the actual historical record, is that of Randall Collins, 'A Comparative Approach to Political Sociology', in Reinhard Bendix, editor, *State and Society: A Reader in Comparative Political Sociology* (Boston: Little, Brown, 1968), pp. 42–67.

31. This is clearly recognized by Collins who writes of the need to separate 'the question of stable coordination *within* groups, from coordination *between* groups'. *Ibid.*, p. 51. That conflict may strengthen solidarity and consensus within the contending groups is, of course, a major proposition of Simmel's sociology as elaborated by Lewis A. Coser in *The Functions of Social Conflict* (Glencoe, Ill.: The Free Press, 1957).

32. I consider it unfortunate, therefore, that Randall Collins chose the title he did for his ambitious and important treatise on sociological theory: *Conflict Sociology: Toward an Explanatory Science* (New York: Academic Press, 1975). In this book no more than in his earlier article does he neglect or minimize the conditions promoting consensus and social cohesion, concerning which, in fact, he advances an original interpretation based on a Durkheimian reading of Goffman's sociology.

33. The phrase is Philip Rieff's from *Freud: The Mind of the Moralist* (New York: Doubleday Anchor Books, 1961), p. 244.

34. William J. Goode, 'The Place of Force in Human Society', *American Sociological Review*, 37 (October 1972), p. 512 (my italics). Goode's overall argument is weakened by his explicit refusal to distinguish between what he calls 'force and force-threat'. He comes close to committing the reverse error from that of the consensualists, who in blurring the distinction between the use and the threat of force minimize

the effectiveness of the latter in light of the limitations of the former. See pp. 26–27 above.

35. For an exceptionally lucid exposition of this argument, see Errol E. Harris, 'Political Power', *Ethics*, 68 (October 1957), pp. 4–5.

36. Niccolo Machiavelli, *The Prince and the Discourses* (New York: Random House, The Modern Library, 1940), p. 45.

37. Michael Polanyi, *Personal Knowledge* (London: Routledge and Kegan Paul, 1958), pp. 224–225.

38. I am grateful to Professor Robert C. Tucker of Princeton University for having given me information bearing on the authenticity of this incident. He says that it is quite possibly apocryphal, although it reached people concerned with Soviet affairs, such as himself, from Soviet sources. He describes it as a 'genuinely Soviet party anecdote' (personal communication).

39. Polanyi, *op. cit.*

40. The *locus classicus* is, of course, Hannah Arendt, *The Origins of Totalitarianism* (New York: Harcourt, Brace, 1951). For an earlier statement, see Leo Lowenthal, 'Terror's Atomization of Man', *Commentary*, 1 (January 1946), pp. 1–8.

41. Walter, *Terror and Resistance*, pp. 110–111.

42. *Ibid.*, p. 29.

43. *Ibid.*, p. 270.

44. I have been unable to locate this phrase in Aron's voluminous writings. It was quoted by Lionel Abel at a public meeting in New York in 1964.

45. Joseph Goebbels had the title of Minister of Propaganda and Public Enlightenment in Nazi Germany.

46. Walter, *Terror and Resistance*, pp. 220–243.

47. For example, Carl J. Friedrich, Michael Curtis, and Benjamin R. Barber, *Totalitarianism in Perspective* (New York: Praeger, 1969); Leonard Schapiro, *Totalitarianism* (London: The Pall Mall Press, 1972), pp. 99–125. For a defence of Hannah Arendt's use of the concept, see Bernard Crick, 'On Rereading *The Origins of Totalitarianism*', *Social Research*, 44 (Spring 1977), pp. 106–126.

48. Neumann, *op. cit.*, p. 9. This is the first of five 'sociological generalizations' about political power in modern societies advanced by Neumann. See also Goode, *op. cit.*, pp. 516–517, where substantially the same point is elaborated.

49. For a valuable discussion of the larger significance of the Oppenheimer case in the early 1950s, see Philip Rieff, 'The Case of Dr. Oppenheimer', in Rieff, editor, *On Intellectuals* (Garden City, N.Y.: Doubleday Anchor Books, 1970), pp. 342–369.

50. On the eventual necessity of de-Stalinization, see Arendt, *On Violence*, pp. 54–56.

51. Zbigniew K. Brzezinski, *The Permanent Purge* (Cambridge, Mass.:

Harvard University Press, 1956). It could not plausibly be maintained today that 'the Soviet system may rightly be called one of the permanent purge' (p. 175).

52. Hobbes, *op. cit.*, p. 107.
53. Orwell, *op. cit.*, pp. 192–215.
54. Arthur L. Stinchcombe, *Constructing Social Theories* (New York: Harcourt, Brace and World, 1968), pp. 158–163.
55. Orwell, *op. cit.*, p. 193.
56. Raymond Aron, *Main Currents in Sociological Thought*, two volumes (New York: Basic Books, 1967), Volume 2, p. 143.
57. Karl Mannheim, *From Karl Mannheim*, edited by Kurt H. Wolff (New York: Oxford University Press, 1971), pp. 65–66.
58. Aron, *op. cit.*, pp. 107–108.
59. Max Weber, *Economy and Society*, three volumes, edited by Guenther Roth and Claus Wittich (New York: Bedminster Press, 1968), Volume 3, p. 953.
60. Gaetano Mosca, *The Ruling Class* (New York: McGraw-Hill, 1939), p. 71.
61. Philip Rahv, 'The Legend of the Grand Inquisitor', *Partisan Review*, 21 (May–June 1954), p. 254.
62. All the direct quotations in the discussion of the Grand Inquisitor are from Fyodor Dostoevsky, *The Brothers Karamazov* (New York: Random House Modern Library College Editions, 1950), pp. 294–312.
63. The three basic needs mentioned here are inferred from Dostoevsky's text, but should not be confused with the three gifts, or temptations, offered by Satan described in the 'Legend', nor with the triad 'miracle' mystery, and authority'. Edward Wasiolek has pointed out that many critics have misinterpreted the three gifts from Satan as consisting of 'miracle, mystery, and authority', presumably because of the salience of the triad with its rhythmic, partly alliterative cadence. Actually, as Wasiolek indicates, 'miracle, mystery, and authority' are instruments of the second temptation only, which is, in his words, 'to prove divinity by miracle'; Wasiolek, *Dostoevsky: The Major Fiction* (Cambridge, Mass.: The M.I.T. Press, 1964), p. 167.
64. D. H. Lawrence, 'Preface to Dostoevsky's *The Grand Inquisitor*', in René Wellek, editor, *Dostoevsky: A Collection of Critical Essays* (Englewood Cliffs, N.J.: Prentice-Hall, 1962), p. 90.
65. Philip Rahv, 'The Unfuture of Utopia', *Partisan Review*, 16 (July 1949), p. 747. In spite of Rahv's assertion, a recent study of the sources of *Nineteen Eighty-Four* does not even refer to the story of the Grand Inquisitor as a possible influence on the book, although it does mention Dostoevsky's *Notes from the Underground* as having helped form Orwell's belief in the fragility of 'objective truth' which is an important ingredient of the novel; see William Steinhoff, *George Orwell and the*

Origins of 1984 (Ann Arbor: University of Michigan Press, 1975). Nor does the index to the four volumes of Orwell's *Collected Essays, Journalism and Letters, op. cit.*, contain more than a single reference to Dostoevsky, which turns out to be a trivial one. Nevertheless, I think one can accept Rahv's surmise that Orwell wrote the dialogue between O'Brien and Winston Smith with the story of the Grand Inquisitor in mind: it echoes and counterpoints it closely in places and Orwell must obviously have been well-acquainted with the story and the novel. Moreover, there is some internal evidence suggesting this: in the first dialogue O'Brien refers with contempt to the Inquisition and the Inquisitor as crude and unsuccessful forerunners of the rulers of Oceania; Orwell, *Nineteen Eighty-Four* (New York: Harcourt, Brace, 1949), p. 257.

66. All quotations, except for the single one indicated in the following note, are from Orwell, *Nineteen Eighty-Four*, pp. 265–267.

67. *Ibid.*, p. 36.

68. Orwell, *Collected Essays* . . . , Volume Four, p. 89.

69. Rahv, 'The Unfuture of Utopia', p. 748.

70. See the perceptive discussion of the relation between 'narcissistic withdrawal' and the leadership of political or religious movements in Philip E. Slater, 'On Social Regression', *American Sociological Review*, 28 (June 1963), pp. 345–348. Slater refers to a short paper by Freud identifying 'narcissistic', 'erotic', and 'obsessional' character types, which Slater then characterizes as 'ego-oriented', 'id-oriented', and 'superego-oriented', respectively; Sigmund Freud, 'Libidinal Types', *Collected Papers*, Volume Five (New York: Basic Books, 1959), pp. 248–249. Freud alludes in passing to narcissistic types as 'independent and not easily overawed' and therefore likely to become leaders. Elsewhere, referring to the 'father of the primal horde' as the prototype of the leader, Freud writes: 'His intellectual acts were strong and independent even in isolation, and his will needed no reinforcement from others. Consistency leads us to assume that his ego had few libidinal ties; he loved no one but himself, or other people only in so far as they served his needs. . . . He, at the very beginning of the history of mankind, was the "superman" whom Nietzsche only expected from the future. Even today the members of a group stand in need of the illusion that they are equally and justly loved by their leader; but the leader himself need love no one else, he may be of a masterful nature, absolutely narcissistic, self-confident and independent' *Group Psychology and the Analysis of the Ego* (New York: Bantam Books, 1960), p. 71. One need not, of course, accept the hypothesis of the primal horde to see this as a valid description of *some* leaders, particularly those, as Slater notes, who are charismatic.

71. It has often been argued that Orwell overestimated, like the Machiavellians, the dominance of 'power-drive' and 'power-worship' in

human conduct, although, unlike the Machiavellians, in his revulsion against totalitarianism he viewed this with despair and hopelessness rather than equanimity. On the other hand, his insistence that the world of 1984 was not inevitable and his arguments against neo-Machiavellians like James Burnham stand in conflict with his more pessimistic views. For a recent critical discussion, see Alex Zwerdling, *Orwell and the Left* (New Haven: Yale University Press, 1974), pp. 27–28, 100–113.

72. Anna Freud, *The Ego and the Mechanisms of Defence* (New York: International Universities Press, 1946), Chapter 9, pp. 117–131.

73. Bruno Bettelheim, *The Informed Heart* (Glencoe, Ill.: The Free Press, 1960), pp. 169–175.

74. Stanley M. Elkins, *Slavery: A Problem in American Institutional and Intellectual Life* (New York: Grosset and Dunlap, The Universal Library, 1963), Part III, pp. 81–139; Eugene D. Genovese, *Roll, Jordan, Roll: The World the Slaves Made* (New York: Pantheon Books, 1974), especially pp. 3–7, 661–665.

75. Stanley M. Elkins, 'The Slavery Debate', *Commentary*, 60 (December 1975), pp. 40–54.

76. Eugene D. Genovese, *In Red and Black* (New York: Pantheon Books, 1971), pp. 94–95.

77. Sigmund Freud, *Civilization and Its Discontents* (New York: W. W. Norton, 1962), pp. 72–74.

78. This is reviewed by George Kateb, *Utopia and Its Enemies* (New York: The Free Press of Glencoe, 1963), especially in Chapter 6, pp. 139–209.

79. Dahrendorf, *Essays . . .* , pp. 107–113, 127–128, 175–178.

80. The phrase is that of Raymond Aron in *La Révolution Íntrouvable, réflexions sur la Révolution de mai* (Paris: Fayard, 1968), p. 41.

81. Steven Lukes, *Power: A Radical View* (London, Macmillan, 1974), pp. 47–50.

82. Dahrendorf, *Class and Class Conflict . . .* , pp. 173–179. Although I obviously am in substantial agreement with Dahrendorf's claim that 'the legitimacy of authority must always be precarious' (p. 176), I find his discussion of what he calls the 'latent interest' of subordinates in resisting their superiors to be singularly confused and confusing. He goes to considerable lengths to argue that these interests are emphatically 'non-psychological'. I shall postpone discussion of the whole question of 'objective' interests and of the views on it of Dahrendorf and others to a later chapter.

83. Erich Fromm, *Escape from Freedom* (New York: Farrar and Rinehart, 1941), pp. 288–289.

84. *Ibid.*, pp. 164–166. In a later book, Fromm repeated verbatim this discussion of 'rational' and 'irrational' authority; *The Sane Society* (New York: Rinehart, 1955), pp. 95–97.

85. Fromm, *Escape from Freedom*, p. 165.

86. John H. Schaar, *Escape from Authority* (New York: Basic Books, 1961), pp. 105–106.
87. Jürgen Habermas, *Knowledge and Human Interests* (Boston: Beacon Press, 1971), pp. 308–315.
88. Anthony Giddens, *Studies in Social and Political Theory* (London: Hutchinson, 1977), pp. 160–161.
89. Giddens makes this criticism very cogently; *ibid.*, pp. 152, 157.
90. Orwell, *Collected Essays* . . . , Volume 4, p. 347.
91. Quoted by Philip Rieff, *Freud: The Mind of the Moralist*, p. 259.
92. *Ibid.*, p. 257.
93. Hannah Arendt, *On Violence*, pp. 39–40.
94. Randall Collins, drawing on Dahrendorf, identifies the power relation with the concrete giving and taking of orders and also stresses 'that being coerced is an intrinsically unpleasant experience'. But, like other writers, he does not distinguish between the unpleasantness of taking orders in and of itself and taking them when there is at least a latent threat of force to compel obedience; *Conflict Sociology*, p. 59; see also Collins's numbered propositions on pp. 73–74 where this distinction is both implied and, it seems to me, blurred.
95. The 'contract' or 'tacit exchange . . . between the few who rule and the many who obey' has recently been stressed by Reinhard Bendix, 'The Mandate to Rule: An Introduction', *Social Forces*, 55 (December 1976), p. 243.

Chapter Six

1. Amitai Etzioni, *The Active Society* (New York: The Free Press, 1968), pp. 357–359.
2. William Gamson, *Power and Discontent* (Homewood, Ill.: The Dorsey Press, 1968), pp. 74–81.
3. Harold Lasswell and Abraham Kaplan, *Power and Society* (New Haven: Yale University Press, 1950), pp. 83–92.
4. Robert A. Dahl, *Who Governs? Democracy and Power in an American City* (New Haven: Yale University Press, 1961), p. 226.
5. Dahl fails to mention coercive resources on either of these lists. A significant omission, because in 1968 blacks in New Haven rioted for several days and, as happened in other American cities at the time, won some concessions to their demands from the city government. New Haven was also the scene of the murder of a member of the Black Panther Party by another member which led to a highly publicized trial of Bobby Seale, one of the national Black Panther leaders, and several other national and local leaders of the Party in 1970. All of the leaders

were in the end acquitted of having been accessories to the murder, but in May, 1970, New Haven was the site of a huge rally of Yale students, local blacks and outside sympathizers addressed by national Black Panther leaders, protesting the indictment of Seale and others for the murder and the American invasion of Cambodia the previous week. The shooting of four students by the Ohio National Guard in the course of anti-war demonstrations on the campus of Kent State University just before the Yale rally enhanced fears of mass violence developing at the rally, although these fears did not materialize. In other works, where he has not been specifically concerned with New Haven or American local government, Dahl has routinely included coercive resources on his lists of political resources; see, for example, *After the Revolution?* (New Haven: Yale University Press, 1970), pp. 105–107; and *Polyarchy: Participation and Opposition* (New Haven: Yale University Press, 1971), p. 82.

6. Dahl, *Who Governs?* p. 305; Gamson, *op. cit.*, pp. 93–109.
7. Nelson W. Polsby, 'Community Power Meets Air Pollution', *Contemporary Sociology*, 1 (March 1972), p. 99.
8. Matthew Crenson, *The Un-Politics of Air Pollution: A Study of Non-Decisionmaking in the Cities* (Baltimore: The Johns Hopkins Press, 1971), pp. 35–82.
9. Nelson W. Polsby, *Community Power and Political Theory* (New Haven: Yale University Press, 1962), pp. 59–63; Schulze's study is summarized in Robert O. Schulze, 'The Role of Economic Dominants in Community Power', *American Sociological Review*, 23 (February 1958), pp. 3–9; and by the same author, 'The Bifurcation of Power in a Satellite City', in Morris Janowitz, editor, *Community Political Systems* (Glencoe, Ill.: The Free Press, 1961), pp. 19–80.
10. Polsby, *Community Power and Political Theory*, p. 117.
11. Robert A. Dahl, 'Equality and Power in American Society', in William V. D'Antonio and Howard J. Ehrlich, editors, *Power and Democracy in America* (Notre Dame: Notre Dame University Press, 1961), pp. 78–79.
12. Dahl, *Who Governs?* pp. 163–165.
13. *Ibid.*, pp. 130–131, 137–138. This is pointed out by Peter Morriss, 'Power in New Haven: A Reassessment of *Who Governs?*' *British Journal of Political Science*, 2 (October 1972), pp. 457–465.
14. For example, *ibid.* I made this point as long ago as 1963 in a review of D'Antonio and Ehrlich, editors, *op. cit.*, *American Sociological Review*, 28 (February 1963), pp. 144–145.
15. Many specific examples, pertaining, significantly, for the most part to the alleged power of individuals rather than of organizations, are given by Raymond E. Wolfinger, 'Reputation and Reality in the Study of "Community Power",' *American Sociological Review*, 25 (October

1960), pp. 636–644; and by the same author, 'A Plea for a Decent Burial', *American Sociological Review*, 27 (December 1962), pp. 840–847.

16. Dahl, *Who Governs?*, p. 138; Wolfinger, 'Reputation and Reality . . .' p. 642.

17. Peter Bachrach and Morton S. Baratz, 'The Two Faces of Power', *American Political Science Review*, 56 (November 1962), pp. 947–952; by the same authors, 'Decisions and Nondecisions: an Analytical Framework', *American Political Science Review*, 57 (September 1963), pp. 641–651; also, *Power and Poverty: Theory and Practice* (New York: Oxford University Press, 1970), especially Part I.

18. Steven Lukes, *Power: A Radical View* (London: Macmillan, 1974), pp. 21–25; Frederick W. Frey, 'Comment: On Issues and Nonissues in the Study of Power', *American Political Science Review*, 65 (December 1971), pp. 1089–1090. Frey was responding to Raymond E. Wolfinger, 'Nondecisions and the Study of Local Politics', *ibid.*, pp. 1063–1080.

19. Or, at least, what is widely taken to be the Weberian view, which as Anthony Giddens has pointed out, either simply omits or ignores the implications of the 'even' in Weber's definition of power as 'the probability that one actor within a social relationship will be in a position to carry out his will *even* against resistance' (my italics). See Chapter 2, Note 1, pp. 261–262 above.

20. This is true also of Lukes's view of power as 'significant affecting', which, however, does not make intentionality a criterion of power. See Lukes, *Power: A Radical View*, pp. 26–27; also, 'Power and Structure', paper prepared for delivery at the 1976 Annual Meeting of the American Political Science Association, pp. 2–5. (In Lukes, *Essays in Social Theory* (New York: Columbia University Press, 1977), pp. 4–29.)

21. Dahl, *Who Governs?*, p. 271.

22. Gamson, *op. cit.*, p. 95.

23. E. E. Schattschneider, *The Semisovereign People* (New York: Holt, Rinehart and Winston, 1960), p. 30 (italics in text).

24. *Ibid.*, p. 35.

25. Robert A. Dahl, *Modern Political Analysis* (Englewood Cliffs, N.J.: Prentice-Hall, 1963), pp. 47–48.

26. Wolfinger, 'Reputation and Reality . . .', p. 642; 'A Plea for a Decent Burial', pp. 842–843.

27. Andrew Hacker, 'What Rules America?' *New York Review of Books*, 1 May 1975, p. 13. Actually, Hacker is here arguing not only against the imputation of power to individuals as such, but also against its attribution to concrete groups composed of persons united by ties of kinship, marriage and shared educational and recreational experiences. His point is that the locus of power lies in organizational structures themselves rather than in an upper class from which organizational leaders are

recruited. He thus carries even further the identification of organization itself as a crucial power resource. Other articles by Hacker developing this theme are: 'Power to do What?' in Irving Louis Horowitz, editor, *The New Sociology* (New York: Oxford University Press, 1964), pp. 134–146; 'The Social and Economic Power of Corporations', in Dennis H. Wrong and Harry L. Gracey, editors, *Readings in Introductory Sociology*, Third Edition (New York: Macmillan, 1977), pp. 502–509; and 'Cutting Classes', *New York Review of Books*, 4 March 1976, pp. 15–18.

28. Lukes, *Power: A Radical View*, p. 22.

29. Gamson, *op. cit.*, p. 94.

30. Dahl, *Who Governs?*, p. 273.

31. *Ibid.*, p. 271.

32. Robert Presthus, *Men at the Top: A Study in Community Power* (New York: Oxford University Press, 1964), p. 430. It should be noted that Dahl appears to have changed his views since the early 1960s and that recent participants in debates over how to study power in communities or at the national level agree that issues raised in an earlier stage of the discussion are independent of the élitist-pluralist controversy with which they were initially associated. See, for example, the exchange between Wolfinger and Frey cited in Note 18 above. Also, Dahl, 'On Removing Certain Impediments to Democracy in the United States', *Dissent*, 25 (Summer 1978), pp. 310–324.

33. Paul F. Lazarsfeld and Herbert Menzel, 'On the Relation between Individual and Collective Properties', in Amitai Etzioni, editor, *Complex Organizations: A Sociological Reader* (New York: Holt, Rinehart and Winston, 1961), pp. 422–440. See also Edward W. and Ethna Lehman, 'Historical Data and the Measurement of Collective Properties', paper presented at the 64th annual meeting of the American Sociological Association, 4 September 1969, San Francisco, pp. 1–13. The Lehmans use the term 'aggregated' for what Lazarsfeld and Menzel call 'analytical' properties in drawing the contrast with what both call 'global' properties.

34. Lazarsfeld and Menzel, *op. cit.*, p. 435.

35. Mancur Olson, Jr., *The Logic of Collective Action*, Revised Edition (New York: Schocken Books, 1971), pp. 53–55.

36. H. H. Gerth and C. Wright Mills, *Character and Social Structure* (New York: Harcourt, Brace, 1953), p. 329.

37. This point is central to Randall Collins's 'conflict theory of organizations', *Conflict Sociology: Toward an Explanatory Science* (New York: Academic Press, 1975), Chapter 6, pp. 286–347.

38. *Ibid.*, p. 300.

39. This assumption is central to what Westhues calls the 'organization paradigm' in contemporary sociology, which he contrasts with the 'class paradigm', in Kenneth Westhues, 'Class and Organization as Paradigms

in Social Science', *The American Sociologist*, 11 (February 1976), pp. 38–49. Hacker also makes it explicitly with reference to corporation executives in 'Cutting Classes'.

40. James S. Coleman, 'Loss of Power', *American Sociological Review*, 38 (February 1973), p. 2.

41. Etzioni, *The Active Society*, pp. 354–357.

42. Lewis A. Coser, *Greedy Institutions* (New York: The Free Press, 1974), Chapter 8, pp. 117–135.

43. Philip A. Selznick, *The Organizational Weapon* (New York: McGraw-Hill, 1952).

44. Paul F. Lazarsfeld, Bernard Berelson and Hazel Gaudet, *The People's Choice* (New York: Duell, Sloan and Pierce, 1944).

45. Stein Rokkan, 'Mass Suffrage, Secret Voting and Political Participation', in Lewis A. Coser, editor, *Political Sociology* (New York: Harper Torchbooks, 1967), pp. 114–119.

46. One of the best-known discussions is that of Ralf Dahrendorf, who develops the concepts of 'latent interests' and 'quasi-groups' in *Class and Class Conflict in Industiral Society* (Stanford, Calif.: Stanford University Press, 1959), especially pp. 173–189.

47. Gamson, *op. cit.*, pp. 94–95.

48. Robert A. Dahl, 'A Critique of the Ruling Elite Model', *American Political Science Review*, 52 (June 1958), pp. 463–469.

49. Hannah Arendt, *On Violence* (New York: Harcourt, Brace and World, 1970), p. 44.

50. Harold Lasswell, *Politics: Who Gets What, When, and How* (New York: Meridian Books, 1958). (Originally published in 1936).

Chapter Seven

1. An example of such an attempt to apply general sociological theory to the mobilization of social movements is Neil J. Smelser's *Theory of Collective Behavior* (New York: The Free Press, 1962).

2. Anthony Oberschall, *Social Conflict and Social Movements* (Englewood Cliffs, N.J.: Prentice-Hall, 1973), p. 102.

3. John Torrance distinguishes between an awareness of *likeness* on the part of the members of a collectivity and an awareness of their *difference* or *estrangement* from others. Conflict represents the logical extreme of estrangement and may create what Torrance calls 'tertiary solidarity' among the members of a group. *Estrangement, Alienation and Exploitation: A Sociological Approach to Historical Materialism* (New York: Columbia University Press, 1977), pp. 122–131. See also the distinction between class *identity* and class *opposition* in Michael Mann, *Consciousness and Action Among the Western Working Class* (London:

Macmillan, 1973), p. 13; also, Anthony Giddens, *The Class Structure of the Advanced Societies* (London: Hutchinson, 1973), pp. 111–114.

4. Torrance, *op. cit.*, p. 126.
5. Nathan Glazer, 'Ethnic Groups in America: From National Culture to Ideology', in Morroe Berger, Theodore Abel, and Charles H. Page, editors, *Freedom and Control in Modern Society* (New York: D. Van Nostrand, 1954), pp. 158–173.
6. Daniel Bell, 'Ethnicity and Social Change', in Nathan Glazer and Daniel Patrick Moynihan, editors, *Ethnicity: Theory and Experience* (Cambridge: Harvard University Press, 1975), p. 169.
7. Nathan Glazer and Daniel Patrick Moynihan, 'Introduction', to *ibid.*, pp. 1–26.
8. Max Weber, *Economy and Society*, three volumes, edited by Guenther Roth and Claus Wittich (New York: Bedminister Press, 1968), Volume Two, pp. 932–938. See also the valuable discussion of Weber's concept of 'status group' in Giddens, *op. cit.*, p. 80.
9. Weber, *op. cit.*, pp. 928–929.
10. Robert M. MacIver, *Society: A Textbook of Sociology* (New York: Rinehart, 1937), pp. 28–30.
11. Karl Marx, *The Eighteenth Brumaire of Louis Bonaparte* (New York: International Publishers, n.d.), p. 109.
12. Karl Marx, *The Poverty of Philosophy* (London: Martin Lawrence, n.d.), pp. 145–146; Karl Marx and Friedrich Engels, *Manifesto of the Communist Party* (New York: International Publishers, n.d.), pp. 17–19.
13. Emile Durkheim, *The Division of Labor in Society* (New York: Macmillan, 1933), pp. 257–258; also, *The Elementary Forms of the Religious Life* (Glencoe, Ill.: The Free Press), 1947, pp. 214–219.
14. Randall Collins advances several formal numbered propositions to this effect in *Conflict Sociology: Toward an Explanatory Science* (New York: Academic Press, 1975), p. 385.
15. See Torrance, *op. cit.*, p. 128, for the concept of 'negative solidarity'; Giddens distinguishes between 'conflict-consciousness' and 'revolutionary-consciousness' in the case of the working class, but the peasantry usually only intermittently achieves even the former, *op. cit.*, pp. 115–117.
16. Barrington Moore, Jr., *Social Origins of Dictatorship and Democracy* (Boston: The Beacon Press, 1966), p. 453.
17. *Ibid.*, p. 475.
18. *Ibid.*, p. 479.
19. Torrance's entire chapter on 'estrangement and solidarity in sociological theory', which classifies simple and complex types of each and their combinations, is invaluable; *op. cit.*, pp. 105–155.
20. Weber, *op. cit.*, p. 929. (I have retained the italics from the translated version in H. H. Gerth and C. Wright Mills, editors, *From Max Weber:*

Essays in Sociology (New York: Oxford University Press, 1946), p. 184.)

21. *Ibid.*, pp. 938–939.

22. The first term is that of William Zartman, 'Toward a theory of Elite Circulation', in Zartman, editor, *The Study of Middle East Elites* (forthcoming, State University of New York Press); the second term is William Gamson's from *The Strategy of Social Protest* (Homewood, Ill.: The Dorsey Press, 1974), p. 14.

23. Theodore J. Lowi distinguishes sharply between established interest groups and social movements and develops a phase theory of the evolution of the latter into the former in *The Politics of Disorder* (New York: Basic Books, 1971), pp. 35–53.

24. Edward W. Lehman, *Political Society: A Macrosociology of Politics* (New York: Columbia University Press, 1977), pp. 95–100.

25. For example, the frequently cited scheme of Lester W. Milbrath, *Political Participation* (Chicago: Rand McNally, 1965), p. 18.

26. Seymour Martin Lipset, *Political Man* (Garden City, N.Y.: Doubleday, 1960), pp. 232–235.

27. For example, the Saskatchewan wheat farmers studied in the 1940s by Seymour Martin Lipset, *Agrarian Socialism* (Berkeley and Los Angeles: University of California Press, 1950).

28. Lipset, *Political Man*, pp. 184–185, 231.

29. Seymour Martin Lipset, *Revolution and Counterrevolution* (New York: Basic Books, 1968), pp. 159–176.

30. Giovanni Sartori, 'From the Sociology of Politics to Political Sociology', in Seymour Martin Lipset, editor, *Politics and the Social Sciences* (New York: Oxford University Press, 1969), pp. 72–74; also, *Parties and Party Systems: A Framework for Analysis*, Volume One (Cambridge: Cambridge University Press, 1976), pp. 20, 27.

31. Joseph A. Schumpeter, *Capitalism, Socialism, and Democracy*, Third Edition (New York: Harper and Brothers, 1950), pp. 269–283.

32. Walter Z. Laqueur, *The Fate of the Revolution: Interpretations of Soviet History* (New York: Macmillan, 1967), pp. 180–182.

33. Raymond Aron, 'Les Sociologues et les Institutions Representatives', *Archives Européenes de Sociologie*, 1 (1960), p. 149.

34. Gerhard Lenski, *Power and Privilege: A Theory of Social Stratification* (New York: McGraw-Hill, 1966), p. 231.

35. Lewis A. Coser, *Greedy Institutions* (New York: The Free Press, 1974), Part I, pp. 21–63.

36. Lenski, *op. cit.*, p. 246.

37. Lenski gives estimates of the proportion of the population for some but not of all the classes above the peasantry, but that collectively they constituted less than ten per cent of the population seems to be an altogether safe assumption. See *ibid.*, pp. 243–285.

38. Franz Neumann, *The Democratic and the Authoritarian State* (Glencoe, Ill.: The Free Press, 1957), pp. 236–243.

39. William Gamson, *Power and Discontent* (Homewood, Ill.: The Dorsey Press, 1968), pp. 2–19.

40. Sartori, *Parties and Party Systems*, pp. 119–125.

41. *Ibid.*, pp. 14–15.

42. The lower classes in pre-industrial societies often did, of course, exercise considerable anticipatory influence on their rulers, but not necessarily in the form of inducing the rulers to make concessions to their interests. For example, a powerful fear of slave uprisings led slaveholders in the American South to maintain and augment their coercive resources in the face of such a possibility even though slave revolts were few in number, largely ineffectual, and the slaves – in contrast to the Caribbean area which was the source of the fears – were greatly outnumbered by the free whites. See Eugene D. Genovese, *Roll, Jordan, Roll: The World The Slaves Made* (New York: Pantheon Books, 1974), pp. 594–598.

43. For reviews of these debates, see Peter Bachrach, *The Theory of Democratic Elitism: A Critique* (Boston: Little, Brown, 1967); Bachrach, editor, *Political Elites in a Democracy* (New York: Atherton Press, 1971); Richard F. Hamilton, *Class and Politics in the United States* (New York: John Wiley and Sons, 1972), pp. 34–46, 515–526; Kenneth Prewitt and Alan Stone, *The Ruling Elites: Elite Theory, Power, and American Democracy* (New York: Harper and Row, 1973).

44. Aron, *op. cit.*, p. 142. See also Lipset, *Political Man*, pp. 22–24.

45. One of the best and most far-ranging reviews and critiques of the nineteenth-century sociological standpoint is that of Sheldon Wolin, *Politics and Vision* (Boston: Little, Brown, 1960), Chapter 10, pp. 352–434.

46. The affinity with socialism with its stress on the primacy of 'the social question' as a moral-political issue has often been pointed out; Saint-Simon was, after all, a founder of both socialism and sociology; see, for example, Alvin W. Gouldner, 'Introduction' to Emile Durkheim, *Socialism* (New York: Collier Books, 1962), pp. 10–13. The affinity with conservatism is preeminently associated with the work in the intellectual history of sociology of Robert A. Nisbet, especially *The Sociological Tradition* (New York: Basic Books, 1966); see also, Leon Bramson, *The Political Context of Sociology* (Princeton, N.J.: Princeton University Press, 1961), pp. 11-26.

47. For an exhaustive examination of the development of 'revolution' from an astronomical to a political-social concept, see Melvin J. Lasky, *Utopia and Revolution* (Chicago: University of Chicago Press, 1976).

48. The phrase is that of Randall Collins and Michael Makowsky, *The Discovery of Society* (New York: Random House, 1972).

49. This provides at least some basis for an intellectual alliance between

'classical' conservatives, stressing pre-industrial and anti-individualist values, and the anti-statism of such advocates of uncontrolled 'free enterprise' as Milton Friedmann, Friedrich von Hayek and their disciples, as is recognized by one classical conservative who writes that 'the discovery of the market and its self-regulating processes in the economy was . . . matched in the nineteenth century by the discovery of comparable processes in the whole social realm: in kinship, local community, voluntary association, and other forms of social life'. Robert A. Nisbet, *Twilight of Authority* (New York: Oxford University Press, 1975), p. 249.

50. Wolin, *op. cit.*

51. Gabriel A. Almond makes the distinction between *articulating* and *aggregating* political demands in Almond and James S. Coleman, editors, *The Politics of the Developing Areas*, 'Introduction' (Princeton, N.J.: Princeton University Press, 1960), pp. 33–45.

52. Sartori, 'From the Sociology of Politics to Political Sociology', p. 84.

53. Maurice Duverger, *Political Parties* (London: Methuen, 1954), pp. 206–255. Lipset makes the seemingly categorical but actually rather qualified statement that: 'Sociologists tend to see party cleavages as reflections of an underlying structure, and hence, wittingly or not, frown on efforts to present the enacted rules of the game as key *causal* elements of a social structure. The sociologist's image of a social system, all of whose parts are interdependent, is at odds with the view of many political scientists, who believe that such seemingly minor differences in systems as variations in the way in which officials are elected can lead to stability or instability. An examination of comparative politics suggests that the political scientists are right, in that electoral laws determine the nature of the party system as much as any other structural variable.' Seymour Martin Lipset, *The First New Nation* (New York: Basic Books, 1963), p. 293.

54. Seymour Martin Lipset and Stein Rokkan, 'Cleavage Structures, Party Systems, and Voter Alignments: An Introduction', in Lipset and Rokkan, editors, *Party Systems and Voter Alignments* (New York: The Free Press, 1967), pp. 50–51.

55. Lowi, *op. cit.*, p. 58.

56. Theodore J. Lowi, *The End of Liberalism* (New York: W. W. Norton, 1969), pp. 68–97.

57. Lowi, *The Politics of Disorder*, p. 54.

58. Smelser, *op. cit.*

59. John D. McCarthy and Mayer N. Zald, 'Resource Mobilization and Social Movements: A Partial Theory', *American Journal of Sociology*, 82 (May 1977), p. 1215.

60. *Ibid.* The term 'resource management' is used to mean the same thing by

Oberschall, *op. cit.*, pp. 27–29; see also Gamson, *The Strategy of Social Protest*, pp. 136–141.

61. Mancur Olson, Jr., *The Logic of Collective Action* (New York: Schocken Books, 1971), Revised Edition, p. 2 (the statement is italicized in the text); see also the incisive review of Olson stressing the implications of his thesis for sociology by Charles B. Perrow, *Social Forces*, 52 (September 1973), pp. 123–125.

62. See, for example, Walter Berns, 'Voting Studies', in Herbert J. Storing, editor, *Essays on the Scientific Study of Politics* (New York: Holt, Rinehart and Winston, 1962), pp. 3–62; V. O. Key, Jr., *The Responsible Electorate* (Cambridge, Mass.: The Belknap Press of Harvard University Press, 1966).

63. Hannah Arendt's Aristotelian conception of politics and the 'public life' should perhaps be considered an exception to this statement. While her classicism is the source of many of her most profound insights, she excludes 'the social question' – the entire realm of material inequalities and social welfare – from the proper concern of politics. Although this view pervades many of her writings, see especially *On Revolution* (New York: The Viking Press, 1963), Chapter 2, pp. 53–110. For criticism of her views that underlines her élitism and her sweeping denial that politics should have any social content, radically isolating it as a human activity from the debased sphere of mere 'society', see Benjamin I. Schwartz, 'The Religion of Politics', *Dissent*, 17 (March–April 1970), pp. 144–161; Noel O'Sullivan, 'Hellenic Nostalgia and Industrial Society', in Anthony de Crespigny and Kenneth Minogue, editors, *Contemporary Political Philosophers* (New York: Dodd, Mead, 1975), pp. 228–251; Jürgen Habermas, 'Hannah Arendt's Communications Concept of Power', *Social Research*, 44 (Spring 1977), pp. 3–24.

64. George Lichtheim, *Marxism in Modern France* (New York: Columbia University Press, 1966), p. 112.

65. One of the most succinct statements of this contrast – not necessarily a contradiction – between theory and practice in Marxism is that of Neumann, *op. cit.*, p. 263.

66. The roots of both views in Marxism as a theory always articulated in response to particular historical events is a theme of George Lichtheim's *Marxism: An Historical and Critical Study* (New York: Frederick A. Praeger, 1961).

67. To my knowledge, one of the first people to formulate systematically the – originally – Stalinist conception of 'revolution from above' was G. L. Arnold (George Lichtheim), in *The Pattern of World Conflict* (New York: The Dial Press, 1955), especially pp. 173–180. Recently, the concept has been more fully elaborated and given roots in Russian history under the Czars by Robert C. Tucker, 'Stalinism as Revolution

from Above', in Tucker, editor, *Stalinism: Essays in Historical Interpretation* (New York: W. W. Norton, 1977), pp. 77–108.

68. Leon Trotsky, *Stalin* (New York: Stein and Day, 1967), New Edition, p. 421. (Trotsky's unfinished biography was first published in 1941).

69. Glencoe, Ill.: The Free Press, 1959.

70. The earliest formulations of the theory of mass society were based almost exclusively on the triumph of National Socialism in Germany. For example, Emil Lederer, *The State of the Masses* (New York: W. W. Norton, 1940). Hannah Arendt has been much criticized for her effort in *The Origins of Totalitarianism* to extend her categories of 'the masses', 'the mob' and 'the élite', clearly derived from the Nazi experience, to the Soviet Union. For an example of such criticism, see H. Stuart Hughes, *The Sea Change* (New York: Harper and Row, 1975), p. 124.

71. Earlier critics have not overlooked the live historical emotions that gave resonance to the demonic theory of the masses. For example, two of my own articles, 'The Perils of Political Moderation', *Commentary*, 27 (January 1959), pp. 1–8; and 'Reflections on the End of Ideology', *Dissent*, 7 (Summer 1960), pp. 286–291. See also Steven Lukes's article, originally published in 1963, 'The New Democracy', in Lukes, *Essays in Social Theory* (New York: Columbia University Press, 1977), pp. 30–51. For a balanced recent discussion, see Lehman, *op. cit.*, pp. 147–152.

72. For a good summary of the many meanings and levels on which the concept has been understood, as well as of its diverse intellectual origins, see E. V. Walter, '"Mass Society": The Late Stages of an Idea', *Social Research*, 31 (Winter 1964), pp. 391–410.

73. Kornhauser, *op. cit.*, p. 64.

74. This useful term I owe to Peter Orleans and Scott Greer, 'Political Sociology', in R. E. L. Faris, editor, *Handbook of Modern Sociology* (Chicago: Rand McNally, 1964), p. 814.

75. Maurice Pinard, 'Mass Society and Political Movements: A New Formulation', *American Journal of Sociology*, 73 (May 1968), pp. 682–690; Pinard, *The Rise of a Third Party: A Study in Crisis Politics* (Englewood Cliffs, N.J.: Prentice-Hall, 1971), pp. 179–219.

76. Kornhauser makes this criticism and attempts to overcome it in his effort to systematize mass theory, *op. cit.*, pp. 32–34.

77. William Sheridan Allen, 'The Appeal of Fascism and the Problem of National Disintegration', in Henry A. Turner, Jr., editor, *Reappraisals of Fascism* (New York: New Viewpoints, 1975), p. 60.

78. Leszek Kolakowski, 'Marxist Roots of Stalinism,' in Tucker, editor, *op. cit.*, p. 287.

79. For an excellent brief sociological account of this process, see Ralf Dahrendorf, *Society and Democracy in Germany* (Garden City, N.Y.: Doubleday Anchor Books, 1969), pp. 384–390.

80. Roy Medvedev, the dissident Soviet historian, has complained that in *contemporary* – not just Stalin's – Russia 'Any small organization, even a club of dog lovers or cactus-growers, is supervised by some appropriate body of the Party'. Quoted by Hedrick Smith, *The Russians* (New York: Ballantine Books, 1976), p. 665.

81. On the dual attitude of the Nazis towards the family, see Max Horkheimer, 'Authoritarianism and the Family', in Ruth Nanda Anshen, editor, *The Family: Its Function and Destiny* (New York: Harper and Brothers, Revised Edition, 1959), pp. 381–398.

82. Lewis A. Coser, 'Some Aspects of Soviet Family Policy', *American Journal of Sociology*, 56 (March 1951), pp. 424–437.

83. Philip E. Slater, 'On Social Regression', *American Sociological Review*, 28 (June 1963), pp. 339–364.

84. Lewis A. Coser, *Greedy Institutions*, pp. 136–149; see also Robert Endleman on the Israeli kibbutz in *Personality and Social Life* (New York: Random House, 1967), pp. 127–180.

85. Bramson, *op. cit.*, pp. 130–139, attributes this view to Marcuse. See also Christopher Lasch on the Frankfurt School theorists in *Haven in a Heartless World: The Family Besieged* (New York: Basic Books, 1977), pp. 85–96. Although Lasch makes no use of the term 'mass society', his entire book deplores the consequences of the decline of the bourgeois family.

86. Hannah Arendt, *The Origins of Totalitarianism* (New York: Harcourt, Brace, 1951), pp. 380–386; Leonard Schapiro emphasizes the primacy of the Leader rather than of the Party in *Totalitarianism* (London: The Pall Mall Press, 1972), pp. 23–29, 102–103.

87. C. B. Macpherson gives an excellent account of the political theory of one such agrarian populist movement, the United Farmers of Alberta, in *Democracy in Alberta* (Toronto: University of Toronto Press, 1953), pp. 38–54. Macpherson describes the replacement in Alberta through electoral victory of the United Farmers of Alberta by the Social Credit Party as a change from a radical corporatist or 'delegate' conception of democracy to 'plebiscitarian democracy' and he sees both as expressions of a *petit-bourgeois* agrarian radicalism' based on 'false consciousness'; *ibid.*, pp. 215–250. For a criticism of Macpherson's particular Marxist version of Albertan and Canadian politics and party-class relations in general, see Seymour Martin Lipset, 'Democracy in Alberta', in two parts, *The Canadian Forum*, 34 (November and December 1954), pp. 175–177, 196–198. The change from the U.F.A. to Social Credit represented a shift from left to right – at least after the immediate distress of the depression which brought Social Credit to power was alleviated. After World War II, the Social Credit Party became a party of the extreme right in Alberta and the other Canadian provinces whereas the U.F.A. was one of the organizations that merged to form the socialist

Cooperative Commonwealth Federation in the early 1930s. See John A. Irving, *The Social Credit Movement in Alberta* (Toronto: University of Toronto Press, 1959), pp. 145–151.

88. Kolakowski, *op. cit.*

89. As by David B. Truman, *The Governmental Process* (New York: Alfred A. Knopf, 1951), pp. 114–115.

90. Guenther Roth, *The Social Democrats in Imperial Germany* (Totowa, N. J.: The Bedminster Press, 1963), especially pp. 159–248.

91. Collins, *op. cit.*, p. 84.

92. An example is the unofficial anthem of the American union movement 'Solidarity Forever,' written by Ralph Chaplin. The traditional slogan of the German labour movement was *Alle Raeder stehen still wenn dein stark Arm es will* ('All wheels stand still when your strong arm wills it'). This is essentially an appeal to the collective resource of job monopoly rather than to solidarity as such.

93. G. L. Arnold (George Lichtheim), 'Collectivism Reconsidered', *British Journal of Sociology*, 6 (March 1955), p. 9.

94. Max Weber referred in this connection to 'the "murmuring" of the workers known in ancient oriental ethics: the moral disapproval of the work-master's conduct, which in its practical significance was probably equivalent to an increasingly typical phenomenon of precisely the latest industrial development, namely, the "slow down" (the deliberate limiting of work effort) of laborers by virtue of tacit agreement'. H. H. Gerth and C. Wright Mills, editors, *op. cit.*, pp. 183–184.

95. See Chapter 5 above, pp. 99–103.

96. Georg Lukács, *History and Class Consciousness* (Cambridge, Mass.: The MIT Press, 1971), pp. 46–82.

97. See, for example, John Westergaard and Henrietta Resler, *Class in a Capitalist Society: A Study of Contemporary Britain* (New York: Basic Books, 1975), p. 248.

98. Ralf Dahrendorf, *Class and Class Conflict in Industrial Society* (Stanford, Calif.: Stanford University Press, 1959), p. 175.

99. *Ibid.*, pp. 176–177.

100. Steven Lukes, *Power: A Radical View* (London: Macmillan, 1974), pp. 34–35.

101. Matthew Crenson, *The Un-Politics of Air Pollution: A Study of Non-Decisionmaking in the Cities* (Baltimore: The Johns Hopkins Press, 1971), pp. 35–82.

102. Lukes, *op. cit.*, p. 34.

103. *Ibid.*, p. 33.

104. See Chapter 3 above, pp. 52–60.

105. Steven Lukes, 'Reply to Bradshaw', *Sociology*, 10 (January 1976), p. 130.

106. Lukes, *Power: A Radical View*, p. 23.

107. Alan Bradshaw, 'A Critique of Steven Lukes' "Power: A Radical View"' *Sociology*, 10 (January 1976), pp. 121–122.

108. Lukes, 'Reply to Bradshaw', p. 129.

109. Martin Green, *The von Richthofen Sisters* (New York: Basic Books, 1974), pp. 62–73.

110. Donald McIntosh, 'Habermas on Freud', *Social Research*, 44 (Autumn 1977), pp. 587–598.

111. Robert Roberts writes of the attitude of most British workers towards trade unions at the beginning of the twentieth century: '. . . general apathy stemmed not from despair at the unions in chains nor the failure of such political action as there was; it sprang from mass ignorance: the millions did not know and did not want to know. At that time one had to work hard indeed to convince the unskilled labourer of the need for trade unions at all. An individualist, he was simply not interested in easing the common lot, but concerned entirely with improving his own, and that not too vigorously. From what little he understood, the aims of trade unions seemed quite impracticable and those of socialism utterly unreal. In the end not persuasion, but dire want, changed his views.' *The Classic Slum: Salford Life in the First Quarter of the Century* (Harmondsworth, Middlesex, England: Penguin Books, 1973), p. 90.

112. Hannah Arendt, *On Violence* (New York: Harcourt, Brace and World, 1970), pp. 77–78.

113. *Ibid.*, p. 78.

114. Henry Miller, *Remember to Remember* (London: Grey Walls Press, 1952), p. 30. For an evocation of the 1970s as the 'Me Decade', see Tom Wolfe, *Mauve Gloves and Madmen, Clutter and Vine* (New York: Farrar, Strauss and Giroux, 1976), pp. 126–167.

115. Giddens, *op. cit.*, pp. 152–154.

116. Mann, *op. cit.*, pp. 34–38.

117. Nathan Glazer, *The Social Basis of American Communism* (New York: Harcourt, Brace and World, 1961), Chap. 4.

118. Weber in Gerth and Mills, editors, *op. cit.*, p. 183.

119. C. Wright Mills often used to play on the dual subjective and objective meaning of the word 'interest' in observing that people are not necessarily 'interested in' what is 'in their interests'.

120. George Kateb treats the view that the costs of 'attaining utopia' are excessive as a major antiutopian argument in *Utopia and Its Enemies* (New York: The Free Press of Glencoe, 1963), pp. 21–67.

121. Weber in Gerth and Mills, editors, *op. cit.*, p. 128.

1. Excluding, of course, a few categories of persons (other than minors) which are nowadays limited in size in most constitutional democracies.

2. The best-known references are Marx's 'Amsterdam speech', partially reported in Hans Gerth, editor, *The First International: Minutes of the Hague Congress* (Madison: University of Wisconsin Press, 1957), pp. 236–237; and Friedrich Engels, 'Introduction' to Marx's *Class Struggles in France* quoted by Bertram D. Wolfe, *Marxism: One Hundred Years in the Life of a Doctrine* (New York: The Dial Press, 1965), pp. 219–223. The controversial translation history of Engels's text is summarized by Wolfe, pp. 222–223, n. 8. Wolfe is highly informative on the attitude of Marx and Engels to universal suffrage and parliamentary democracy.

3. For broad reviews and summaries, see Gerhard Lenski, *Power and Privilege: A Theory of Social Stratification* (New York: McGraw-Hill, 1966), pp. 308–433; Frank Parkin, *Class Inequality and Political Order* (London: Granada, 1972).

4. Edward W. Lehman, *Political Society: A Macrosociology of Politics* (New York: Columbia University Press, 1977), p. 152.

5. Parkin, *op. cit.*, pp. 181–182.

6. This perhaps needs to be stated, because I recall reading an anti-left polemic in a British periodical that quoted Parkin as a sinister example of left-wing anti-democratic beliefs.

7. Herbert Marcuse, Robert Paul Wolff and Barrington Moore, Jr., *A Critique of Pure Tolerance* (Boston: Beacon Press, 1966).

8. Parkin, *op. cit.*, p. 184.

9. Guenther Roth, *The Social Democrats in Imperial Germany* (Totowa, N. J.: Bedminster Press, 1963), pp. 249–284.

10. In Michels's words: 'Thus the social revolution would not effect any real modification of the internal structure of the mass. The socialists might conquer, but not socialism, which would perish in the moment of its adherents' triumph.' Robert Michels, *Political Parties* (New York: Dover Publications, 1959), p. 391.

11. These overall conclusions of Lipset's well-known summary still broadly hold. See Seymour Martin Lipset, *Political Man* (Garden City, N. Y.: Doubleday, 1960), pp. 179–263. See also Dowse and Hughes's 'Inventory of Some Social Correlates of Political Participation' in Robert E. Dowse and John A. Hughes, *Political Sociology* (New York: John Wiley and Sons, 1972), pp. 297–300.

12. Seymour Martin Lipset, *Revolution and Counterrevolution* (New York: Basic Books, 1968), pp. 159–176.

13. *Ibid.*, p. 160.

14. Stanislaw Ossowski, *Class Structure in the Social Consciousness* (New York: The Free Press of Glencoe, 1963), pp. 30–37, 142–147.

15. Parkin, *op. cit.*, p. 81.
16. Niccolo Machiavelli, *The Prince and the Discourses* (New York: The Modern Library, Random House, 1940), p. 21.
17. Lipset, *Revolution and Counterrevolution*, p. 165. The last proposition does not, of course, imply that the use of political anti-Semitism and racial agitation is always, or even primarily, a right-wing tactic. As long ago as the late nineteenth century, Auguste Bebel's famous statement that 'Anti-Semitism is the socialism of fools' recognized that it might also be found on the left.
18. See Stein Rokkan's valuable comparative survey of progress towards full democratization in Western Europe: 'Mass Suffrage, Secret Voting and Political Participation', in Lewis A. Coser, editor, *Political Sociology* (New York: Harper and Row, 1966), pp. 101–131.
19. I have in this section drawn on and revised an earlier article, 'The Rhythm of Democratic Politics', which has been reprinted in *Skeptical Sociology* (New York: Columbia University Press, 1976), pp. 226–241.
20. This paragraph is adapted from my contribution to a symposium entitled 'What is a Liberal – Who is a Conservative?' in *Commentary*, 62 (September 1976), pp. 111–113.
21. The blurring, of course, is in accordance with Anthony Downs's expectations in his well-known *An Economic Theory of Democracy* (New York: Harper and Row, 1957).
22. For an excellent argument developing the partial mutual entailment of liberty and equality, see Michael Walzer, 'In Defense of Equality' in Lewis A. Coser and Irving Howe, editors, *The New Conservatives: A Critique from the Left* (New York: Quadrangle, 1974), pp. 107–123; see also Steven Lukes, *Essays in Social Theory* (New York: Columbia University Press, 1977), pp. 96–117.
23. Karl Mannheim, *Ideology and Utopia* (New York: Harcourt, Brace, 1946), p. 207.
24. The combination of the *content* of a movement's ideology with its *social base* leads Lipset to use the unfortunate, apparently oxymoronic phrase 'extremism of the centre' to characterize fascism in *Political Man*, pp. 132–133.
25. A case in point was the defeat in Alberta in 1935 of the agrarian socialist United Farmers of Alberta by the Social Credit Party which at the time was widely perceived as one of several radical movements responding to the economic distress of the depression, although its doctrines were upheld elsewhere by thinkers and political sectarians on the extreme right. The Canadian and Albertan parties ultimately moved to the far right after World War II.
26. See the arguments of Karl Popper, *The Poverty of Historicism* (New York: Harper Torchbooks, 1964); Ernest Gellner, *Thought and Change* (London: Weidenfeld and Nicolson, 1964), pp. 15–20; Robert A. Nisbet,

Social Change and History (New York: Oxford University Press, 1969), pp. 160–188.

27. O. Utis (Isaiah Berlin), 'Generalissimo Stalin and the Art of Government', *Foreign Affairs*, 30 (January 1952), pp. 197–214.

28. Arthur Schlesinger, Sr., *Paths to the Present* (New York: Macmillan. 1949), pp. 77–92.

29. Arthur Schlesinger, Sr., *In Retrospect: The History of a Historian* (New York: Harcourt, Brace and World, 1963), p. 108.

30. *Ibid.*, pp. 190–191.

31. See the old but still valuable account by Adolf Sturmthal, *The Tragedy of European Labor, 1918–1939* (New York: Columbia University Press, 1943), pp. 35–97, 129–143.

32. The Canadian Conservative Party re-named itself the 'Progressive-Conservative' Party in order to increase its appeal to an electorate favourable towards social reform immediately after World War II.

33. President Eisenhower used the label 'moderate Republicanism' to distinguish his outlook from that of the traditional anti-New Deal Republicans shortly after his election in 1952.

34. Schlesinger, *Paths to the Present*, p. 84.

35. I owe the suggestion of this image to Robert L. Heilbroner.

36. Seymour Martin Lipset and Everett Carll Ladd, Jr., 'College Generations – from the 1930's to the 1960's', *The Public Interest*, No. 25 (Fall, 1971), pp. 111–112 (italics in text).

37. Schlesinger, *Paths to the Present*, p. 88.

38. Lipset, *Revolution and Counterrevolution*, p. 164. See also pp. 206–208.

39. I have drawn on Raymond Aron's valuable account of how democracy generates both a Left and a Right Opposition in *The Century of Total War* (Garden City, N. Y.: Doubleday, 1954), pp. 241–261.

40. John Rex, *Key Problems of Sociological Theory* (London: Routledge and Kegan Paul, 1961), pp. 127–129.

41. R. G. Collingwood, *The New Leviathan* (Oxford: The Clarendon Press, 1942), pp. 209–210.

42. See the impressive attempt to support this with comparative evidence by Robert A. Dahl, *Polyarchy: Participation and Opposition* (New Haven: Yale University Press, 1971), pp. 105–123. See also Tom Nairn's brilliant argument concerning the oldest capitalist nation: *The Break-Up of Britain: Crisis and Neo-Nationalism* (London: New Left Books, 1977); also Ernest Gellner's searching discussion of Nairn in 'Nationalism, or the New Confessions of a Justified Edinburgh Sinner', *Political Quarterly*, 49 (January–March, 1978), pp. 103–111.

43. See the useful brief discussion by Herminio Martins, 'Portugal', in Margaret Scotford Archer and Salvador Giner, editors, *Contemporary Europe: Class, Status and Power* (New York: St. Martin's Press, 1971), pp. 60–63; also Ernest Gellner, *Thought and Change*, pp. 66–172.

44. One of the very few discussions of this as a future possibility is that of Stimson Bullitt, *To Be a Politician* (Garden City, N.Y.: Doubleday Anchor Books, Revised Edition, 1961), pp. 177–184.

45. Richard F. Hamilton, *Class and Politics in the United States* (New York: John Wiley and Sons, 1972), pp. 83–151, 534–559; also Hamilton's *Restraining Myths: Critical Studies of U.S. Social Structure and Politics* (Beverly Hills, Calif.; Sage Publications, 1975).

46. Mancur Olson, Jr., *The Logic of Collective Action* (New York: Schocken Books, Revised Edition, 1971).

47. See, for example, Robert Bierstedt on 'the sociology of majorities' in *Power and Progress: Essays in Sociological Theory* (New York: McGraw-Hill, 1974), pp. 199–219; Tom Bottomore, *Elites and Society* (London: C. A. Watts, 1964).

48. As in the recent work of Peter M. Blau, who treats size as a crucial variable in social organization in *Inequality and Heterogeneity: A Primitive Theory of Social Structure* (New York: The Free Press, 1977).

Chapter Nine

1. Thomas Hobbes, *Leviathan* (Indianapolis: Bobbs-Merrill, 1958), p. 86.

2. *Ibid.*, p. 86.

3. *Ibid.*, p. 105.

4. Talcott Parsons, *Politics and Social Structure* (New York: The Free Press, 1969), pp. 352–429; Niklas Luhmann, *Macht* (Stuttgart: Ferdinand Enke, 1975).

5. Hobbes, *op. cit.*, p. 106.

6. C. B. Macpherson, *The Political Theory of Possessive Individualism* (Oxford: Oxford University Press, 1964), pp. 44–45. Macpherson correctly maintains that to Hobbes the desire for honour and glory is ultimately reducible to the desire for power (see especially Hobbes, *op. cit.*, p. 68). His major argument is that Hobbes's conception of human nature was essentially a 'bourgeois' one characterized by what Macpherson calls 'possessive individualism' and reflecting the emerging capitalist social and economic relations of the seventeenth century. Yet Hobbes's constant stress throughout his writings on man's pride, vanity, lust for 'vainglory', and extreme touchiness about honour – as in the passage cited in note 5 above, which is only one of many – seems to me to be redolent of aristocratic values and sensibility rather than of the sober, calculating, prudential kind of self-interest we usually regard as bourgeois. Leo Strauss has argued that Hobbes's early writings reveal a high esteem for 'aristocratic virtue' but that 'the more Hobbes elaborated his political philosophy, the further he departed from his original recognition of honour as virtue, from the original recognition of

aristocratic virtue' to the point where in *Leviathan* he arrived at 'the establishment of a peculiarly bourgeois morality'. Strauss, *The Political Philosophy of Thomas Hobbes* (Oxford: The Clarendon Press, 1936), p. 50.

Aside from the question of whether Hobbes's view of man is 'aristocratic' or 'bourgeois', another commentator, John Plamenatz, has criticized his 'reduction' of the motive of pride to concern over reputation for power as a means of averting violent death: 'For men, Hobbes tells us, are full of pride. They desire to be important in the eyes of other men and their own. That being so, fear of disgrace or insignificance must often be stronger in them than fear of death or wounds or imprisonment. It is then more their interest to preserve their reputation (or even their self-respect) than their lives or their health or their freedom of movement. It may be that men come to desire power as a means to other things, and learn to care for reputation and superiority as they compete for power; it may be that the possessions which overcome the fear of death in them arise as effects of what they do to provide for natural appetites which must be satisfied if they are to keep alive and healthy. But, once they have these passions, no matter how they came by them, they have needs which it is just as reasonable to strive to satisfy as the appetites necessary to life and health'. John Plamenatz, 'Introduction' to Hobbes, *Leviathan* (London: Collins, Fontana Library of Philosophy, 1962), pp. 54–55.

Plamenatz's view of motivation here is suggestive of the psychologist Gordon W. Allport's conception of the 'functional autonomy of motives' which views motives as capable of being severed from their origins in organic drives. Allport, *Personality: A Psychological Interpretation* (New York: Henry Holt, 1937), pp. 191–212.

7. Macpherson, *op. cit.*, p. 40: 'He [Hobbes] has moved from the definition of power as present means to obtain future good, through a redefinition of power as the excess or eminence of one man's means in comparison with another's . . . Hobbes has described, and in effect defined, acquired power as power to command the services of other men.'

8. Macpherson, *ibid.*, p. 42, correctly criticizes Strauss's contention that to Hobbes 'man desires power and ever greater power, spontaneously and continuously, in one jet of appetite . . .' Strauss, *op. cit.*, p. 10.

9. Sigmund Freud, *Civilization and Its Discontents* (New York: Doubleday Anchor Books, 1958), pp. 60–61.

10. Hobbes, *op. cit.*, p. 106.

11. Norman O. Brown, *Life Against Death* (Middletown, Conn.: Wesleyan University Press, 1959); Herbert Marcuse, *Eros and Civilization* (Boston: Beacon Press, 1955). The last section of Brown's book is entitled 'The Way Out'.

12. Bertrand Russell, *Power: A New Social Analysis* (London: George Allen and Unwin, 1938), p. 21.

13. This is especially true of much of his 'Thoughts for the Times on War and Death', *Collected Papers*, Volume Four (New York: Basic Books, 1959), pp. 288–317. It is less true of his 'Why War?', *ibid.*, Volume Five, pp. 273–287, written seventeen years later.

14. Philip Rieff, *Freud: The Mind of the Moralist* (Garden City, N.Y.: Doubleday Anchor Books, 1961), pp. 273–274. In 'Why War?', however, Freud does virtually acknowledge Rieff's point, pp. 281–282.

15. Robin Fox, 'The Inherent Rules of Violence' in Peter Collett, editor, *Social Rules and Social Behaviour* (Oxford: Basil Blackwell, 1977), pp. 132–149.

16. The effects on behaviour of the verbal and visual depiction of both sex and violence have long been debated in terms that scarcely differ.

17. Robert E. Lane, *Political Life* (Glencoe, Ill.: The Free Press, 1959), p. 127.

18. Gerald Reitlinger, *The SS, Alibi of a Nation, 1922–1945* (New York: The Viking Press, 1957), p. 288.

19. *Ibid.*, p. 183.

20. Philip E. Slater, 'On Social Regression', *American Sociological Review*, 28 (June 1963), pp. 346–348.

21. Russell, *op. cit.*, pp. 8–9.

22. Harold D. Lasswell, *Power and Personality* (New York: W. W. Norton, 1948), pp. 27–32; also Lasswell and Abraham Kaplan, *Power and Society* (New Haven: Yale University Press, 1950), pp. 74–97.

23. Lasswell, *op. cit.*, p. 39.

24. *Ibid.*, pp. 59–93. Lasswell rejects the extreme image of 'the power-hungry man, the person wholly absorbed in getting and holding power, utterly ruthless in his insatiable lust to impose his will upon all men everywhere' (p. 54), but his own identification of 'political man' remains far too loose.

25. Elias Canetti, quoted by W. G. Runciman, *Sociology in its Place* (Cambridge: Cambridge University Press, 1970), p. 108.

26. *Ibid.*, p. 108.

27. Richard H. Rovere, *Senator Joe McCarthy* (New York: Harcourt, Brace, 1959), pp. 253–254.

28. J. L. Austin, *How to Do Things with Words* (Cambridge, Mass.: Harvard University Press, 1962).

29. C. Wright Mills, *Power, Politics and People* (New York: Oxford University Press, 1963), pp. 310–315.

30. C. B. Macpherson, *Democratic Theory: Essays in Retrieval* (Oxford: The Clarendon Press, 1973), pp. 41–42. Macpherson's contrast between 'extractive power' and 'developmental power' is a version of the distinction between 'power over' and 'power to'.

31. I have used the most recent translation in W. G. Runciman, editor, *Max Weber: Selections in Translation* (Cambridge: Cambridge University Press, 1978), p. 43.

32. Hans Gerth and C. Wright Mills, editors, *From Max Weber: Essays in Sociology* (New York: Oxford University Press, 1946), p. 84.

33. Runciman, editor, *op. cit.*, p. 212. Where possible, I have chosen to use the recent but partial translation of 'Politics as a Vocation' in the Runciman volume.

34. David Riesman, *Individualism Reconsidered* (Glencoe, Ill.: The Free Press, 1954), pp. 46–47.

35. Gerth and Mills, editors, *op. cit.*, p. 128. I have reverted here to the older Gerth-Mills translation because I like its rendition of this passage better if only for reasons of long familiarity with it.

36. Hannah Arendt, *The Origins of Totalitarianism* (New York: Harcourt, Brace, 1951), p. 397.

37. I quote these lines from memory having read fragmentary reproductions of them in English in the writings of such critics and commentators on Brecht as Hannah Arendt, Daniel Bell, Martin Esslin, and Herbert Lüthy. I did not consult the English translation of *Die Massnahme* which only recently appeared: Bertolt Brecht, *The Measures Taken* (London: Eyre Methuen, 1977). The line in the next sentence is from Brecht's most famous poem, 'To Posterity', from *Selected Poems*, translated by H. R. Hays (New York: Reynal and Hitchcock, 1947), p. 177.

38. The distinction between *intended* and *foreseen* consequences which I stressed in Chapter 1 is crucial to the understanding of Weber's two types of ethics. See above, pp. 4–5.

39. See my earlier discussion of this issue in Dennis H. Wrong, 'Introduction' to *Max Weber* (Englewood Cliffs, N.J.: Prentice-Hall, 1970), pp. 61–69. Reprinted in Wrong, *Skeptical Sociology* (New York: Columbia University Press, 1976) as 'Ends and Means in Politics', pp. 266–276.

40. Roderick Martin, *The Sociology of Power* (London: Routledge and Kegan Paul, 1977), p. 19.

41. See the discussion of this problem by Nelson W. Polsby, *Community Power and Political Theory* (New Haven: Yale University Press, 1963), pp. 98–105.

42. William E. Connolly, *The Terms of Political Discourse* (Lexington, Mass.: D. C. Heath, 1974), pp. 88–89. Connolly is too inclined to see 'power to' and 'power over' as opposed rather than as complementary perspectives on power. See also the discussion by Lewis A. Coser, 'The Notion of Power: Theoretical Developments' in Coser and Bernard Rosenberg, editors, *Sociological Theory: A Book of Readings* (New York: Macmillan, Fourth Edition, 1976), pp. 150–161.

43. Hobbes, *op. cit.*, p. 106.

44. *Ibid.*, p. 127.

45. *Ibid.*, p. 152.

46. C. Wright Mills, *The Power Elite* (New York: Oxford University Press, 1956); Parsons's original review of *The Power Elite* is included in his *Politics and Social Structure, op. cit.*, pp. 185–233. I reviewed the Mills-Parsons debate in *Commentary* as early as 1959 in an article reprinted in *Skeptical Sociology*, pp. 25–27. For later discussions, see Connolly, *op. cit.*, pp. 114–115; Coser, *op. cit.*, pp. 158–160. Many others might be cited.

47. C. Wright Mills, *The Sociological Imagination* (New York: Oxford University Press, 1959), p. 37.

48. Two of these articles are included in Parsons, *op. cit.*, pp. 352–429. I have relied for Parsons's views on them and on the earlier review of *The Power Elite*, pp. 185–223.

49. The social democrat was myself and the pro-Soviet Marxist was Paul Sweezy. Both of us quoted the same passage about America living 'in a military neighorhood' as evidence of Mills's ambiguity in reviews of *The Power Elite* reprinted in G. William Domhoff and Hoyt S. Ballard, editors, *C. Wright Mills and The Power Elite* (Boston: Beacon Press, 1968): Wrong, 'Power in America', p. 93; Sweezy, 'Power Elite or Ruling Class?' pp. 126–127.

50. Parsons, *op. cit.*, p. 201.

51. *Ibid.*, p. 199.

52. *Ibid.*, pp. 362–364, 410–413.

53. *Ibid.*, p. 362.

54. See above, p. 3.

55. See above, pp. 27–28, 38. A recent writer who has sharply distinguished between force and coercion is F. Chazel, 'Power, Cause and Force' in Brian Barry, editor, *Power and Political Theory: Some European Perspectives* (London: John Wiley and Sons, 1976), pp. 60–65; the distinction is also clearly drawn by Jack Lively, 'The Limits of Exchange Theory' in *ibid.*, p. 8.

56. See above, pp. 86–87.

57. Anthony Giddens, *Studies in Social and Political Theory* (London: Hutchinson, 1977), p. 341.

58. *Ibid.*, pp. 338–346.

59. Parsons, *op. cit.*, p. 353.

60. Edward W. Lehman, 'Towards a Macrosociology of Power', *American Sociological Review*, 34 (August 1969), p. 461.

61. Bliss C. Cartwright and R. Stephen Warner, 'The Medium is Not the Message' in Jan J. Loubser and others, *Explorations in General Theory in Social Science: Essays in Honor of Talcott Parsons*, two volumes (New York: The Free Press, 1976), Volume Two, xeroxed copy, pp. 1–52.

62. Giddens, *op. cit.*, p. 340.

63. Peter M. Blau, *Exchange and Power in Social Life* (New York: John Wiley and Sons, 1964), pp. 208–209.

64. Robert S. Lynd, 'Power in American Society as Resource and Problem' in Arthur Kornhauser, editor, *Problems of Power in American Democracy* (Detroit: Wayne State University Press, 1957), pp. 1–45. Seymour Martin Lipset calls attention to the apparent agreement between Lynd and Parsons in *Revolution and Counterrevolution* (New York: Basic Books, 1968), pp. 147–149, as does Coser, *op. cit.*, p. 159. C. B. Macpherson, who clearly writes from a socialist and a Marxist perspective, also maintains: 'The power of a whole society is defined as its capacity to attain its goals' and refers as an example to 'modernization' which 'increases the society's control over Nature' (p. 48). Macpherson then criticizes the 'zero-sum' view of power for ignoring the fact that the power holder can increase the economic productivity of the power subjects by controlling them more efficiently and making them work harder (as I noted above, p. 47). See Macpherson, *Democratic Theory*, pp. 46–50.

65. Giddens, *op. cit.*, p. 340.

66. As noted by Steven Lukes, 'Power and Authority', xeroxed manuscript, pp. 46–47, scheduled to appear in Tom Bottomore and Robert A. Nisbet, editors, *History of Sociological Analysis* (New York: Basic Books, forthcoming). I am grateful to Dr. Lukes for having given me the opportunity to read in advance of publication his terse but staggeringly comprehensive survey of the concepts of power and authority in Western thought.

67. Robert Michels, *Political Parties* (New York: Dover Publications, 1959), p. 401.

68. Parsons, *op. cit.*, p. 370.

69. See above, pp. 140–141.

70. Hannah Arendt, *On Violence* (New York: Harcourt, Brace and World, 1970), pp. 35–52.

71. Ralf Dahrendorf was the first to equate Parsons's general conception of human society with literary images of utopia in his influential 1958 article 'Out of Utopia' reprinted in his *Essays in the Theory of Society* (Stanford, Calif.: Stanford University Press, 1968), pp. 107–128.

72. Edward W. Lehman, *Political Society: A Macrosociology of Politics* (New York: Columbia University Press, 1977), p. 57.

73. I have in mind such writers as Etzioni, Gamson, and Lehman, whom I have frequently cited throughout this book. Poulantzas and Offe are among the Marxists who occasionally cite Parsons approvingly in criticism of 'zero-sum' views though rejecting other aspects of his concept of power.

74. R. G. Collingwood, *The New Leviathan* (Oxford: The Clarendon Press, 1942), pp. 153–154.

75. Friedrich Engels, 'On Authority' in Karl Marx and Friedrich Engels, *Selected Works*, three volumes (Moscow: Progress Publishers, 1969), Volume Two, pp. 377–379.

76. Karl Marx, *Capital*, Volume Three (Moscow: Foreign Languages Publishing House, 1962), pp. 275–279. Marx may have borrowed the metaphor of the orchestra leader from Saint-Simon who often used it: see Daniel Bell, *The Coming of Post-Industrial Society* (New York: Basic Books, 1973), pp. 77, 263.

77. Engels, *op. cit.*, p. 379.

78. The concept of 'head roles' is used by Hans Gerth and C. Wright Mills, *Character and Social Structure* (New York: Harcourt, Brace, 1953), pp. 22–23. Mills uses the term 'command post' to mean essentially the same thing in *The Power Elite*, p. 4.

79. Alvin W. Gouldner, *For Sociology* (New York: Basic Books, 1974), p. 400.

80. Michael Evans, *Karl Marx* (London: George Allen and Unwin, 1975), p. 163. George Lichtheim's comments are of similar import in *Marxism: An Historical and Critical Study* (New York: Praeger, 1961), pp. 391–392.

81. Eliot Freidson, *Profession of Medicine* (New York: Dodd, Mead, 1972).

82. Peter Bachrach and Morton S. Baratz, *Power and Poverty: Theory and Practice* (New York: Oxford University Press, 1970).

83. Arendt, *On Violence*, p. 81.

84. Steven Lukes contrasts power as 'subjective' human agency with structure as 'objective' constraint in his essay 'Power and Structure' in *Essays in Social Theory* (New York: Columbia University Press, 1977), pp. 3–29. However, in his earlier book, *Power: A Radical View* (London: Macmillan, 1974), he identified power with the constraint exercised by some persons, groups, or institutions over others. Clearly, there is a shift here from a view of power as a constraint on the freedom to act of the power subject to a view of power as precisely the capacity to act, to choose between alternatives, in the face of 'structural' constraints. The distinction is essentially a variation on the contrast between 'power to' and 'power over'. More recently, Lukes has recognized the similarity between the 'structural determinism' of Parsonian structural-functionalism and that of Althusserian Marxism, especially as represented in the work of Poulantzas. See Lukes, 'Power and Authority', pp. 46–48; also 'On the Relativity of Power', xeroxed, 1978, pp. 4–6, 9–10.

85. As, for example, William Outhwaite, *Understanding Social Life* (London: George Allen and Unwin, 1975); Anthony Giddens, *New Rules of Sociological Method* (New York: Basic Books, 1976); Richard J. Bernstein, *The Restructuring of Social and Political Theory* (New York: Harcourt Brace Jovanovich, 1976). William E. Connolly presents

a compelling, philosophically sophisticated argument for identifying power with intentionality, *op. cit.*, pp. 104–107.

86. Giddens, *New Rules of Sociological Method*, p. 69. Giddens made this point more explicitly in a seminar at New York University in April 1977.

87. As represented, for example, in the anthology edited by John O'Neill, *Modes of Individualism and Collectivism* (London: Heinemann Educational Books, 1973). See also Steven Lukes, *Individualism* (Oxford: Basil Blackwell, 1973), pp. 110–122.

88. Martin discusses the question of consciousness from this standpoint, *op. cit.*, pp. 165–170, where he argues against the concept of 'objective interests' in terms close to my own in Chapter 7 above, pp. 179–196.

89. See the exemplary lucid statement by Frank Parkin: 'Once we come to consider power as an aspect of stratification and not simply of role differentiation, we cannot easily separate it from the material and symbolic elements of inequality already examined. To some extent, in fact, to conceive of stratification in terms of power may simply be another way of conceptualizing the distribution of class and status advantages. That is, to speak of the distribution of power could be understood as another way of describing the flow of rewards; the very fact that the dominant class can successfully claim a disproportionate share of rewards *vis-à-vis* the subordinate class, is in a sense a *measure* of the former's power over the latter. In other words, power need not be thought of as something which exists over and above the system of material and social rewards; rather, it can be thought of as a concept or metaphor which is used to depict the flow of resources which constitutes this system. And as such it is not a separate dimension of stratification at all. Weber himself advocated this way of looking at the matter by claiming that "classes", "status groups", and "parties" are *phenomena of the distribution of power* within a community'. Parkin, *Class Inequality and Political Order* (London: Granada, 1972), p. 46.

90. Weber in Runciman, editor, *op. cit.*, pp. 40, 55–56.

91. Nicos Poulantzas, *Political Power and Social Classes* (London: New Left Books, 1973), pp. 136, 191, 256, 273, 282, and 326, among the many page references that might be cited from this book; see also Claus Offe, 'Political Authority and Class Structures', in Paul Connerton, editor, *Critical Sociology* (Harmondsworth, Middlesex, England: Penguin Books, 1976), pp. 393–394.

92. Poulantzas, *op. cit.*, p. 115.

93. On this point, see Anthony Giddens, *The Class Structure of the Advanced Societies* (London: Hutchinson, 1973), p. 106.

94. Kenneth Westhues, 'Class and Organization as Paradigms in Social Science', *The American Sociologist* 11 (February 1976), pp. 38–49.

95. Weber in Runciman, editor, *op. cit.*, p. 260.

96. See the important argument by Andrew Hacker, 'What Rules America?'

New York Review of Books, 1 May 1975, pp. 9–13. See also the discussion above, pp. 140–141.

97. I have drawn here on an earlier article in *Skeptical Sociology*, pp. 202–206.

98. Robert A. Dahl, 'A Critique of the Ruling Elite Model', *American Political Science Review*, 52 (June 1958), pp. 463–469. On the fallacy of imputing power on the basis of functional indispensability, Weber wrote: 'If "indispensability" were decisive, then where slave labor prevailed and where freemen usually abhor work as a dishonor, the "indispensable" slaves ought to have held the positions of power, for they were at least as indispensable as officials and proletarians are today'. Gerth and Mills, editors, *op. cit.*, p. 232.

99. Parkin, *op. cit.*, pp. 45–46.

100. Robert Redfield, *The Primitive World and Its Transformations* (Ithaca, N.Y.: Cornell University Press, 1953), pp. 111–138. Redfield regards the absence of the idea of reforming their institutions as one of the major characteristics of primitive or 'precivilized' societies.

Preface, 1988

1. I agree entirely with Gianfranco Poggi's criticism that, although I "put forward very early in the book the vital distinction between 'power to' and 'power over,' " I do not make use of the distinction until the discussion of the Mills-Parsons debate in the final chapter, which should, accordingly, "have come much earlier in the book." "A Masterful Conceptual Map," *Contemporary Sociology*, 10 (January 1981), p. 89.

2. Giddens's earliest discussion of the concept of power, from which he has scarcely deviated in later works, is to be found in Anthony Giddens, *New Rules of Sociological Method* (New York: Basic Books, 1976), pp. 110–111. His fullest discussion of the concept and its relation to other concepts such as "action," "agency," and "structure" is in Giddens, *Central Problems in Social Theory* (Berkeley and Los Angeles: University of California Press, 1979), pp. 88–93.

3. Giddens, *New Rules*, pp. 112–113.

4. For example, "Action involves intervention in events in the world, thus producing definite outcomes . . ." *Central Problems*, p. 88.

5. *Ibid.*, p. 91.

6. Michel Foucault, *The History of Sexuality, Volume I: An Introduction* (New York: Vintage Books, 1980), pp. 93, 94.

7. Michael Walzer, "The Politics of Michel Foucault," *Dissent*, 30 (Fall 1983), p. 483.

8. Erving Goffman, "The Interaction Order," *American Sociological Review*, 48 (February 1983), pp. 1–17.

9. Morris Janowitz has attempted to revive what he calls the "social-control perspective" in *The Last Half-Century* (Chicago and London: University of Chicago Press, 1978).

10. Michel Foucault, *Power/Knowledge: Selected Interviews and Other Writings, 1972–1977* (New York: Pantheon Books, 1980), p. 119.

11. Anthony Giddens, *The Constitution of Society* (Cambridge: Polity Press, 1984), p. 15.

12. Anthony Giddens, *Profiles and Critiques in Social Theory* (Berkeley and Los Angeles: University of California Press, 1982), pp. 218–227.

13. Giddens, *The Constitution of Society,* p. 257; *Profiles and Critiques,* p. 219.

14. Michel Foucault, *Discipline and Punish* (New York: Vintage Books, 1979), p. 27.

15. Eliot Freidson, *Professional Powers: A Study of the Institutionalization of Formal Knowledge* (Chicago and London: University of Chicago Press, 1986), p. 217.

16. Michael Mann has contended that beginning on p. 156 of *Power: Its Forms, Bases, and Uses* "we are being hijacked by the tenets of orthodox American political sociology." He objects in particular to my discussion of voting, seeing it as an abandonment of concern with "collective power relations" in turning instead to "aggregations of individuals." Mann's review is instructive and I learned much from it, but I think he overlooks the fact that my discussion of voting dealt less with aggregates of individuals than with voting *blocs* considered as loosely organized, diffusely solidary collectivities. I intended to stress that even these amorphous and incoherent collectivities still had to be understood as *more* than mere aggregates of individuals, as requiring reference to such collective resources as solidarity and organization in order to make sense of such limited action in concert as casting votes for the same party or candidate. I thought that I had made this plain on pp. 155–156 and had thus immunized myself against criticism of the inherent "individualism" or even "psychologism" of most survey research. See Michael Mann's review of *Power: Its Forms, Bases, and Uses,* in the *American Journal of Sociology,* 88 (March 1983), pp. 1030–1032.

17. For example, Anthony Giddens, *The Nation-State and Violence* (Berkeley and Los Angeles: University of California Press, 1985); Daniel Chirot, *Social Change in The Modern Era* (New York: Harcourt Brace Jovanovich, 1986); Randall Collins, *Weberian Sociological Theory* (Cambridge: Cambridge University Press, 1986), part 2, pp. 145–209.

Bibliography

(All citations in the text and notes.)

Adorno, Theodore W., Else Fenkel-Brunswik, Daniel J. Levinson, and R. Nevitt Sanford, *The Authoritarian Personality*, New York: Harper and Brothers, 1950.

Allen, William Sheridan, 'The Appeal of Fascism and the Problem of National Disintegration', in Henry A. Turner, Jr., editor, *Reappraisals of Fascism*, New York: New Viewpoints, 1975, 44–68.

Allport, Gordon W., *Personality: A Psychological Interpretation*, New York: Henry Holt, 1937.

Almond, Gabriel A., 'Introduction' to Almond and James S. Coleman, editors, *The Politics of the Developing Areas*, Princeton, N.J.: Princeton University Press, 1960, 3–64.

Anscombe, G. E. M., *Intention*, Ithaca, N.Y.: Cornell University Press, Second Edition, 1966.

Arendt, Hannah, *The Origins of Totalitarianism*, New York: Harcourt, Brace, 1951.

——, *The Human Condition*, Chicago: University of Chicago Press, 1958.

——, *Between Past and Future*, New York: Viking Press, 1961.

——, *On Revolution*, New York: Viking Press, 1963.

——, *Eichmann in Jerusalem*, New York: Viking Press, 1963.

——, *On Violence*, New York: Harcourt, Brace and World, 1970.

Aristotle, *Politics and Poetics*, Cleveland: Fine Editions Press, 1952.

Aron, Raymond, *The Century of Total War*, Garden City, N.Y.: Doubleday, 1954.

——, 'Les Sociologues et les Institutions Représentatives', *Archives Européenes de Sociologie*, 1 (1960), 142–157.

——, 'Macht, Power, Puissance: prose démocratiques ou poésie démoniacque?' *Archives Européenes de Sociologie*, 5 (1964), 27–51.

——, *Main Currents in Sociological Thought*, two volumes, New York: Basic Books, 1967.

——, *La Révolution Introuvable, reflexions sur la Révolution de mai*, Paris, Fayard, 1968.

Atkinson, Dick, *Orthodox Consensus and Radical Alternative*, London: Heinemann Educational Books, 1971.

Austin, J. L., *How to Do things with Words*, Cambridge, Mass.: Harvard University Press, 1962.

Bachrach, Peter, *The Theory of Democratic Elitism*, Boston: Little Brown, 1967.

——, editor, *Political Elites in a Democracy*, New York: Atherton Press, 1967.

——, and Morton S. Baratz, 'The Two Faces of Power', *American Political Science Review*, 56 (November 1962), 947–952.

——, 'Decisions and Nondecisions: An Analytical Framework', *American Political Science Review*, 57 (September 1963), 641–651.

——, *Power and Poverty: Theory and Practice*, New York: Oxford University Press, 1970.

Bambrough, Renford, 'Plato's Political Analogies', in Peter Laslett, editor, *Philosophy, Politics and Society*, New York: Macmillan, 1956, 98–115.

Bell, Daniel, 'Marxian Socialism in the United States', in Donald Drew Egbert and Stow Persons, editors, *Socialism and American Life*, two volumes, Princeton, N.J.: Princeton University Press, 1952, 213–405.

——, *The Coming of Post-Industrial Society*, New York: Basic Books, 1973.

——, 'Ethnicity and Social Change', in Nathan Glazer and Daniel Patrick Moynihan, editors, *Ethnicity: Theory and Experience*, Cambridge, Mass.: Harvard University Press, 1975, 141–174.

Bendix, Reinhard, *Max Weber: An Intellectual Portrait*, Garden City, N.Y.: Doubleday Anchor Books, 1962.

——, 'Reflections on Charismatic Leadership', in Dennis H. Wrong, editor, *Max Weber*, Englewood Cliffs, N.J.: Prentice-Hall, 1970, 166–181.

——, 'The Mandate to Rule: An Introduction', *Social Forces*, 55 (December 1976), 242–255.

Berlin, Isaiah (O. Utis), 'Generalissimo Stalin and the Art of Government', *Foreign Affairs*, 30 (January 1952), 197–214.

——, 'The Question of Machiavelli', *New York Review of Books*, 4 November 1971, 20–32.

Berns, Walter, 'Voting Studies', in Herbert J. Storing, editor, *Essays on the Scientific Study of Politics*, New York: Holt, Rinehart and Winston, 1962, 3–62.

Bernstein, Richard J., *The Restructuring of Social and Political Theory*, New York: Harcourt Brace Jovanovich, 1975.

Bettelheim, Bruno, *The Informed Heart*, Glencoe, Ill.: The Free Press, 1960.

Bierstedt, Robert, *Power and Progress: Essays on Sociological Theory*, New York: McGraw-Hill, 1974.

Blau, Peter M., *Exchange and Power in Social Life*, New York: John Wiley and Sons, 1964.

——, *Inequality and Heterogeneity: A Primitive Theory of Social Structure*, New York: The Free Press, 1977.

Bottomore, Tom, *Elites and Society*, London: C. A. Watts, 1964.

Boulding, Kenneth, 'Toward a Pure Theory of Threat Systems', in Roderick Bell, David V. Edwards and R. Harrison Wagner, editors, *Political Power: A Reader in Theory and Research*, New York: The Free Press, 1969, 285–292.

Bradshaw, Alan, 'A Critique of Steven Lukes' "Power: A Radical View",' *Sociology*, 10 (January 1976), 121–128.

Bramson, Leon, *The Political Context of Sociology*, Princeton, N.J.: Princeton University Press, 1961.

Brecht, Bertolt, *Selected Poems*, translated by H. R. Hays, New York: Grove Press, 1947.

——, *The Measures Taken*, London: Eyre Methuen, 1977.

Brown, Norman O., *Life Against Death*, Middletown, Conn.: Wesleyan University Press, 1959.

Brzezinski, Zbigniew, *The Permanent Purge*, Cambridge, Mass.: Harvard University Press, 1956.

Cartwright, Bliss C. and R. Stephen Warner, 'The Medium is Not the Message', in Jan J. Loubser, Rainer C. Baum, Andrew Effrat and Victor Meyer Lidz, editors, *Explorations in General Theory in Social Science: Essays in Honor of Talcott Parsons*, two volumes, New York: The Free Press, 1976, xeroxed copy.

Chazel, F., 'Power, Cause and Force', in Brian Barry, editor, *Power and Political Theory: Some European Perspectives*, London: John Wiley and Sons, 1976, 60–65.

Coleman, James S., 'Loss of Power', *American Sociological Review*, 38 (February 1973), 1–17.

Collingwood, R. G., *The New Leviathan*, Oxford: The Clarendon Press, 1942.

Collins, Randall, 'A Comparative Approach to Political Sociology', in Reinhard Bendix, editor, *The State and Society*, Boston: Little, Brown, 1968, 42–67.

——, *Conflict Sociology: Toward an Explanatory Social Science*, New York: Academic Press, 1975.

——, and Michael Makowsky, *The Discovery of Society*, New York: Random House, 1972.

Connolly, William E., *The Terms of Political Discourse*, Lexington, Mass.: D. C. Heath, 1974.

Coser, Lewis A., 'Some Aspects of Soviet Family Policy', *American Journal of Sociology*, 56 (March 1951), 424–437.

——, *The Functions of Social Conflict*, Glencoe, Ill.: The Free Press, 1956.

Coser, Lewis A. *Greedy Institutions: Patterns of Undivided Commitment*, New York: The Free Press, 1974.

——, 'The Notion of Power: Theoretical Developments', in Coser and Bernard Rosenberg, editors, *Sociological Theory: A Book of Readings*, New York: Macmillan, Fourth Edition, 1976, 150–161.

Crenson, Matthew E., *The Un-Politics of Air Pollution: A Study of Non-Decisionmaking in the Cities*, Baltimore: The Johns Hopkins Press, 1971.

Crick, Bernard, 'On Rereading *The Origins of Totalitarianism*', *Social Research*, 44 (Spring 1977), 106–125.

Dahl, Robert A., 'A Critique of the Ruling Elite Model', *American Political Science Review*, 52 (June 1958), 463–469.

——, *Who Governs? Democracy and Power in an American City*, New Haven: Yale University Press, 1961.

——, 'Equality and Power in American Society', in William V. D'Antonio and Howard J. Ehrlich, editors, *Power and Democracy in America*, Notre Dame, Ind.: Notre Dame University Press, 1961, 73–89.

——, *Modern Political Analysis*, Englewood Cliffs, N.J.: Prentice-Hall, 1963.

——, *After the Revolution?* New Haven: Yale University Press, 1970.

——, *Polyarchy: Participation and Opposition*, New Haven: Yale University Press, 1971.

——, 'On Removing Certain Impediments to Democracy in the United States', *Dissent*, 25 (Summer 1978), 310–324.

——, and Charles E. Lindblom, *Politics, Economics and Welfare*, New York: Harper and Brothers, 1953.

Dahrendorf, Ralf, *Class and Class Conflict in Industrial Society*, Stanford, Calif.: Stanford University Press, 1959.

——, *Essays on the Theory of Society*, Stanford, Calif.: Stanford University Press, 1968.

——, *Society and Democracy in Germany*, Garden City, N.Y.: Doubleday Anchor Books, 1969.

Dostoevsky, Feodor, *Notes from Underground*, New York: New American Library, 1961.

——, *The Brothers Karamazov*, New York: Random House, The Modern Library, 1950.

Downs, Anthony, *An Economic Theory of Democracy*, New York: Harper and Brothers, 1957.

Dowse, Robert E. and John A. Hughes, *Political Sociology*, New York: John Wiley and Sons, 1972.

Durkheim, Emile, *The Division of Labor in Society*, New York: Macmillan; 1933.

——, *The Elementary Forms of the Religious Life*, Glencoe, Ill.: The Free Press, 1947.

Duverger, Maurice, *Political Parties*, London: Methuen, 1954.

Easton, David, 'The Perception of Authority and Political Change', in Carl J. Friedrich, editor, *Authority*, Nomos I, Cambridge, Mass.: Harvard University Press, 1958, 170–196.

Elkins, Stanley M., *Slavery: A Problem in American Institutional and Intellectual Life*, New York: Grosset and Dunlap, The Universal Library, 1963.

——, 'The Slavery Debate', *Commentary*, 60 (December 1975), 40–54.

Ellis, Desmond P., 'The Hobbesian Problem of Order', *American Sociological Review*, 36 (August, 1971), 692–703.

Emerson, Richard M., 'Power-Dependence Relations', *American Sociological Review*, 27 (February 1962), 31–41.

Endleman, Robert, *Personality and Social Life*, New York: Random House, 1967.

Etzioni, Amitai, *A Comparative Analysis of Complex Organizations*, New York: The Free Press, 1961.

——, *The Active Society*, New York: The Free Press, 1968.

Evans, Michael, *Karl Marx*, London: George Allen and Unwin, 1975.

Fox, Robin, 'The Inherent Rules of Violence', in Peter Collett, editor, *Social Rules and Social Behavior*, Oxford: Basil Blackwell, 1977, 132–149. .

Freidson, Eliot, 'The Impurity of Professional Authority', in Howard S. Becker, Blanche Geer, David Riesman and Robert S. Weiss, editors, *Institutions and the Person*, Chicago: Aldine, 1968, 25–34.

——, *Profession of Medicine*, New York: Dodd, Mead, 1972.

Freud, Anna, *The Ego and the Mechanisms of Defense*, New York: International Universities Press, 1946.

Freud, Sigmund, *Group Psychology and the Analysis of the Ego*, New York: Bantam Books, 1960.

——, *Civilization and Its Discontents*, Garden City, N.Y.: Doubleday Anchor Books, 1958, Joan Riviere translation; New York: W. W. Norton, 1961, James Strachey translation.

——, *Collected Papers*, five volumes, New York: Basic Books, 1959.

Frey, Frederick W., 'Comment: On Issues and Nonissues in the Study of Power', *American Political Science Review*, 65 (December 1971), 1081–1101.

Friedrich, Carl J., *Constitutional Government and Politics*, New York: Harper and Brothers, 1937.

——, 'Authority, Reason, and Discretion', in Friedrich, editor, *Authority*, Cambridge, Mass., 1958, 28–48.

——, *Man and Government*, New York: McGraw-Hill, 1963.

——, Michael Curtis, and Benjamin R. Barber, *Totalitarianism in Perspective*, New York: Praeger, 1969.

Fromm, Erich, *Escape from Freedom*, New York: Farrar and Rinehart, 1941.

Fromm, Erich, *The Sane Society*, New York: Rinehart, 1955.

Gamson, William, 'Reputation and Resources in Community Politics', *American Journal of Sociology*, 72 (September 1966), 121–131.

——, *Power and Discontent*, Homewood, Ill.: The Dorsey Press, 1968.

——, *The Strategy of Social Protest*, Homewood, Ill.: The Dorsey Press, 1975.

Garfinkel, Harold, 'Conditions of Successful Degradation Ceremonies', *American Journal of Sociology*, 61 (March 1956), 420–424.

——, 'Aspects of the Problem of Common-sense Knowledge of Social Structures', *Transactions of the Fourth World Congress of Sociology*, International Sociological Association, 1959, Volume Four, 51–65.

Gellner, Ernest, *Thought and Change*, London: Weidenfeld and Nicolson, 1964.

——, 'Nationalism, or the New Confessions of a Justified Edinburgh Sinner', *The Political Quarterly*, 49 (January–March 1978), 103–111.

Genovese, Eugene D., *In Red and Black: Marxist Explorations in Southern and Afro-American History*, New York: Pantheon Books, 1971.

——, *Roll, Jordan, Roll: The World the Slaves Made*, New York: Pantheon Books, 1974.

Gerth, Hans, editor, *The First International: Minutes of the Hague Congress*, Madison: University of Wisconsin Press, 1958.

——, and C. Wright Mills, editors, *From Max Weber: Essays in Sociology*, New York: Oxford University Press, 1946.

——, and C. Wright Mills, *Character and Social Structure*, New York: Harcourt, Brace, 1953.

Giddens, Anthony, *The Class Structure of the Advanced Societies*, London: Hutchinson, 1973.

——, *New Rules of Sociological Method*, New York: Basic Books, 1976.

——, *Studies in Social and Political Theory*, London: Hutchinson, 1977.

——, *Durkheim*, Glasgow: Collins/Fontana, 1978.

Glazer, Nathan, 'Ethnic Groups in America: From National Culture to Ideology', in Morroe Berger, Theodore W. Abel, and Charles H. Page, editors, *Freedom and Control in Modern Society*, New York: D. Van Nostrand, 1954, 158–173.

——, *The Social Basis of American Communism*, New York: Harcourt, Brace and World, 1962.

——, and Daniel Patrick Moynihan, editors, *Ethnicity: Theory and Experience*, Cambridge, Mass., 1975.

Goffman, Erving, *Encounters*, Indianapolis: Bobbs-Merrill, 1962.

Goode, William J., 'The Place of Force in Human Society', *American Sociological Review*, 37 (October 1972), 507–519.

Goodman, Paul, *New Reformation: Notes of a Neolithic Conservative*, New York: Random House, Vintage Books, 1971.

Goldhamer, Herbert and Edward A. Shils, 'Types of Power and Status', *American Journal of Sociology*, 45 (September 1939), 171–182.

Gouldner, Alvin W., 'Introduction' to Emile Durkheim, *Socialism*, New York: Collier Books, 1962, 7–31.

——, *The Coming Crisis of Western Sociology*, New York: Basic Books, 1970.

——, *For Sociology*, New York: Basic Books, 1974.

Green, Martin, *The von Richthofen Sisters*, New York: Basic Books, 1974.

Greer, Scott and Peter Orleans, 'Political Sociology', in R. E. L. Faris, editor, *Handbook of Modern Sociology*, Chicago: Rand McNally, 1964, 808–851.

Habermas, Jürgen, *Toward a Rational Society*, Boston: Beacon Press, 1970.

——, *Knowledge and Human Interests*, Boston: Beacon Press, 1971.

——, *Legitimation Crisis*, Boston: Beacon Press, 1975.

——, 'Hannah Arendt's Communications Concept of Power', *Social Research*, 44 (Spring 1977). 3–24.

Hacker, Andrew, 'Power to do What?' in Irving Louis Horowitz, editor, *The New Sociology*, New York: Oxford University Press, 1964, 134–146.

——, 'What Rules America?' *New York Review of Books*, 1 May 1975, 9–13.

——, 'The Social and Economic Power of Corporations', in Dennis H. Wrong and Harry L. Gracey, editors, *Readings in Introductory Sociology*, New York: Macmillan, Third Edition, 1977, 502–509.

——, 'Cutting Classes', *New York Review of Books*, 4 March 1976, 15–18.

Hamilton, Richard J., *Class and Politics in the United States*, New York: John Wiley and Sons, 1972.

——, *Restraining Myths: Critical Studies of U.S. Social Structure and Politics*, Beverly Hills, Calif.: Sage Publications, 1975.

Harris, Errol E., 'Political Power', *Ethics*, 68 (October 1957), 1–10.

Hobbes, Thomas, *Leviathan*, Indianapolis: Bobbs-Merrill, 1958.

Homans, George, *The Human Group*, New York: Harcourt, Brace, 1950.

——, *Social Behavior: Its Elementary Forms*, New York: Harcourt Brace Jovanovich, Revised Edition, 1974.

Horkheimer, Max, 'Authoritarianism and the Family', in Ruth Nanda Anshen, editor, *The Family: Its Function and Destiny*, New York: Harper and Brothers, Revised Edition, 1959, 381–398.

Howe, Mark DeWolfe, editor, *Holmes-Laski Letters*, two volumes, Cambridge, Mass.: Harvard University Press, 1953.

Hughes, H. Stuart, *The Sea Change*, New York: Harper and Row, 1975.

Irving, John A., *The Social Credit Movement in Alberta*, Toronto: University of Toronto Press, 1959.

Jouvenel, Bertrand de, 'Authority: The Efficient Imperative', in Friedrich, editor, *Authority*, Cambridge, Mass., 1958, 159–169.

Kateb, George, *Utopia and Its Enemies*, New York: The Free Press of Glencoe, 1963.

Key, V. O., *The Responsible Electorate*, Cambridge, Mass.: The Belknap Press of Harvard University Press, 1966.

Koestler, Arthur, *Darkness at Noon*, London: Jonathan Cape, 1940.

Kolakowski, Leszek, 'Marxist Roots of Stalinism', in Robert C. Tucker, editor, *Stalinism: Essays in Historical Interpretation*, New York: W. W. Norton, 1977, 283–298.

Kornhauser, William, *The Politics of Mass Society*, Glencoe, Ill.: The Free Press, 1959.

Lane, Robert E., *Political Life*, Glencoe, Ill.: The Free Press, 1959.

Lasch, Christopher, *Haven in a Heartless World: The Family Besieged*, New York: Basic Books, 1977.

Lasky, Melvin J., *Utopia and Revolution*, Chicago: University of Chicago Press, 1976.

Lasswell, Harold, *Politics: Who Gets What, When, How*, New York: Meridian Books, 1958.

——, *Power and Personality*, New York: W. W. Norton, 1948.

——, and Abraham Kaplan, *Power and Society*, New Haven: Yale University Press, 1950.

Laqueur, Walter Z., *The Fate of the Revolution: Interpretations of Soviet History*, New York: Macmillan, 1967.

Lawrence, D. H., 'Preface to Dostoevsky's *The Grand Inquisitor*', in René Wellek, editor, *Dostoevsky: A Collection of Critical Essays*, Englewood Cliffs, N.J.: Prentice-Hall, 1962, 90–97.

Lazarsfeld, Paul F., Bernard Berelson, and Hazel Gaudet, *The People's Choice*, New York: Duell, Sloan and Peirce, 1944.

——, and Herbert Menzel, 'On the Relation between Individual and Collective Properties', in Amitai Etzioni, editor, *Complex Organizations: A Sociological Reader*, New York: Holt, Rinehart and Winston, 1961, 422–440.

Lederer, Emil, *The State of the Masses*, New York: W. W. Norton, 1940.

Lehman, Edward W., 'Towards a Macrosociology of Power', *American Sociological Review*, 34 (August 1969), 453–465.

——, *Political Society: A Macrosociology of Politics*, New York: Columbia University Press, 1977.

——, and Ethna Lehman, 'Historical Data and the Measurement of Collective Properties', paper presented at the 64th annual meeting of the American Sociological Association, San Francisco, 4 September, 1969, 1–13.

Lenski, Gerhard, *Power and Privilege: A Theory of Social Stratification*, New York: McGraw-Hill, 1966.

Levi, Carlo, *Christ Stopped at Eboli*, New York: Farrar, 1947.

Lichtheim, George (G. L. Arnold), *The Pattern of World Conflict*, New York: The Dial Press, 1955.

——, (G. L. Arnold), 'Collectivism Reconsidered', *British Journal of Sociology*, 6 (March 1955), 1–15.

——, *Marxism: An Historical and Critical Study*, New York: Praeger, 1961.

——, *Marxism in Modern France*, New York: Columbia University Press, 1966.

Lifton, Robert Jay, *Thought Reform and the Psychology of Totalism*, New York: W. W. Norton, 1963.

——, 'On the Hearst Trial', *New York Times*, 16 April 1976, 27.

Lipset, Seymour Martin, *Agrarian Socialism*, Berkeley and Los Angeles: University of California Press, 1950.

——, 'Democracy in Alberta', in two parts, *The Canadian Forum*, 34 (November and December, 1954), 175–177, 196–198.

——, *Political Man*, Garden City, N.Y.: Doubleday, 1960.

——, *The First New Nation*, New York: Basic Books, 1963.

——, *Revolution and Counterrevolution*, New York: Basic Books, 1968.

——, and Stein Rokkan, editors, *Party Systems and Voter Alignments*, New York: The Free Press, 1967.

——, and Everett Carll Ladd, Jr., 'College Generations – from the 1930's to the 1960s', *The Public Interest*, No. 25 (Fall, 1971), 99–113.

Lively, Jack, 'The Limits of Exchange Theory', in Barry, editor, *Power and Political Theory: Some European Perspectives*, London, 1976, 1–9.

Lowenthal, Leo, 'Terror's Atomization of Man', *Commentary*, 1 (January 1946), 1–8.

Lowenthal, Richard, 'Social Transformation and Democratic Legitimacy', *Social Research*, 43 (Summer 1976), 246–275.

Lowi, Theodore J., *The End of Liberalism*, New York: W. W. Norton, 1969.

——, *The Politics of Disorder*, New York: Basic Books, 1971.

Luhmann, Niklas, *Macht*, Stuttgart: Ferdinand Enke, 1975.

Lukács, Georg, *History and Class Consciousness*, Cambridge, Mass.: The MIT Press, 1971.

Lukes, Steven, *Individualism*, Oxford: Basil Blackwell, 1973.

——, *Power: A Radical View*, London: Macmillan, 1974.

——, 'Reply to Bradshaw', *Sociology*, 10 (January 1976), 127–132.

——, *Essays in Social Theory*, New York: Columbia University Press, 1977.

——, 'Power and Authority', xeroxed, 1978, to appear in Tom Bottomore and Robert A. Nisbet, editors, *History of Sociological Analysis*, New York: Basic Books, forthcoming, 1–53.

Lukes, Steven, 'On the Relativity of Power', xeroxed, 1978, 1–13.

Lynd, Robert S., 'Power in American Society as Resource and Problem', in Arthur Kornhauser, editor, *Problems of Power in American Democracy*, Detroit: Wayne State University Press, 1957, 1–45.

McCarthy, John D. and Mayer N. Zald, 'Resource Mobilization and Social Movements: A Partial Theory', *American Journal of Sociology*, 82 (May 1977), 1208–1217.

McDermott, John, 'Technology: The Opiate of the Intellectuals', *New York Review of Books*, 31 July, 1969, pp. 25–35.

MacFarlane, L. J., *Violence and the State*, London: Thomas Nelson and Sons, 1974.

Machiavelli, Niccolo, *The Prince and the Discourses*, New York: Random House, The Modern Library, 1940.

McIntosh, Donald, 'Habermas on Freud', *Social Research*, 44 (Autumn 1977), 562–598.

MacIntyre, Alasdair, 'The Idea of a Social Science', in Bryan Wilson, editor, *Rationality*, New York: Harper and Row, 1970, 112–130.

MacIver, Robert M., *The Modern State*, Oxford: Oxford University Press, 1926.

——, *Society: A Textbook of Sociology*, New York: Rinehart, 1937.

——, *The Web of Government*, New York: Macmillan, 1947.

Macpherson, C. B. *Democracy in Alberta*, Toronto: University of Toronto Press, 1953.

——, *The Political Theory of Possessive Individualism*, Oxford: Oxford University Press, 1964.

——, *Democratic Theory: Essays in Retrieval*, Oxford: Oxford University Press, 1973.

Mann, Michael, *Consciousness and Action Among the Western Working Classes*, London: Macmillan, 1973.

Mannheim, Karl, *Ideology and Utopia*, New York: Harcourt, Brace, 1946.

——, *Essays in Sociology and Social Psychology*, New York: Oxford University Press, 1953.

——, *From Karl Mannheim*, edited and with an introduction by Kurt H. Wolff, New York: Oxford University Press, 1971.

Marcuse, Herbert, *Eros and Civilization*, Boston: Beacon Press, 1955.

——, Robert Paul Wolff, and Barrington Moore, Jr., *A Critique of Pure Tolerance*, Boston: Beacon Press, 1966.

Martin, Roderick, *The Sociology of Power*, London: Routledge and Kegan Paul, 1977.

Martins, Herminio, 'Portugal', in Margaret Scotford Archer and Salvador Giner, editors, *Contemporary Europe: Class, Status and Power*, New York: St. Martin's Press, 1971, 60–89.

Marx, Karl, *The Poverty of Philosophy*, London: Martin Lawrence, no date.

Marx, Karl, *The Eighteenth Brumaire of Louis Bonaparte*, New York: International Publishers, no date.

——, *Capital*, three volumes, Moscow: Foreign Languages Publishing House, 1962.

——, and Friedrich Engels, *Manifesto of the Communist Party*, New York: International Publishers, no date.

——, and Friedrich Engels, *Selected Works*, three volumes, Moscow: Progress Publishers, 1969.

Merriam, Charles E., *Political Power*, New York: McGraw-Hill, 1934.

Merton, Robert K., *Mass Persuasion: The Social Psychology of a War Bond Drive*, New York: Harper and Brothers, 1946.

——, *Social Theory and Social Structure*, New York: The Free Press, Revised and Enlarged Edition, 1957.

Michels, Robert, *Political Parties*, New York: Dover Publications, 1959.

Milbrath, Lester W., *Political Participation*, Chicago: Rand McNally, 1965.

Miller, Henry, *Remember to Remember*, London: Grey Walls Press, 1952.

Mills, C. Wright, *The Power Elite*, New York: Oxford University Press, 1956.

——, *The Sociological Imagination*, New York: Oxford University Press, 1959.

——, *Power, Politics and People*, New York: Oxford University Press, 1963.

Moore, Barrington, Jr., *Political Power and Social Theory*, Cambridge, Mass., Harvard University Press, 1958.

——, *Social Origins of Dictatorship and Democracy*, Boston: Beacon Press, 1967.

Mosca, Gaetano, *The Ruling Class*, New York: McGraw-Hill, 1939.

Morriss, Peter, 'Power in New Haven: A Reassessment of "Who Governs?"' *British Journal of Political Science*, 2 (October 1972), 457–465.

Nagel, Jack H., 'Some Questions about the Concept of Power', *Behavioural Science*, 13 (March 1969), 129–137.

——, *A Descriptive Analysis of Power*, New Haven: Yale University Press, 1975.

Nairn Tom, *The Break-Up of Britain: Crisis and Neo-Nationalism*, London: New Left Books, 1977.

Neumann, Franz, *The Democratic and the Authoritarian State*, Glencoe, Ill.: The Free Press, 1957.

Nietzsche, Friedrich, *Beyond Good and Evil*, Chicago: Henry Regnery, 1955.

Nisbet, Robert A., *The Sociological Tradition*, New York: Basic Books, 1966.

——, *Social Change and History*, Oxford: Oxford University Press, 1969.

——, *Twilight of Authority*, Oxford: Oxford University Press, 1975.

Oberschall, Anthony, *Social Conflict and Social Movements*, Englewood Cliffs, N.J.: Prentice-Hall, 1973.

Offe, Claus, 'Political Authority and Class Structures', in Paul Connerton, editor, *Critical Sociology*, Harmondsworth, Middlesex, England: Penguin Books, 1976, 388–421.

Olson, Mancur, Jr., *The Logic of Collective Action*, New York: Schocken Books, Revised Edition, 1971.

O'Neill, John, editor, *Modes of Individualism and Collectivism*, London: Heinemann Educational Books, 1973.

Oppenheim, Felix, E., *Dimensions of Freedom*, New York: St. Martin's Press, 1961.

Orwell, George, *Homage to Catalonia*, London: Secker and Warburg, 1938.

——— , *Nineteen Eighty-Four*, New York: Harcourt, Brace, 1949.

——— , *Collected Essays, Journalism and Letters*, four volumes, Harmondsworth, Middlesex, England: Penguin Books, 1970.

Ossowski, Stanislaw, *Class Structure in the Social Consciousness*, New York: The Free Press of Glencoe, 1963.

O'Sullivan, Noel, 'Hellenic Nostalgia and Industrial Society', in Anthony de Crespigny and Kenneth Minogue, editors, *Contemporary Political Philosophers*, New York: Dodd, Mead, 1975, 228–251.

O'Toole, Roger, *The Precipitous Path: Studies in Political Sects*, Toronto: Peter Martin Associates, 1977.

Outhwaite, William, *Understanding Social Life*, London: George Allen and Unwin, 1975.

Parkin, Frank, *Class Inequality and Political Order*, London: Granada, 1972.

Parsons, Talcott, *The Structure of Social Action*, New York: McGraw Hill, 1937.

——— , 'Introduction' to Max Weber, *Theory of Social and Economic Organization*, New York: Oxford University Press, 1947, 3–86.

——— , *The Social System*, Glencoe, Ill.: The Free Press, 1951.

——— , 'Max Weber', *American Sociological Review*, 25 (October, 1960), 750–752.

——— , *Politics and Social Structure*, New York: The Free Press, 1969.

Partridge, P. H., 'Some Notes on the Concept of Power', *Political Studies*, 11 (June, 1963), 107–125.

——— , *Consent and Consensus*, New York: Praeger, 1971.

Perrow, Charles B., *Complex Organizations: A Critical Essay*, Glenview, Ill.: Scott, Foresman, 1972.

——— , review of Mancur Olson, Jr., *The Logic of Collective Action* in *Social Forces*, 52 (September 1973), 123–125.

Pinard, Maurice, 'Mass Society and Political Movements: A New Formulation', *American Journal of Sociology*, 73 (May 1968), 682–690.

——— , *The Rise of A Third Party: A Study in Crisis Politics*, Englewood Cliffs, N.J.: Prentice-Hall, 1971.

Plamenatz, John, 'Introduction' to Thomas Hobbes, *Leviathan*, London: Collins, Fontana Library of Philosophy, 1962, 3–55.

Polanyi, Michael, *Personal Knowledge*, London: Routledge and Kegan Paul, 1958.

Plato, *The Republic and Other Works*, Garden City, N.Y.: Doubleday Anchor Books, 1973.

Polsby, Nelson W., *Community Power and Political Theory*, New Haven: University Press, 1963.

——, 'Community Power Meets Air Pollution', *Contemporary Sociology*, 1 (March 1972), 99–101.

Popper, Karl, *The Poverty of Historicism*, New York: Harper and Row, Harper Torchbooks, 1964.

Poulantzas, Nicos, *Political Power and Social Classes*, London: New Left Books, 1973.

Presthus, Robert, *Men At The Top: A Study in Community Power*, New York: Oxford University Press, 1964.

Prewitt, Kenneth and Alan Stone, *The Ruling Elites: Elite Theory, Power, and American Democracy*, New York: Harper and Row, 1973.

Rabinowitz, Dorothy, 'The Hostage Mentality', *Commentary*, 63 (June 1977), 70–72.

Rahv, Philip, 'The Unfuture of Utopia', *Partisan Review*, 16 (July 1949), 743–749.

——, 'The Legend of the Grand Inquisitor', *Partisan Review*, 21 (May–June 1954), 249–271.

Redfield, Robert, *The Primitive World and Its Transformations*, Ithaca, N.Y.: Cornell University Press, 1953.

Reitlinger, Gerald, *The SS, Alibi of a Nation, 1922–1945*, New York: Viking Press, 1957.

Rex, John, *Key Problems in Sociological Theory*, London: Routledge and Kegan Paul, 1961.

——, *Sociology and the Demystification of the Modern World*, London: Routledge and Kegan Paul, 1974.

Rieff, Philip, *Freud: The Mind of the Moralist*, Garden City, N.Y.: Doubleday Anchor Books, 1961.

——, 'The Case of Dr. Oppenheimer', in Rieff, editor, *On Intellectuals*, Garden City, N.Y.: Doubleday Anchor Books, 1970, 341–369.

Riesman, David, in collaboration with Reuel Denny and Nathan Glazer, *The Lonely Crowd*, New Haven: Yale University Press, 1951.

——, *Individualism Reconsidered*, Glencoe, Ill.: The Free Press, 1953.

Roberts, Robert, *The Classic Slum: Salford Life in the First Quarter of the Century*, Harmondsworth, Middlesex, England: Penguin Books, 1973.

Rokkan, Stein, 'Mass Suffrage, Secret Voting and Political Participation', in Lewis A. Coser, editor, *Political Sociology*, New York: Harper and Row, Harper Torchbooks, 1967, 101–131.

Rose, Arnold M., *The Power Structure: Political Process in American Society*, New York: Oxford University Press, 1967.

Roth, Guenther, *The Social Democrats in Imperial Germany*, Totowa, N.J.: Bedminster Press, 1963.

Rougemont, Denis de, 'The Crisis of the Modern Couple', in Anshen, editor, *The Family: Its Function and Destiny*, New York, 1959, 449–462.

Rousseau, Jean-Jacques, *The Social Contract*, Harmondsworth, Middlesex, England: Penguin Books, 1968.

Rovere, Richard H., *Senator Joe McCarthy*, New York: Harcourt, Brace, 1959.

Runciman, W. G., *Sociology in Its Place*, Cambridge: Cambridge University Press, 1970.

——, *A Critique of Max Weber's Philosophy of Social Science*, Cambridge: Cambridge University Press, 1972.

Russell, Bertrand, *Power: A New Social Analysis*, London: George Allen and Unwin, 1938.

Ryle, Gilbert, *The Concept of Mind*, New York: Barnes and Noble, 1949.

Sartori, Giovanni, 'From the Sociology of Politics to Political Sociology', in Seymour Martin Lipset, editor, *Politics and the Social Sciences*, New York: Oxford University Press, 1969, 65–100.

——, *Parties and Party Systems*, Volume One, Cambridge: Cambridge University Press, 1975.

Schaar, John H., *Escape from Authority*, New York: Harper and Row, Harper Torchbooks, 1961.

Schapiro, Leonard, *Totalitarianism*, London: Pall Mall Press, 1972.

Schattschneider, E. E., *The Semisovereign People*, New York: Holt, Rinehart and Winston, 1960.

Schlesinger, Arthur, Sr., *Paths to the Present*, New York: Macmillan, 1949.

——, *In Retrospect: The History of a Historian*, New York: Harcourt, Brace and World, 1963.

Schulze, Robert O., 'The Role of Economic Dominants in Community Power Structure', *American Sociological Review*, 23 (February 1958), 3–9.

——, 'The Bifurcation of Power in a Satellite City', in Morris Janowitz, editor, *Community Political Systems*, Glencoe, Ill.: The Free Press, 1961, 19–80.

Schumpeter, Joseph, *Capitalism, Socialism, and Democracy*, New York: Harper and Brothers, Third Edition, 1950.

Schwartz, Benjamin I., 'The Religion of Politics', *Dissent*, 17 (March–April 1970), 144–161.

Selznick, Philip, *The Organizational Weapon*, New York: McGraw-Hill, 1952.

Shils, Edward A., 'Charisma, Order and Status', *American Sociological Review*, 30 (April 1965), 199–213.

Simmel, Georg, *The Sociology of George Simmel*, translated, edited, and with an introduction by Kurt H. Wolff, Glencoe, Ill.: The Free Press, 1950.

Simon, Herbert A., 'Notes on the Observation and Measurement of Power', in Bell, Edwards, and Wagner, editors, *Political Power: A Reader in Theory and Research*, New York, 1969, 69–78.

Slater, Philip E., 'On Social Regression', *American Sociological Review*, 28 (June 1963), 339–364.

Smelser, Neil J., *Theory of Collective Behavior*, New York: The Free Press, 1962.

Smith, Hedrick, *The Russians*, New York: Ballantine Books, 1976.

Solzhenitsyn, Alexandr I., *The First Circle*, New York: Harper and Row, 1968.

Steinhoff, William, *George Orwell and the Origins of Nineteen Eighty-Four*, Ann Arbor: University of Michigan Press, 1975.

Stinchcombe, Arthur L., *Constructing Social Theories*, New York: Harcourt, Brace and World, 1968.

Strauss, Leo, *The Political Philosophy of Thomas Hobbes*, Oxford: The Clarendon Press, 1937.

Stretton, Hugh, *The Political Sciences*, New York: Basic Books, 1969.

Sturmthal, Adolf, *The Tragedy of European Labor, 1918–1939*, New York: Columbia University Press, 1943.

Sweezy, Paul, 'Power Elite or Ruling Class?' in G. William Domhoff and Hoyt B. Ballard, editors, *C. Wright Mills and the Power Elite*, Boston: Beacon Press, 1968, 115–132.

Torrance, John, *Estrangement, Alienation and Exploitation: A Sociological Approach to Historical Materialism*, New York: Columbia University Press, 1977.

Trotsky, Leon, *Stalin*, New York: Stein and Day, New Edition, 1967.

Truman, David B., *The Governmental Process*, New York: Alfred A. Knopf, 1951.

Tucker, Robert C., 'Stalinism as Revolution from Above', in Tucker, editor, *Stalinism: Essays in Historical Interpretation*, New York, 1977, 77–108.

Turner, Jonathan H., *The Structure of Sociological Theory*, Homewood, Ill.: The Dorsey Press, 1974.

Van Doorn, J. A. A. 'Sociology and the Problem of Power', *Sociologia Neerlandica*, (Winter 1962–1963), 3–51.

Vidich, Arthur J. and Joseph Bensman, *Small Town in Mass Society*, Princeton, N.J.: Princeton University Press, 1958.

Walter, E. V., 'Power and Violence', *American Political Science Review*, 58 (June 1964), 350–360.

——, '"Mass Society": The Late Stages of an Idea', *Social Research*, 31 (Winter, 1964), 391–410.

——, *Terror and Resistance*, New York: Oxford University Press, 1969.

Walzer, Michael, 'In Defense of Equality', in Lewis A. Coser and Irving Howe, editors, *The New Conservatives: A Critique from the Left*, New York: Quadrangle Books, 1974, 107–123.

Wasiolek, Edward, *Dostoevsky: The Major Fiction*, Cambridge, Mass.: The MIT Press, 1964.

Weber, Max, *The Theory of Social and Economic Organization*, New York: Oxford University Press, 1947.

——, *Economy and Society*, three volumes, translated and edited by Guenther Roth and Claus Wittich, Totowa, N.J.: Bedminster Press, 1968.

——, *Selections in Translation*, edited by W. G. Runciman, Cambridge: Cambridge University Press, 1978.

Weingart, Peter, 'Beyond Parsons? A Critique of Ralf Dahrendorf's Conflict Theory', *Social Forces*, 48 (December 1969), 151–165.

Weldon, T. D., *The Vocabulary of Politics*, Harmondsworth, Middlesex, England: Penguin Books, 1953.

Westergaard, John and Henrietta Resler, *Class in a Capitalist Society: A Study of Contemporary Britain*, New York: Basic Books, 1975.

Westhues, Kenneth, 'Class and Organization as Paradigms in Social Science', *The American Sociologist*, 11 (February 1976), 38–49.

Winch, Peter, *The Idea of a Social Science*, London: Routledge and Kegan Paul, 1958.

Wolfe, Bertram D., *Marxism: One Hundred Years in the Life of a Doctrine*, New York: Dial Press, 1965.

Wolfe, Tom, *Mauve Gloves and Madmen, Clutter and Vine*, New York: Farrar, Strauss and Giroulx, 1976.

Wolfinger, Raymond E., 'Reputation and Reality in the Study of Community Power', *American Sociological Review*, 25 (October, 1960), 636–644.

——, 'A Plea for a Decent Burial', *American Sociological Review*, 27 (December 1962), 840–847.

——, 'Nondecisions and the Study of Local Politics', *American Political Science Review*, 65 (December 1971), 1063–1080.

Wolin, Sheldon, *Politics and Vision*, Boston: Little, Brown, 1960.

Wrong, Dennis H., 'Power in America', *Commentary*, 22 (September 1956), 278–280. Reprinted in Domhoff and Ballard, editors, *C. Wright Mills and the Power Elite*, Boston, 1968, 88–94.

——, 'The Perils of Political Moderation', *Commentary*, 27 (January 1959), 1–8.

——, 'Reflections on the End of Ideology', *Dissent*, 7 (Summer 1960), 286–291.

——, review of William V. D'Antonio and Howard J. Ehrlich, editors, *Power and Democracy in America*, in *American Sociological Review*, 28 (February 1963), 144–145.

——, editor, *Max Weber*, Englewood Cliffs, N.J.: Prentice-Hall, 1970.

——, *Skeptical Sociology*, New York: Columbia University Press, 1976.

——, 'What is a Liberal – Who is a Conservative?' contribution to a symposium, *Commentary*, 62 (September 1976), 111–113.

Zartman, William I., editor, *The Study of Middle East Elites*, State University of New York Press, forthcoming.

Zwerdling, Alex, *Orwell and the Left*, New Haven: Yale University Press, 1974.

Index